MW00612343

Writing & Grammar 7

Third Edition
for Christian Schools™

for Christian Schools™

Hannah Landis
Mrs. Eichenmuller
Per. 2

June W. Cates
Elizabeth Rose
Kimberly Y. Stegall
Dawn L. Watkins

BJU PRESS
GREENVILLE, SOUTH CAROLINA

WRITING AND GRAMMAR 7
Third Edition

Produced in cooperation with the Bob Jones University Division of English Language
and Literature of the College of Arts and Science, the School of Education, and
Bob Jones Academy.

Coordinating Writers
June W. Cates
Elizabeth Rose, M.Ed., M.A.
Kimberly Y. Stegall, M.Ed.
Dawn L. Watkins, M.Ed., M.A.

Contributing Writers
Alicia M. Bernson
Jill M. Blackstock, M.Ed.
Eileen M. Berry
Denise Zutter Cevela, M.Ed.
Dana Gibby Gage
Wendy M. Harris
Ellen M. Howell, M.S.
Judith W. Lanier, M.A.
Lois Oldenburg
Karen Rowe, M.Ed.
Christina Hatfield Scheiderer
Lesa M. Seibert, M.Ed.
Sarah Shanks
Maggie Smeltzer Sloan, M.A.

E. Anne Smith
Sandra R. Utt, M.S.

Consultants
Grace Collins Hargis, Ph.D.
Daniel P. Olinger, Ph.D.
Steven N. Skaggs, M.Ed.

Bible Integration
Bryan Smith, Ph.D.
Will Gray, M.A.

Editor
Rebecca S. Moore

Designers
Duane A. Nichols
Timothy French

Compositors
Nancy C. Lohr
Bonnijean Marley

Project Manager
Nathan Huffstutler

Photo Acquisition
Rachel Carper
Brenda Hansen
Joyce Landis
Terry Latini

Illustrators
Timothy D. Banks
Vincent Barnhart
John Bjerk
Johanna Ehnis
Justin Gerard
Preston Gravely Jr.
Deborah King
Stefanie Kubina
Asher Parris
Scotty Pruitt
Dick Sheets
Lynda Slattery
Melissa Smith

Acknowledgements and Photograph credits appear on page x.

© 2005 BJU Press
Greenville, South Carolina 29614
First Edition © 1982 BJU Press
Second Edition © 1999 BJU Press

Printed in the United States of America
All rights reserved

ISBN 1-59166-368-7

15 14 13 12 11 10 9 8 7 6 5 4

Congratulations

Your search for the very best educational materials available has been completely successful! You have a textbook that is the culmination of decades of research, experience, prayer, and creative energy.

The facts
Nothing overlooked. Revised and updated. Facts are used as a springboard to stimulate thoughtful questions and guide students to broader applications.

The foundation
Nothing to conflict with Truth, and everything to support it. Truth is the pathway as well as the destination.

The fun
Nothing boring about this textbook! Student (and teacher) might even forget it's a textbook! Brimming with interesting extras and sparkling with color!

TABLE OF CONTENTS

GRAMMAR

Chapter 5: Adjectives

GRAMMAR

Chapter 6: Adverbs

GRAMMAR

Chapter 7: Prepositions, Conjunctions, and Interjections

GRAMMAR

Chapter 8: Clause Structure

USAGE

Chapter 9: Subject-Verb Agreement

Chapter 10: Pronoun-Antecedent Agreement

Chapter 11: Pronoun Usage

Chapter 12: Using Adjectives and Adverbs Correctly

Chapter 13: Using Troublesome Words Correctly

Chapter 14: Capitalization

Chapter 15: Punctuation

Chapter 16: Spelling

Chapter 17: Dictionary Skills

Chapter 18: Library Skills

Chapter 19: Study Skills

Chapter 20: Composition Skills: The Writer's Toolbox

Chapter Reviews

Acknowledgments

A careful effort has been made to trace the ownership of selections included in this textbook in order to secure permission to reprint copyrighted material and to make full acknowledgment of their use. If any error or omission has occurred, it is unintentional and will be corrected in subsequent editions, provided written notification is made to the publisher.

CHAPTER 1
Excerpt from "The Drummer Boy of Shiloh" by Ray Bradbury. Reprinted by permission of Don Congdon Associates, Inc. Copyright © 1960 by Curtis Publishing Company, renewed 1988 by Ray Bradbury.

CHAPTER 2
From *The Cay* by Theodore Taylor, copyright © 1969 by Theodore Taylor. Used by permission of Doubleday, a division of Random House, Inc.

CHAPTER 6
"Those Winter Sundays." Copyright © 1966 by Robert Hayden, from *Collected Poems of Robert Hayden* by Robert Hayden, edited by Frederick Glaysher. Used by permission of Liveright Publishing Corporation.

CHAPTER 8
Excerpt from "The Son from America" from *A Crown of Feathers* by Isaac Bashevis Singer. Copyright © 1973 by Isaac Bashevis Singer. Reprinted by permission of Farrar, Straus and Giroux, LLC.

CHAPTER 11
Excerpt from *The Count of Monte Cristo* by Alexandre Dumas. Used by permission of Bantam Books, a division of Random House, Inc.

CHAPTER 17
Page 1567 from *The American Heritage Dictionary.* Copyright © 1997 by Houghton Mifflin Company. Adapted and reproduced by permission from *The American Heritage College Dictionary, Third Edition.*

Photograph Credits

The following agencies and individuals have furnished materials to meet the photographic needs of this textbook. We wish to express our gratitude to them for their important contribution.

The Biltmore Company, Asheville, North Carolina
The Bob Jones University Collection
The British Library
B.W. Carper
George R. Collins
Corel Corporation
Denver Metro Convention and Visitors Bureau
The Dr Pepper Museum, Waco, TX
Dwight D. Eisenhower Library
George Bush Presidential Library and Museum
Hemera Technologies, Inc.

Brian D. Johnson
Library of Congress
NASA
National Archives
National Basketball Hall of Fame, Springfield, MA
OMF International
PhotoDisc/Getty Images
Unusual Films
Dawn L. Watkins
The White House
www.arttoday.com

Chapter 1
George R. Collins 4; Used with permission from the Biltmore Company, Asheville, North Carolina 6

Chapter 2
© 2004 Hemera Technologies, Inc. All rights reserved. 40

Chapter 3
PhotoDisc/Getty Images 52; © 2004 Hemera Technologies, Inc. All rights reserved. 53; National Basketball Hall of Fame, Springfield, MA 57; By permission of the British Library (Cott Vit A XV; folio 132) 59; OMF International 67; George Bush Presidential Library and Museum 74

Chapter 4
Corel Corporation 97

Chapter 5
www.arttoday.com 109; Denver Metro Convention & Visitors Bureau 118

Chapter 6
PhotoDisc/Getty Images 136, 138

Chapter 7
Official White House Photograph 145; Library of Congress 148; NASA 151 (both); Courtesy of the Dr Pepper Museum, Waco, TX 154

Chapter 8
PhotoDisc/Getty Images 174

Chapter 9
Brian D. Johnson 182; NASA 187; Library of Congress 189

Chapter 10
B. W. Carper 196; Corel Corporation 198, © 2004 Hemera Technologies, Inc. All rights reserved. 203

Chapter 11
Dawn L. Watkins 208

Chapter 12
Brian D. Johnson 232

Chapter 13
PhotoDisc/Getty Images 246; Unusual Films 258

Chapter 14
Dawn L. Watkins 266; Library of Congress 278; © 2004 Hemera Technologies, Inc. All rights reserved. 279

Chapter 15
Brian D. Johnson 286; George R. Collins 288; Dwight D. Eisenhower Library 296; National Archives 303, 308; Library of Congress 313; Unusual Films 314

Chapter 16
Brian D. Johnson 318

Chapter 17
PhotoDisc/Getty Images 336

Chapter 18
PhotoDisc/Getty Images 344

Chapter 19
PhotoDisc/Getty Images 358

Chapter 20
PhotoDisc/Getty Images 374; *Esther before Ahasuerus* by Claude Vignon, From the Bob Jones University Collection 380

To the STUDENT

Why do we study language? Some would argue that we need this study because people who know their language can make a lot of money. Others may say that good language training helps a person appear educated.

The Christian knows that he should take his language study seriously because of God. Our God is a God of language and communication. He brought the world into existence through language (Gen. 1:3), He made mankind in His image and called him to have dominion over the earth partly through his use of language (Gen. 1:28; 2:19-20), and He is redeeming this world to Himself through language (John 1:1-18). Christians are the instruments of God's redemption, and God has called us who love Him to use language for redemptive purposes. By taking language study seriously, a Christian may demonstrate obedience to the two most important commands in the Bible (Mark 12:29-31). The Christian who studies language shows that he loves God, who displays part of His glory in His use of language and in His gift of language to us. The Christian student also shows that he loves those around him, who will understand God's work of redemption only as they hear about it through human language.

But why do we study English? We learn how to understand and how to speak English while we are very young. Why, then, do we spend so much of our lives studying something we already know?

English is a living language. It changes—constantly. New words appear; obsolete words fade away as they are no longer needed. Usage patterns change; even rules occasionally change. Without a thorough understanding of English, we cannot communicate effectively with others.

English is also a flexible language. We use different levels of formality for different audiences. For example, we speak and write to our friends differently than we speak and write to our pastor or teacher.

WRITING AND GRAMMAR 7 for Christian Schools, Third Edition, will help you learn to communicate in English more effectively. The first step toward the goal of better speaking and writing is to acquaint yourself with the text. Take a few minutes to become familiar with these features:

- *Combine the Skills Boxes point you to other pages with information about the topic:*

     A grammar box refers to a grammar concept in Chapters 1-8.

     A usage box sends you to material in Chapters 9-16 about correct usage.

     A reference box refers to helpful tips in Chapters 17-20.

    A writing box tells you about an important writing concept.

- *Etymology boxes tell you the histories and definitions of certain English words.*
- *ESL notes explain concepts that can be difficult for students from another language background (ESL is an abbreviation for English as a Second Language). Every student can learn more about English from these helpful explanations.*
- *Grand Slam: Writing Across the Curriculum brings your writing skills into contact with other areas of study, such as geography, history, and science.*
- *Between Innings offers tips for improving your writing style.*
- *Pinch Hitter: Critical Thinking develops your critical thinking skills as you try to solve the mysteries that confront Inspector Jameson and Officer Bell.*
- *History of the English Language explains how our language has developed.*
- *The Glossary is a collection of definitions of the terms used throughout the book.*
- *Learning Christianly notes encourage you to step back from what you are learning and to look at it from a Christian worldview.*

The personal satisfaction of becoming an effective communicator is a good feeling to have—just like hitting a home run in a baseball game. So go for it; make an A+ home run this year.

CHAPTER 1

SENTENCES

THE DRUMMER BOY OF SHILOH
BY RAY BRADBURY

The boy turned on his side. A moth brushed his face, but it was peach blossom. A peach blossom flicked him, but it was a moth. Nothing stayed put. Nothing had a name. Nothing was as it once was.

If he stayed very still when the dawn came up and the soldiers put on their bravery with their caps, perhaps they might go away, the war with them, and not notice him lying small here, no more than a toy himself.

"Well, by thunder now," said a voice. The boy shut his eyes to hide inside himself, but it was too late. Someone, walking by in the night, stood over him. "Well," said the voice quietly, "here's a soldier crying *before* the fight. Good. Get it over. Won't be time once it all starts."

And the voice was about to move on when the boy, startled, touched the drum at his elbow. The man above, hearing this, stopped. The boy could feel his eyes, sense him slowly bending near. A hand must have come down out of the night, for there was a little *rat-tat* as the fingernails brushed and the man's breath fanned the boy's face.

"Why, it's the drummer boy, isn't it?"

The boy nodded, not knowing if his nod was seen. "Sir, is that you?" he said.

"I assume it is." The man's knees cracked as he bent still closer. He smelled as all fathers should smell, of salt-sweat, horse and boot leather, and the earth he walked upon. He had many eyes. No, not eyes, brass buttons that watched the boy.

He could only be, and was, the general. "What's your name, boy?" he asked.

"Joby, sir," whispered the boy, starting to sit up.

"All right, Joby, don't stir." A hand pressed his chest gently, and the boy relaxed. "How long you been with us, Joby?"

"Three weeks, sir."

"Run off from home or join legitimate, boy?"

Silence.

"Fool question," said the general. "Do you shave yet, boy? Even more of a fool. There's your cheek, fell right off the tree from overhead. And the others here, not much older. Raw, raw, the lot of you. You ready for tomorrow or the next day, Joby?"

"I think so, sir."

"You want to cry some more, go on ahead. I did the same last night."

- *This conversation takes place in a peach orchard on the night before a bloody battle. Does the dialogue between the two characters seem realistic to you? Why or why not?*

- *Which characters in this story ask questions? Which character gives commands or requests?*

- *If you had to choose a favorite sentence from this passage, which one would it be? Why?*

- *What do you think of the general at the end of this conversation? What do you think of Joby?*

Learning Christianly

At the beginning of a course like this, you might wonder how important this subject really is. You may think, "Why do I have to study grammar? I can understand what I speak and write, and all my friends can too!" Is it really fair to expect students to learn standard grammar when they already understand each other? Read Proverbs 4:7 and James 4:6. In what distinctive ways can Christians profit from the study of grammar?

The types of sentences used in the dialogue show the relationship between the characters. Joby, who is fourteen, does not speak in commands; he is not in a position to give orders to his general. Instead he asks a polite question ("Sir, is that you?") and answers the general's questions ("Three weeks, sir"). Notice how many commands the general gives. ("Get it over. . . . All right, Joby, don't stir. . . . You want to cry some more, go on ahead.") Even though the commands are gentle, they express the general's position of authority over Joby. They paint a picture of the general as a strong, tough leader with a compassionate heart.

Sentences that are commands have a special name: *imperative.* Questions have another name: *interrogative.* In this chapter, you will learn about imperatives, interrogatives, and two other types of sentences. This excerpt from "The Drummer Boy of Shiloh" uses different kinds of sentences to make the characters real to us. At the end of this chapter, you will be able to identify the types of sentences Bradbury uses.

Sentences

There are several ways of explaining what a sentence is. One way would be to say that everything on this page that ends with a period or a question mark is a sentence. That is true, but it is not much of a definition. After all, people do make mistakes in placement of punctuation.

Another way is to say that a sentence expresses a complete thought, or a whole thought. That is not very exact, but it may help. Smaller groups of words, called phrases (such as "in the house" and "as fast as possible"), seem to express pieces of thoughts rather than whole thoughts. Of course, it sometimes takes several sentences before we really understand what a person is talking about. Still, each sentence is a complete thought-link in the chain of ideas.

Four Types of Sentences

Sentences can be of four different types, each of which serves a different purpose in our language. We vary word order and change punctuation to express statements, questions, commands, and strong emotion.

A **declarative sentence** makes a statement, usually a fact, and ends with a period.

> Andrew will go fishing.
> Jamal ran with the ball.

An **interrogative sentence** asks a question and ends with a question mark.

> Will Andrew go fishing?
> Will anyone catch Jamal?

Interrogative is a combination of the Latin words *inter*, "between," and *rogare,* "ask." The word *interrogate* means "to question formally."

An **imperative sentence** gives a command or a request and usually ends with a period.

> Go fishing, Andrew.
> Run faster, Jamal.

Imperative comes from two Latin words that mean "to prepare against." The phrase later came to mean a command or an order to prepare.

An **exclamatory sentence** expresses strong emotion or feeling and ends with an exclamation point.

> Andrew caught a huge fish!
> That was a great play, Jamal!

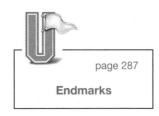

page 287

Endmarks

In English, one of the major differences in the types of sentences is the rising and falling of pitch, called the *intonation*. Intonation of a sentence can be a hint about what type the sentence is.

1. Declarative sentences have falling intonation at the end.
2. Many interrogative sentences have rising intonation at the end.
3. Imperative sentences have falling intonation at the end.
4. Exclamatory sentences are stated at a higher pitch than other sentences or with a greater difference between the high and the low pitches.

ETYMOLOGY   *Intonation* comes from two Latin words: *in,* meaning "in," and *tonus,* meaning "a musical sound." To intone, then, is to give words a musical sound.

1-1   PRACTICE THE SKILL

Identify each sentence as declarative, interrogative, imperative, or exclamatory. Place the appropriate punctuation mark at the end of each sentence.

_____ 1. Deserts do not receive much rainfall

_____ 2. Whew, it is hot

_____ 3. Have you ever lived in the desert

_____ 4. Most people must adjust to the dry climate

_____ 5. Where is the Mojave Desert located

_____ 6. How many national parks have you visited

_____ 7. The beautiful scenery attracts thousands of visitors to the parks every year

_____ 8. Watch for interesting wildlife in the Great Smoky Mountains National Park

_____ 9. Wow! The sequoia trees in Redwood National Park are huge

_____ 10. Can you trace Daniel Boone's exploration through the Cumberland Gap near the borders of Kentucky and Tennessee

Identify each sentence as declarative, interrogative, imperative, or exclamatory. Place the appropriate punctuation mark at the end of each sentence.

_____ 1. Listen to Rich's story of the game

_____ 2. That was an exciting game

_____ 3. Why was the game so exciting

_____ 4. At the beginning of the fourth quarter, our team was behind by eighteen points

_____ 5. Well, with our best two players fouled out, there seemed to be no hope of winning

_____ 6. Coach Rhodes put in Doug Riselle, a new student in our school

_____ 7. Doug made fifteen points in just one quarter

_____ 8. Did you see Doug's face when he sank the winning twenty-foot jump shot

_____ 9. Come to the game next Tuesday

_____ 10. Maybe we will win again

Finding Subjects and Predicates

All sentences have two main parts: a subject and a predicate. The following example is a complete sentence because it has the two parts necessary to any sentence.

The young man on the platform spoke to the audience.

The **subject** of a sentence is the person, place, thing, or idea that the sentence is about. The subject usually comes at or near the beginning of the sentence, and it may be one word or many words. In the example above, _The young man on the platform_ is the **complete subject.** _Man_ is the **simple subject** because it is the main word in the complete subject. In every sentence, the simple subject will be a noun or a pronoun.

The **predicate,** which follows the subject in most sentences, makes a statement about the subject. Every predicate has a verb. In the example, _spoke to the audience_ is the **complete predicate.** The **simple predicate** is the verb _spoke_. The complete predicate either describes the subject in some way or tells about an action of the subject.

Some imperative sentences seem to have only a predicate. The subject may not actually appear in the sentence, but we understand the sentence as if it were there. Rather than saying, "You go to the store," we usually say, "Go to the store." The _you_ is understood to be the subject even when we do not say it. Only imperative sentences can have understood subjects.

page 51

Verbs

However, not all imperative sentences have understood subjects because the *you* may actually appear in the sentence.

> You mail this letter right away.
> (you) Mail this letter right away.

Both examples are complete sentences because both include a simple subject (either *you* or understood *you*) and both include a simple predicate *(mail)*.

page 164

Clauses

ETYMOLOGY

Predicate comes from two Latin words meaning "to say in public" or "to proclaim." A predicate in a sentence makes some "proclamation" about the subject.

Word Order: In English, unlike some other languages, the subject almost always comes before the verb.

1. Tim ordered pizza for dinner.
2. Tim was hungry for the pizza.
3. His mother said, "(you) Eat a sandwich now, Tim."

IN SUMMARY

The **subject** of a sentence is what the sentence is about. The **simple subject** is the main noun or pronoun in a sentence.

The **predicate** of a sentence makes a statement about the subject. The **simple predicate** is the main verb in a sentence.

1-3　PRACTICE THE SKILL

A. Draw a vertical line between the complete subject and the complete predicate. One of the sentences has an understood subject. When you find it, draw a vertical line before the verb.

1. George W. Vanderbilt built a huge mansion in Asheville, North Carolina.

2. He named his mansion Biltmore House.

3. Beautiful European furniture fills Biltmore House.

4. Vanderbilt's heirs opened the house and gardens for public tours.

5. Visit Biltmore Estate on your next vacation.

B. List the simple subjects and the simple predicates of the sentences above. If the subject is understood *you*, put it in parentheses.

      Subject   Predicate

1. _____   _____

2. _____   _____

3. _____   _____

4. _____   _____

5. _____   _____

 1-4   REVIEW THE SKILL

    A. Draw a vertical line between the complete subject and the complete predicate in each sentence.

    B. Underline each simple subject once and each simple predicate twice.

    C. If the subject is understood *you*, draw a vertical line before the sentence and write *you* in parentheses.

1. Read about education in colonial times.

2. Few people attended school.

3. Some children went to school for only a short time.

4. Benjamin Franklin left school at age ten.

5. His father stopped his education after only two years.

6. He studied for the rest of his life, however.

7. Franklin taught himself mathematics and science.

8. Grammar was another of his subjects.

9. He learned five foreign languages.

10. His example amazes us today.

    Some sentences may have more than one subject or predicate. Look at the following examples.

        Pedro went to the parade.
        Pedro and his sister went to the parade.

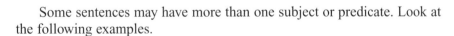

In the first sentence, *Pedro* is the subject. In the second sentence, *Pedro* is joined by *sister*. The compound simple subject of the sentence is *Pedro* and *sister*. A **compound subject** is two or more subjects joined by a conjunction.

A sentence can also have a compound predicate. A **compound predicate** is two or more simple predicates joined by a conjunction.

Manuel buys apples at the market.
Manuel buys apples at the market and eats them on the way home.

In the first sentence *buys* is the simple predicate. In the second sentence the subject, *Manuel,* not only *buys* apples but also *eats* them. The compound simple predicate is *buys* and *eats*.

Sentences can have both a compound subject and a compound predicate.

George and Maria built and decorated a new house.

Be sure to look carefully at each sentence to find all the subjects and all the predicates.

page 151

Conjunctions

page 188

Subject-Verb agreement

In Summary

A **compound subject** is two or more subjects joined by a conjunction.
A **compound predicate** is two or more predicates joined by a conjunction.

1-5 PRACTICE THE SKILL

Underline each simple subject once. Underline each simple predicate twice.

1. Hudson Taylor preached God's Word and administered medical treatment to the wounded.

2. The China Inland Mission began under Hudson Taylor's leadership and employed John and Betty Stam.

3. John Stam and Betty Scott attended Moody Bible Institute.

4. John Stam studied the Chinese language and wrote letters to Betty Scott.

5. John and Betty Stam traveled to Suancheng and visited with the Birches there.

6. Helen Priscilla Stam and the Los' son traveled far to the Wuhu Methodist Hospital.

7. The Red forces invaded and pillaged the city of Tsingteh.

8. John wrote to the China Inland Mission about his capture and requested twenty thousand dollars in ransom money.

9. John's faith and Betty's faith influenced many Chinese.

10. Evangelist Lo rescued Helen Priscilla and took her to her grandparents.

1-6 REVIEW THE SKILL

Combine the following pairs of sentences. Some sentences may need a compound subject; others may need a compound predicate.

1. Ice cream was sold commercially in 1851.
   Ice cream did not become popular until the 1900s.

   _____

   _____

2. Whole milk can be used in ice cream.
   Two percent milk can be used in ice cream.

   _____

   _____

3. Flavorings are added to ice cream.
   Nuts are added to ice cream.

   _____

   _____

4. Jenna baked some cookies.
   Jenna ate some cookies.

   _____

   _____

5. Sasha likes gingerbread.
   Sasha dislikes gingersnaps.

   _____

   _____

6. Jenna made a gingerbread house.
   Jenna gave it as a gift.

   _____

   _____

Learning Christianly

Learning how sentences work may not seem very important at first. How significant can a sentence be, anyway? Pretty significant—if you take the Bible seriously. Consider the power of one of God's sentences in Genesis 1:3. What does this verse suggest about language in general?

7. Sasha baked for the party.
   Jenna baked for the party.

   _____

   _____

8. Jenna made a cake.
   Jenna brought some ice cream.

   _____

   _____

9. Jorge came to the party.
   Sasha came to the party.

   _____

   _____

10. Jorge ate only a few cookies.
    Jorge became quite ill.

    _____

    _____

page 192

Inverted Order

Finding Subjects and Predicates in Inverted Order

In the natural order of most declarative sentences, the subject comes first and the predicate follows.

          S   P
The young man spoke to the audience.

   S   P
He is speaking about his trip to Australia.

Some declarative sentences reverse the **natural order:** the predicate comes first and the subject follows. These sentences are in **inverted order.**

               P   S
Behind the podium stood the young man.

           P   S
There were the notes for his speech.

Look again at the second sentence. The word *there* is almost never the subject of a sentence. If you see a sentence that begins with *there* followed by a verb, look for the subject after the predicate.

Usually, you can rearrange the words in an inverted sentence to follow natural order. Doing so may help you to find the subject and the predicate more easily.

        S   **P**

The young man stood behind the podium.

      S   **P**

The notes for his speech were there.

Interrogative sentences also can be in both natural order and inverted order. Many interrogative sentences are in the same order as most declarative sentences.

      S **P**

Who spoke to the audience?

Other interrogative sentences are in inverted order.

        P   **S**

When is the program?

In many interrogative sentences with inverted order, the subject comes between the two verbs that make up the simple predicate.

      P   **S** **P**

Did the young man speak to the audience?

   P S   **P**

Is he speaking about his trip to Australia?

You can turn inverted interrogative sentences around to make sure that you have found the subject and the verb.

       S **P**

The program is when?

        S   **P**

The young man did speak to the audience.

   S **P**

He is speaking about his trip to Australia.

Be sure to include both parts of the simple predicate for any interrogative sentences that follow this order.

IN SUMMARY

Most sentences follow the **natural** subject/predicate order.

Some sentences, especially interrogative sentences, may use **inverted order,** with the predicate first and the subject second.

1-7 PRACTICE THE SKILL

Underline each simple subject once and each simple predicate twice.

1. Where do you live?

2. There stands your mother.

3. Into the house walks your dog.

4. Where is his leash?

5. Did you see it in the house?

6. There is the leash.

7. Where was your dog going?

8. On the porch sits your dog.

9. Who called her name?

10. Your mother called from the house.

1-8 REVIEW THE SKILL

Underline each simple subject once and each simple predicate twice.

1. Did you see the marines?

2. Where did they go?

3. There went the corps of marines.

4. Will they travel on a boat?

5. Yes, into the ocean went their boat.

6. Upon land walked another group of soldiers.

7. By whom were their orders issued?

8. Into the tent marched their commanding officer.

9. By his hand came the orders.

10. Where is he?

Recognizing Fragments

In formal usage a sentence needs to be complete, not a **fragment.** As you have learned, a sentence contains both a subject and a predicate. A **complete sentence** also expresses a complete thought. It is properly capitalized and punctuated.

> Charles Lindbergh flew across the ocean.

The group of words above is a complete sentence because it meets all the criteria for a complete sentence.

A fragment is a group of words that is not a complete sentence but is wrongly capitalized and punctuated as if it were complete. In other words, a fragment leaves out important information. It may lack a subject or a predicate or both. Sometimes a fragment has a subject and a predicate but also includes a word or phrase that makes it too weak to stand alone. The words *after, although, as, because, if, unless,* or *while* often introduce a group of words that, unless combined with a complete sentence, will result in a sentence fragment.

> Was named the *Spirit of St. Louis. (What was named?)*
> The people of Paris. *(What did the people of Paris do?)*
> Because he was the first pilot to cross the Atlantic Ocean alone without stopping. *(What happened because he was the first?)*

You can correct a fragment that lacks a subject or a predicate by supplying the missing element. You can correct a fragment that cannot stand alone by joining it to a sentence or adding information that completes the thought.

> **Lindbergh's plane** was named the *Spirit of St. Louis.*
> The people of Paris **welcomed him enthusiastically.**
> **We remember Lindbergh today** because he was the first pilot to cross the Atlantic Ocean alone without stopping.

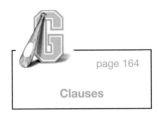

page 164

Clauses

IN SUMMARY

A **complete sentence** must express a complete thought and contain both a subject and a predicate.

Fragments are incomplete sentences. Correct a fragment by supplying the missing information or by joining it to a complete sentence.

1-9   PRACTICE THE SKILL

A. Label each group of words *S* (sentence) or *F* (fragment). Be prepared to explain your answers.

_____ 1. We do not know the origin of cheese making.

_____ 2. European cheese making, a family tradition since the seventeenth century.

_____ 3. Today the United States.

_____ 4. Produces more cheese than any other country.

_____ 5. James Kraft, an American, introduced the process of cheese pasteurization.

_____ 6. High-protein cow's milk is the main ingredient in most cheeses.

_____ 7. If sour milk replaces sweet milk.

_____ 8. The flavor of cheese will be strong.

_____ 9. Cottage cheese is creamy.

_____ 10. Because cheese makers use a variety of methods.

B. Rewrite the fragments from numbers 1-10 above to make complete sentences. You may combine groups of words. If a group of words is already a sentence, write *sentence* in the blank.

1. _____

_____

2. _____

_____

3. _____

_____

4. _____

_____

5. _____

_____

6. _____

_____

7. _____

_____

8. _____

_____

9. _____

_____

10. _____

_____

A. Label each group of words _S_ (sentence) or _F_ (fragment).

_____ 1. In almost every country around the world.

_____ 2. People use the metric system for measuring.

_____ 3. The metric system can be used for the measurement of weight, length, time, and temperature.

_____ 4. Because it is extremely simple.

_____ 5. Came up with the metric system in the 1790s.

_____ 6. A team of talented French scientists.

_____ 7. Seven base units make up all metric measurements.

_____ 8. Part of what makes the metric system so simple.

_____ 9. Even though the metric system is simple.

_____ 10. Most Americans prefer the inch–pound system of measurement.

B. Rewrite the fragments from numbers 1-10 above to make complete sentences. You may combine groups of words. If a group of words is already a sentence, write _sentence_ in the blank.

1. _____

_____

2. _____

_____

3. _____

_____

4. _____

_____

5. _____

_____

6. _____

_____

7. _____

_____

meters

grams

liters

8. _____

   _____

9. _____

   _____

10. _____

    _____

Recognizing Other Sentence Errors

A correct sentence must be a single sentence, not two or more sentences written as if they were one. These joined sentences are sentence errors. A **comma splice** consists of two sentences incorrectly joined by only a comma. One way to correct a comma splice is to change the incorrect comma to a period at the end of the first sentence and to capitalize the next word to form the beginning of a second sentence.

> **Wrong:** Charles Lindbergh flew across the Atlantic Ocean, his airplane was called the *Spirit of St. Louis.*

> **Right:** Charles Lindbergh flew across the Atlantic Ocean. His airplane was called the *Spirit of St. Louis.*

A **fused sentence** consists of two or more sentences incorrectly joined without any punctuation at all. You can correct a fused sentence by adding the missing punctuation at the end of the first sentence and capitalizing the first word of the second sentence.

> **Wrong:** His flight captured the world's attention the reporters gave Lindbergh the nickname "Lone Eagle."

> **Right:** His flight captured the world's attention. The reporters gave Lindbergh the nickname "Lone Eagle."

page 166

Compound sentences

page 291

Commas

page 301

Semicolons

IN SUMMARY

Comma splices and **fused sentences** are two or more sentences incorrectly written as if they were one sentence.

Correct these sentence errors by separating them into individual sentences.

A. Label each group of words S (sentence), CS (comma splice), or FS (fused sentence).

_____ 1. Tennis has changed greatly since the game's invention.

_____ 2. The French played a game like tennis over seven hundred years ago, the players hit the ball with their hands instead of rackets.

_____ 3. In the 1870s Major Walter Clopton Wingfield, an Englishman, developed modern tennis.

_____ 4. Wingfield played on grass courts the game became known as lawn tennis.

_____ 5. The players used rackets they did not hit the ball with their hands.

_____ 6. Mary Ewing Outerbridge brought lawn tennis to the United States, she organized the first American tennis court in New York.

_____ 7. Today we rarely play tennis on grass.

_____ 8. Most American tennis courts consist of asphalt or concrete, carpet covers many indoor courts.

_____ 9. Table tennis is a miniature version of tennis a table replaces the court.

_____ 10. Tennis is a popular sport all over the world today.

B. Rewrite part A, changing the comma splices and fused sentences to correct sentences. If a group of words is already a sentence, write _sentence_ in the blank.

1. _____

    _____

2. _____

    _____

3. _____

    _____

4. _____

    _____

5. _____

_____

6. _____

_____

7. _____

_____

8. _____

_____

9. _____

_____

10. _____

_____

1-12 REVIEW THE SKILL

Rewrite the sentences to correct the fragments, comma splices, and fused sentences. Write *sentence* for a correct sentence.

1. Benjamin Franklin accomplished many remarkable things in his lifetime.

_____

_____

2. He started his career at age twelve, he worked in his brother's print shop.

_____

_____

3. Ten years later, Franklin owned his own print shop, he published newspapers and books.

_____

_____

4. Although he was originally a printer.

_____

_____

5. Franklin enjoyed scientific experiments too.

_____

_____

6. He developed many useful inventions he improved the efficiency of heating stoves.

_____

_____

7. The colonial postal service.

_____

_____

8. Owed its efficiency to Franklin's reforms.

_____

_____

9. He also established a fire department and a city police department.

_____

_____

10. Franklin started an academy the school became the University of Pennsylvania.

_____

_____

1-13 PRACTICE THE SKILL

A. Label each group of words *S* (sentence), *Frag* (fragment), *CS* (comma splice), or *FS* (fused sentence).

_____ 1. Julia Ward Howe lived from 1819 to 1910, she was quite famous during her lifetime.

_____ 2. She wrote, lectured, and crusaded in the antislavery and women's movements.

_____ 3. Her best-known writing is perhaps "The Battle Hymn of the Republic" she borrowed the tune from a popular song.

_____ 4. The tune "John Brown's Body."

_____ 5. At a military encampment she wrote the song she later published it.

_____ 6. After its publication in 1861, "The Battle Hymn of the Republic" was sung often by Union soldiers.

_____ 7. Howe wrote plays and poems she also edited an antislavery newspaper with her husband.

_____ 8. In 1872 crusaded for a national Mother's Day.

_____ 9. About voting rights for women, there were different views.

_____ 10. Howe was the first president of the New England Woman Suffrage Association, her influence as a writer for women's voting rights was great.

B. Rewrite part A, changing the fragments, comma splices, and fused sentences to correct sentences. If a group of words is already a sentence, write _sentence_ in the blank.

1. _____

_____

2. _____

_____

3. _____

_____

4. _____

_____

5. _____

_____

6. _____

_____

7. _____

_____

8. _____

_____

9. _____

_____

10. _____

_____

≡SLIDING HOME

The dialogue in "The Drummer Boy of Shiloh" is realistic, much like our everyday speech. When we talk to our friends, we don't always speak in complete, logical sentences. Notice the fragments in the general's speech. "Won't be time once it all starts. . . . Even more of a fool. . . . There's your cheek, fell right off the tree from overhead." The general's meaning is clear to us, even though his sentences are not grammatically perfect. There is even a fragment in the narration: "Silence." Bradbury's choice to use only one word makes the "sentence" short and blunt, and it makes us "hear" the silence more powerfully.

- *What types of sentences (declarative, interrogative, imperative, exclamatory) does Bradbury use in the excerpt at the beginning of the chapter?*

- *Only one type of sentence is used in the first paragraph. What type is it? Why do you think the author uses so many short sentences in a row? Read the first paragraph out loud. Does it make you think of someone tossing and turning, trying to go to sleep?*

Genesis 1:1
In the beginning God created the heaven and the earth.

Acts 9:6
And he trembling and astonished said, Lord, what wilt thou have me to do? And the Lord said unto him, Arise, and go into the city, and it shall be told thee what thou must do.

Psalm 8:9
O Lord our Lord, how excellent is thy name in all the earth!

- *Which types of sentences are represented in the passages above?*

CREATING A BOOK JACKET

Man looketh on the outward appearance.
I Samuel 16:7

Years ago, the book jacket was a kind of dirt and dust protector. Now, book jackets serve as advertisements. An eye-catching picture or title or a favorite author's name makes you want to select one book above others. The information on the jacket influences you to reshelve the book or to buy it.

Your Turn

Design a book jacket for a favorite novel. Write material for the back cover and the inside flaps and illustrate the front cover.

Planning

Think about the books you have read recently. Which one was your favorite? What made it stand out above the others?

Identify your favorite part of the book. Did one chapter stand out? Or did the storyline make you want to keep reading? Perhaps one character became your favorite. Choose one thing to highlight in your review.

Consider your audience. Your purpose is to describe the book and to persuade someone else to read it. Write in a way that will appeal to your audience and answer questions someone considering this book might have.

page 381

Reasons

Drafting

Write a short "review" of the book for the back cover. Pretend you are a critic and list your reasons for recommending the book. Make sure that your reasons are supported well, not simply based on preference.

Summarize the beginning of the story on the inside front flap. Here is an excerpt of a student summary of *The Cay* by Theodore Taylor:

> As *The Cay* begins, Phillip, an eleven-year-old American boy, is living on the island of Curaçao off the coast of Venezuela. His father is working for the Royal Dutch Shell company. During February of 1942 German submarines blow up some ships and an oil refinery nearby. Phillip's mother is frightened about what might happen if the family stays on the island. As Phillip and his mom leave to return to Virginia, the ship on which they are sailing sinks. Timothy, a really old West Indian man, rescues Phillip. Phillip becomes blind because of an injury from the explosion.

When summarizing, be careful not to give away the ending!

Ask "teaser" questions. Will Timothy and Phillip ever be rescued? How will Phillip and Timothy get along? Will Phillip ever get his sight back? Questions will make the reader want to find out more about the book.

Include a short biographical paragraph on the inside back flap. Find out something about the author's life. Theodore Taylor, author of *The Cay*, became interested in the Caribbean because he spent time there. That fact and other facts about him and his books will increase reader interest.

Draw a front-cover illustration. The illustration should represent the main idea of the book. Include both the title and the author's name.

Revising

Re-view the draft for ways to improve it. Does the cover convey the message of the book? Does the inside front flap make the reader want to read the story? Does the back flap include interesting facts about the author? Does the back cover include a review based on facts, not opinion?

Let someone else look at your book jacket. Someone who has never read the book could check for interest level; someone who is familiar with the work could check for accuracy. Consider the suggestions as you revise.

Check your work for precision. Now is the time to find the best words for the context. The student who wrote about *The Cay* made the following changes to the first draft after examining it for precise words.

> As Phillip and his mom leave to return to Virginia, the ship on
> which they are sailing ~~sinks~~ *is torpedoed and sunk*. Timothy, ~~a really old~~ *an elderly* West Indian
> man, rescues Phillip.

Proofread your book jacket for errors. If you run the spell checker on your computer, remember that it cannot catch certain errors. It will not notice if you write about someone who is a "close fried" (friend).

Publishing

Display your book jacket somewhere that others will see it. Perhaps the school librarian would be interested in your book jacket for an exhibit.

Add your book jacket to your portfolio. A well-done book jacket will be an example of your persuasive and informative writing skills.

Adopting Words

Between Innings

Many words we use every day in English come from other languages. When you order a *hamburger,* you acknowledge the German city of Hamburg, where the dish originated. When you say you want a *cookie,* you are using a word from Holland. Having *goulash* for supper? That is a Hungarian dish. And that "all-American" favorite *spaghetti* comes from Italy.

Even the names of many American places reflect other languages. *Tioga, Omaha, Susquehanna, Dakota,* and *Kansas* are Native American terms. What others can you think of? Other places have Spanish names: *Colorado, Los Angeles, Florida,* and *Nevada. New Orleans* comes from the French, and *Philadelphia* is Greek in origin. What about the name of your town or city?

Grand Slam: Writing Across the Curriculum

Cut a cartoon strip from a newspaper. Then cut the "bubbles" of words out and cut the frames apart. Glue the frames onto white paper, perhaps changing the order.

Into the blank spaces where the words had been, write your own script. This time, though, relate the script to something you have studied or experimented with in science class or in another class that you particularly like.

Try to make the script "match" the pictures and remember to add some humor too.

CHAPTER 2

NOUNS

THE CAY
BY THEODORE TAYLOR

In the morning, the air was crisp and the cay smelled fresh and clean. Timothy cooked a small fish, a pompano, that he'd speared at dawn down on the reef. Neither of us had felt so good or so clean since we had been aboard the *Hato*. And without discussing it, we both thought this might be the day an aircraft would swing up into the Devil's Mouth, if that's where we were.

The pompano, broiled over the low fire, tasted good. Of course, we were eating little but what came from the sea. Fish, langosta, mussels, or the eggs from sea urchins, those small, black round sea animals with sharp spines that attach themselves to the reefs.

Timothy had tried to make a stew from seaweed but it tasted bitter. Then he'd tried to boil some new sea-grape roots but they made us ill. The only thing that ever worked for him was sea-grape leaves, boiled first in sea water and then cooked in fresh water.

But above us, forty feet from the ground, Timothy said, was a feast. Big, fat green coconuts. When we'd landed, there were a few dried ones on the ground, but the meat in them was not very tasty. In a fresher one, there was still some milk, but it was rancid.

- *What names of things in this passage are not familiar to you?*

- *If you had to guess what these things are, what clues does this passage give you?*

- *Which names in the passage seem to have a Caribbean sound to them?*

- *Do you think you would like to eat with Timothy and the narrator?*

Some of the names in this passage begin with capital letters. The capitals signal that these are names of specific things or places. *Hato* is the name of a ship. What other words in the passage lead you to believe that the *Hato* is a ship?

The list in the second paragraph gives many specific details. Writers use details like these to make you feel that you are a part of the scenes they are describing.

Names of people, places, things, and ideas are called *nouns*. Nouns are just one of the parts of speech that good writers learn to use to advantage. After you finish this chapter, you will better understand how this writer used nouns to make us feel as if we were on the cay with Timothy and the narrator.

page 381

Developing the Supporting Sentences

Nouns

The largest group of words in the English language is nouns; the next largest group is verbs, then adjectives, and then adverbs. There are thousands of words in each group. New words can be added to these classes by invention, by changing or combining other words, or by taking words from another language. In any complete sentence, it is the nouns, verbs, adjectives, and adverbs that carry most of the meaning in the sentence.

Nouns are words that name. Traditionally, nouns have been defined as the names of persons, places, things, and ideas.

Person:	girl, Moira
Place:	town, Boise
Thing:	book, *Swiss Family Robinson*
Idea:	emotion, happiness

2-1 **PRACTICE THE SKILL**

Underline the nouns.

1. Critics believe Edgar Allan Poe wrote a poem when a friend tragically died.

2. Poe chose to name his heroine after the legendary Helen of Troy.

3. Her circumstances led to the Trojan War.

4. In the poem, Poe alludes to Ulysses, who returned to his home after ten years of travel.

5. The themes of his poems often deal with death or terror.

6. "The Raven" is the most famous poem by Edgar Allan Poe.

7. The poem brought Poe his first taste of fame.

8. The structure of the poem is developed around questions asked by the speaker.

9. The death of a beautiful woman is the theme.

10. The raven repeats the same word at the end of several stanzas.

Fill in each blank with an appropriate noun.

_____ 1. (person) and Denise worked at camp during the summer.

_____ 2. Denise's (idea) of water inspired her to be a lifeguard.

_____ 3. The camp was in (place).

_____ 4. The campers played many (thing).

_____ 5. Out in the (place), Justin hid from the other team.

_____ 6. Amy's (idea) of snakes affected her enjoyment.

_____ 7. (person) borrowed clothes from her sister.

_____ 8. From camp, Todd sent (thing) to his best friend at home.

_____ 9. Ted wrote to his grandparents who live in (place).

_____ 10. (person) was practicing for his swim test.

Forms of Nouns

Another way to define nouns is by how they change when they are used in different ways. In English most nouns have four forms: the **singular,** the **singular possessive,** the **plural,** and the **plural possessive.** Any word that can appear in these four forms is a noun.

boy The singular form of the noun shows that just one person or thing is being named.

boy's The singular possessive form shows ownership by one person or thing. It usually modifies another noun.

boys The plural shows that at least two persons or things are being named.

boys' The plural possessive form shows ownership by more than one person or thing. It usually modifies another noun.

Learning Christianly

Nouns are important in language because naming is important in life. Read Genesis 1:3-5 and 2:19. What does the similarity between these two portions suggest about using language to name things?

page 320

Plural nouns

Spelling the Plurals of Nouns

A singular noun indicates that there is only one person, place, thing, or idea. Plural nouns indicate that there are two or more persons, places, things, or ideas.

Regular plural formation

Pronunciation of Plurals (and Possessives)

English has three different pronunciations for its plural (and possessive) noun forms.

1. Plurals after *s, x, z, ch,* or *sh* sounds are pronounced /ez/.
   Examples: buses, boxes, quizzes, churches, dishes.
2. Plurals after *b, d, g, l, m, n, r, v, w,* or vowel sounds are pronounced /z/.
   Examples: dogs, dolls, cans, cows, arias.
3. Plurals after *f, k, p,* or *t* sounds are pronounced /s/.
   Examples: laughs, larks, shops, cots.

Add *s* to the singular form of most nouns to form the plural.

>   dog   dogs

Add *es* to singular nouns ending with *s, x, z, ch,* and *sh.*

>   dish   dishes

If the noun ends with a consonant followed by *y,* change the *y* to *i* and then add *es.*

>   city   cities

If the noun ends with a vowel followed by *y,* add only *s.*

>   monkey   monkeys

If the word ends in *f* or *fe,* consult your dictionary. For some nouns, add *s;* for others, change the *f* to *v* and add *es.*

>   chief   chiefs
>   wolf   wolves

If the word ends in *o,* consult your dictionary. For some nouns, add *s;* for others, add *es.*

>   piano   pianos
>   potato   potatoes

Irregular plural formation

Change the spelling.

>   man   men
>   goose   geese
>   mouse   mice

Change nothing.

deer   deer
Chinese   Chinese

Add *'s* to form the plurals of letters being discussed.

the *d*   the *d*'s

IN SUMMARY

Nouns name persons, places, things, and ideas.

Most nouns have four forms: **singular, singular possessive, plural,** and **plural possessive.**

Add *s* or *es* to most singular nouns to form the plural.

Some nouns have irregular forms for the plural.

2-3 **PRACTICE THE SKILL**

Change the underlined nouns to the plural form. Write the answer in the blank.

_____ 1. Black darkness cloaked the <u>mountain</u>.

_____ 2. The wind tore the leaves from the <u>tree</u>, and rain-drops hammered the <u>housetop</u>.

_____ 3. The <u>branch</u> of the tree hung low from the weight of the rain.

_____ 4. Rain overflowed in the <u>gutter</u> of the old farm-house.

_____ 5. The <u>sky</u> flashed lightning blue.

_____ 6. The lightning <u>flash</u> looked like a <u>z</u> in the sky.

_____ 7. Moments later, a <u>crash</u> of thunder rumbled through the <u>valley</u>.

_____ 8. The <u>man</u> ran quickly onto the <u>porch</u> to get out of the storm.

_____ 9. After the rain the <u>child</u> went outside to play.

_____ 10. The day turned out to be perfect for fishing for <u>trout</u>.

Underline any error with plural forms of nouns. Rewrite the nouns correctly on the lines below the paragraph.

Minnesota is home to many wild animalses. The northern forestes are home to bears and mooses. Some of the most interesting creatures in the state are the wolfs. You can see smaller animals in Minnesota too. Beavers and foxs are abundant. Wildfowl, such as ducks and turkies, also live there. The state is famous for the fishs that live in its lakes. Some people fish all year long. Many people have buildinges called shanties to protect them from the cold. The shantys have holes in their floors that allow the fishermen to fish through holeses in the ice.

_____

_____

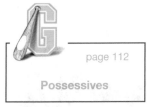

page 112

Possessives

page 310

Apostrophe

Forming the Possessives of Nouns

Possessive nouns show ownership or belonging. They tell who or what owns a thing. All possessive nouns have apostrophes.

To form the singular possessive, add 's to the singular form of the noun (even if the noun already ends in *s*).

house	house's roof
Mr. Charles	Mr. Charles's car
child	child's toy
goose	goose's feathers

Traditionally, add only ' to the proper names *Jesus* and *Moses*.

Jesus   Jesus' disciples

To form the plural possessive, add ' or 's to the plural form of the noun. If a plural ends with *s*, add only ' to make it possessive.

houses	houses' foundations
the Bateses	the Bateses' vacation

If a plural does not end with *s*, add 's.

children	children's playground
geese	geese's pond

IN SUMMARY

To form the singular possessive, add 's to the singular form.

To form the plural possessive, add ' or 's to the plural form.

2-5 PRACTICE THE SKILL

Rewrite each phrase on the line beside it, changing each *of* phrase to a possessive noun form.

1. the car of Mrs. Peterson

2. the collars of the dogs

3. the sister of Moses

4. the food of the mice

5. the basketball of Angelo

6. the suits of the men

7. the daughter of the Joneses

8. the passport of the tourist

9. the attention of the people

10. the color of the flowers

Rewrite each sentence, changing each underlined noun to its possessive form.

1. The <u>boy</u> hastily written lesson is illegible.

   _____

2. The <u>teacher</u> suggestion was to exert more effort.

   _____

3. Mrs. Connelly complimented the <u>children</u> progress.

   _____

4. At the <u>teachers</u> meeting, the principal announced new policies.

   _____

   _____

5. Our <u>choir</u> song won first place in interscholastic competition.

   _____

   _____

6. The <u>boys</u> choir and the <u>girls</u> choir will combine for a special concert.

   _____

   _____

7. In history class we heard the <u>president</u> speech.

   _____

   _____

8. In my book report I told a few facts about the <u>author</u> life.

   _____

   _____

9. In our book reports we are not to tell the <u>stories</u> endings.

   _____

   _____

10. In a science report Ted told about <u>sheep</u> aversion to fast-running water.

   _____

   _____

Choosing Between Possessive and Plural

If you have trouble deciding whether a noun should be possessive or plural, try putting the noun into a prepositional phrase beginning with the word *of*. The *of* phrase, like the possessive form, shows ownership. The prepositional phrase may sound a little strange, but it will almost always make sense.

The *boys'* ride to the old barn took four hours.
The *ride of the boys* to the old barn took four hours.

Although the second sentence sounds wordy, it makes sense. The correct form of the noun is the plural possessive.

Usually the *of* phrase will not work when the plural form is needed. Sometimes you cannot substitute an *of* phrase for the noun without changing the meaning of the sentence.

Wrong: The ride of the boys their bicycles to the park.
Right: The boys ride their bicycles to the park.

The sentence with the *of* phrase does not make sense. The plural form, not the possessive form, is correct.

page 144
Prepositional phrases

IN SUMMARY

Use an *of* phrase to test whether the possessive form or the plural form of a noun is correct.

2-7 PRACTICE THE SKILL

Fill in each blank with the correct singular, singular possessive, plural, or plural possessive form of a word from the list below.

        body   dolphin   fin   sound

_____ 1. The __?__ is one of a group of mammals similar to the whale.

_____ 2. The __?__ of dolphins are shaped like torpedoes.

_____ 3. __?__ differ from porpoises in the shapes of their snouts and teeth.

_____ 4. Their __?__ abilities to slow the heart rate and collapse the lungs enable dolphins to dive deeply.

_____ 5. __?__ flippers and __?__ balance and propel them through the ocean.

_____ 6. Scientists speculate that its _?_ blubber helps keep a dolphin afloat.

_____ 7. The two tail _?_ purposes are both propulsion and communication.

_____ 8. While underwater, a _?_ blowhole, located on the top of its head, remains closed.

_____ 9. Dolphins are able to hear many _?_ .

_____ 10. A _?_ built-in sonar system helps it locate and identify objects.

2-8 REVIEW THE SKILL

Using one of the words from the list, fill in the blank with the correct singular (S), singular possessive (SP), plural (P), or plural possessive (PP) form. Then use the abbreviations to tell which form you used.

bee   beekeeper   hive   honey

_____ 1. The only source of _?_ is honeybees.

_____ 2. Beeswax, another of the _?_ products, is an ingredient in chewing gum.

_____ 3. Some beekeepers are able to handle _?_ with their bare hands.

_____ 4. All worker _?_ hind legs have baskets that are used to carry pollen.

_____ 5. A worker _?_ dance tells other bees where they can find nectar.

_____ 6. Worker _?_ guard all of the hive's entrances against unwanted invaders.

_____ 7. If a _?_ movements around the hive are too quick, a bee is more likely to sting.

_____ 8. Many _?_ hives are transported cross-country in order to expose the bees to a variety of plants.

_____ 9. _?_ flavor varies according to the plant that supplied the nectar.

_____ 10. God's design in nature can be seen in the structure of the _?_ .

Underline any errors with plurals or possessives. Rewrite the words correctly on the lines below. Be prepared to explain your answers.

Andorra is one of the smallest country's in the world. (Notice that the country's name has two *r*s in it.) Andorra is located between France and Spain. The Pyrenees Mountains surround Andorra's vallies.

For more than seven hundred years, two prince's, one from each of Andorra's neighbors, ruled Andorra. The peoples wishs for self-rule became reality in 1993 when they adopted their countries first constitution. This constitution limits the princes' power.

Today tourism is popular in Andorra, and many men and womans work in store's and hotel's. In the past, however, most Andorrans were farmers or shepherds. Many Andorran familys still live in their ancestors' farmhouses.

_____

_____

Identifying Common and Proper Nouns

Whether singular or plural, possessive or not possessive, all nouns are either **common** or **proper.** Common nouns are general words for persons, places, or things. Proper nouns name specific people, places, or things. We capitalize proper nouns.

Recognizing Common and Proper Nouns

	Common	**Proper**
Persons	son	Randall
	pastor	Lloyd Harrison
	real estate agent	Pam Gossette
Places	park	Eder Park
	airport	O'Hare International Airport
	mountain	Mount McKinley
Things	flag	Old Glory
	magazine	*National Geographic*
	beagle	Snoopy

page 116

Proper adjectives

page 277

Capitalization

Common nouns are general words for persons, places, things, and ideas. Common nouns are not generally capitalized.

Proper nouns are specific words for persons, places, things, and ideas. Proper nouns must be capitalized.

2-10 **PRACTICE THE SKILL**

Underline the nouns in the sentences below. Label each noun C (common) or P (proper).

1. Jason flew on a plane to France.

2. His vacation to this new country was exciting.

3. Jason left his family at the LaGuardia International Airport.

4. The plane stopped in Paris.

5. In this city, people can see the Louvre.

6. Jason walked down the Champs-Elysees.

7. Cafes are located along this street.

8. The Duponts took him to see Notre Dame, the famous cathedral.

9. Then the family rode the metro back to their chalet.

10. Jason traveled to Normandy on a train.

2-11 **REVIEW THE SKILL**

Replace each common noun in parentheses by writing a proper noun in the blank.

_____ 1. (girl) is in the seventh grade.

_____ 2. She attends (school).

_____ 3. The school is located in (city).

_____ 4. (boy), her older brother, attends the same school.

_____ 5. They live nearby in (another city).

_____ 6. On (weekday) her history class took a field trip.

_____ 7. They visited (historic site).

_____ 8. There, the students learned about (historical figure).

_____ 9. That person was an important figure in the history of (state).

_____ 10. (teacher) and the students enjoyed their trip.

Identifying Count and Noncount Nouns

So far you have studied three pairs of noun characteristics: singular and plural, possessive and nonpossessive, and common and proper. In addition to these characteristics, common nouns (and only common nouns) are also **count** and **noncount.** Normally we make distinctions between count and noncount nouns automatically.

Count nouns, unlike noncount nouns, can be made plural to show *how many.* Changing a singular count noun to plural changes the number but not the meaning of the word. We can speak of *a book, one book,* or *two books.* Count nouns can be singular or plural in form. You can test a singular noun to see whether it is a count noun by putting either the word *a* or the word *one* in front of it. When a count noun is plural, it can have a number word other than *one* before it.

A *book* lay on the desk.
One *book* lay on the desk.
Two *books* lay on the desk.

Noncount nouns are always singular, never plural, in form. Noncount nouns will not take *a* or *one* before them.

Wrong: The pitcher is for *a milk.*
Right: The pitcher is for *milk.*
Wrong: The glass would not hold *milks.*
Right: The glass would not hold much *milk.*

Count and Noncount Nouns

1. Use *many* with plural count nouns and *much* with noncount nouns.
   We ate *many rolls* and *much rice* at dinner last night.
2. Use *a few* with plural count nouns and *a little* with noncount nouns.
   We ate *a few* biscuits with *a little* gravy.
3. Do not put an *s* on the end of a noncount noun.
   Wrong: We ate many rices for dinner.
        They have many knowledges.
   Right: We ate a lot of rice for dinner.
       They have much knowledge.

Count nouns can be made plural to show how many.
Noncount nouns are always singular in form.

2-12 PRACTICE THE SKILL

Label each underlined noun CO (count) or N (noncount).

_____ 1. Did the glass hold much <u>cola</u>?

_____ 2. Did you wear your <u>socks</u> today?

_____ 3. Can you bring me the <u>water</u>?

_____ 4. The aspirin gave me some <u>relief</u> for my headache.

_____ 5. Do you like my new <u>coat</u>?

_____ 6. My mom bought me matching <u>mittens</u> to wear also.

_____ 7. It's fun to go shopping with my <u>mom</u>.

_____ 8. Occasionally, we leave the stores with many <u>bags</u>.

_____ 9. After driving around town so much, we have to refill the car with <u>gas</u>.

_____ 10. At the end of the day, we are out of <u>cash</u>.

2-13 REVIEW THE SKILL

Label each underlined noun CO (count) or N (noncount).

_____ 1. Dolley Madison was a prominent citizen of Washington, D.C., under two different <u>presidents</u>.

_____ 2. Because his wife had died, President Thomas Jefferson asked Dolley to act as official White House <u>hostess</u>.

_____ 3. Later, her <u>husband</u> became president of the United States.

_____ 4. She is famous today for her <u>courage</u> during the War of 1812 when the British invaded the city and threatened to burn the White House.

_____ 5. Dolley refused to flee until she arranged for the <u>safety</u> of important state papers and a historic painting of George Washington.

_____ 6. Lucy Hayes, the <u>wife</u> of President Rutherford B. Hayes, was also a remarkable woman.

_____ 7. She graduated from Wesleyan Female College in Ohio during a time when many women did not attend a <u>college</u>.

_____ 8. Lucy was the first president's wife to earn a college <u>degree</u>.

_____ 9. She believed <u>slavery</u> and alcohol were ruining the country and became famous for her opposition to them.

_____ 10. In fact, critics nicknamed her "Lemonade Lucy" because she served <u>lemonade</u> instead of alcohol in the White House.

Identifying Compound Nouns

Some nouns have been formed by combining two words. These nouns are called **compound nouns.** The meaning of a compound word is often a special combination of the meanings of the two original words.

> Compound nouns in English have their main stress (loudest syllable) in the first part of the compound: <u>high</u>chair, <u>bas</u>ketball, <u>red</u>head, <u>son</u>-in-law.
> However, when an adjective modifies a noun, the noun has the main stress: a high <u>chair</u>, a red <u>head</u>.

book + mark   =   bookmark

son + in + law   =   son-in-law

thunder + bolt   =   thunderbolt

red + head   =   redhead

page 337

Finding the word

Notice the different ways that compound nouns are written. Some are written as one word; others are hyphenated. Because the hyphen has been omitted from many compound nouns in modern spelling, you must often check a dictionary for spellings.

IN SUMMARY

Compound nouns are made by joining two or more words or by hyphenating two or more words.

2-14 PRACTICE THE SKILL

Underline each compound noun.

1. Yellowstone is the oldest national park in America and a popular vacation spot.

2. Many families enjoy the campgrounds and the famous geysers.

3. The park is known for its abundance of wildlife too.

4. Wildflowers such as fringed gentian and mountain bluebell cover the meadows during the summer.

5. But in the winter, heavy snow covers the park; in fact, three of the park's five entrances are closed because of the snowfall.

6. Another famous campsite is the Grand Canyon.

7. Many people have seen minor rockslides at the Grand Canyon.

8. The pathway into the Grand Canyon is very narrow in some places.

9. One of the highlights of the hike is to see the massive stone formations from the bottom.

10. The Grand Canyon is one of the biggest outspreads of rock in the United States.

2-15 REVIEW THE SKILL

Underline each compound noun.

1. The thunderstorm was finally over, and Alison and Katy decided to go for a hike.

2. They borrowed backpacks from their great-uncle.

3. Alison and Katy set off down the footpath.

4. Yesterday, the riverbed had been almost dry.

5. Now the trickle of water made a beautiful waterfall.

6. Once they reached the mountaintop, Alison and Katy decided to turn around.

7. The thunderstorm returned with heavier rainfall.

8. The massive amount of rain began to form its own watercourse.

9. The raindrops were so large they looked almost like hailstones.

10. Alison and Katy found shelter at the campground.

A. Label the underlined nouns *C* (common) or *P* (proper).
B. Label each underlined common noun *CO* (count) or *N* (non-count).
C. Correct any incorrect spelling of plurals or any incorrect possessives by writing the correct word above the error.

Lois Lenski grew up in a small Ohio town in the early 1900s. After college, she moved to New York and then to London to study art. She soon was writing and illustrating bookes. Many of Loises' books tell about childs growing up in small towns across the United States, reflecting her fondness for her own childhood. Her illustrations help to tell the story by depicting the people and places her words describe. Her book *Strawberry Girl* won the 1946 Newbery Medal, an award for an outstanding contribution to childrens literature. Lois Lenski also wrote storyes for very young readers. One of her books is a frontier tale about Cowboy Small, who carries his bedroll and dishs tied to his saddle. He and the other cowboies use their lassos to rope calfs. They eat their lunches at the chuckwagon where the cook serves them beef, red beans, and coffee. Lois Lenski wrote or illustrated approximately one hundred books in her career.

A. Rewrite the paragraph, changing the underlined words to the correct possessive forms or plural forms.

B. Correct any fragments, comma splices, or fused sentences. There are five errors of this type.

Daniel Boone was born in Pennsylvania his <u>family</u> move to North Carolina happened in 1750. As an adult he devoted his life to exploring and settling <u>Americas</u> <u>frontier</u>. A wagon driver, John Findley. Told Daniel Boone a story about a hunter's paradise. There were many <u>buffalo</u> as well as <u>deer</u> and <u>turkey</u>. Boone traveled over the Appalachian Mountains through rugged wilderness, he reached the unexplored area of Kentucky. His path is now called the Cumberland Gap. His knowledge of the Indians saved many <u>settlers</u> <u>life</u>. Two years later on a return trip to North Carolina. The Indians attacked a group of settlers after they left against <u>Boones</u> <u>wish</u>.

_____

_____

_____

_____

_____

_____

_____

_____

_____

_____

_____

_____

_____

_____

SLIDING HOME

The more specific a writer's nouns are, the sharper and clearer the picture in the reader's mind will be. For example, the noun *fish* in the second paragraph of *The Cay* excerpt is general; there are thousands of kinds of fish. But *langosta, mussels,* and *sea urchins* each name a specific type of sea creature. Can you see why it is important for a writer to be as precise as possible?

- *Can you find any compound nouns in the excerpt?*

- *What nouns would you change to make this passage be set in Alaska rather than the Caribbean?*

page 386

Precise words

I Kings 7:47-51

47 And Solomon left all the vessels unweighed, because they were exceeding many: neither was the weight of the brass found out.

48 And Solomon made all the vessels that pertained unto the house of the Lord: the altar of gold, and the table of gold, whereupon the shewbread was,

49 And the candlesticks of pure gold, five on the right side, and five on the left, before the oracle, with the flowers, and the lamps, and the tongs of gold,

50 And the bowls, and the snuffers, and the basons, and the spoons, and the censers of pure gold; and the hinges of gold, both for the doors of the inner house, the most holy place, and for the doors of the house, to wit, of the temple.

51 So was ended all the work that king Solomon made for the house of the Lord. And Solomon brought in the things which David his father had dedicated; even the silver, and the gold, and the vessels, did he put among the treasures of the house of the Lord.

- *How many different nouns are in this passage? How many can you classify?*

> And they brought up an evil report of the land . . . saying, The land, through which we have gone to search it, is a land that eateth up the inhabitants thereof; and all the people that we saw in it are men of great stature. . . . And all the congregation lifted up their voice, and cried; and the people wept that night.
>
> *Numbers 13:32; 14:1*

Observation journals—sometimes called field notes—are used by writers of many professions. Scientists, teachers, and artists all use field notes when they record their observations of persons, objects, or places. Writers must look closely at a subject and take notes on what they see. Some famous observation journals record such events as the fall of the Berlin Wall or the sinking of the *Titanic*; others may tell about everyday happenings such as the student sitting in the bus seat in front of you or a lady feeding the ducks.

Your observation journal, because it will record *things*, will no doubt be filled with many nouns. Use a variety of specific nouns as you write so that your reader can envision what you describe.

Your Turn

Watch something or someone over a period of time; record and describe your observations in a journal. One of the following may be a possibility for the subject of your journal.

- A growing thing (tree, plant, flower)—Observe the growing thing for two weeks, at different times of the day, in different lights, in different types of weather. Record any changes, such as leaves falling or withering, buds forming, petals opening and closing, and so on.

- The moon—Watch the moon for a period of two weeks, every night if possible. Describe how the moon looks each night or describe how the sky looks if the moon is not visible one night.

- A baby—Watch a baby or a toddler for a prolonged period of time (at least an hour) and keep a log of your observations. Record how the child reacts to his physical surroundings, to people he comes in contact with, and to problems he encounters.

Learning Christianly

Genesis 2:20-24 records the climax of Adam's naming of God's creatures. How does Adam name this final creature? What does this manner of naming indicate about how humans should use language?

Planning

Brainstorm with friends for ideas. Questions may help to get the ideas flowing. Ask members of your brainstorming group about the places they like to go or the strangest things they have ever seen. Consider having each person start with the statement "You won't believe what I saw yesterday/last week. I saw. . . ." This discussion should give you some starter ideas of where to go or whom to go to for some good observation.

Decide on something to observe. The ideas for observation mentioned above are merely a starting point. You will want to use the brainstorming session or some other method for coming up with an idea to make your decision. Below is a list of ideas that one student came up with by writing just the next thing that came to his mind—a sort of word association technique:

local pond
scum/algae
fish
water lilies
fishing
ducks
* watching people feed the ducks

When the student thought of people feeding ducks, she decided to visit a nearby pond and observe people in action. Try to vary your observations as much as possible—different times of day, different situations, different angles, and so on. This will give a well-developed picture of your subject.

Take all of your senses with you. The tendency may be to write only what you see. (This is an *observation* journal after all.) Remember to include smells, sensations, tastes, sounds, and sights in your journal. Taylor uses several of the senses in *The Cay.* Notice on page 25 his sentences that describe the smell of the air; the taste of seaweed, sea-grape leaves, and coconuts; the feel of finally being clean; and the sight of the sea urchins. Try thinking about the thing you are describing using a sense not ordinarily associated with that subject, for example, the smell of a penny or the taste of the wind. Be prepared to include some of these types of observation in your journal entry.

pages 375-77

Chapter 20

Drafting

Write in complete sentences. This will help you to be as specific as possible as you write. Remember that your journal will be read by others, so you want your reader to be able to understand exactly what you mean—short, choppy phrases or single words, although fine for your own use, may be difficult for a reader to decipher.

Take special care with the nouns and verbs you select. Make sure that they are precise and strong. The following excerpt from an observation journal shows how the right nouns and verbs make an entry come alive.

page 381

Developing the supporting sentences

> A lady sits by the lake in a floppy hat, eating something and throwing pieces of bread to the ducks. Two children, a girl and a boy, play hide-and-seek in the trees. On a park bench a teenage boy wears a denim jacket, listening to headphones. A young man and woman walk slowly around the lake, talking. The woman gestures often with her arms, and her laugh comes across the water. Several yards behind them a mother pushes a stroller. A tiny, long-haired dog walks beside her, pausing now and then to sniff at something in the grass.

Choose a title. After you have written your journal entries, decide on a title that encompasses the whole work. The title should let a reader know what the group of entries is about and should make the reader want to read on. The writer of the observation by the lake might have titled her work "Lakeside Wanderers" or "At Carisbrooke Pond."

Revising

Check for complete sentences. If you were rushed when you wrote your observations, you may have needed to use your own version of shorthand or to write in incomplete sentences in portions of your journal. As you revise, be sure to eliminate these fragments from your writing.

Revise your entry before publishing. The student who wrote about the people at the lake made the following changes to the entry. Notice how much stronger the new words are. (The newer words are printed in italics.) Specific nouns like *hot dog* and *pines* and vibrant verbs like *slouches* and *trots* show rather than tell about your topic.

A lady sits by the lake in a floppy hat, eating *a hot dog* and throwing pieces of *a bun* to the ducks. Two children, a girl and a boy, play hide-and-seek in the *pines*. On a park bench a teenage boy *slouches deep into* his denim jacket, listening to headphones. A young man and woman walk slowly around the lake, talking. The woman gestures often with her arms, and her laugh echoes across the water. Several yards behind them a mother pushes a stroller. A tiny, long-haired dog *trots* beside her, pausing now and then to sniff at something in the grass.

Proofread your journal. Look at the grammar, usage, and punctuation as well as the capitalization and spelling in each entry. Try reading the entries aloud—your ear might help you hear an error that your eyes might miss.

Publishing

Stage a public reading. Encourage class members to read portions of their journals aloud. Allow for commentary from others who have visited the place or who know the person being described.

Illustrate and bind the observation journals. Display the book in the classroom. Include several blank pages for comments.

Post the entries on the class webpage. If you post your journal, try to take a photograph of the person or place to post with it. Then add to the journal as you continue your observations. Encourage feedback from site visitors by including a link to your e-mail address.

Mail the observation journal. The person you described or someone who knows the place you observed would probably enjoy reading your journal. Send him a copy of your journal or give him the address of your website.

HISTORY of the ENGLISH LANGUAGE

The United States of America is just a little over two hundred years old. But America's common language, English, is much older. Ancient people in Europe and Asia spoke a language that we now call Indo-European. Some believe that the Indo-European language, called a *parent language,* was spoken as early as 3000 B.C. It was from this ancient language that English was born.

People who spoke the Indo-European language spread out into different parts of the world. As groups moved farther and farther away and interacted with people who spoke other languages, the Indo-European language changed. One of these groups moved into northern and western Europe; these people developed the *Germanic* languages.

Around A.D. 450, three of the Germanic tribes sailed across the North Sea and settled in Britain. They were the Angles, the Saxons, and the Jutes. The language they spoke in Britain until A.D. 1100 is now called Old English or *Anglo-Saxon,* after the two largest tribes. The largest tribe gave its name to the country ("Angle-land") and to the language ("Angle-ish"). Can you see how we got our word *English?*

CHAPTER 3

VERBS

FOUL SHOT
BY EDWIN A. HOEY

With two 60's stuck on the scoreboard
And two seconds hanging on the clock,
The solemn boy in the center of eyes,
Squeezed by silence,
Seeks out the line with his feet,
Soothes his hands along his uniform,
Gently drums the ball against the floor,
Then measures the waiting net,
Raises the ball on his right hand,
Balances it with his left,
Calms it with fingertips,
Breathes,
Crouches,
Waits,
And then through a stretching of stillness,
Nudges it upward.
The ball
Slides up and out,
Lands,
Leans,
Wobbles,
Wavers,
Hesitates,
Exasperates,
Plays it coy
Until every face begs with unsounding screams—

And then

     And then

          And then,

Right before ROAR-UP,
Dives down and through.

- *Hoey's poem breaks down into many smaller actions the single act of a boy shooting a free throw—drums the ball, raises it, balances it on his hand, and so on. What effect does naming all of these minor actions have on the poem?*

- *How do you feel throughout most of the poem?*

Hoey's poem describes only a brief moment in time. But notice how Hoey draws out the moment by mentioning small details of action: the player "soothes his hands along his uniform," "drums the ball against the floor," "measures the waiting net," "raises the ball," "calms it with fingertips," and so on. The details slow the pace of the poem. They make us hold our breath. They build anticipation, capitalizing on the feeling of suspense that builds inside all of us as we wait for a climax: will the ball go through the net or not? Slowing the pace of the poem is like replaying a shot in slow motion: it draws out the waiting so that the moment of triumph is even more exhilarating.

Action words like *seeks, drums, measures,* and *raises* are called *verbs.* Hoey uses many action verbs in his poem because the scene he is describing is an active one. But not every verb in our language expresses action. In this chapter, you will learn more about action verbs and other types of verbs.

Verbs

Probably there is no word in a sentence more important than the verb. Verbs give life to sentences, and they connect with other words in important ways. For example, in the clause "The player dribbled the ball," *dribbled* not only describes the action but also tells two other things: what the player did and what was done to the ball. Understanding verbs—both the types and the various forms they can take—will help you use them correctly.

Recognizing Verbs

A **verb** shows action or tells state of being. In other words, a verb can tell what someone or something does or is. A verb that shows state of being is often a form of the word *be (am, is, are, was, were, be, being, been).*

Harley *ran* down the court. *(action)*
He *threw* the ball. *(action)*
His shot *was* good. *(state of being)*
Mr. Chavez *is* the coach. *(state of being)*

As you have learned, a verb acts as the main word in the predicate in any sentence. Therefore, it is important that you know how to find verbs in sentences. All verbs appear in similar forms. Nearly every verb can have *s* or *ing* added to it without changing the meaning: *play, plays, playing.* Any word that will fit into the following test frames can be a verb.

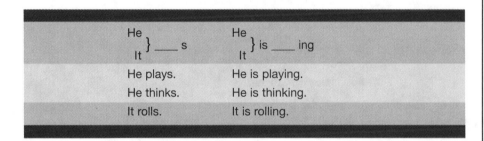

A verb shows action or state of being.
Almost any verb will fit in the verb test frame.

3-1 PRACTICE THE SKILL

Underline each verb.

1. The black-footed ferret is one of the rarest mammals in North America.

2. The ferret grows up to two feet long.

3. A domestic ferret weighs more than a black-footed ferret.

4. A domestic ferret is looking at me with its red eyes.

5. The ferret is hunting underground by scent and sound.

page 184

Special forms of the verb *be*

page 5

Finding subjects and predicates

page 320

Spelling rules

6. Ferrets chase prairie dogs.

7. They also catch rabbits.

8. That tame ferret is wearing a muzzle.

9. The muzzle prevents the death of the prey.

10. Some people confuse ferrets and weasels.

3-2 REVIEW THE SKILL

Supply the missing verbs. Use a different verb in each blank.

_____ 1. Tomorrow Gary will ? an operation on his knee.

_____ 2. He ? nervous about the procedure.

_____ 3. His church ? for him last night.

_____ 4. He ? his knee in a soccer game last week.

_____ 5. He was ? the ball when another player slid into him.

_____ 6. He has been ? ever since then.

_____ 7. The surgery will ? at 9:00 A.M.

_____ 8. Gary's parents will ? in the lobby during the operation.

_____ 9. Gary ? his friends to visit him later.

_____10. Everybody ? about him.

Transitive and Intransitive Verbs

Transitive Verbs and Direct Objects

Just as a sentence fragment needs additional information to make it a complete sentence, a verb may need a receiver for its action in order to express a complete thought. This receiver is called a **direct object** (DO). A verb that needs a direct object is a **transitive verb** (TrV). A direct object is a noun or pronoun that receives the action of the verb.

> Dmitri baked a cake.
> Dmitri baked *what? (a cake)*

In the sentence above, *cake* is the direct object of the action verb *baked. Cake* follows the verb, receives the action of the verb, and answers the question "whom or what?" about the verb. To identify the direct object, first find the subject and the verb; then ask "whom or what?" The direct object is compound if more than one word answers the question "whom or what?"

> Dmitri baked a *cake* and a *pie*.

Sentences that contain these elements follow the pattern **S-TrV-DO.** Look at the diagram for this sentence:

> Dmitri baked a cake.

 Transitive comes from the Latin word *transire,* "to go over or across." The action of a transitive verb goes across to a receiver.

Intransitive Verbs

Some verbs do not need objects to express a complete thought. These verbs are **intransitive** (InV). An intransitive verb is a verb that needs nothing to complete it. It does not send its action toward anyone or anything. The sentence pattern is **S-InV.**

> Dmitri baked in the kitchen.

In this example, the words *in the kitchen* follow the verb *baked,* but they do not answer the question "what?" about the verb. *Kitchen* is not a direct object because it is not receiving the action of being baked. *Baked* is an intransitive verb in this sentence. Look at the diagram for this sentence:

> Dmitri baked in the kitchen.

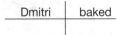

Transitive Verbs and Indirect Objects

Sometimes a sentence with a transitive verb and a direct object may include another word that tells who or what was affected by the verb's action on the direct object. This word is called an **indirect object** (IO).

page 247

Troublesome verbs

An indirect object is a noun or pronoun that tells *to whom* or *for whom* the subject does something. It always comes after the verb but before the direct object.

> Dmitri baked Katya a cake.
> Dmitri baked a cake *for whom? (Katya)*

In the example, *Katya* is the indirect object. The noun *Katya* tells us for whom Dmitri baked a cake. To identify the indirect object, find the simple subject, the verb, and the direct object; then ask, "To whom or for whom was the action done?" The next example contains a compound indirect object.

> Dmitri baked Katya and Angela a cake.

Sentences with both a direct object and an indirect object follow the pattern **S-TrV-IO-DO.** The diagram for this pattern is similar to the diagram for S-TrV-DO. Look at the diagram for this sentence:

> Dmitri baked Katya a cake.

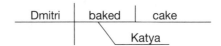

║N SUMMARY

A **transitive verb** needs a direct object to receive its action.

An **intransitive verb** does not need a direct object to receive its action.

A **direct object** is a noun or pronoun that receives the action of a transitive verb.

An **indirect object** is a noun or pronoun that tells to whom or for whom the verb's action was done.

3-3　 PRACTICE THE SKILL

Label the sentence patterns *S-InV, S-TrV-DO,* or *S-TrV-IO-DO.* Above each word of the sentence pattern, write its label.

1. The banker called the police.

2. Many policemen arrived quickly.

3. The captain showed his men the plans.

4. He unfolded a map.

5. He told the policemen their orders.

6. The men ran to their positions.

7. They surprised the thieves.

8. The thieves gave the police the stolen funds.

9. The police arrested the thieves.

10. Then the police handed the happy banker his money.

3-4 ⚾ REVIEW THE SKILL

Label the sentence patterns *S-InV, S-TrV-DO,* or *S-TrV-IO-DO*. Above each word of the sentence pattern, write its label.

1. Belshazzar gave a great feast.

2. Many lords came to the palace.

3. The servants brought them golden vessels.

4. Mysterious fingers wrote Belshazzar a message.

5. The message frightened him.

6. Belshazzar offered his wise men fine clothes.

7. The queen gave the king a suggestion.

8. Belshazzar promised a reward.

9. Daniel supplied Belshazzar the interpretation.

10. Belshazzar died during the night.

Linking Verbs, Predicate Nouns, and Predicate Adjectives

A "being" verb usually acts in a sentence as a **linking verb.** A linking verb links the subject with a word that renames or describes the subject. It functions almost like an equal sign.

> David was a shepherd.
> David = shepherd.

The word *shepherd* renames the subject *David*. The simple predicate *was* acts as a linking verb because it links *David* to *shepherd*.

If the word that follows the linking verb is a noun or a pronoun, it is called a **predicate noun.** A predicate noun renames the subject.

> Tom is the goalie.

In the example, *goalie* is a predicate noun. You recognize *Tom* as the subject. *Tom* and the *goalie* are the same person. *Goalie* follows the verb and renames *Tom*.

page 192

Predicate noun

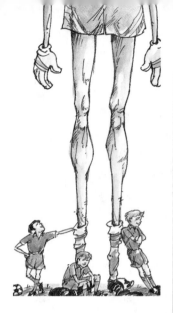

page 102

Adjectives

This sentence follows the pattern **S-LV-PN.**

If the word that follows a linking verb is an adjective, it is called a **predicate adjective.** A predicate adjective usually describes the subject.

> Tom is tall.

In this example, *tall* is a predicate adjective. If you try putting *tall* in front of *Tom (tall Tom)*, you can see that *tall* describes *Tom,* but it does not rename him. This sentence follows the pattern **S-LV-PA.** Both S-LV-PN and S-LV-PA can contain compounds.

> Tom is the goalie and the team captain.
> Tom is tall and thin.

The patterns S-LV-PN and S-LV-PA are diagrammed the same way. Look at the diagram for this sentence.

> Tom is the goalie.

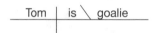

Now look at the diagram for this sentence.

> Tom is tall.

I̲N̲ S̲U̲M̲M̲A̲R̲Y̲

A **linking verb** links the subject of a sentence to a word that renames or describes the subject.

A **predicate noun** is a noun in the complete predicate that follows a linking verb and renames the subject.

A **predicate adjective** is an adjective in the complete predicate that follows a linking verb and describes the subject.

3-5   PRACTICE THE SKILL

Underline each linking verb. Label the sentence patterns *S-LV-PN* or *S-LV-PA*. Above each word of the sentence pattern, write its label.

1. James Naismith was a creative gym teacher.

2. In 1891 he was responsible for the invention of a new game.

3. He and his boss were eager for an indoor team sport for the winter.

4. The legacy of that desire is basketball.

5. Two peach baskets attached to balcony railings were the first hoops.

6. The first ball was a soccer ball.

7. The first players were members of Naismith's gym class.

8. The sport was popular then.

9. But its popularity is even greater now.

10. Both neighborhood kids and professional athletes are enthusiastic about Naismith's creation.

 3-6 REVIEW THE SKILL

Underline each linking verb. Label the sentence patterns *S-LV-PN* or S-LV-PA. Above each word of the sentence pattern, write its label.

1. The United States Marine Corps is a separate military branch within the Department of the Navy.

2. Marines were unique from the beginning in their dual operations on land and sea.

3. The commandant is the top officer of the corps.

4. He is a member of the Joint Chiefs of Staff.

5. "Boots" are new recruits.

6. Their instruction is rigorous.

7. The result is highly disciplined soldiers.

8. Marines are the first troops in battle in most major conflicts.

9. The corps is capable and courageous in its conduct.

10. The Marines are indispensable to the military system.

As you may have noticed, forms of the verb *be* often function as linking verbs. Certain other words can act as either linking verbs or action verbs, depending on the sentences they are in. These words include *become, stay, remain, grow, seem, appear, smell, sound, feel, taste,* and *look.* Remember that these words are not always linking verbs. To determine whether a verb is a linking verb, you must see how that verb is used in a particular sentence.

Halley's Comet *appears* bright. (linking)
Halley's Comet *appears* every 77 years. (intransitive)
The horn *sounded* loud. (linking)
I *sounded* the horn. (transitive)
This chocolate *tastes* delicious. (linking)
He *tastes* the chocolate. (transitive)

 **Learning Christianly**

One of the most fascinating uses of a linking verb in the Bible is found in Exodus 3. Here God calls Moses to lead His people. Moses responds by asking what God's name is. God answers, "I AM THAT I AM" (v. 14). This statement is very difficult to translate. Some scholars have suggested the following translation: "I am I AM." In other words, God is telling Moses that His name is I AM. If this translation is correct, the sentence is a good example of the pattern S-LV-PN. What is fascinating is that the predicate noun in this sentence also has a subject and a linking verb. But this predicate noun does not have its own predicate adjective or noun. What do you think God meant to communicate through the S-LV pattern of this PN in Exodus 3:14?

Remember to distinguish between nouns used as predicate nouns and nouns used as direct objects. A predicate noun renames the subject and follows a linking verb. It is "equal to" the subject.

Landon is a fisherman.
Landon = fisherman.

A direct object does not rename the subject; it is a receiver of the verb's action. The verb before a direct object is always a transitive verb.

Devin ate the cake.
Devin ate *what? (the cake)*

No verb can be both a transitive verb and a linking verb at the same time in the same sentence.

	Part of speech	Position in sentence	Function
Direct Object	Noun or pronoun	Follows a transitive verb	Receives the action of the verb. Answers "S + V + whom/what?" Does not normally rename the subject.
Indirect Object	Noun or pronoun	Follows a transitive verb but comes before the direct object	Tells who or what was affected by the verb's action. Answers "S + V + to/for whom/what?" + DO
Predicate Noun	Noun or pronoun	Follows a linking verb	Renames (in other words, is another name for) the subject. We can usually put an equal sign between the S and the PN.
Predicate Adjective	Adjective	Follows a linking verb	Describes the subject.

IN SUMMARY

Some verbs can be either transitive verbs or linking verbs; however, no verb can be both action and linking at the same time in the same sentence.

Underline each verb. In the blank, identify each *linking* verb.

_____ 1. Andre goes to Calvary High School.

_____ 2. He is a freshman.

_____ 3. He appears tall for his age.

_____ 4. Andre gives the team his best effort at each soccer game.

_____ 5. His junior varsity squad remains undefeated.

_____ 6. His sister participated in the band last year.

_____ 7. LaTasha played the flute.

_____ 8. This year she is an excellent cheerleader.

_____ 9. Their parents come to all of their games.

_____ 10. They support Calvary High loyally.

Underline each linking verb. Label the sentence patterns *S-LV-PN* or *S-LV-PA*. Above each word of the sentence pattern, write its label.

1. The first notable work of English literature is *Beowulf*.

2. The author remains unknown to this day.

3. The language of the poem is Old English.

4. In battle, Beowulf seems strong and courageous.

5. Beowulf's opponent was Grendel.

6. Grendel's roar sounded ferocious.

7. He looked extremely fierce.

8. He appeared much stronger than Beowulf.

9. After the battle, Beowulf became a hero.

10. The Danish people were thankful for Beowulf's help.

Underline each verb. Label the sentence patterns _S-InV, S-TrV-DO, S-TrV-IO-DO, S-LV-PN,_ or _S-LV-PA._ Above each word of the sentence pattern, write its label.

1. The Mitchells are missionaries to the Philippines.

2. They became quite busy with the local church in the area.

3. Mila attends their church.

4. She comes faithfully each Sunday.

5. Mila sang a solo.

6. Her voice echoed throughout the sanctuary.

7. It sounded beautiful.

8. Her parents bought her a new dress for the occasion.

9. Mila's friend came with her.

10. He gave Mila a corsage.

Auxiliaries

Auxiliaries, sometimes called _helping verbs,_ are words that help the **main verb** in a sentence to express special meaning. The following are common auxiliaries.

- am, is, are, was, were, be, being, been

- have, has, had

- do, does, did

- will, would, shall, should, can, could, may, might, must

An auxiliary and a main verb together form a complete verb. A complete verb may consist of the main verb alone (if there are no auxiliaries) or one or more auxiliaries along with the main verb.

Billy Sunday once _played_ baseball for the Chicago White Sox.
By 1896 he _had become_ a preacher of the gospel.
Our Sunday school class _will be studying_ his life this week.

Be sure to include the complete verb when you diagram a sentence that uses auxiliaries.

class	will be studying

Some auxiliaries can be used alone as main verbs. You have already learned that *be* can act as a linking verb. *Have* and *do* can also act alone as main verbs. These three auxiliaries and all their forms are listed at the beginning of this section.

They *are learning* more every week. *(auxiliary + main)*
They *are* young. *(main)*
They *have remembered* to take their books home. *(auxiliary + main)*
They *have* their tickets. *(main)*
He *does forget* his books sometimes. *(auxiliary + main)*
He *does* it frequently. *(main)*

ETYMOLOGY

Auxiliary comes from the Latin word *auxilium,* meaning "help."

IN SUMMARY

Auxiliaries and **main verbs** together form complete verbs.

3-10 PRACTICE THE SKILL

Underline each complete verb. Write each auxiliary verb in the blank.

_____ 1. Mexico City has been the capital of Mexico since 1821.

_____ 2. People will fill the downtown of Mexico City all day.

_____ 3. José and Elena Hernandez have a house on the outskirts of Mexico City.

_____ 4. They can walk to church on Sundays.

_____ 5. José's friend must travel downtown each day.

_____ 6. Many wealthy people live along the Paseo de la Reforma.

_____ 7. The College of Mexico may be found in downtown Mexico City.

_____ 8. Mountains surround the city.

_____ 9. Soccer is played by people of all ages.

_____ 10. José and Elena have bought tickets for the final soccer game of the season.

Underline each complete verb. Write the auxiliaries in the blanks.

_____ 1. Some of the men of Cameroon hunt pythons.

_____ 2. The hunters must be smart and courageous.

_____ 3. The pythons will hide in old animal holes.

_____ 4. The hunters must crawl through narrow tunnels after the snakes.

_____ 5. Some hunters have encountered snakes as long as twenty feet.

_____ 6. The hunter grabs the snake behind its head and pulls it slowly out of the hole.

_____ 7. The hunter's friends are waiting for him outside the hole.

_____ 8. The python might try an escape or an attack.

_____ 9. The men must kill the snake quickly.

_____ 10. The meat of the snake is eaten, and the skin of the snake is preserved.

Principal Parts of Verbs

Every verb has three basic forms. These basic forms are called the principal parts of the verb. The first principal part is called the **present.** The second principal part is called the **past.** The third principal part is called the **past participle.** The past participle is used with some form of the auxiliary *have.* As you study tenses, you will learn how to use these parts.

For most verbs the second and third principal parts are just alike, usually ending in *ed.* We call these verbs regular verbs. Irregular verbs form their past and past participle in some other way.

page 340

Pronouncing the word

	Present	Past	Past Participle
Regular	work	worked	(have) worked
Irregular	set	set	(have) set
	stand	stood	(have) stood
	take	took	(have) taken

Learning the principal parts of irregular verbs is necessary in order to avoid mistakes in usage. You can find the principal parts of a verb in any standard dictionary. The principal parts are usually given right after the pronunciation of the word. The principal parts for some troublesome verbs are given below.

Present	Past	Past Participle
bring	brought	brought
burst	burst	burst
choose	chose	chosen
climb	climbed	climbed
come	came	come
do	did	done
drag	dragged	dragged
draw	drew	drawn
drink	drank	drunk
drive	drove	driven
drown	drowned	drowned
eat	ate	eaten
fall	fell	fallen
get	got	gotten, got
give	gave	given
go	went	gone
grow	grew	grown
lay	laid	laid
lie	lay	lain
ride	rode	ridden
ring	rang	rung
rise	rose	risen
run	ran	run
see	saw	seen
set	set	set
shrink	shrank, shrunk	shrunk, shrunken
sing	sang, sung	sung
sit	sat	sat
slay	slew	slain
sneak	sneaked	sneaked
speak	spoke	spoken
steal	stole	stolen
swim	swam	swum
take	took	taken
throw	threw	thrown

 IN SUMMARY

All verbs have three principal parts: **present, past, past participle.**

The past participle is always used with a form of the auxiliary *have*.

Underline the correct verb form in parentheses. Be prepared to explain your answers.

1. Joshua had *(went, gone)* to spy out the land with eleven other men.

2. Of the twelve, only he and Caleb *(chose, chosen)* to take the land God had promised.

3. The Israelites wandered for forty years because they did not obey what the Lord had *(spoke, spoken)*.

4. Because of their disobedience, they *(fell, fallen)* into wickedness.

5. They *(broke, broken)* God's law, but God was merciful to them.

6. While they wandered in the wilderness, the children of Israel *(saw, seen)* the Lord provide for them.

7. Because Joshua and Caleb had *(did, done)* what God had told them, they were allowed to cross the Jordan; but other men their age who had not believed were not permitted to cross.

8. Joshua *(took, taken)* the children of Israel to Jericho.

9. When God destroyed Jericho, His people *(knew, known)* His power.

10. Joshua *(wrote, written)* the events of Jericho's destruction in Joshua 6.

3-13  **REVIEW THE SKILL**

Underline the correct verb form in parentheses.

1. Jim had *(open, opened)* a letter his friend had written.

2. The wind *(blown, blew)* Jim's letter away.

3. Before he could reach it, it *(fell, fallen)* into the fountain.

4. He had *(took, taken)* a rest at a small café in Madrid.

5. After ordering a pastry, he had *(drank, drunk)* a glass of mineral water.

6. Then he had opened his letter and had *(threw, thrown)* the envelope into the trash can.

7. His letter landed in the fountain; everyone at the café *(saw, seen)* it.

8. Jim thought no one there *(spoke, spoken)* English.

9. But one old man finally *(broke, broken)* the silence.

10. "Well, that *(did, done)* it, my boy."

Simple Tenses

Tense tells a verb's time: present, past, or future. Without tense we could not separate in conversation what happened yesterday from what is happening today and what will happen tomorrow. We form all the tenses from the three principal parts of the verb.

The simple tenses are the present, the past, and the future. A verb in one of the first two tenses is a one-word verb. A verb in the future tense includes the auxiliary *will* or *shall*.

Tense comes from the Latin word *tempus,* meaning "time."

Present Tense

The present tense of a verb comes from the first principal part of that verb. With some verbs, the present tense tells present time—that the action or state of being is occurring right now.

> God *sees* you.
> He *knows* the truth.

With action verbs, the present tense tells what is done as habit or usual practice.

> My brother and I *ride* our bikes in the park every day.

When a singular noun or *it, he,* or *she* is the subject of the sentence, we add *s* or *es* to the first principal part.

> My *brother* ride*s* his bike on the trail.
> *He* ride*s* his bike on the trail.

For a plural subject, the verb never takes the added *s*. The following sentences show the differences between singular and plural forms of a present-tense verb.

page 183

Subject-Verb agreement

Singular	Plural
I *ride* my bike to the bridge.	We *ride* our bikes to the bridge.
You *ride* your bike to the bridge.	You *ride* your bikes to the bridge.
He *rides* his bike to the bridge.	They *ride* their bikes to the bridge.

Past Tense

The second principal part is the form used for the past tense. The past tense expresses an action that has already occurred.

> Scott *opened* the door.
> Kylee *typed* her book report yesterday.

Future Tense

The auxiliary *will* or *shall* and the first principal part combine to form the future tense of a verb. (The first principal part is the same one used for the present tense.) The future tense refers to events that have not yet occurred. It is made the same way for every verb.

> Sid *will open* the presents after we sing to him.
> You and my sister *will ride* your bicycles to meet us.

When you identify a verb in the future tense, be sure to include both the auxiliary *will* or *shall* and the first principal part.

IN SUMMARY

The **present tense** of a verb comes from its first principal part.

Use the present tense to express an action that is occurring now or occurs habitually.

The **past tense** of a verb is its second principal part.

Use the past tense to express an action that has already occurred.

The **future tense** of a verb is the auxiliary *will* or *shall* and the verb's first principal part.

Use the future tense to express action that has yet to occur.

3-14 ⚾ PRACTICE THE SKILL

Fill in each blank with the given verb in the tense indicated.

_____ 1. Juwan _?_ this book about the lives of missionaries in China. *(enjoy, future)*

_____ 2. Some missionaries in China _?_ well known by Christians. *(be, present)*

_____ 3. The Communist forces _?_ John and Betty Stam in 1934. *(slay, past)*

_____ 4. Their deaths _?_ many Chinese to salvation. *(bring, past)*

_____ 5. Many people still _?_ about the Stams' effect on China. *(read, present)*

_____ 6. The Stams _?_ strong for God. *(stand, past)*

_____ 7. Their story _?_ throughout China and the United States. *(ring, past)*

_____ 8. The Chinese _?_ at their faith in God. *(marvel, past)*

_____ 9. God _?_ His children. *(empower, present)*

_____ 10. They _?_ God with their lives. *(glorify, future)*

3-15 PRACTICE THE SKILL

Fill in each blank with the given verb in the tense indicated.

_____ 1. Even some missionaries _?_ spiritually while growing up. *(struggle, present)*

_____ 2. At one point during college, Isobel Miller _?_ God's existence. *(doubt, past)*

_____ 3. God made Himself real to her, and she _?_ Him control of her life. *(give, past)*

_____ 4. On November 4, 1929, she _?_ John Kuhn. *(marry, present)*

_____ 5. After the ceremony they _?_ to France for their honeymoon. *(go, future)*

_____ 6. Before the wedding, John _?_ time in Chengchiang. *(spend, past)*

_____ 7. He still _?_ the need for Christians there. *(recognize, present)*

_____ 8. John and Isobel _?_ the Lord's will for their lives. *(seek, past)*

_____ 9. They _?_ back to Chengchiang after their honeymoon. *(come, future)*

_____ 10. They _?_ there for nearly a year until they transfer to Tali. *(minister, future)*

Rewrite each underlined verb, changing it to the tense in parentheses.

_____ 1. Thomas Jefferson <u>will write</u> the first draft of the Declaration of Independence. *(past)*

_____ 2. The colonists <u>blamed</u> the British government for many infringements on their freedom. *(present)*

_____ 3. Our Founding Fathers <u>will state</u> their rights in this document. *(present)*

_____ 4. The Stamp Act <u>required</u> the colonists to pay taxes on newspapers and other items. *(future)*

_____ 5. The British government <u>will repeal</u> the act because of protests. *(past)*

_____ 6. King George III <u>rejects</u> the appeal of the colonists. *(future)*

_____ 7. In history classes, many students <u>memorize</u> parts of the Declaration of Independence. *(future)*

_____ 8. The writing of the Bill of Rights <u>followed</u> the writing of the Declaration of Independence. *(present)*

_____ 9. Someone <u>copies</u> the declaration on parchment. *(past)*

_____ 10. All fifty-six members of Congress <u>sign</u> the document on August 2, 1776. *(past)*

Perfect Tenses

The **perfect tenses** express actions that are completed, or perfected. The perfect tenses include the present perfect, the past perfect, and the future perfect. So far, we have studied two of the three principal parts. We have learned how to form the present and future tenses from the first principal part, and we have learned that the second principal part is the same as the past tense.

The third principal part is the past participle. The three perfect tenses use this principal part along with some form of the auxiliary verb *have*. The present perfect, the past perfect, and the future perfect are named for the simple tense of *have* used to form them.

Tense	Auxiliary
Present Perfect	*have* or *has*
Past Perfect	*had*
Future Perfect	*will have* (or *shall have*)

Present Perfect Tense

The present perfect tense expresses action completed during the present time period, often up to the present moment. This tense is made by combining the present tense of the auxiliary *have* and the past participle of the main verb.

Present perfect tense = *have* or *has* + past participle

Scott *has opened* the door for the girls every day this week.
Kylee *has typed* all of her book reports for her English class.
The boys *have opened* the door for the girls every day this week.
They *have typed* all of their book reports for English class.

IN SUMMARY

The three **perfect tenses** use forms of the auxiliary *have* and the past participle of the main verb.

Use the **present perfect tense** to express action completed during the present time period, often up to the present moment.

3-17 PRACTICE THE SKILL

Fill in each blank with the given verb in the present perfect tense.

_____ 1. Susannah Thompson _?_ the Olneys. *(visit)*

_____ 2. They _?_ to the New Park Street Chapel. *(go)*

_____ 3. Charles Spurgeon _?_ Susannah a poignant question. *(ask)*

_____ 4. They _?_ a small, simple wedding ceremony. *(choose)*

_____ 5. Mrs. Spurgeon has not gone with her husband, but Spurgeon _?_ to many places. *(travel)*

_____ 6. Charles _?_ Susannah many letters. *(write)*

_____ 7. Susannah _?_ a book fund for poor men in the ministry. *(begin)*

_____ 8. God _?_ many needed donations. *(send)*

_____ 9. Susannah _?_ her time with this needed work. *(occupy)*

_____ 10. She _?_ her own ministry there in Great Britain. *(has)*

3-18   REVIEW THE SKILL

Fill in each blank with the given verb in the present perfect tense.

_____ 1. Washington Irving _?_ a story about Rip Van Winkle. (*write*)

_____ 2. Rip always _?_ helpful in the neighborhood. (*be*)

_____ 3. However, he _?_ to avoid work at home whenever possible. (*try*)

_____ 4. To get away one fine day, Rip and his dog _?_ into the mountains to hunt squirrels. (*climb*)

_____ 5. A strange little man _?_ for Rip's help to carry a large keg. (*ask*)

_____ 6. The man _?_ Rip into a hollow where a group is playing ninepins. (*lead*)

_____ 7. Rip _?_ much from the keg during the game. (*drink*)

_____ 8. He _?_ for twenty years. (*sleep*)

_____ 9. The townspeople _?_ surprised to see him again. (*be*)

_____ 10. Rip _?_ his new life in the village. (*enjoy*)

Past Perfect Tense

The past perfect tense expresses an action completed before some past time or event. The past perfect tense is formed using *had* (the past tense of the auxiliary *have*) along with the past participle of the verb.

Past perfect tense = *had* + past participle

When we talk about something that happened before a certain time or before something else happened, we use the past perfect tense.

The Vikings *had discovered* America before Columbus arrived.
Before the Pilgrims established Plymouth Colony, colonists *had settled* at Jamestown.

IN SUMMARY

Use the **past perfect tense** to express action completed before some past time or event.

3-19 PRACTICE THE SKILL

Underline each simple predicate. In the blank to the left, identify the tense of the simple predicate as past or past perfect.

_____ 1. Mutual mistrust had affected the relationship between the white people and Indians for years.

_____ 2. The last battle between the Indians and the settlers occurred at Wounded Knee Creek.

_____ 3. Several Indian tribes had lived in the area between the Missouri River and the Rocky Mountains.

_____ 4. Eventually, the white settlers forced treaties on the various Indian tribes.

_____ 5. The treaties gave the Indian land to the settlers.

_____ 6. Soon the Indians had moved onto reservations.

_____ 7. Ranchers had moved into the Plains area.

_____ 8. Texas became a cattle empire.

_____ 9. The westward expansion of the railroads contributed to the rise of the cattle industry.

_____ 10. Ranches and the railroad spread quickly from Texas into Colorado, Oregon, and Wyoming.

Fill in each blank with the given verb in the tense indicated.

_____ 1. Christopher Columbus _?_ across the Atlantic Ocean. *(sail, past)*

_____ 2. Many of the European explorers _?_ as far as Africa. *(travel, past perfect)*

_____ 3. Christopher _?_ together with his brothers. *(work, past perfect)*

_____ 4. His father _?_ him to work in business. *(persuade, past)*

_____ 5. Columbus _?_ Felipa Perestrello Moniz in 1479. *(marry, past)*

_____ 6. When he had planned his trip, Columbus _?_ the location of Japan. *(mistake, past perfect)*

_____ 7. By 1483 Columbus _?_ his plan to King John II of Portugal. *(propose, past perfect)*

_____ 8. He _?_ the gold, silk, and spices of the East Indies. *(seek, past)*

_____ 9. King John II _?_ Columbus's plan. *(reject, past)*

_____ 10. Finally, by 1492 Spanish monarchs _?_ his plan. *(approve, past perfect)*

Future Perfect Tense

The future tense of *have (will have* or *shall have)* and the past participle of a verb make the future perfect tense. This tense tells about an action that will be done before a future time or event.

Future perfect tense = *will* (or *shall*) *have* + past participle

By the time Tristan visits next year, I *will have moved* to Illinois. Dad *will have closed* the store when I get there after soccer practice.

We do not use this tense very often, but there are times when only the future perfect tense will say exactly what we mean.

IN SUMMARY

Use the **future perfect tense** to express action that will be completed before a future time or event.

3·21 PRACTICE THE SKILL

A. Underline each complete verb.
B. Label the auxiliaries *aux*.
C. Write in the blank the tense of each complete verb: *present, past, future, present perfect, past perfect,* or *future perfect.*

_____ 1. The Spanish invaded the Aztec Empire in Mexico in 1521.

_____ 2. By 1821 the Mexicans had gained their independence from Spain.

_____ 3. The population has increased for years.

_____ 4. Pablo and his parents live with his grandparents in Tampico.

_____ 5. He goes to the school in town.

_____ 6. For a year he has studied about the Aztecs.

_____ 7. His sister will start school next year.

_____ 8. On May 2 their Aunt Dina will have taught at their school for five years.

_____ 9. Pablo had walked to school every day.

_____ 10. Aunt Dina will drive him to school next year.

Fill in each blank with the given verb in the tense indicated.

_____ 1. By the end of each two-year session, Congress _?_ over ten thousand bills. (*introduce, future perfect*)

_____ 2. A bill is not passed until both houses _?_ committee and floor debates on it. *(hold, present perfect)*

_____ 3. Perhaps Congress _?_ all the bills by the end of its session. (*debate, future perfect*)

_____ 4. Some people _?_ in opposition to the bill. (*filibuster, past perfect*)

_____ 5. Often special interest groups _?_ the bills. (*support, present perfect*)

_____ 6. Some committees _?_ meetings to discuss specific issues. (*hold, future perfect*)

_____ 7. Sometimes before a bill passed, the president _?_ to veto it. (*decide, past perfect*)

_____ 8. Because of the veto, Congress _?_ the bill again. (*discuss, present*)

_____ 9. Later, the bill _?_ law after it had received a two-thirds majority. (*become, past*)

_____ 10. Congressional members _?_ other bills next session. (*propose, future*)

Remember that the main verb in all three perfect tenses is identical—the third principal part. Therefore, you must look at the auxiliary forms to determine the tense.

3·23  **USE THE SKILL**

Write a sentence using the tense indicated. Use verbs other than *be* verbs wherever possible.

1. Describe your neighbor's shoes. (*present*)

_____

_____

2. Tell about the most memorable gift you ever gave someone. (*present perfect*)

_____

_____

3. Describe how your appearance will have changed fifty years from now. (*future perfect*)

_____

_____

4. Write a sentence about cars of the future. (*future*)

_____

_____

5. Tell about the last thing that made you sad. (*past perfect*)

_____

_____

6. Write a sentence about your hobby. (*present*)

_____

_____

7. Describe your favorite family vacation. (*present perfect*)

_____

_____

8. Tell about a job you would like to have in twenty-five years. (*future perfect*)

_____

_____

Learning Christianly

Think for a moment about the people in your family and your friends. What do you think of when you think of each person? What is it that makes each person unique? Now try to pick a verb for each person that matches that person well. For instance, you might choose the verb *think* in relation to your dad and the verb *laugh* in relation to your best friend. In the Bible God is often called names that are verbs. Read the following passages: Job 19:25; Psalm 40:17; Romans 11:26. What do these verb names reveal about God?

Verbs **75**

9. Write a sentence about what major you hope to have in college. *(future)*

_____

_____

10. Describe your most recent birthday. *(past perfect)*

_____

_____

3-24   CUMULATIVE REVIEW

Locate and correct the fifteen errors in the paragraph: fused sentences, comma splices, fragments, noun plurals, and verb principal parts. Use the lines below to write the paragraph correctly.

Some people moved west for quick riches some moved west for a new beginning. Along the trail. Many people and cattles died from diseases or starvation. Indians occasionally waylaid the travelers. Sometimes the Indians and the travelers fighted. Large groups emigrated across the land and settled in the West. The Gold Rush in the 1840s. Enticed many mans to California. Often mans left their families and comed out West alone. Some familys moved. Not many womans had came initially. Some towns had only one woman some towns had none. As towns grew. More women came to the West.

_____

_____

_____

_____

_____

_____

_____

_____

_____

═Sliding Home

Read the poem at the beginning of the chapter again. Notice the variety of verbs that Hoey uses in describing the action of the ball after it leaves the basketball player's hands. The ball *slides, lands, leans, wobbles, wavers, hesitates, exasperates, plays,* and finally *dives.* Does it seem to you as though the ball takes on a personality all its own at this point? How do these creative verbs enhance the picture of this scene in your mind?

page 386

Precise words

- *Which verbs in "Foul Shot" surprise you the most? Which please you the most?*

- *What verbs might Hoey have used at the end of the poem if the ball had not gone through the net?*

> *Proverbs 30:25-27*
>
> *25 The ants are a people not strong, yet they prepare their meat in the summer;*
>
> *26 The conies are but a feeble folk, yet make they their houses in the rocks;*
>
> *27 The locusts have no king, yet go they forth all of them by bands.*

- *How many action verbs are in this passage? How many linking verbs?*

- *Why do you think there are more of one kind than the other?*

Persuading an Audience

And he reasoned in the synagogue every sabbath, and persuaded the Jews and the Greeks.

Acts 18:4

page 378

Determining purpose

Every time you hear a radio announcement about a school concert or a new restaurant that is opening, read in the newspaper about a clothing sale, or look at a billboard telling about a vacation resort, you are seeing or hearing a kind of persuasion.

Advertising tries to persuade you to do something or to buy something. Have you ever thought about how advertising works? Good ads target a specific audience and thrust forward one message to that audience. Incorporating strong verbs helps convey the message to the target audience.

By following a few rules you can become an effective advertiser. A good advertisement should contain the *what,* the *when,* and the *where.* The *what* tells about the product, place, or event; the *when* gives the time, if needed, or the date a new product will be available; the *where* explains at what place the event will be held or the product can be found.

Perhaps an announcement will need a *how* in it. That is a section to explain, for example, how to get to a meeting, how to sign up for a contest, or how to get tickets for a play. If there is a *how* part in an advertisement, it should be simple and orderly.

Not all ads are visual; some must rely on the imagination for images. For example, compare the following two radio ads:

Canine Gourmet is now on sale at your local grocer's. The most delicious dog food available. Isn't your dog worth it?

[Sound of silverware on fine china; light barking in background]

Gruff voice: **I say, Muffie, what's that you're eating?**

Lighter "poodle" voice: **Canine Gourmet. My human just got it for me at the market. Want to try it?**

The second ad makes more use of the special advantages of radio. Some people may think that a radio ad, because it does not have a picture, is more limiting than a television or magazine ad. But consider how much harder it would be for film to portray the effect of rich dogs eating in a fancy restaurant. Radio ads can often do far more adventurous advertising at far less cost.

Your Turn

Write a radio announcement designed to persuade someone to try a product, use a service, or attend an event.

Planning

Choose a product, service, or event to highlight. Think of what is going on in your school or community. Is there an upcoming fitness run or craft show that would interest someone in your audience? Have you discovered a product that you really enjoy? Or do you have a service to offer, such as doing yard work or walking dogs?

Decide on a target audience. Once you have chosen what to advertise, you must think about *who* would be interested in your product/service/event. Will you target families? the elderly? young people? Think about who will be buying or using your product.

page 378

Considering audience

Write a statement of the message you want to project. What is the purpose of your ad? The purpose of the Canine Gourmet ad is to sell dog food. Will the audience remember the poodle's voice or the name of the dog food? The most memorable part of any advertisement really should be the event, the product, or the service being advertised. But sometimes the "gimmick" of the ad can overpower the message. Although many people may talk about an entertaining advertisement, it is useless if they cannot remember the purpose.

Decide on your approach. In a short radio announcement, a good opening is crucial. It gets the listeners' attention. Notice the difference between the following announcements.

Next Friday at seven-thirty in the auditorium on Rodeville Road, the choirs and band of Emmanuel Christian High School will present a free concert. Everyone is invited to attend.

At this joyous season of Christmas, the students of Emmanuel Christian High School invite you to "The Lord is Come," a concert of Christmas music performed by the choirs and band in the Emmanuel Christian Church Auditorium. The concert will be presented on Friday, December 18, at 7:30 P.M. Emmanuel Christian School is located at 9345 Rodeville Road in Cheyenne. Admission is free.

Which is more effective in its opening?

Drafting

Write a rough draft. The message of your advertisement should be short, appealing, and simple. Identify your product, the *what* of your ad. Then include the *when, where,* and *how* if these are applicable. As you wwrite your ad, use action verbs to convey your message and choose words that fit your target audience. Since many radio advertisements are thirty seconds or shorter, make every word count toward your purpose.

Revising

Examine your ad to see that you have a single message and that the message comes through in the ad. You do not want to overload the listener with too much information that is not relevant to your main message. Radio advertisements are usually no longer than sixty seconds and some are as short as fifteen seconds; therefore, you must focus on your main idea. Use strong verbs that convey the message you are trying to get across to your audience.

Proofread for correctness. Check for errors in grammar and mechanics. Your credibility as an advertiser is diminished if your ad contains grammatical errors. Remember, however, that ad writers sometimes use fragments for emphasis or appeal.

Ask a peer to read your ad. Does the ad get the reader's attention? Does the ad persuade him to do what you wanted? Ask the reader to tell you what is most appealing about the ad. What is most effective about the ad?

Publishing

Make an audio recording of your ad. Ask your classmates to assume the parts of speakers in your advertisement. Play the recording of your ad for the class or another group.

Exchange ads with classmates and read the ads to the class. You may be interested in hearing how others orally interpret the words and phrases in your ad.

Include the script in your writing folder. Writing a radio advertisement is a different type of writing assignment from many that you do. Adding this to your folder will provide another sample of your writing.

PINCH HITTER: CRITICAL THINKING

Inspector Jameson's current case had brought him to the lavishly decorated Brindle Antiques. A soft tone sounded as he and Officer Bell crossed the threshold. Attractive pieces of furniture of various styles were carefully and interestingly arranged throughout the store. Inspector Jameson stopped to run his hand along the top of a beautiful chest. Officer Bell took the opportunity to pop a peppermint candy into his mouth. Jameson studied the chest. Its feet were worn and several nicks showed along the bottom of one side. Yet the piece had character in spite of use, and Mrs. Jameson would certainly like it.

"May I help you, sir?" A young woman stood beside Jameson.

"Oh, thank you. Not just now. I'm waiting for someone." She nodded and went to another customer.

Soon a man came to him. "Good morning, Inspector. I'm Hector Montgomery. I understand you need to determine the authenticity of these furnishings."

"Dr. Montgomery, thank you for meeting us. I got your name from this brochure from another store. Yes, we need your expertise."

"Glad to help if I can," said Dr. Montgomery.

"There is strong suspicion of fraud here, and personally I am quite curious about the methods you use to determine the age of furniture. Have you come to any conclusions yet?" asked Inspector Jameson.

"Well, let me show you what I have found and satisfy your curiosity about my procedures. Step over to this hutch. It's a good example of my findings. This one is advertised as an authentic 1860s Irish pine hutch. Notice the overall color, or patina, of the wood. The color is consistent and the general style and size of this hutch are typical of pine pieces from the 1860s."

Officer Bell, whose curiosity was not as keen as Inspector Jameson's when it came to furniture, had wandered over to an ostentatious hat stand, an odd-looking Victorian relic. He absent-mindedly turned over the price tag. When the tag's figure registered in his mind, he gasped, lodging the peppermint in his throat. He coughed and lurched forward, becoming entangled with the hat stand. Inspector Jameson and Dr. Montgomery watched in amazement. It appeared to the onlookers as though Officer Bell were waltzing with the hat stand while gasping admiration. The encounter was soon over as the peppermint dislodged and the stand righted itself. Officer Bell straightened his uniform and dutifully returned to Inspector Jameson's side.

Dr. Montgomery continued. "Now look at the drawers. See how the runners are worn smooth and have a concave appearance from being pulled in and out? That indicates years of use. The hardware is all original also. There are no telltale signs of previous hardware on the drawer back. The key works and shows real signs of age and use."

"So you believe this hutch to be a genuine antique?" asked the Inspector.

"The lesson is not quite over, Inspector Jameson! Notice one last item. The glass in the hutch doors . . ."

Jameson put his hand behind one pane of glass. "It seems wavy to me," said Jameson.

"Yes," said Montgomery, "old glass is wavy. Perhaps you've noticed this in old houses?" Officer Bell joined the conversation. He had suddenly become very interested in furniture.

"Has this fellow found genuine but damaged antiques and repaired them to sell at first quality prices? That is not illegal unless the furniture is advertised as completely original," said Officer Bell.

"Well," said Montgomery, "I think Inspector Jameson can answer that now."

Jameson ran his hand behind all the panes in the hutch. Near the top he stopped and looked at Montgomery. "Fraud." Montgomery nodded.

"Yes, Inspector. The case, wood, hardware, patina, and wear are original 1860s. This glass pane is not. The discrepancy could be an honest mistake, except that I myself appraised this piece for the owner and pointed out this discrepancy. There is no doubt that the owner of this store is practicing fraud."

Officer Bell was astonished. "'How did you know, Inspector?"

"Why, my old friend, it was clear as a bell!"

1. *What did Jameson mean when he said that the answer "was clear as a bell"?*

2. *From looking at the brochure, why do you think Jameson felt he could trust Dr. Montgomery?*

3. *If Officer Bell wants to find out more about the hat stand he encountered, which evening of the week should he keep open?*

Featherstone Antiques & Art

441 West Adams Avenue 371-9555

Only the Best

Are you interested in quality, genuine antiques?

Look no further!

Not only do we offer the finest antique furniture in town, but we also offer classes to teach you to be a furniture expert.

Honesty is our Byword
Quality is our Goal

OCTOBER ONLY

Art Appreciation
Mondays   7:30-9:30 $45

Determining Age of Furniture
Thursdays   7:00-9:00 $50

History of Upholstery
Fridays   6:00-7:30 $35

All classes will be taught by world-renowned expert Hector Montgomery

While Dr. Montgomery is well versed in every era, his specialty is furniture from the 1700s and 1800s.

Come join us this month!

CHAPTER 4

PRONOUNS

CHIEF COCHISE

Excerpt from a speech at a conference where Cochise was told the Apaches would be sent to a reservation

I have no father or mother. I am alone in the world. Nobody cares about Cochise. That is why I do not care to live and want the rocks to fall and cover me up. If I had a father and mother like you, I would be with them and they with me.

When I was going around the world, everybody was asking for Cochise. Now he is here. You see him and hear him. Are you glad? If so, say so. Speak, Americans and Mexicans. I do not want to hide anything from you nor have you hide anything from me. I will not lie to you. Do not lie to me.

I want to live in these mountains. I do not want to go to Tularosa. That is a long way off. The flies on those mountains eat out the eyes of the horses. The bad spirits live there. I have drunk of these waters, and they have cooled me. I do not want to leave this place.

- *To whom is Cochise speaking?*

- *What words would you use to describe the way Cochise is feeling as he delivers this speech?*

- *When Cochise makes this speech, he is a prisoner. What request is he making of his captors?*

- *How is the way Cochise refers to himself in the third sentence different from the way he refers to himself in the first two sentences? Can you find other places where he uses this technique?*

Cochise is pleading that he not be sent to a reservation at Tularosa, New Mexico. Sometimes he uses *I* and *me;* sometimes he calls himself *Cochise.* When he speaks using *I* and *me,* he seems strong and independent. But when he calls himself *Cochise,* he seems to be speaking of someone else for whom he has much pity. His manner of speaking had a great effect on his audience. General Oliver Howard petitioned the United States government to let Cochise stay on his own land. Cochise was granted that right.

Words like *I, me, you, they,* and *that* are used in this passage as *pronouns.* They take the place of the nouns *Cochise, Americans and Mexicans, father and mother,* and *Tularosa.* Cochise also uses the words *nobody, everybody,* and *anything,* which are also pronouns.

Pronouns and Antecedents

Pronouns are words that substitute for nouns. Using pronouns simplifies our writing and speaking. Usually, repeating the same nouns over and over makes writing awkward and wordy.

> When *Sven* was riding *Sven's* bicycle home from school, *Sven* saw a wallet on the sidewalk.
> When Sven was riding his bicycle home from school, he saw a wallet on the sidewalk.

ETYMOLOGY

Pro means "in place of." What does *pronoun* mean?

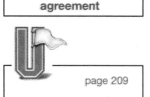

page 197

Pronoun-Antecedent agreement

page 209

Pronoun reference

The noun that a pronoun refers to is called the **antecedent**. In the example, *Sven* is the antecedent of *his* and *he*. The antecedent usually appears before the pronouns that refer to it. The antecedent may even appear in a previous sentence. Occasionally an antecedent will appear after the pronoun.

> *Sven* stopped *his* bicycle.
> *Sven* picked up the *wallet*. *He* opened *it* curiously.
> As soon as *he* saw *it*, *Sven* recognized the owner's *name*.

In Summary

A **pronoun** is a noun substitute. An **antecedent** is the noun that a pronoun refers to.

4-1 PRACTICE THE SKILL

Underline the pronouns. Write each pronoun and its antecedent on the line below the sentence.

1. Keesha, have you read about Mark Twain? His real name was Samuel Clemens.

   _____

2. He took that pen name from the river term for "two fathoms deep."

   _____

3. Clemens is remembered best for his humorous writings, for they captured people's imaginations.

   _____

4. Clemens's life produced its share of sadness, though.

   _____

5. Clemens and his wife, Olivia, had three daughters in their family: Susy, Clara, and Jean.

   _____

6. When Susy died from spinal meningitis in 1896, they were devastated.

_____

7. Even before her death, though, Clemens had been having financial troubles.

_____

8. He had to spend several years working his way out of debt.

_____

9. Olivia died in 1904, and her youngest daughter followed her mother to the grave only five years later.

_____

10. These disappointments certainly affected Clemens, and they probably contributed to the pessimism of his later writings.

_____

 4·2 REVIEW THE SKILL

Underline each pronoun. Write its antecedent in the blank.

_____ 1. Jochebed, the mother of Moses, put him in a basket.

_____ 2. Miriam watched her brother in the river.

_____ 3. He floated in a small basket.

_____ 4. His mother had made the basket.

_____ 5. It was made of bulrushes and waterproofed.

_____ 6. Pharaoh's daughter sent her maids to get the basket.

_____ 7. When the maids opened it, they saw Moses.

_____ 8. Miriam brought Moses' mother to care for him.

_____ 9. Pharaoh's daughter named him.

_____ 10. Moses loved the Israelites and their God.

Personal Pronouns

The pronouns we most frequently use are the **personal pronouns**. All personal pronouns have four characteristics: **person**, **number**, **gender**, and **case**. Refer to the chart as you study these four characteristics.

Singular

	Subjective Case	Objective Case	Possessive Case
First Person	I	me	my, mine
Second Person	you	you	your, yours
Third Person			
neuter	it	it	its
masculine	he	him	his
feminine	she	her	her, hers

Plural

	Subjective Case	Objective Case	Possessive Case
First Person	we	us	our, ours
Second Person	you	you	your, yours
Third Person	they	them	their, theirs

page 112

Possessives

page 209

Pronoun case

page 217

Courtesy order

Person tells whether the personal pronoun refers to the speaker, the person spoken to, or the person spoken of.

> **First person is the person speaking:** *I* am here.
> **Second person is the person spoken to:** *You* are here.
> **Third person is the person spoken of:** *He* is here.

Number tells whether the personal pronoun is singular or plural.

> **Singular:** *He* is here.
> **Plural:** *They* are here.

Gender tells whether the personal pronoun is masculine, feminine, or neuter. A difference of gender is shown only with the third-person singular pronouns.

> **Masculine:** *He* is here.
> **Feminine:** *She* is here.
> **Neuter:** *It* is here.

Case tells how the personal pronoun is being used in a sentence. The three cases of personal pronouns are subjective, objective, and possessive. Later you will study how these three cases are used correctly. For now, notice the case forms for the third-person singular masculine pronoun.

> **Subjective:** *He* is the pastor.
> **Objective:** The congregation likes *him*.
> **Possessive:** *His* sermons teach us God's Word.

IN SUMMARY

Personal pronouns reflect **person** (first, second, third), **number** (singular, plural), **gender** (masculine, feminine, neuter), and **case** (subjective, objective, possessive).

4·3 PRACTICE THE SKILL

Replace each underlined word with an appropriate pronoun.

_____ 1. <u>Diana</u> read the story about David and Goliath.

_____ 2. <u>Diana's</u> teacher asked her to read the story.

_____ 3. <u>Mr. Reynolds</u> is the Bible teacher.

_____ 4. <u>The story</u> is found in I Samuel 17.

_____ 5. Goliath challenged <u>David</u> to fight.

_____ 6. David accepted <u>Goliath's</u> challenge.

_____ 7. Saul offered <u>Saul's</u> armor to David.

_____ 8. David collected five stones; he put one of <u>the stones</u> in his sling.

_____ 9. <u>David</u> used the sling, and the stone that David threw hit Goliath.

_____ 10. <u>The Israelites</u> praised David.

Learning Christianly

Subjects like writing and grammar can be difficult to learn and even more difficult to master. Why should we spend so much time learning to excel in these areas? Read Genesis 1:27-28. These verses explain that since God made humans in His image, they are able to be like Him in some ways and to act like Him in some ways. In light of these verses, how can refining your writing and grammar skills allow you to act more like God?

Replace each underlined word or phrase with an appropriate pronoun.

———— 1. The story of Elijah and the prophets of Baal should encourage every Christian.

———— 2. The story's description of how God worked in and through Elijah gives hope to others.

———— 3. Elijah challenged the prophets of Baal to a contest to determine who served the true God.

———— 4. Elijah would offer a bullock on an altar, and the prophets of Baal would do the same thing.

———— 5. The God that sent fire down to consume the sacrifice would be acknowledged to be the true God.

———— 6. The prophets of Baal spent hours trying to get Baal to listen to the prophets' cries, but Baal remained silent.

———— 7. When it was Elijah's turn, Elijah ordered that twelve barrels of water be poured over the sacrifice and wood.

———— 8. Immediately after Elijah prayed, God responded to Elijah with fire that consumed not only the sacrifice but also everything in and around the altar, even the water.

———— 9. Surprisingly, Elijah fled after this great victory because Queen Jezebel threatened to kill him.

————10. Yet God did not allow Jezebel's threats to ruin Elijah's service but showed Elijah that there was still work to be done and people to help do it.

Demonstrative Pronouns

The **demonstrative pronouns** *this, these, that,* and *those* point out objects, persons, places, or ideas. These pronouns may function as subjects, predicate nouns, direct objects, indirect objects, and objects of prepositions. Use *this* (singular) or *these* (plural) for objects that are near and *that* (singular) or *those* (plural) for objects that are far away.

Subject:	*These* are mine.
Predicate Noun:	His favorite cookies are *those*.
Direct Object:	I gave her *that*.
Indirect Object:	She gave *this* more attention.
Object of Preposition:	She has three of *these*.

page 215

Who and *whom*

page 217

Whose and *who's*

Interrogative Pronouns

The five **interrogative** pronouns are often used to ask questions.

Which of us will enter the battle?
What does the Lord require of you?
Who is on the Lord's side?
Whom shall I send?
Whose are the commands?

IN SUMMARY

Demonstrative pronouns point out objects, persons, places, or ideas; they can be used any way a noun can be used in a sentence.

Interrogative pronouns are generally used to ask questions.

4·5 PRACTICE THE SKILL

Underline the demonstrative and interrogative pronouns. Label each underlined pronoun *Dem* (demonstrative) or *Inter* (interrogative).

_____ 1. Please take that to Mika.

_____ 2. Which do you mean?

_____ 3. This is the one.

_____ 4. Who gets the item?

_____ 5. We choose these.

_____ 6. What do you want?

_____ 7. I prefer those.

_____ 8. Whom shall I choose?

_____ 9. Who handles problems well?

_____10. That stumps many people.

A. Label each underlined pronoun *Per* (personal), *Dem* (demonstrative), or *Inter* (interrogative).

B. Write the antecedent of each personal and each demonstrative pronoun.

_____ 1. <u>Who</u> was Jacques Cousteau?

_____ 2. <u>He</u> was a well-known French oceanographer.

_____ 3. <u>What</u> made Cousteau famous?

_____ 4. The Aqua-Lung was invented by <u>him</u>.

_____ 5. <u>This</u> is a breathing device used to allow divers to move freely in the ocean.

_____ 6. <u>It</u> was an important piece of equipment for Cousteau and his sons.

_____ 7. <u>Their</u> research ship was named *Calypso*.

_____ 8. <u>It</u> became famous as Cousteau's reputation grew.

_____ 9. <u>That</u> allowed Cousteau to produce television programs.

_____ 10. <u>These</u> emphasized marine conservation and dramatized ocean exploration.

Reflexive and Intensive Pronouns

Reflexive pronouns and **intensive pronouns** are made from pronoun forms with *self* or *selves* added. Only certain pronoun forms can become reflexive or intensive.

Singular	
First Person	myself
Second Person	yourself
Third Person	
neuter	itself
masculine	himself
feminine	herself
Plural	
First Person	ourselves
Second Person	yourselves
Third Person	themselves

page 219

Reflexive and Intensive pronouns

Reflexive pronouns are used as direct objects, indirect objects, and objects of prepositions. They always refer to the same person or thing as the subject. Therefore, the subject is the antecedent. Reflexive pronouns are the only direct objects that refer to the subject.

> **Direct Object:** The parrot bit *itself.*
> **Indirect Object:** Joey asked *himself* a question.
> **Object of Preposition:** We looked for *ourselves* in the picture.

Intensive pronouns do not function as part of a sentence pattern. Instead, they emphasize a noun or a pronoun already used in the sentence. The antecedent is the word that the intensive pronoun emphasizes. Because intensive pronouns are not part of the sentence pattern, they can be removed without changing the basic meaning of the sentence.

> We met the author *himself.*
> We *ourselves* met the author.

IN SUMMARY

Reflexive pronouns are used as direct objects, indirect objects, and objects of prepositions; they always refer to the subject.

Intensive pronouns emphasize a noun or a pronoun already in the sentence, but they do not function as part of the sentence pattern.

PRACTICE THE SKILL

Label the sentence patterns *S-InV, S-TrV-DO, S-TrV-IO-DO, S-LV-PN,* or *S-LV-PA.* In the blank, label the underlined pronouns *Int* (intensive) or *Ref* (reflexive).

_____ 1. Samuel Wesley <u>himself</u> was Samuel Westley originally.

_____ 2. Wesley gave <u>himself</u> the new name during his years at Oxford.

_____ 3. Wesley's father and grandfather made names for <u>themselves</u> as

Nonconformist ministers.

_____ 4. Wesley <u>himself</u> returned to the established church and

contributed to its defense with his writing and speaking.

_____ 5. Ironically, Wesley's name is <u>itself</u> famous because of his sons'

work with the new Methodist movement.

_____ 6. Susanna Wesley was a remarkable woman <u>herself</u>.

_____ 7. From a family of twenty-five children, she could read Greek

and Hebrew for <u>herself</u> by the age of thirteen.

_____ 8. Her faith spoke for <u>itself</u> in the lives her many children led.

_____ 9. They provided <u>themselves</u> entertainment on many occasions.

_____ 10. Susanna <u>herself</u> talked with each child for an hour every week.

REVIEW THE SKILL

Label the sentence patterns *S-InV, S-TrV-DO, S-TrV-IO-DO, S-LV-PN,* or *S-LV-PA.* In the blank, label the underlined pronouns *Int* (intensive) or *Ref* (reflexive).

_____ 1. Harriet Tubman made a name for <u>herself</u> as a leader of the

Underground Railroad.

_____ 2. The Railroad <u>itself</u> owed much of its success to Tubman.

_____ 3. In fact, Tubman earned <u>herself</u> the nickname Moses for her efforts.

_____ 4. Tubman <u>herself</u> was a slave from birth.

_____ 5. Her husband had been a slave <u>himself</u> but was free by the time of their marriage.

_____ 6. Tubman escaped to Philadelphia by <u>herself</u> in 1849.

_____ 7. After her own escape, Tubman gave <u>herself</u> to the work of the Underground Railroad.

_____ 8. About three hundred slaves owed <u>themselves</u> and their freedom to Tubman's nineteen trips on their behalf.

_____ 9. Several rewards for her arrest appeared, but the hunters <u>themselves</u> never could catch Tubman.

_____ 10. In later years, Tubman assigned <u>herself</u> the job of caring for the elderly, the needy, and the uneducated.

Indefinite Pronouns

Unlike personal pronouns, **indefinite pronouns** do not always refer to specific persons or things. These pronouns usually do not have clear antecedents.

Some Common Indefinite Pronouns			
anybody	everybody	nobody	somebody
anyone	everyone	no one	someone
anything	everything	nothing	something
all	both	many	none

Indefinite pronouns can be used as subjects, predicate nouns, direct objects, indirect objects, or objects of prepositions.

Subject:	_Everyone_ has a favorite meal.
Predicate Noun:	My mother's cooking is really _something_.
Direct Object:	She can make _anything_.
Indirect Object:	She tells _nobody_ her secret recipes.
Object of Preposition:	The meals are a pleasant surprise for _all_.

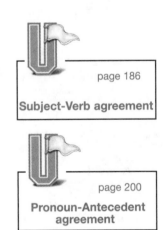

page 186

Subject-Verb agreement

page 200

Pronoun-Antecedent agreement

Indefinite pronouns do not refer to specific persons or things.
Indefinite pronouns usually do not have antecedents.

4-9 PRACTICE THE SKILL

Underline the indefinite pronouns.

1. Brenda has invited everyone to the picnic.

2. May we bring anything?

3. Somebody will want salad.

4. No one offered us cake.

5. Is anyone bringing anything for a tablecloth?

6. Is everybody coming at noon?

7. Some will be late.

8. Is everything ready?

9. Someone dropped the hamburgers.

10. The work for the picnic will be nothing.

4-10 REVIEW THE SKILL

Underline the indefinite pronouns.

1. Does anyone play the trumpet?

2. Probably everybody has at least heard a trumpet.

3. It is a popular instrument for many in bands and orchestras.

4. Anybody can see that trumpeters push down valves.

5. Mouth movement is not as obvious to everyone.

6. Both are important, though, for making music.

7. Musicians started playing something like a trumpet around 1200 B.C.

8. But none of the original trumpets had valves to help create different notes.

9. Mouth position and breath support were everything.

10. Today's trumpet is definitely easier to play, but no one would deny that it still requires much hard work.

Underline the pronouns. Label each pronoun above the word: *P* (personal), *Dem* (demonstrative), *Inter* (interrogative), *Ref* (reflexive), *Int* (intensive), or *Ind* (indefinite).

Phillis Wheatley came to America on a slave ship when she was about eight years old. A wealthy merchant named John Wheatley bought her as a slave for his wife. Although most slaves were uneducated, both of the Wheatleys recognized that Phillis was intelligent, and Phillis proved that by learning to read and write. She also studied geography, history, and Latin; at age fourteen Phillis taught herself to write poems. Many of these were published in Phillis's book *Poems on Various Subjects: Religious and Moral*. It was published in England in 1773. The poems themselves discussed Phillis's deep religious convictions. Phillis also wrote about life as a slave. Who could better write about this? Almost everything Phillis wrote was deeply personal. As a young woman, Phillis was freed, and she married John Peters. Although she died almost unknown, everyone reading Phillis's work today recognizes her important contribution to American poetry. She was the first important black poet of the New World.

Underline each pronoun. Fill in the blank with the type of pronoun:
demonstrative, indefinite, intensive, interrogative, **or** *reflexive.*

1. Who joined the League of Nations?

   _____

2. The absence of the United States was a surprise to all.

   _____

3. This baffled the proponents of the League.

   _____

4. What barred the United States from joining this?

   _____

5. Whom was the League protecting?

   _____

6. The League maintained safety and protection for itself.

   _____

7. However, not everyone was concerned for other nations.

   _____

8. Many of the nations defeated themselves and the purpose of the
   League.

   _____

9. This was proved when France itself would not aid Ethiopia.

   _____

10. In the end, no one helped anyone for the fear of everyone.

    _____

Locate and correct the ten errors in the paragraph: fragments, comma splices, noun plurals, singular and plural noun possessives, verb forms (for example, *had wrote*), and spellings of verb forms. Use the lines below to write the paragraph correctly.

One of the most docile and timid creatures of the sea is the manatee. Sometimes called a sea cow. There are three species of manatees, the types of manatees are Caribbean, Amazon, and African. Another name for manatees is "Sirenia." Because of their resemblance to mermaids or sirens. The legend of the mermaid probably originated when sailors had seed some dugongs in the Red Sea. Dugong's are similar to manatees. Most manatees lives in tropical areas. Manatees are the largest of all plant-eating animals that live their entire lives in the water, a manatees diet might consist of a hundred pounds of water plants in a day! Female manatees take good care of their young. A mother plays with her baby and sometimes carrys it on her back. Manatees's lives are generally solitary, but occasionally they will come together in a group. This occurs in winter in places where the water is unusually warm.

_____

_____

_____

_____

_____

_____

_____

_____

_____

_____

_____

≡Sliding Home

Try reading the passage from Cochise's speech again, substituting nouns for each pronoun. Do you see how valuable pronouns are in making writing clearer and more concise?

- *What is the personal pronoun Cochise uses most frequently in the last paragraph?*

- *How does the use of* I *make the ending stronger?*

> *Isaiah 14:13-15*
>
> *13 For thou hast said in thine heart, I will ascend into heaven, I will exalt my throne above the stars of God: I will sit also upon the mount of the congregation, in the sides of the north:*
>
> *14 I will ascend above the heights of the clouds; I will be like the most High.*
>
> *15 Yet thou shalt be brought down to hell, to the sides of the pit.*

- *To whom does the pronoun* I *refer? What does this pronoun reveal about its antecedent?*

Writing to a Pen Pal

The elder unto the wellbeloved Gaius, whom I love in the truth. Beloved, I wish above all things that thou mayest prosper and be in health, even as thy soul prospereth.

III John 1-2

Notice how Cochise introduced himself through his speech. He made it very personal by his numerous references to *I*. How would you introduce yourself through a letter to someone who had never seen you before?

Your Turn

Imagine that you have been assigned a pen pal in another state and that this person knows nothing about you. Write a letter introducing yourself.

Planning

Make a list of the things that you want your pen pal to know about you. Take a few minutes and write down what you like, what you like to do, and where you like to go. Be sure to include things that make you *you.* Do not try to organize the ideas yet but be as specific as possible.

Group related ideas. After you complete your list, use colored pens to mark similar items. For example, you could mark items about your parents, brothers, sisters, pets, house, and room with the same color and then list them under the category *family.* Continue to mark and categorize your ideas until you have organized all of them.

Drafting

Write the salutation. Begin with a friendly salutation. Since you know the name of your pen pal, be sure to include his or her name.

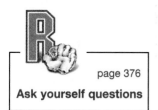

page 376

Ask yourself questions

Determine the order of your ideas. What do you want your pen pal to know first? next? last? When you have decided, you are ready to begin writing your letter.

Choose your words carefully. Remember that your reader has only your words; the reader cannot see your face or hear your voice. Be sure that you give your pen pal honest details about yourself.

Write well-organized paragraphs. Begin each paragraph with a topic sentence that presents the main idea of that paragraph. Adapt the categories that you used to organize your list of ideas. Remember, though, that your letter should not be simply a list. Add details and bits of humor. Let your personality shine through. Use personal pronouns as you write.

Write the closing. The closing should be friendly and appropriate, such as *Your friend* or *Sincerely.* Be sure to sign your name legibly too.

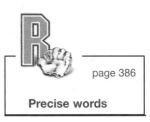

page 386

Precise words

Revising

Question yourself about your letter. Are all the words spelled correctly? Are the ideas within the paragraphs arranged in a logical way? Have you presented an accurate picture of yourself? Did you include an appropriate salutation and closing? Are the paragraphs indented neatly?

Write a clean copy of your letter. Use your best penmanship for the final copy of your letter. A handwritten letter is more personal than a letter generated from a word processor. Remember that this letter is your pen pal's first impression of you. You want to make a positive impression.

Publishing

Prepare your letter for mailing. Fold your letter carefully and insert it into an appropriately sized envelope. Write the complete address for your pen pal on the front of the envelope. Be sure to include your return address in the upper left corner of the envelope.

Create a memory book. If you establish a writing relationship with a pen pal, save the letters that you receive from your pen pal and preserve them in an album. Read through previous letters before you write a new letter.

Dear Pen Pal,

My name is Angelique Randall, and I am twelve years old. I am in seventh grade at Trinity Christian School. My dad is the science teacher at the school, and my mom works part-time in the school office. I have three younger brothers and one little sister. My sister, Meghan, is my favorite person to play with. She is only three years old, and since I'm the oldest of us kids, I get to be Meghan's baby sitter lots of times.

I like to do a lot of different things. I play volleyball for our school team. We had our first game last night and won. I am still learning the overhand serve, but I'm getting better at it. I also love little kids. I help my mom teach the kindergarten Sunday school class at our church. Mom and I get along great. Just last week, she taught me how to bake cinnamon rolls. I think that's going to become one of my favorite things to do, because I love to eat them!

I think my favorite subject at school is science, maybe because I have such a great teacher. A lot of kids ask me if I want to be a science teacher when I grow up, like my dad. I'm not sure what I want to do yet. I love to study about weather and storms and things like that, so I think it would be fun to be a meteorologist. But I'll just have to wait and see. Whatever else I do, I know I want to be a mom, because I think kids are so much fun.

Please write soon and tell me all about yourself. I can't wait to hear from you.

Your friend,
Angelique

P.S. I'm sending you my school picture from sixth grade. My hair is longer now, and I have braces.

P.S. is an abbreviation for the term *post script*, which means "to write after." *P.S.* introduces an additional message after the main part of a letter.

CHAPTER 5

ADJECTIVES

THE SPECKLED BAND
BY SIR ARTHUR CONAN DOYLE

It was a singular sight which met our eyes. On the table stood a dark lantern with the shutter half open, throwing a brilliant light upon the iron safe, the door of which was ajar. Beside the table, on the wooden chair, sat Dr. Grimesby Roylott, clad in a long gray dressing gown, his bare ankles protruding beneath, and his feet thrust into red heelless Turkish slippers. Across his lap lay the short stock with the long lash which we had noticed during the day. His chin was cocked upward and his eyes were fixed in a dreadful rigid stare at the corner of the ceiling. Round his brow he had a peculiar yellow band, with brownish speckles, which seemed to be bound tightly round his head. As we entered he made neither sound nor motion.

"The band! The speckled band!" whispered Holmes.

I took a step forward. In an instant his strange headgear began to move, and there reared itself from among his hair the squat diamond-shaped head and puffed neck of a loathsome serpent.

- *How do you think the author wants the reader to feel as he reads this passage?*

- *What details add to the suspense of the scene?*

- *Could you draw a picture of the room? Of the way the doctor is dressed?*

You would probably be able to draw this scene because the author describes it meticulously. He uses words like *wooden, gray, heelless, dreadful, brownish,* and *diamond-shaped.* These words appeal to the senses. Suppose Doyle had told us only that the doctor wore slippers. There are many kinds of slippers. But Doyle uses descriptive words to narrow our choices. These are "red heelless Turkish slippers." Without the words *red, heelless,* and *Turkish*, we might imagine that he wore pink bunny slippers.

Descriptive words that sharpen our understanding of nouns are called *adjectives.* As you study this chapter, you may be surprised to find how many adjectives you use all the time.

Adjectives

A **modifier** is a word that tells more about another word. It describes the other word. Modifiers help us say exactly what we mean. Without modifiers many of our sentences would be dull. Modifiers enrich the meanings of our nouns and verbs.

As we use modifiers in our writing, we should remember that the modifiers alone cannot get our ideas across. The basic sentence parts are always the most important words of our sentences. We must begin with strong nouns and verbs. Then we add modifiers to make the meanings of these words clearer.

Adjectives are words that modify nouns. In other words, an adjective gives details that make the noun's meaning clearer. Adjectives tell *what kind, which one, how many,* or *whose* about the nouns they modify.

What kind?   The *weary* hiker trudged through the *dark* forest.

Which one?   Would *this* trail lead him home?

How many?   He checked the map for the *third* time.

Whose?   *His* compass would help.

In these sentences adjectives give details about the hiker, the forest, the trail, the time, and the compass. The adjectives *weary, dark, this, third,* and *his* help us create a picture.

Most adjectives come just before the nouns they modify. Other adjectives come after a linking verb; these adjectives are called predicate adjectives. A predicate adjective always describes the subject of the sentence.

The long, dusty trail was *steep.*

To determine whether a word is an adjective, ask if it answers any of the adjective questions. You can also use the adjective test frame. Any word that will fit into the frame may be used as an adjective. Some adjectives will fit the test frame, but some will not. Remember, if a word modifies a noun it is an adjective.

The _____ thing (or person) is very _____ .

The *bright* thing is very *bright.*

The *tall* person is very *tall.*

Adjectives modify nouns and tell what kind, which one, how many, or whose. Many adjectives will fit the adjective test frame.

page 56

Predicate adjectives

page 144

Prepositional phrases

page 233

Adjective or Adverb?

Underline the adjectives. Draw an arrow from each adjective to the noun it modifies.

1. Many people enjoy golf.

2. Historically, the British royalty played this sport.

3. Queen Mary of Scotland was an avid golfer.

4. The sport became popular in America.

5. People made the early clubs from wood.

6. American golfers changed to steel clubs.

7. Initially, golfers used leather balls.

8. The leather balls became soggy in the rain.

9. Someone designed a solid, dimpled ball.

10. That cheap little ball changed the game.

5-2 **REVIEW THE SKILL**

Underline the adjectives.

1. Thomas Alva Edison was a famous inventor.

2. He married Mary Stillwell, and they had three children.

3. After Mary's death, he married the daughter of a wealthy industrialist.

4. Thomas Edison spent his early years in Milan, Ohio.

5. In later years, he became nearly deaf.

6. Despite physical problems, Edison masterminded many new inventions.

7. In 1886 he moved to an improved laboratory in West Orange, New Jersey.

8. Edison invented the cylindrical phonograph.

9. His inventions introduced new concepts to several other industries also.

10. Edison's inventions brought him worldwide honor.

Write descriptive sentences using the instructions below. Check for adjectives in your sentences.

1. Describe an invention of your own.

   _____

   _____

2. Tell about a fantastic sports play you have witnessed.

   _____

   _____

3. Write an interesting fact about a book you have enjoyed recently.

   _____

   _____

4. Use words to show what your brother's, sister's, or parents' (or your own!) hair looks like in the morning.

   _____

   _____

5. Describe what your toothpaste tastes like.

   _____

   _____

6. Proverbs 17:22 says, "A merry heart doeth good like a medicine." Whom do you know who has a merry heart? Describe that person.

   _____

   _____

7. Write specifics about a pet you would like to own someday.

   _____

   _____

8. Tell about your favorite flower, tree, or plant.

   _____

   _____

Learning Christianly

Adjectives are a grammatical way of separating things into categories. Some things are tall and others are short. Some are green and others are red. Have you ever realized that animals and plants don't have the ability to recognize the categories to the extent that humans do? Since God has made humans to be distinctive in their awareness of His creation, why are words like adjectives so valuable?

9. The Bible has much to say about friends. Briefly describe one of your friends.

_____

_____

10. If you could come up with a new soda product, what would it taste like? Write a one-sentence advertisement for your soda.

_____

_____

Comparing with Adjectives

Most adjectives answer the question "what kind?" and come just before the nouns they modify. These are adjectives that can show comparison. They have **comparative** and **superlative** forms in addition to the stem, or **positive,** form. The comparative form compares two people or things; the superlative form compares three or more people or things. For most adjectives the comparative form is the stem + *er.* The superlative form for most of the common adjectives is the stem + *est.* For adjectives that would sound awkward with *er* or *est,* we use the words *more* and *most* before the adjectives.

Positive	Comparative	Superlative
cool	cooler	coolest
weary	wearier	weariest
beautiful	more beautiful	most beautiful

Jon is tall, but Stephen is taller. Eric is the tallest boy in the class.

February is a popular month for weddings, but summer months are more popular. In fact, June is the most popular month for weddings.

Irregular adjectives do not follow these simple rules for forming the comparative and superlative. Rather than simply adding *er* and *est* or *more* and *most,* irregular adjectives may have entirely different forms to show comparison.

Positive	Comparative	Superlative
good	better	best
well	better	best
bad	worse	worst
many	more	most
little	less	least

Adjectives that can be compared will always fit into the test frame. But be sure to use the stem form of the word when using the test frame.

page 237

Comparisons

Wrong: The *loudest* thing is very *loudest.*
Right: The *loud* thing is very *loud.*

As you can see, using the superlative form of the adjective in the test frame results in an illogical sentence.

IN SUMMARY

Regular adjectives show comparison by adding *er* and *est* or *more* and *most* to the stem form of the adjective.

Irregular adjectives may have entirely different forms to show comparison.

5-4 PRACTICE THE SKILL

Fill in each blank with the correct form of the adjective.

_____ 1. Many Bible scholars consider Martin Luther the _?_ reformer. *(great, superlative)*

_____ 2. Martin Luther's _?_ work was his Ninety-five Theses. *(famous, superlative)*

_____ 3. His _?_ years were spent in Mansfeld, Saxony. *(early, comparative)*

_____ 4. Luther's _?_ criticism came from the religious leaders of the day. *(harsh, superlative)*

_____ 5. His wife Katie was the _?_ person in his life. *(helpful, superlative)*

_____ 6. The _?_ death of Martin and Katie's daughter Magdalena grieved them. *(sudden, positive)*

_____ 7. Martin's health became _?_ after her death. *(bad, comparative)*

_____ 8. His writings were _?_ during his bouts of pain. *(sharp, superlative)*

_____ 9. Martin's death in 1546 caused Katie's _?_ sorrow. *(great, superlative)*

_____ 10. After Martin's death, Katie and her children began a _?_ flight from Wittenberg. *(dangerous, positive)*

Fill in each blank with the correct form of the adjective in parentheses.

_____ 1. John Stallworth was one of the _?_ wide receivers in the NFL. *(good, superlative)*

_____ 2. However, in school he was _?_ than his friends. *(clumsy, comparative)*

_____ 3. His _?_ size gave him an edge over his opponents. *(large, comparative)*

_____ 4. He broke his foot and leg in his _?_ season. *(bad, superlative)*

_____ 5. John had the _?_ Super Bowl average yards per catch. *(high, superlative)*

_____ 6. His reception over his opponent's back was one of the _?_ plays ever. *(sensational, superlative)*

_____ 7. On the Steelers' team, John Stallworth played with the _?_ Lynn Swann. *(popular, comparative)*

_____ 8. Many times it was questioned who was _?_ . *(quick, comparative)*

_____ 9. The characteristic that was _?_ was their catching style: Stallworth used his hands while Swann used his body. *(different, superlative)*

_____ 10. Some people believe that Stallworth and Swann were the _?_ receiver pair in the NFL. *(good, superlative)*

More Adjectives

page 291

Commas in a series

Sometimes other parts of speech act like adjectives. For instance, some nouns and pronouns function as adjectives when they modify another noun. Nouns and pronouns functioning as adjectives will not fit the adjective test frame. Remember that these words are adjectives only when they modify nouns. If these words are functioning as subjects or objects, they are not adjectives.

Adjective: Robert Louis Stevenson wrote *this* book.

               S LV   PN
Pronoun: *This* is my favorite book.

Adjective: *Treasure Island* is an *adventure* story.

           S TrV   DO
Noun: It describes the *adventures* of Jim Hawkins.

Do not be confused by nouns that function as adjectives. A noun that functions as an adjective always comes right before the noun that it modifies and after any other adjectives that may be there. When you see a word that may be either a noun or an adjective, determine how the word is functioning in the sentence.

S TrV   DO
He polished the brass.

S TrV   DO
He polished the large brass bell.

In the first example *brass* is a noun because it functions as the direct object of the transitive verb *polished. Brass* is the main noun in the phrase *the brass.* In the second example *brass* is an adjective because it modifies the noun *bell. Brass* is not the main noun. The complete phrase is *the large brass bell.*

To diagram an adjective, write it on a slanted line beneath the word it modifies. Look at the diagram for this sentence:

He polished the large brass bell.

To the left of the number tell whether the italicized word is an adjective, noun, or pronoun.

_____ 1. Francis Marion was a *farm* boy from South Carolina.

_____ 2. His first experience with *war* was a skirmish with the Cherokee Indians in 1761.

_____ 3. In 1775, Marion left his parents' *farm* and joined the Revolutionary War effort.

_____ 4. He defended Charleston, South Carolina, from a *British* attack.

_____ 5. By the time the *British* had captured Charleston in 1780, Marion had left the city.

_____ 6. But his *war* experience was not over.

_____ 7. Marion soon formed a small band of fighters to run *surprise* attacks on the British.

_____ 8. *These* attacks frustrated British troops, who spent much time chasing Marion through the swamplands of northeastern South Carolina.

_____ 9. The British had never seen fighters like *these!*

_____ 10. Attacks by *surprise* were Marion's specialty and earned him the nickname "Swamp Fox."

To the left of the number tell whether the italicized word is an adjective, noun, or pronoun.

_____ 1. You have no doubt heard of *mistletoe.*

_____ 2. However, many people have never seen the *mistletoe* plant.

_____ 3. The plant is actually a parasite that grows on *tree* branches.

_____ 4. *This* sometimes damages the host trees.

_____ 5. One variety of mistletoe grows primarily on the apple *tree.*

_____ 6. Mistletoe has oblong green leaves and white berries. Birds find the mistletoe *berry* quite tasty.

_____ 7. When the bird eats the berry, *berry* seeds stick to his beak, and he carries the seeds to his next perch.

_____ 8. In *this* way, the mistletoe plant is spread to other trees.

_____ 9. The mistletoe plant plays a role in *Christmas* tradition.

_____ 10. At *Christmas,* a person caught under the mistletoe gets a kiss!

Articles

The most common adjectives are the **articles** *a, an,* and *the. The* is a **definite article** because it points to specific things. *A* and *an* are **indefinite articles** because they point to nonspecific things.

> Today we will plant *a* flower in our garden. (any flower)
> My favorite flower is *the* rose. (a specific flower)

page 251

Troublesome words

> Use *a* before a consonant (*b, c, d, f, g,* etc.): What *a* beautiful day! Before a vowel, *a* changes to *an* (vowels: *a, e, i,o, u*): He gave *an* apple to his teacher.

In Summary

Some nouns and pronouns can also function as adjectives.

The **articles** *a, an,* and *the* are the most common adjectives.

5-8 PRACTICE THE SKILL

Underline the articles.

1. Christians should develop a strong daily prayer life.

2. The God of heaven desires daily prayers.

3. For some people, prayer is a last resort.

4. Intercessory prayer benefits the welfare of others.

5. Jesus is the heavenly intercessor.

6. God hears a sincere request.

7. An immediate answer does not always come.

8. The infinite plans of God outweigh finite human ones.

9. We must offer an earnest, heartfelt request.

10. Godly, fervent prayers produce the result of closeness to God.

Underline the articles. Draw an arrow from each to the noun it modifies.

The hedgehog is a small nocturnal animal with a pointed nose and stiff spines covering its back. The spines of the hedgehog do not come out as easily as do the quills of the porcupine, an alarmingly prickly creature that is often confused with the hedgehog. When a hedgehog is threatened, it rolls itself into a ball. This protects the underpart of its body, which has no spines. This action is one of the few defenses of the timid hedgehog.

Hedgehogs also exhibit an unexplained behavior. First, they produce a foamy saliva. Then they spread the sticky foam all over their bodies. Scientists believe this froth may have a cooling effect on the hedgehog, but they are not sure. Hedgehogs have an average life span of three or four years, with some animals living to be as old as six years.

Possessives

A **possessive** is a noun form or pronoun form that shows ownership. Possessives usually function as adjectives. A possessive that functions as an adjective answers the question "whose?" about the noun it modifies.

page 30

Forming possessives

page 86

Possessive pronouns

Possessive Pronouns		
Person	**Singular**	**Plural**
first	my, mine	our, ours
second	your, yours	your, yours
third	its, his,	their, theirs
	her, hers	

A possessive noun usually signals that another noun will follow in the sentence.

Connie's bicycle is new.

The possessive noun *Connie's* modifies the noun *bicycle* to tell us who owns the bicycle. Possessive nouns usually act as adjectives rather than as nouns. Possessive pronouns act like possessive nouns and can take the place of possessive nouns.

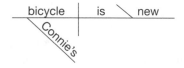

Connie's bicycle is new.

Her bicycle is new.

The possessive pronoun *her* replaces the possessive noun *Connie's*. The possessive pronoun modifies the noun *bicycle* and shows ownership. To diagram a possessive noun or pronoun used as an adjective, follow the diagram for any other adjective:

Connie's bicycle is new.

```
bicycle  |  is  \  new
    \Connie's
```

Sometimes an entire phrase (a group of words) shows possession. A possessive phrase consists of a possessive noun modified by at least one other adjective.

Her brother's old bicycle has a new seat.

In this example, the word *brother's* is not the complete possessive. The possessive phrase *her brother's* tell us exactly who owns the bicycle. Possessive pronouns can also replace an entire possessive phrase.

Her brother's old bicycle has a new seat.

His old bicycle has a new seat.

The possessive pronoun *his* replaces the possessive phrase *her brother's*. The possessive pronoun is an adjective because it modifies the noun *bicycle*. A possessive phrase is diagrammed slightly differently than other adjectives are diagrammed. The adjective that precedes the possessive word is attached to the possessive itself rather than to the main noun:

Her brother's old bicycle has a new seat.

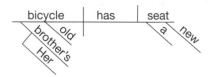

```
bicycle  |  has  |  seat
   \old            \a  \new
   \brother's
   \Her
```

Sometimes a possessive noun or pronoun can replace more than just a noun or a possessive phrase. A possessive noun or pronoun can also replace an entire phrase.

Her brother's old bicycle has a new seat.
His has a new seat.

In this example, the possessive pronoun *his* does not modify any noun in the sentence. Instead, the word *his* replaces the entire phrase *her brother's old bicycle.* When a possessive acts in place of a noun or a noun and its adjectives, it is called an **independent possessive.** Independent possessives are not adjectives because they do not modify nouns. An independent possessive replaces the noun and all of its modifiers.

> *Jill's birthday* was last week.
> *Jill's* was last week.

In the first sentence, the possessive noun *Jill's* is an adjective. It modifies the noun *birthday.* In the second example, *Jill's* does not modify any other noun. It is an independent possessive functioning as the subject of the sentence.

> She opened *my gift.*
> She opened *mine.*

The possessive pronoun *my* is an adjective because it modifies the noun *gift* and shows ownership. The possessive pronoun *mine* is an independent possessive. It does not modify any noun in the sentence. Instead, *mine* replaces the phrase *my gift* and acts as the direct object in the sentence.

Because independent possessives replace other nouns or pronouns, they should be diagrammed according to the function of the word or phrase they replace. Look at the diagram for this sentence:

His has a new seat.

Now look at the diagram for this sentence:

She opened mine.

She | opened | mine

Learning Christianly

Adjectives allow us to describe our reactions to things in different ways. If you smell something good, there are plenty of adjectives you can use to describe it. Or if you smell something awful, there are many other adjectives at your service. Many adjectives allow us to categorize things in ways that suggest a thing to be bad or good. What does this reality suggest about the way God created people and nature?

IN SUMMARY

Possessives are nouns and pronouns that show ownership and signal that a noun will follow.

Independent possessives are not adjectives; they replace nouns and function as nouns.

5-10   PRACTICE THE SKILL

A. Label the sentence patterns *S-InV, S-TrV-DO, S-TrV-IO-DO, S-LV-PN, or S-LV-PA.*

B. Underline each possessive noun or pronoun functioning as an adjective twice and the other adjectives once.

C. Draw an arrow from each adjective to the noun it modifies.

D. Circle any independent possessives.

1. Williamsburg is one of the colonists' beautiful cities.

2. The Virginia Colony chose Williamsburg as its capital.

3. Virginia's highest court met twice during the year.

4. A session attracted many Virginian families.

5. The sessions became a favorite social event of theirs.

6. Also, the American colonies' first mental institution opened here.

7. Today, Williamsburg's businesses benefit from many tourists.

8. Their shops exhibit many of the original craftsmen's trades.

9. One notable colonial shop is the blacksmith's shop.

10. His was a useful service.

5-11   REVIEW THE SKILL

A. Underline each possessive noun or pronoun functioning as an adjective twice and any other adjectives once.

B. Draw an arrow from each adjective to the noun it modifies.

C. Circle the independent possessives.

1. A young Katie von Bora married the distinguished Martin Luther in 1525.

2. Martin's father supported their marriage.

3. Katie gave Martin's hectic household order.

4. The busy Martin benefited from Katie's constant encouragement and faithful prayers.

5. God blessed the Luthers with a baby son early in their marriage.

6. Their daughter died from a mysterious disease.

7. His wife helped strengthen Luther in his downcast state.

8. His grief was more intense than hers.

9. Later, Duke George desired Luther's death.

10. Theirs was not an easy life.

Proper Adjectives

page 35

Common and Proper nouns

page 277

Proper adjectives

You have already learned that nouns can be common or proper. Adjectives can also be **common** or **proper.** Proper adjectives are adjectives that are made from proper nouns.

> Last night we ate dinner at a Chinese restaurant.
> Charles Dickens wrote his stories during the Victorian era in England.

In the first example *Chinese* is a proper adjective made from the proper noun *China*. In the second example the proper adjective *Victorian* is made from the proper noun *Victoria*.

Adjectives cannot be made plural in English.
Wrong: Some Indians chiefs were extremely brave.
Right: Some Indian chiefs were extremely brave.

Proper adjectives are adjectives made from proper nouns.

5-12 PRACTICE THE SKILL

Underline the proper adjectives.

1. Yes, let's go to the mall and get some Chinese food.

2. How does a Mexican enchilada sound?

3. Have you ever tried Cajun food?

4. Italian pasta appeals more to me.

5. I could order French bread with it.

6. My friend Anne prefers Thai beef salad.

7. Suzanne enjoys an Indian dish called chicken curry.

8. The Japanese restaurant also serves other Oriental foods.

9. A Hong Kong fried rice dish is a favorite with many diners.

10. For children, a good old American cheeseburger is always a possibility.

5-13 REVIEW THE SKILL

Underline each proper adjective.

1. Have you seen the Renaissance furniture at the mall? We studied the Renaissance in history.

2. The Spanish style exhibited a Moorish influence through the intricate geometric designs.

3. I prefer the Gothic style of furniture for my living room.

4. If you like rococo furniture, then you may also like the Chippendale style of furniture.

5. Biedermeier furniture presents an informal style that many like too. This furniture was named for Gottlieb Biedermeier, an imaginary person.

6. Far Eastern influences can be seen in the pine Scandinavian furniture.

7. Some of the handpainted pieces are often mistaken for the Pennsylvania Dutch furniture of the 1920s.

8. My mother enjoys many different styles of furniture. She has a beautiful Queen Anne desk in her study.

9. Plain Shaker rockers line the front porch of our home.

10. Her favorite piece is a Hepplewhite chair designed by George Hepplewhite.

5-14 REVIEW THE SKILL

A. Underline the adjectives.
B. Draw an arrow from each adjective to the noun it modifies.
C. Label each predicate adjective *PA*. Circle any independent possessives.

1. On the North American continent there are approximately seven hundred types of poisonous plants.

2. Some of these plants are extremely toxic.

3. Some mushrooms are deadly.

4. The berries from many forest plants can cause severe illness.

5. Perhaps the most infamous poisonous shrub is poison ivy.

6. This plant is part of the cashew family.

7. Its tissues discharge an acidlike oil that irritates human skin.

8. Yours will probably feel as though it is on fire if you come in contact with the plant.

9. This oil causes a painful rash.

10. However, the ugly eruptions themselves are not infectious.

5-15 CUMULATIVE REVIEW

A. Locate and correct the ten errors in the paragraph: fragments, comma splices, fused sentences, noun plurals, singular and plural noun possessives, verb forms (e.g., *had throwed*), and spellings of verb forms. Use the lines below to write the paragraph correctly.

B. Improve the paragraph by replacing each underlined noun with a more precise noun.

Colorado has been called "The Centennial State." Because it becomed a state on the hundredth anniversary of the Declaration of Independence. The capital of Colorado is Denver two earlier territorial capitals were Colorado City and Golden. The <u>building</u> in Denver has a gold-plated dome. Some other <u>things</u> also represent Colorado. Colorados state flag is as colorful as the state itself. The red *C* symbolizes a Spanish word for red, *colorado*. The gold ball represents Colorado's gold production, the blue and white stripes represent blue skys and mountain snow. The state bird is the lark bunting, and the state flower is the Rocky Mountain columbine. Recognized for its symmetrical blue and white petals. Colorado is also known for the quality of it's mountain-growed <u>food</u>. The Rocky Ford cantaloupe is popular throughout the entire United States. Above all else, Colorado has been knowed for its great beauty. It well deserves its recognition as a paradise of the Rocky Mountains.

═Sliding Home

Good writers choose their adjectives carefully, using only those they really need. You can think of adjectives as the salt of writing. A little seasoning goes a long way.

• *Read the last paragraph of "The Speckled Band" excerpt without the adjectives. How is the scene different? Has it lost some tension?*

• *Try replacing the adjectives with some that will make the snake a garter snake. Does the scene now seem funny instead of scary?*

> **Esther 1:3-6**
>
> **3 In the third year of his reign, he made a feast unto all his princes and his servants; the power of Persia and Media, the nobles and princes of the provinces, being before him:**
>
> **4 When he shewed the riches of his glorious kingdom and the honour of his excellent majesty many days, even an hundred and fourscore days.**
>
> **5 And when these days were expired, the king made a feast unto all the people that were present in Shushan the palace, both unto great and small, seven days, in the court of the garden of the king's palace;**
>
> **6 Where were white, green, and blue, hangings, fastened with cords of fine linen and purple to silver rings and pillars of marble: the beds were of gold and silver, upon a pavement of red, and blue, and white, and black, marble.**

• *What do the adjectives do for this description?*

• *Read the passage without the adjectives. How does it change?*

CREATING A POEM FROM PROSE

A word fitly spoken is like apples of gold in pictures of silver.
Proverbs 25:11

What is the difference between poetry and prose? Prose is what you read in the newspaper, in a textbook, and in your favorite adventure novel. Prose is very much like conversation, although it is usually more formal than everyday speech. Prose also lacks metrical structure. Poetry, on the other hand, could be compared to music. A poem is arranged in lines, has qualities of sound, and compresses ideas into fewer words than prose. Metered poetry has a set pattern of stresses and nonstresses in its rhythm. Remember, however, that a poem does not have to rhyme. One type of poem, a "found" poem, uses descriptive words and phrases adapted from a prose text.

Your Turn

Write a "found poem" based on a descriptive prose selection.

Planning

Choose a prose selection. As you consider what to select, keep in mind that your text should be a particularly descriptive passage that brings specific pictures, or images, to your mind or inspires a certain emotion inside you. The text of your poem should come directly from the prose text of something else. Look for an appropriate passage in a novel, in a letter, in a newspaper or a magazine, on a billboard, or in an advertisement. Be sure to have a copy of the text for your use as you work.

One student chose to use a portion of a letter written to him by his grandfather.

> I often thought about Abraham and Job when I was your age. Those stories used to bother me. Really. I wondered why Abraham should have to live through those agonies of climbing the hill with his son, expecting to have to kill him when they reached the top. I wondered why Job would be required to lose everything, not knowing that all would be restored—and not all restored even then, but replaced.
>
> Later I thought that the ordeals of Abraham and Job made them stronger, better. Then I thought—who wants to be that strong and good? Then I thought—if God in omniscience already knew how Job and Abraham would respond, why did He test them so? And then, finally, it appeared that God was not showing Himself how they would respond—but rather He was showing them. Aha.

Read the selection several times. After you have become familiar with the prose selection by reading it silently, try reading it aloud to discover where a speaker would pause in reading the words.

Use slash marks to indicate the natural breaks in thought. Read the selection aloud again and divide each paragraph into its natural phrases. Think about how to break the lines to make the most of the text's natural rhythm and to emphasize its most important ideas. Consider using a highlighter to mark selected words, phrases, and sentences that contain vivid and clear descriptions. Be sure that your selected descriptions portray a clear picture for the reader.

Notice how the student used slashes to indicate the natural breaks.

I often thought about Abraham and Job when I was your age. / Those stories used to bother me. / Really. / I wondered why Abraham should have to live through those agonies / of climbing the hill with his son, / expecting to have to kill him when they reached the top. / I wondered why Job would be required to lose everything, / not knowing that all would be restored— / and not all restored even then, / but replaced.

Later I thought that the ordeals of Abraham and Job made them stronger, / better. Then I thought / —who wants to be that strong and good? / Then I thought— / if God in omniscience already knew how Job and Abraham would respond, / why did He test them so? / And then, / finally, / it appeared that God was not showing Himself how they would respond— / but rather He was showing them. / Aha.

Drafting

Edit the prose selection. Look at the portions of the text that you have marked. Delete any words and phrases that you decide are unnecessary.

Evaluate sentence breaks. You may want to alter these breaks. Keep in mind the text's natural rhythm and emphasize its most important ideas. Remember that your poem does not have to rhyme.

Arrange the lines of your poem. Using the slash marks, determine which ideas to put into each line. You may incorporate a few phrases into a single line. Other phrases are important enough to stand alone, each on its own line. Use a variety of line lengths to emphasize the descriptive portions.

Write your found poem. Write a rough draft of your poem without stopping to fix errors. Use your marks to guide you as you write out each line.

Abraham and Job.
Those stories used to bother me.
Really.
I wondered why Abraham
should have to live through
those agonies
of climbing the hill with his son,
expecting to have to kill him
when they reached the top.
I wondered why Job
would be required to lose everything,
not knowing that all would be restored—
and not all restored even then,
but replaced.
Later I thought that the ordeals
of Abraham and Job
made them stronger, better.
Then I thought—but who wants to be
that strong and good?
Then I thought—if God in omniscience
already knew how Job and Abraham would respond,
why did He test them so?
And then, finally,
it appeared that God was not showing Himself
how they would respond—
but rather He was showing them.
Aha.

Re-examine your poem to be sure that the arrangement emphasizes the important ideas. Notice that the most important idea of the example poem comes last: God tested Abraham and Job, not to show *Himself* how they would respond but to show *them* how they would respond. The poem progresses as a series of thoughts, put into the form of questions, and finally leads to this conclusion. Ending a poem immediately after the most important idea is one of the best ways to emphasize that idea. Readers tend to remember best what was said at the end, not at the beginning, of a poem. Including the word *Aha,* a surprising word of discovery, immediately draws our attention to what was said right before it to make sure we have made the same discovery as the speaker in the poem. If necessary, rearrange the line breaks in your poem so that the most important ideas are easy for the reader to find.

Proofread for correctness. Remember that when you create a found poem, you may drop words from the text but you may not add your own words to the text. Once you have determined that you have not added any words of your own, check for correct grammar, spelling, and punctuation.

Make a final, error-free copy of your found poem. Include an appropriate title for your found poem. Write or type the poem according to standard manuscript form, with correct margins and spacing.

Post your poem on a poetry bulletin board. Choose a title for the poem and display them together on the bulletin board. You may wish to post not only your found poem but also the text from which you created your poem.

Present your poem orally. Read through your poem several times before you present it for the class. Include the title of the poem when you read it.

page 382

Organizing sentences

Officer Bell searched through the coupon section of the Yellow Pages. "A unit 10 x 8 x 12—just what I need, and Compact Storage company has an address on my side of town too. I'll just give them a call at lunch." He sighed in relief and circled the telephone number printed on the coupon. "Why I ever bought that hat stand! What was I thinking? A Victorian hat stand and me in an apartment. I'll take it to Grandmother Bell next summer; then this mistake will be over. What would Inspector Jameson think if he knew I bought that thing. I hope the storage unit is tall enough!"

Officer Bell reviewed Inspector Jameson's instructions for the day. "Earlier this year counterfeiters began flooding the area with products produced in Mexico bearing fake name-brand logos. I want a list of all the local flea markets in the area. We'll visit each market during the next few weeks and interview each manager. We must find the vendors. Most of them are honest and will help lead us to the source of these fakes. Have the list ready by tomorrow morning." Officer Bell began combing through the Yellow Pages compiling a list of flea markets the counterfeiters might try to misuse.

However, lunchtime found him on the phone with Compact Storage working out the details of delivery, lease, insurance, and size. "That seemed simple enough," he thought. "Saved me a trip too, calling ahead like that. One trip this afternoon and one trip next summer—very neat. It's done."

Delivery of the hat stand was accomplished as smoothly as the phone call. The manager even offered to help him secure the hat stand in a storage unit.

"Not a scratch; thank you for your help, Mr. Boyd. The job was a lot easier with two doing it," said Officer Bell as he also placed a bowling ball bag inside the unit. It was an old ball he didn't use, and it was forever in his way in the bottom of the closet. "Getting more value for my dollar storing it here with the hat stand," he thought.

He noticed Mr. Boyd staring at the unlikely match, hat stand with bowling ball. "They're an odd pair. The hat stand is for my Grandmother. The ball's just here to be out of the way," Bell explained.

"Oh, don't mind my looking," said Mr. Boyd. "I'm just naturally curious. I've seen odder things than that. A woman once wanted to store her husband's snake while he was away. She couldn't stand the thing and didn't want it in the house while he was gone. I told her it wouldn't be right. Snake or no, it's a living creature and shouldn't be shut up like that. Now your hat stand isn't as odd as that! One guy had a windmill from Texas that he had taken apart and brought here! Can you believe that? Officer, I'm a curious man in a curious business! But that was years ago. The oddest thing lately has been a guy who comes every Monday. He takes out a dozen boxes and puts them in his truck. But I never see him put any boxes in. Surely he must. But then I just work days."

Bell asked, "What's in the boxes?"

"I don't know. The labels are in Spanish. So, here's your key, sir."

Officer Bell was still reliving the conversation when he arrived at work the next morning. He told Inspector Jameson every detail about the odd people Mr. Boyd had met.

"What were you doing at Compact Storage?" asked the Inspector.

His own mistake took Officer Bell completely by surprise. "Oh, I just stored some stuff that was in my way. You know, small apartment and all. It's just temporary till summer."

"Those are odd stories, Bell. Tell me—where is Compact Storage?"

"On Trail Drive. It was the only one near my place."

"Really," said Jameson. "Where are the others?"

Bell flopped open the Yellow Pages. "Here. You can see for yourself. They're all in the busier sections than the one I use."

The Inspector studied the ads. "Aha," he said. "Your storage unit may be close, but it certainly isn't the safest!

"I have a new theory. It's a good thing you have a small apartment. Otherwise we could have spent weeks trying to solve the counterfeit case. Let's go visit your hat stand, Bell!"

"How did you know I bought the hat stand? Oh never mind; how did you come up with a new theory on the counterfeit case?"

1. *Supposing Officer Bell did not know the names of all the streets in town, how else could he have known all the other storage units were across town from him?*

2. *What details in Bell's recounting of his visit to Compact Storage alerted Jameson to a possible link with the counterfeiter?*

3. *What do you think Jameson noticed about the ads that made him say it was not the safest storage?*

4. *How do you think the lack of safety helped Jameson form a new theory?*

CHAPTER 6

ADVERBS

THOSE WINTER SUNDAYS
BY ROBERT HAYDEN

Sundays too my father got up early
and put his clothes on in the blueblack cold,
then with cracked hands that ached
from labor in the weekday weather made
banked fires blaze. No one ever thanked him.

I'd wake and hear the cold splintering, breaking.
When the rooms were warm, he'd call,
and slowly I would rise and dress,
fearing the chronic angers of that house,

Speaking indifferently to him,
who had driven out the cold
and polished my good shoes as well.
What did I know, what did I know
of love's austere and lonely offices?

- *Who is the speaker in this poem?*

- *What word in the second stanza tells you that the speaker did not like to get up in the morning?*

- *What word in the last stanza reveals how the speaker, as a teenager, viewed his father?*

- *How old do you think the speaker is at the time he recalls this memory? How has his view of his father changed since his youth?*

The speaker in this poem is looking back on his younger days at home. He seems a bit ashamed of his behavior. He says he spoke indifferently to his father; he says he responded slowly when his father called. He seems to have been more concerned with his own comfort than with the sacrifices his father was making for him. Words like *indifferently* and *slowly* help to show that the writer is now sorry for how he spoke and responded to his father.

Just as adjectives sharpen our focus on nouns, adverbs add information to verbs and other words. In this chapter you will learn that we can recognize adverbs by asking certain questions.

page 146

Prepositional phrases

page 149

Preposition or Adverb?

page 237

Double negatives

page 310

Apostrophes

Adverbs

Adverbs are words that modify verbs, adjectives, or other adverbs. Adverbs that modify verbs tell *when, where,* or *how* about the verbs they modify. Adverbs that modify adjectives and other adverbs tell *to what extent*. They strengthen or weaken the meaning of the words they modify.

Adverb comes from the latin *ad-* (additional) and *verbum* (word). *Adverb* literally means "additional word."

When?	The soccer team is at Locke Park *now*.
Where?	They practice *there*.
How?	Mr. Schmidt coaches them *well*.
To what extent?	Their schedule is *somewhat* full already.
	The goalie watches the ball *very* carefully.

Even though *not* does not answer any of the common adverb questions, we do consider it to be an adverb. It is used to make a sentence negative.

Raoul is *not* playing today.
He did *not* quit the team.
He can*not* play soccer with a broken leg.
The other players have*n't* heard the news.

6-1 PRACTICE THE SKILL

Underline the adverbs in the following sentences.

1. One of the most attractive qualities a person can have is a spirit of gratefulness.

2. Numerous people, including parents, doctors, and teachers, have unselfishly contributed to our lives.

3. We often do not give them the credit they deserve.

4. One of the very best rewards a person can receive is gratitude.

5. You may have worked exceptionally hard and been disappointed because you received no word of appreciation.

6. Can you think of some people who have especially helped you to succeed?

7. You should send a thank-you note and sincerely thank them.

8. You would be quite surprised at their reaction.

9. Have you said "Thank you" to your parents lately?

10. Scripture specifically reminds us, "In every thing give thanks" (I Thess. 5:18).

6-2 **REVIEW THE SKILL**

Underline the ten adverbs in the following paragraph.

The men stood in a tight huddle and painfully raised their hands to shield the brightness from their eyes. The sun shone relentlessly on the men's excessively white skin. All ten of them looked anxiously down the dusty road to see Him. The Man and His followers were quickly approaching. They all had heard of this Man and how He liberally healed diseases such as leprosy. Soon they stood before Him. He spoke few words. The ten men watched the decaying flesh on their hands gradually transform into exceptionally smooth and healthy skin. Only one man returned to give thanks to Jesus, who had healed him.

Positions of Adverbs

You have already learned that adjectives usually come just before the nouns they modify. Adverbs that modify adjectives or other adverbs also come just before the words that they modify.

The bread tasted *quite* good.

She ate it *too* quickly.

Adverbs that modify verbs, however, can appear many different places in the sentence.

After the verb: They will eat *now*.

After the verb and direct object: They will eat the bread *now*.

After the auxiliary verb: They will *now* eat the bread.

Before the complete verb: They *now* will eat the bread.

At the beginning of the sentence: *Now* they will eat the bread.

Notice that the adverb sometimes appears between parts of the complete verb. For example, if an adverb appears after an auxiliary verb, the adverb is interrupting the complete verb. The complete verb is the auxiliary verb and the main verb; the adverb that appears between them is not part of the complete verb.

The diagram format for adverbs is similar to the format for adjectives. Be sure to attach the adverb line to the word it modifies. Look at the diagram for this sentence.

She ate it quickly.

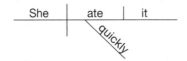

IN SUMMARY

Adverbs modify verbs, adjectives, or other adverbs.

Adverbs tell *when, where, how,* or *to what extent* about the words they modify.

Most adverbs can appear in many different places in the sentence.

6-3 PRACTICE THE SKILL

A. **Underline the adverbs.**

B. **Draw an arrow from each adverb to the word it modifies.**

C. **Label each modified word *V* (verb), *Adj* (adjective), or *Adv* (adverb).**

_____ 1. Daily Duane reads his Bible.

_____ 2. Duane nearly always finishes his devotions before breakfast.

_____ 3. Proverbs is usually Duane's choice for study.

_____ 4. Duane likes the exceptionally beautiful language of Proverbs.

_____ 5. He studies the verses carefully.

_____ 6. Duane also memorizes many Proverbs passages.

_____ 7. The verses seem easily applicable to his daily life.

_____ 8. Regularly Duane offers a friend help in a study of Proverbs.

_____ 9. His study of Proverbs is almost complete.

_____ 10. He does not neglect other parts of the Bible.

A. **Underline the adverbs.**

B. **Draw an arrow from each adverb to the word it modifies.**

C. **Label each modified word** *V* **(verb),** *Adj* **(adjective), or** *Adv* **(adverb).**

_____ 1. The Sargasso Sea lies somewhat east of the North American continent.

_____ 2. It is most notable for its seaweed surface.

_____ 3. Christopher Columbus first scientifically described the surface in 1492.

_____ 4. The Sargasso Sea often appears in legends of ships lost at sea.

_____ 5. Only recently have scientists discovered several interesting facts about the Sargasso Sea.

_____ 6. The seaweed somehow floats by its own air sacs.

_____ 7. These small air sacs appear strategically on the leaves' undersides.

_____ 8. The water of the Sargasso Sea is not typical.

_____ 9. It is extremely clear with a high salt content.

_____ 10. The temperature sometimes reaches 83°F.

North America

Atlantic Ocean

Sargasso Sea

South America

Fill in each blank with an adverb that answers the question in parentheses.

_____ 1. The soldiers _?_ marched in their formations. *(how?)*

_____ 2. Their sergeant commanded them to halt _?_ . *(when?)*

_____ 3. His orders could be heard by _?_ all the base. *(to what extent?)*

_____ 4. One general commented _?_ that the sergeant must be having a good day. *(how?)*

_____ 5. Colonel Villiers commanded that the soldiers return _?_ ! *(when?)*

_____ 6. March _?_ ! File _?_ ! *(where?)*

_____ 7. _?_ the drill was finished. *(when?)*

_____ 8. Anthony marched _?_ to the barracks and fell into his bed. *(where?)*

_____ 9. He had rarely felt so _?_ exhausted! *(to what extent?)*

_____ 10. He could _?_ keep his eyes open for long. *(negative)*

Fill in each blank with an adverb that answers the question at the end of the sentence.

_____ 1. _?_ I rode in a hot-air balloon for the first time. *(when?)*

_____ 2. The experience was _?_ exciting! *(to what extent?)*

_____ 3. I did _?_ know what to expect. *(negative)*

_____ 4. The pilot _?_ filled the balloon with hot air. *(how?)*

_____ 5. The balloon _?_ rose into the air. *(how?)*

_____ 6. We watched the people _?_ . *(where?)*

_____ 7. The crowd watched the balloon flying high _?_ . *(where?)*

_____ 8. The pilot opened the vent _?_ . *(when?)*

_____ 9. We descended _?_ gently. *(to what extent?)*

_____ 10. I will _?_ forget the adventure. *(negative)*

page 233

Adjective or Adverb?

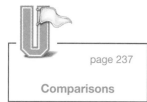

page 237

Comparisons

Comparing with Adverbs

Like adjectives, many adverbs have **comparative** and **superlative** forms; the comparative form is used for two people or things, and the superlative form is used for three or more people or things. These forms are made by adding *er* and *est* to some adverbs or by using *more* and *most* with others. Irregular adverbs form comparative and superlative in other ways. A reliable dictionary will give you the comparative and the superlative forms of any irregular adverb.

	Positive	Comparative	Superlative
Regular			
	fast	faster	fastest
	early	earlier	earliest
	fairly	more fairly	most fairly
	neatly	more neatly	most neatly
Irregular			
	well	better	best
	badly	worse	worst

Javier runs <u>faster</u> than Greg, but Ivan runs the <u>fastest</u> of all on the track team.

Tomatoes grow <u>well</u> in my garden, but Brussels sprouts grow even <u>better</u>.

Many common adverbs, especially those that modify adjectives or other adverbs, do not have comparative or superlative forms. To make comparisons with these (among others) would not make sense: *not, daily, now, almost, here, very, really, somewhat, almost,* and *too.*

IN SUMMARY

Regular adverbs show comparison by adding *er* and *est* or *more* and *most* to the stem form of the adverb.

Irregular adverbs have different forms to show comparison.

Some adverbs cannot be compared.

 **PRACTICE THE SKILL**

Fill in each blank with the correct form of the adverb in parentheses. Some adverbs may need two words to make the comparative or superlative form.

_____ 1. The seventh grade class took their science experiments _?_. *(seriously, superlative)*

_____ 2. They built model rockets to see whose would fly _?_. *(well, superlative)*

_____ 3. Rules were _?_ enforced to ensure a safe launch. *(strictly, positive)*

_____ 4. At first, the science teacher talked _?_ than did the students. *(enthusiastically, comparative)*

_____ 5. Once construction started, however, the students arrived at school _?_ than usual and worked on their rockets. *(early, comparative)*

_____ 6. Prizes were to be given to those whose rockets flew _?_ and _?_. *(fast, superlative; far, superlative)*

_____ 7. After a lot of preparation, everyone watched _?_ as the students approached the launch pads. *(excitedly, positive)*

_____ 8. Josie's model rocket climbed _?_ into the sky than she had expected. *(quickly, comparative)*

_____ 9. However, Fritz's soared _?_ and stayed up longer than hers did. *(high, comparative)*

_____ 10. Fiona's rocket floated to earth _?_ because it had the largest and most elaborate parachute. *(slowly, superlative)*

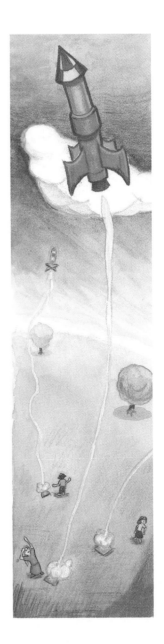

Fill in each blank with the correct form of the adverb in parentheses.

_____ 1. Generally, people believe that turtles travel _?_ than any other animal. *(slowly, comparative)*

_____ 2. However, some turtles can move _?_ than you would think. *(quickly, comparative)*

_____ 3. Sea turtles swim the _?_ of all of the turtle species. *(rapidly, superlative)*

_____ 4. The green turtle is the _?_ of all the sea turtles, reaching speeds of twenty miles per hour. *(fast, superlative)*

_____ 5. That turtle swims _?_ than we humans do. *(well, comparative)*

_____ 6. Turtles live _?_ than most animals. Some can live over one hundred years. *(long, comparative)*

_____ 7. Turtle markings differ _?_. Shells can be black, brown, green, yellow, orange, or red. *(greatly, positive)*

_____ 8. Of all turtles, snapping turtles strike the _?_ at strangers. *(aggressively, superlative)*

_____ 9. Some people eat turtles _?_ and use their shells for ornamentation. *(frequently, positive)*

_____ 10. Young people _?_ keep turtles as pets than older people do. *(frequently, comparative)*

Insert at least one adverb into each sentence. Try to use a variety of adverbs.

1. The beautiful city of Tokyo, Japan, was founded in 1457 by a mighty Japanese warrior.

   _____

   _____

2. This lovely city is the Japanese capital and is the center of Japan's important commerce.

   _____

   _____

3. Conditions in Tokyo are crowded.

   _____

   _____

4. At the center of the city proper lies the gorgeous Imperial Palace, which is surrounded by ornate parks.

   _____

   _____

5. Many of the crowded streets in Tokyo do not have names; instead, sections of the city, called wards, are named.

   _____

   _____

6. Over eight million people live in Tokyo, and there is a serious housing shortage.

   _____

   _____

7. Since World War II, Tokyo's economy has been strong, and electrical machinery and publishing has played an active role.

   _____

   _____

Learning Christianly

Insert several different adverbs into the following sentence: "The knight rescued the damsel." How do the different adverbs change your view of the knight? If you're trying to be more than a little creative, you're probably discovering that adverbs can have a significant impact on how we view the people and events presented in a sentence. What does the importance of adverbs in language suggest about the importance of how we do what we do in life?

8. At the respected Tokyo Stock Exchange, enthusiastic members trade large numbers of valuable stocks.

_____

_____

9. Tokyo has twice been destroyed: by earthquake in 1923 and by fearful bomb raids during World War II.

_____

_____

10. Modern Tokyo features both the old and the new Japan. Visitors to this diverse city may see residents in traditional kimonos side by side with those in Western dress.

_____

_____

_____

A. **Locate and correct the ten errors in the paragraphs: fragments, comma splices, fused sentences, noun plurals, singular and plural noun possessives, verb forms (e.g., *had wrote*), and spellings of verb forms.**

B. **Add a descriptive adjective or adverb where you see a caret (^).**

Are you traveling to Hong Kong? You might visit the Kansu Street Jade Market. Full of ^ jade ornaments and ^ jewelry. Several different types of jade exist. Emperor's jade is ^ expensive, it is deep green in color. Mutton fat jades' color is white, and mauve jade is light purple. Other jade color's are yellow, brown, and orange.

Australian jade and soapstone look like jade, but they are much ^ common. They are softer and ^ valuable than true jade, wise jade buyers will avoided these ^ stones. Sometimes salesmans trick buyers. They dye cheap stones then they sell buyers these impostors. Occasionally, careless tourists have took home worthless jade. You should stay away from false jade! On your trip to Hong Kong.

Hong Kong

_____

_____

_____

_____

_____

_____

_____

_____

_____

_____

Adverbs   **139**

SLIDING HOME

If adjectives are the salt of writing, adverbs are the pepper. Most good writers use even fewer adverbs than adjectives. So the ones they choose must be exactly right.

- *Hayden included two adverbs in the poem's first line. Try reading the line, leaving them out. What meaning do they add? Do you think they make the first line stronger?*

- *Can you think of any "austere and lonely offices" that your parents perform for you? When was the last time you thanked them?*

I Samuel 18:14-15

14 And David behaved himself wisely in all his ways; and the Lord was with him.

15 Wherefore when Saul saw that he behaved himself very wisely, he was afraid of him.

- *What adverb is used twice? How is it different the second time?*

- *What adverb would describe how you behave yourself?*

REPORTING A FAMILY TRADITION

Honour thy father and mother; (which is the first commandment with promise;) That it may be well with thee, and thou mayest live long on the earth.
Ephesians 6:2-3

Whether it means eating popcorn on Saturday or trimming a tree each Christmas, your family has traditions, special activities to celebrate special moments. Look at this example of a student report about family tradition.

My family has a special way of celebrating the first day of school every fall. When school gets out at noon on the first day, Mom meets us with a big picnic basket and drives to our favorite park. It has a creek with lots of smooth stones sticking out of the water. While Mom organizes the food, my brother and I have races crossing the creek on the rocks. Last year he tried to jump too far and landed in the creek. He was so surprised that he just sat there in the water. I thought Mom would be mad but she just laughed.

After our creek race, we sit on the blanket and have our lunch. Mom always makes special sandwiches on thick, crusty bread. My brother and I can always eat at least two. We drink lemonade out of brightly colored plastic cups. But the best part is dessert. Every year Mom tries out a new cheesecake recipe. Last year's was the best ever. It was chocolate with cherries on top.

After lunch is over, Mom takes out a notebook and asks us what our favorite thing about the past summer was. When we tell her, she writes it down. Then she reads us what we said in the past about the other summers. It's a neat way to remember things.

Your Turn

Write a report about a special tradition that is unique to your family.

Planning

Choose a tradition that is unique to your family. List the ways that your family spends birthdays, vacations, and holidays. Considering what you know about other families, choose one of your family's unique traditions.

Determine the details that the reader will need to know. Whom does this tradition include? When and where does it take place? Why does your family keep it? Use descriptive words that appeal to your reader's senses.

Organize the facts in chronological order. Analyze the facts that you have compiled and group them to represent a clear time sequence.

Drafting

Begin your report. The first sentence should indicate who participates in the family tradition, what the tradition is, and when it takes place.

Write your report. Record the details that explain your family tradition clearly. Use a new paragraph to indicate another aspect of the tradition.

Revising

Evaluate your report for word choice and correctness. Be sure that you used specific words to give vivid details. Eliminate any unnecessary exaggerations. Correct any errors of grammar, spelling, or punctuation.

Prepare a clean copy of your report. Include necessary changes.

Publishing

Deliver a speech. Read your report to the class if your teacher allows.

Post your report on a bulletin board. Include family photographs.

HISTORY of the ENGLISH LANGUAGE

"Angle-ish" was different from the English we speak today. Over the centuries "Angle-ish" changed and developed as it was influenced by many other languages.

In A.D. 597, a group of Roman monks came to England as missionaries. They brought many religious words with them, such as *disciple* and *nun*. Later, daring seamen from the north, called Vikings, invaded England. They brought words such as *reindeer* and *window* to the language.

France took over the government of England for a time. Because the French were in power, French became the language of the upper class. Many English people peppered their sentences with French words and phrases to be fashionable. Even today words like *government, pastor,* and *captain* reflect the French influence on the English language.

CHAPTER 7

PREPOSITIONS, CONJUNCTIONS, & INTERJECTIONS

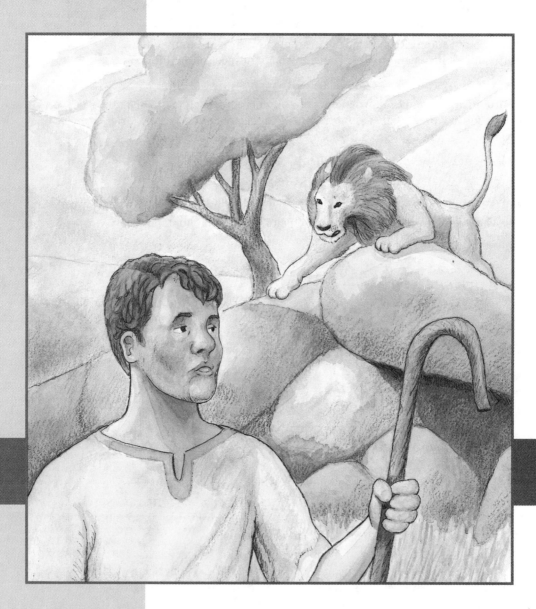

PSALM 70

ake haste, O God, to deliver me; make haste to help me, O Lord.

2 Let them be ashamed and confounded that seek after my soul: let them be turned backward, and put to confusion, that desire my hurt.

3 Let them be turned back for a reward of their shame that say, Aha, aha.

4 Let all those that seek thee rejoice and be glad in thee: and let such as love thy salvation say continually, Let God be magnified.

5 But I am poor and needy: make haste unto me, O God, thou art my help and my deliverer; O Lord, make no tarrying.

- *What do you think "Aha, aha" in verse 3 means? Has anyone ever said something like this to you? How did he mean it?*

- *What is David's response?*

- *How can you tell that David wants an answer very soon?*

In this psalm, David is asking the Lord to deliver him from those who seek after his soul, who mock him. We can see the earnestness in his request by the way he says "O God" rather than "God" and "O Lord" rather than "Lord," and by the way he describes himself. He says that there are those who seek after his soul and that he is poor and needy.

When the letter *O* is used as a word, it is called an *interjection*. Interjections usually show strong feeling. In this chapter you will learn about interjections, prepositions, and conjunctions.

Prepositions

A **preposition** is a word that shows the relationship between its object and another word in the sentence. An **object of the preposition** is the noun or pronoun that follows the preposition. All prepositions have objects.

Preposition (pre + position) literally means something "placed in front of."

The baseball *on* the box is a gift.
The baseball *under* the box is a gift.
The baseball *in* the box is a gift.
The baseball *behind* the box is a gift.
The baseball *outside* the box is a gift.

In each of these sentences, a preposition links the subject *baseball* to *box,* the object of the preposition. The preposition shows how the baseball is related to the box. Notice that the relationship between the baseball and the box changes whenever the preposition changes.

Commonly Used Prepositions				
about	behind	except	on	to
above	below	for	onto	toward
across	beside	from	out	under
after	between	in	outside	until
against	beyond	inside	over	upon
among	but	into	past	with
around	by	like	since	within
at	down	near	through	without
before	during	of	throughout	

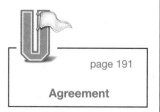

page 191

Agreement

Prepositional Phrases

A preposition and its object together form a **prepositional phrase.** If the object has any modifiers, they are also part of the prepositional phrase. The object itself is the simple object of the preposition. The object and its modifiers together are the complete object of the preposition.

The baseball *with the red stitches* is a gift *from my favorite uncle.*

This example contains two prepositional phrases. Each prepositional phrase consists of a preposition followed by a noun and its modifiers. The preposition *with* links the complete object of the preposition *the red stitches* to the subject *baseball.* The preposition *from* shows the relationship between its object *my favorite uncle* and the predicate noun *gift.*

Sometimes a prepositional phrase may contain a compound object. In the prepositional phrase *of David and Goliath,* both *David* and *Goliath* are objects of the preposition *of.*

The story *of David and Goliath* appears in I Samuel 17.

page 33

Choosing between Possessive and Plural

IN SUMMARY

A **preposition** relates its object to another word in the sentence.

The **object of a preposition** is the noun or pronoun that follows the preposition.

A **prepositional phrase** consists of the preposition and the complete object of the preposition.

7-1 PRACTICE THE SKILL

A. **Place parentheses around each prepositional phrase.**

B. **Label each preposition *P.***

C. **Label each object of the preposition *OP.***

1. Ronald Reagan's birthplace is (near Chicago, Illinois.)

2. (On March 4, 1952,) Reagan married Nancy Davis.

3. California elected him (to the governor's office.)

4. The 1980 election pitted Reagan (against President Carter.)

5. The race (among the Republican candidates) was close.

6. Ronald Reagan finished well everywhere (except Iowa and Michigan.)

7. He split the votes (in the Michigan primary) (with George Bush.)

8. George Bush campaigned (until May 26, 1980.)

9. Finally, the Republicans chose Reagan (for their nominee.)

10. George Bush became Reagan's vice presidential nominee (in the 1980 presidential campaign.)

A. Place parentheses around each prepositional phrase.

B. Label the object of the preposition *OP*.

C. Label the sentence patterns *S-InV*, *S-TrV-DO*, or *S-TrV-IO-DO*.

1. (In the sixteenth century) French immigrant workers greatly advanced the art of papier-mâché.

2. This art casts paper strips (onto a mold.)

3. Some people place petroleum jelly (underneath the strips.)

4. The artist should tear the paper (along its grain.)

5. Smaller pieces (against the mold) form better.

6. (For variety,) you may use different-colored paper.

7. (Across the first layer) you should place the second layer.

8. Each layer (of strips) covers the previous layer.

9. Each piece must lie smoothly (upon the mold.)

10. Otherwise, air may stay (beneath the layers.)

Functions of Prepositional Phrases

One use of prepositional phrases is to modify nouns. These prepositional phrases are called adjectival prepositional phrases because they function like adjectives. These phrases add information about the nouns they modify.

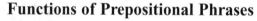

Naaman was a captain *of the host*.

The prophet *of God* taught Naaman a lesson *in obedience*.

In the first example the prepositional phrase *of the host* tells more about the noun *captain*. In the second example the prepositional phrase *of God* describes *prophet,* and *in obedience* describes *lesson*. Notice that the prepositional phrases in these examples come right after the nouns they modify. A prepositional phrase that modifies a noun normally comes just after the noun.

Another use of prepositional phrases is to modify verbs. These prepositional phrases are called adverbial prepositional phrases because they are functioning like adverbs. These phrases add information about the verbs they modify.

page 102

Adjectives

page 128

Adverbs

At the airport we waited *inside the terminal.*

The airplane coasted *to a smooth stop at 6:45.*

Both examples contain two prepositional phrases. In the first example, *at the airport* and *inside the terminal* both modify the verb *waited.* They tell *where* about the verb. They are both adverbial prepositional phrases. In the second example, *to a smooth stop* tells *how* about the verb *coasted. At 6:45* tells *when* about the verb *coasted.* Because both phrases modify the verb, both are adverbial prepositional phrases.

A prepositional phrase that is acting like an adverb can appear in different places in the sentence.

After the verb:	We met *at the gate.*
After the direct object:	I met my father *at the gate.*
At the beginning of the sentence:	*At the gate* I met my father.

Sometimes adjectival prepositional phrases and adverbial prepositional phrases occur in the same sentence.

He carried his suitcase *to the trunk of our car.*

In this example the prepositional phrase *to the trunk* modifies the verb *carried;* therefore, it is an adverbial prepositional phrase. The prepositional phrase *of our car* modifies the noun *trunk.* It is an adjectival prepositional phrase. Notice that one prepositional phrase can modify the object of another prepositional phrase.

A prepositional phrase is always diagrammed under the word it modifies. Look at the diagram for this sentence:

He carried his suitcase to the trunk of our car.

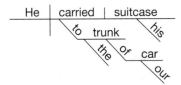

―――――― ‖N ⟨UMMARY ――――――

Prepositional phrases can be used like adjectives to modify nouns or like adverbs to modify verbs.

Place parentheses around each prepositional phrase. Draw an arrow from each prepositional phrase to the word it modifies.

1. Many people admire the work (of Benjamin West.)

2. Benjamin West lived (in a Quaker community) (in Swarthmore, Pennsylvania.)

3. His first paintbrushes came (from the hairs) (of the family cat.)

4. King George III (of England) commissioned West.

5. Benjamin West became the history painter (for King George III.)

6. West's paintings were commissioned (for the new chapel) (in Windsor Castle.)

7. West had divided the Bible (into four dispensations.)

8. Without instruction (from the king,) he could not work quickly.

9. (During years) (of work,) West's frustration grew.

10. Finally, the king abandoned his plans (for the paintings.)

A. Underline each adjectival prepositional phrase with one line.
B. Underline each adverbial prepositional phrase with two lines.
C. Draw an arrow from each prepositional phrase to the word it modifies.

"Well, Arby, this is a big day for you."

"Yes sir," I said. "I'm a little scared about the speech." No one in our family had ever given a speech at a graduation ceremony. Later I practiced my speech on my mom four times. When we got to school, the parents went into the auditorium, and we went to our classroom. I was sure that I would go blank right up in front of the whole entire world. I would stumble. I would crash. I would get a little piece of dust under my contact. I marched in with the other students. The principal said a bunch of good things about the school. Then it was time for my speech. I walked behind the pulpit and stood up on a little step. I could feel my hands shaking, and I stuffed them into my pockets. Then I saw Mr. Watson sitting in the back row.

Selected passages from *Arby Jenkins* by Sharon Hambrick (BJU Press, 1996).

Preposition or Adverb?

Some words used as prepositions can also be used as adverbs. To determine whether a word in a sentence is a preposition or an adverb, look for an object of the preposition.

The runner ran *down* the road.
The runner fell *down*.

In the first sentence, *down* is a preposition. It is followed by the object *road*. In the second sentence, *down* is an adverb that tells where the runner fell. It has no object. A word is not a preposition if it does not have an object.

page 128

Adverbs

Some words used as prepositions can also be used as adverbs.

A preposition is followed by an object; an adverb does not have an object.

7-5 PRACTICE THE SKILL

Label each italicized word *Prep* (preposition) or *Adv* (adverb).

 1. As they grow *up*, many people cherish their teddy bears.

 2. A cartoonist named the first teddy bear *after* President Theodore (Teddy) Roosevelt.

 3. Roosevelt's fame grew as the story spread *around*.

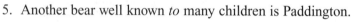 4. *From* that point, teddy bears increased in popularity.

 5. Another bear well known *to* many children is Paddington.

 6. Paddington's adventures amuse children *of* many ages.

 7. One time Paddington dressed *up* for the opera.

 8. Another time, for his birthday, he put a magic show *on*.

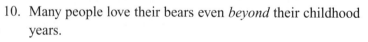 9. *During* their lifetimes, most children love many bears.

10. Many people love their bears even *beyond* their childhood years.

Label each underlined word *Prep* (preposition) or *Adv* (adverb).

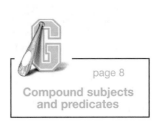

_____ 1. The time drew <u>near</u> for the announcement of the winner.

_____ 2. A private citizen had never traveled into space <u>before</u>.

_____ 3. NASA chose Christa McAuliffe as the first teacher <u>in</u> space.

_____ 4. She was glad not to be left <u>behind</u> when the mission started.

_____ 5. Christa had grown close <u>to</u> the other nine candidates.

_____ 6. In the weeks <u>after</u> her selection, Christa sat for many interviews and publicity shots.

_____ 7. She spent hours training <u>with</u> the other astronauts.

_____ 8. Finally, they were prepared <u>for</u> their mission.

_____ 9. Tragically, the shuttle exploded in flight while the spectators watched <u>below</u>.

_____ 10. <u>Despite</u> the tragedy, the memory of Christa McAuliffe inspires courage.

Conjunctions

A **conjunction** is a connecting word that joins words or groups of words in a sentence. A **coordinating conjunction** joins sentence parts of the same type. The parts of a sentence joined by a coordinating conjunction make up a **compound part** of the sentence. Some commonly used coordinating conjunctions in English are *and, but, or, nor,* and *yet.*

page 8
Compound subjects
and predicates

ETYMOLOGY

Conjunction comes from the Latin prefix *con-,* meaning "together," and the Latin verb *jungere,* meaning "to join."

ETYMOLOGY

Coordinating comes from our word *coordination. Coordination* is from the Latin prefix *co-,* meaning "same," and the Latin noun *ordinatio,* meaning "arrangement." In English, words joined by a coordinating conjunction have the same basic function.

Joining Words

A coordinating conjunction may join single words of the same function within a sentence.

Compound subject

Jeff and *Kim* memorized the verses.

Compound predicate

Jeff *memorized* and *recited* Psalm 103.

Compound direct object

He will memorize *Romans 12* or *James 1* next.

Compound predicate noun

Kim's favorite passages are *Psalm 103*, *Proverbs 3*, and *I Corinthians 13*.

Compound adjective

The *eleventh* and *twelfth* verses of Psalm 103 are Jeff's favorites.

Compound adverb

He recited them *quickly* but *correctly*.

In each sentence the words joined by the coordinating conjunction have the same function. For example, in the first sentence *Jeff* and *Kim* are both subjects. Together *Jeff* and *Kim* form the compound subject. Coordinating conjunctions must join words that share the same function in the sentence.

Joining Phrases

A coordinating conjunction can also join phrases.

Compound complete subject

A group of oceanographers and *a team of salvagers* recovered an ancient ship.

Compound complete predicate

A violent storm *sank the ship* and *killed the crew*.

Compound prepositional phrases

The old wooden ship *with a full crew* and *under Henry VIII's flag* had been part of the war fleet.

Compound complete predicate noun

Some observers at the recovery were *Prince Charles of England* and *other officials of the British government*.

Remember that coordinating conjunctions join only those phrases that share the same function.

Learning Christianly

We can use prepositions and conjunctions in sentences in order to show a relationship between things. In fact, in the previous sentence, the preposition *between* relates the words *relationship* and *things*. And the conjunction *and* connects the words *prepositions* and *conjunctions*. The more you study in school, the more you will be able to see the connections between different aspects of reality. It is interesting to note that we even refer to what we know of reality as the "universe." Why is a term like this especially appropriate for the Christian to use?

A compound part is always diagrammed in the same general way that a similar single part would be diagrammed. The line is split into two lines, and the parts of the compound are written on the lines. The conjunction is written on a broken line joining the two lines. Look at the diagram for this sentence:

Jeff and Kim memorized the verses.

When diagramming a compound part made of phrases, be sure to include all parts of the phrase on the correct line. Now look at the diagram for this sentence:

A violent storm sank the ship and killed the crew.

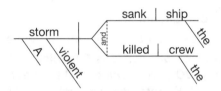

page 166

Compound sentences

page 291

Commas in a series

IN SUMMARY

A **conjunction** is a connecting word that joins words or groups of words in a sentence.

A **coordinating conjunction** joins sentence parts of the same type.

The parts of a sentence joined by a coordinating conjunction make up a **compound part** of the sentence.

 7-7 PRACTICE THE SKILL

A. Circle each coordinating conjunction.

B. Underline the words or phrases that the conjunction joins.

C. Label each underlined compound part *S* (subject), *V* (verb), *Pred* (complete predicate), *DO* (direct object), *IO* (indirect object), *PN* (predicate noun), *PA* (predicate adjective), *Adj* (adjective), *Adv* (adverb), or *OP* (object of the preposition).

 1. Joseph Haydn played the violin and sang at an early age.

 2. He was alone and independent at age eight.

 3. After his time in a church choir, Haydn was a musician and teacher in Vienna.

 4. In 1761 Haydn became the composer for Prince Nicholas Esterhazy and his court.

DO   5. Haydn left the <u>court</u> (and) his <u>job</u> after the Prince's death.

S   6. <u>Symphonies</u>, <u>string quartets</u>, (and) <u>sonatas</u> are Haydn's most famous works.

V   7. People rarely <u>perform</u> (or) <u>mention</u> Haydn's operas.

PrN   8. On a trip through Germany, Ludwig von Beethoven became Haydn's <u>friend</u> (and) <u>pupil</u>.

Adj.   9. Haydn probably wrote not <u>104</u> (but) <u>108</u> symphonies.

Adv.   10. Haydn traveled <u>often</u> (yet) <u>unwillingly</u> away from his Austrian home.

7-8   REVIEW THE SKILL

A. Circle each coordinating conjunction.

B. Underline the words or phrases that the conjunction joins.

C. Label the underlined words or word groups *S* (subject), *V* (verb), *Pred* (complete predicate), *DO* (direct object), *IO* (indirect object), *PN* (predicate noun), *PA* (predicate adjective), *Adj* (adjective), *Adv* (adverb), or *OP* (object of the preposition).

1. In the 1800s physicians practiced <u>medicine</u> *DO* (and) <u>pharmacy</u> *DO* in the same building.

2. Some <u>tasty</u> *Adj.* (yet) <u>ineffective</u> *Adj.* medicines became quite popular.

3. The products available at Old Corner Drug Store in Waco, Texas, included <u>medicines</u> *DO*, <u>foodstuffs</u> *DO*, (and) <u>flavored carbonated beverages</u>.

4. Pharmacist Charles C. Alderton of the Old Corner Drug Store <u>mixed</u> *V* (but) <u>did not name</u> *V* the first Dr Pepper drink in 1885.

5. Named by the drugstore's owner, the new drink made its national debut at the 1904 World's Fair along with <u>the hot dog bun</u> *OP* (and) <u>the ice-cream cone</u> *OP*.

6. The original Dr Pepper tasted <u>spicy</u> *PA* (or) <u>tangy</u> *PA* (but) <u>not sour</u> *PA*.

7. After Dr Pepper's invention, <u>Coca-Cola</u> *S* (and) <u>Pepsi Cola</u> *S* entered the carbonated beverage market.

8. The Pepsi Cola Company <u>acquired national distribution rights for Dr Pepper</u> *Pred* (and) <u>increased competition with the Coca-Cola Company</u> *Pred*.

9. In 1939 Dr Pepper scientists <u>removed the caffeine</u> *Pred* (and) <u>added vitamin B-1 to the drink</u> *Pred*.

10. Because consumers did not like the bad-tasting product, they <u>quickly</u> *Adv* (and) <u>loudly</u> *Adv* mandated a return to the original formula.

Interjections

Interjections are words that indicate emotion, agreement or disagreement, greeting, politeness, and hesitation or beginning. Many interjections show strong feeling.

From the Latin *interjicere,* meaning "to throw between," we get our English word *interjection.*

Emotion:	*Wow!* We're finally at the top.
Agreement:	*Yes,* we climbed one hundred steps.
Greeting:	*Hello!* When did you arrive?
Politeness:	I enjoyed the view. *Thank you.*
Hesitation:	*Well,* you can come back anytime.

Interjections can stand alone, punctuated as sentences; or they can appear along with a regular sentence in which they have no real part. Unlike prepositions and conjunctions, interjections do not show relationships between other words in the sentence. They do not function as subjects, predicates, objects, or modifiers. Because an interjection has no grammatical function, it can be omitted from a sentence without changing the meaning much—except, of course, that the emotion would be lost.

> Oh, no!
> Sorry, I didn't see you there.

Some words used as interjections can also be used as other parts of speech.

Verb:	Your visit will *please* her.
Interjection:	Leave your dog outside, *please.*
Adjective:	She allows *no* dogs in her house.
Interjection:	*No,* she will not make an exception for your dog.

In the first set of examples, the word *please* first functions as a transitive verb. *Please* is an interjection expressing politeness in the next sentence. In the second set of examples, the word *no* first functions as an adjective modifying the noun *dogs.* In the last sentence, the word *no* does not have a grammatical function. It is an interjection expressing disagreement. To decide whether a word is an interjection or another part of speech, determine whether it has a grammatical function in the sentence.

Because interjections do not function as parts of the sentence, they are diagrammed on a separate line above the sentence. Look at the diagram for this sentence:

Yes, we climbed the steps.

page 287

Punctuation

An **interjection** is a word that stands alone, not modifying other words nor working as part of the sentence pattern.

Interjections show emotion, agreement or disagreement, greeting, politeness, and hesitation or beginning.

Some words used as interjections can also be used as other parts of speech.

7-9   PRACTICE THE SKILL

Underline the interjections in the following sentences.

1. Would you please tell Laurie that she needs to come to the office right away?

2. Yes, I will tell her as quickly as possible.

3. Tell Stephen that he needs to come too. Thank you.

4. Uh-oh! I think they are in trouble.

5. No, Mr. Conrad just wants to ask them about the winter banquet.

6. How was the meeting? Good!

7. I didn't think the meeting would take that long. Sorry.

8. Well, I know meetings can take a long time.

9. Hey, is our banquet going to be fun?

10. That sounds great. Wow!

Learning Christianly

Have you ever heard someone curse or swear? Some interjections like this are called profanity, and the Bible prohibits us from using them (Eph. 4:29). Read I Corinthians 10:31. Why is using interjections like profanity a misuse of language?

7-10   USE THE SKILL

Fill in each blank with a conjunction or a preposition.

The story of Queen Esther _____ her cousin Mordecai is evidence

_____ God's care for His people. Because Vashti would not appear

_____ King Ahasuerus, the king was angered _____ decreed that she

be banished _____ the royal palace. Many candidates were brought

_____ the king to replace Vashti, _____ the king preferred Esther

_____ all of the others. Soon after Esther was made queen, the king promoted Haman _____ a high rank in the kingdom; _____ Haman was an evil man. Because Mordecai refused to bow _____ Haman, Haman wanted to destroy Mordecai _____ his people, the Jews. Neither Haman _____ the king knew that Queen Esther was also a Jew. After three days of fasting, Esther came _____ the king's court _____ requested an audience _____ him and with Haman. _____ the banquet that Esther had prepared, the queen told Ahasuerus about the plan to destroy all Jews. She requested that her life be spared. The king was furious _____ the man who dared try to kill his queen. Soon it was revealed that Haman was the man, _____ Haman was hanged _____ the gallows that he had prepared for Mordecai.

7-11 REVIEW THE SKILL

Underline the interjections and conjunctions in the following sentences. Label each underlined word *Conj* (conjunction) or *Inter* (interjection).

_____ 1. Hey, did you read about Dave Dravecky?

_____ 2. Dave played for the San Diego Padres and the San Francisco Giants.

_____ 3. Wow! He played on both teams!

_____ 4. Would you please lend me the book about him?

_____ 5. His story is realistic yet amazing.

_____ 6. Dravecky had cancer surgery and lost most of his deltoid muscle.

_____ 7. He endured a vigorous but surprisingly short rehabilitation.

_____ 8. Yes, his recovery astounded everyone.

_____ 9. His quick comeback to baseball surprised his doctors and his teammates.

_____ 10. Did you enjoy his story? Good!

7·12 REVIEW THE SKILL

A. Label each underlined word *Adv* (adverb), *Prep* (preposition), *Conj* (conjunction), or *Inter* (interjection).

B. Draw an arrow from each adverb to the word it modifies.

C. Place parentheses around each prepositional phrase.

D. Label each prepositional phrase *Adj P* (adjectival phrase) or *Adv P* (adverbial phrase).

   The <u>highly</u> unusual Mexican jumping bean is named <u>for</u> its fast popping movements. The bean is <u>actually</u> a seed <u>from</u> a shrub found in Mexico. <u>Oh</u>, it is not really the bean that is jumping! A caterpillar lives <u>inside</u>, <u>and</u> its movements cause the bean's jumping. The caterpillar grabs the bean's inner walls <u>with</u> its tiny legs and snaps its body. <u>Presto</u>! The bean pops! The caterpillar hollows the inside <u>of</u> the seed, <u>but</u> the outside remains a hard shell. The seed's jumping helps scare <u>away</u> birds <u>or</u> animals that would eat the seed. <u>After</u> several months, the caterpillar cuts an escape hatch <u>for</u> itself, <u>yet</u> it cannot <u>quite</u> leave the bean. <u>First</u>, it must spin a cocoon. Then it changes <u>into</u> a moth. The moth <u>very</u> <u>soon</u> emerges <u>through</u> the lid it cut earlier.

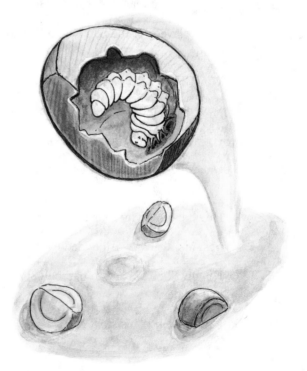

Complete each sentence by giving a word whose part of speech is indicated.

_____, have you _____ heard Beethoven's *Ninth*
　　Interjection　　　　　　*adverb*

Symphony? It is a(n) _____ _____! From an early age,
　　　　　　　adjective　　　*noun*

Beethoven showed signs of becoming a(n) _____ musician. He
　　　　　　　　　　　　　　　　　　　　adjective

played both the violin _____ the piano and wrote many pieces for
　　　　　　　　　　conjunction

piano and strings. Beethoven's only opera _____ *Fidelio*, which is
　　　　　　　　　　　　　　　　　　verb

_____ performed _____. Unfortunately, Beethoven had a
　adverb　　　　　　　*adverb*

difficult family life. His mother died when Beethoven was _____
　　　　　　　　　　　　　　　　　　　　　　　　　adverb

seventeen. As a result of several visits to Vienna, Beethoven _____
　　　　　　　　　　　　　　　　　　　　　　　　　　verb

there permanently. _____ his twenties, Beethoven began to lose his
　　　　　　　　Preposition

hearing. Soon he became almost _____ deaf, _____ this
　　　　　　　　　　　　　　adverb　　　　*conjunction*

did not keep him from writing music. In fact, _____ the last years
　　　　　　　　　　　　　　　　　preposition

of his life, it is reported that in order to compose he removed the legs from

his piano. This allowed him to feel the vibrations from the instrument.

_____, Beethoven _____ overcame a lot to become an
　Interjection　　　　　*adverb*

accomplished musician.

≡Sliding Home

Notice in Psalm 70 that David says "O God" and "O Lord" in the first verse and the last verse. He opens and closes his prayer with the same intensity. In his request, he uses conjunctions to heighten the emotion: "be ashamed and confounded," "turned backward, and put to confusion," and "poor and needy." In each phrase, the words after the conjunction build onto the meaning of the first word. For example, David wants his enemies not only to be embarrassed but also to be defeated (one meaning of *confounded*).

- *Notice the prepositional phrase in verse 4 of this psalm. What question does the phrase answer? Why is the object of the preposition so important?*

- *How many conjunctions can you find in this psalm? Find the two conjunctions in verse 5. Compare the sets of words that they link. What important contrast exists between the words linked by the first conjunction and the words linked by the second?*

Prepositions

> **II Timothy 3:16-17**
>
> *16 All scripture is given by inspiration of God, and is profitable for doctrine, for reproof, for correction, for instruction in righteousness:*
>
> *17 That the man of God may be perfect, throughly furnished unto all good works.*

- *How many prepositions are used in this passage?*

- *How do all of the objects of the preposition* for *relate to* profitable?

Conjunctions

> **Revelation 5:11-12**
>
> *11 And I beheld, and I heard the voice of many angels round about the throne and the beasts and the elders: and the number of them was ten thousand times ten thousand, and thousands of thousands;*
>
> *12 Saying with a loud voice, Worthy is the Lamb that was slain to receive power, and riches, and wisdom, and strength, and honour, and glory, and blessing.*

- *Read verse 12 without the* ands. *Read it with the* ands. *Why do you think the second reading is more powerful?*

Interjections

> **Proverbs 24:5**
>
> *A wise man is strong; yea, a man of knowledge increaseth strength.*

- *What is the interjection in this verse?*

- *How does the interjection add a special emphasis to the point this verse is making?*

DESCRIBING A PROCESS

So they read in the book in the law of God distinctly, and gave the sense, and caused them to understand the reading.
Nehemiah 8:8

Have you ever studied the instructions for something and still been confused? If so, you understand the importance of *thoroughness*. A thorough writer gives complete information and answers all the reader's questions.

Your Turn

Write a paragraph explaining how to make something.

Planning

Choose your process. Decide on a topic that interests you, preferably something that you have experience doing.

Identify your audience. Consider what your audience knows about the process already and what information the audience will need to know.

Organize your information. List each necessary item. Then list the steps of the process in the correct order. Take notes as you perform the process.

page 382

Organizing sentences

Drafting

Write your draft. First, name the process and tell why it is important. Then name the necessary materials and explain each step of the process. To conclude, congratulate your reader on completing the process.

Anticipate difficulties. Tell the reader what might be done to make the process easier. Mention options in case the process does not work.

Use smooth transitions. Transition words such as first, next, then, after, while, and last help the reader follow the sequence of the steps.

Revising

Ask a peer to read your paragraph. A reader can detect problems that you have missed. Encourage your peer to comment on weaknesses.

Revise for correction. Make changes that clarify the steps in the process. Identify and correct any errors in grammar, punctuation, and spelling.

Make a clean copy with changes and corrections. Here is one example:

Gelatin is a delicious and easy-to-prepare dessert. Before you begin, gather a saucepan, a measuring cup, a three-ounce package of gelatin, a gelatin mold, and two cups of water. To begin, pour one cup of water into the saucepan. Turn the stove to high and wait for the water to boil. When bubbles form on the water, pour three ounces of gelatin into the water. Turn the stove off and remove the pan. Stir the mixture until the gelatin dissolves. When you can see no more powder, pour one cup of cold water into the mixture. Finally, pour the mixture into the mold and place it in the refrigerator. When the gelatin is firm, it is ready.

Publishing

Make a visual recording of the process. Demonstrate the process while you explain it orally. Contribute your recording to the school library.

Demonstrate your process for the class. On the day of your presentation, remember to bring the items necessary to complete the entire process.

CHAPTER 8

CLAUSE STRUCTURE

THE SON FROM AMERICA
BY ISAAC BASHEVIS SINGER

The village of Lentshin was tiny—a sandy marketplace where the peasants of the area met once a week. It was surrounded by little huts with thatched roofs or shingles green with moss. The chimneys looked like pots. Between the huts there were fields, where the owners planted vegetables or pastured their goats.

In the smallest of these huts lived old Berl, a man in his eighties, and his wife, who was called Berlcha (wife of Berl). Old Berl was one of the Jews who had been driven from their villages in Russia and settled in Poland. In Lentshin, they mocked the mistakes he made while praying aloud. He spoke with a sharp "r." He was short, broad-shouldered, and had a small white beard, and summer and winter he wore a sheepskin hat, a padded cotton jacket, and stout boots. He walked slowly, shuffling his feet. He had a half acre of field, a cow, a goat, and chickens.

The couple had a son, Samuel, who had gone to America forty years ago. It was said in Lentshin that he became a millionaire there. Every month, the Lentshin letter carrier brought old Berl a money order and a letter that no one could read because many of the words were English. How much money Samuel sent his parents remained a secret. Three times a year, Berl and his wife went on foot to Zakroczym and cashed the money orders there. But they never seemed to use the money. What for? The garden, the cow, and the goat provided most of their needs. Besides, Berlcha sold chickens and eggs, and from these there was enough to buy flour for bread.

- *Are Berl and Berlcha rich or poor? What do you think they think "rich" is?*

- *Do you think the story is told by a person who lives in Lentshin or America?*

- *Why do you think Berl's son wrote his parents in English?*

This story reads as though it were told in the village of Lentshin. For one thing, we see the letters arriving rather than being sent. Another clue is the simple way in which the story is told. The words are plain, and the sentences are short. This style gives the reader the feeling of listening to someone who is not a native English speaker.

In this chapter, you will learn different ways sentences are put together.

Phrases

A **phrase** is a group of words that does not contain both a subject and a predicate. You have learned already about verb phrases, possessive phrases, and prepositional phrases. Every sentence includes phrases.

<u>Miss Chen's class</u> <u>is reading</u> <u>a biography</u> <u>about William Carey</u>.

The example above has four phrases underlined. *Miss Chen's class* is a phrase that functions as the complete subject of the sentence. The simple predicate of the example is the verb phrase *is reading*. Another phrase, *a biography,* acts as the direct object. *About William Carey* is an adjectival prepositional phrase that modifies the simple direct object. Some of these phrases include words that could be subjects; one is a simple predicate; but no phrase includes both a subject and a predicate.

Clauses

A **clause** is a group of words that has both a subject and a predicate working together (a subject-predicate pair). There are two kinds of clauses. An **independent clause** can stand alone as a sentence; it expresses a complete thought. A **dependent clause** is unable to stand alone as a sentence; it contains an introductory or connecting word that makes it express an incomplete thought. The word that makes the clause dependent is called a subordinating word. A dependent clause actually relies on the independent clause for its complete meaning. Dependent clauses that are left to stand alone are sentence fragments.

page 5

Finding subjects and predicates

                     S   TrV   DO

Independent: William Carey obeyed God's Word.

                                   S   TrV   DO

Dependent: Although the English preachers rejected Carey's idea

page 13

Recognizing fragments

The first example is labeled *independent* because it contains a subject-predicate pair and expresses a complete thought. The second example also contains a subject-predicate pair. However, it is a dependent clause because the subordinating word *although* leaves unanswered questions. It does not express a complete thought. It cannot stand alone as a sentence. The chart below lists some common subordinating words.

Common Subordinating Words		
after	if	though
although	since	unless
as	so	until
as if	so that	when
because	than	where
before	that	while

IN SUMMARY

A **phrase** is a group of words that does not contain both a subject and a predicate.

A **clause** is a group of words that contains both a subject and a predicate.

An **independent clause** can stand alone as a sentence.

A **dependent clause** contains a subordinating word that makes it unable to stand alone as a sentence.

8-1 **PRACTICE THE SKILL**

Label each underlined group of words *P* (phrase), *IC* (independent clause), or *DC* (dependent clause).

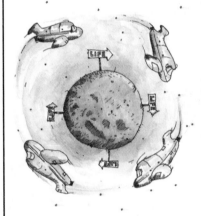

DC 1. The planet Mars is approximately 78,840,000 miles farther from the sun <u>than is Earth</u>.

DC 2. <u>Although Mars is more than 34,000,000 miles from Earth</u>, it is Earth's second closest planet.

IC 3. <u>Mars orbits the sun</u> approximately every 687 days.

P 4. <u>At 4,223 miles in diameter</u>, Mars is only slightly larger than half of Earth's size.

DC 5. Mars travels in an elliptical pattern <u>as it orbits the sun</u>.

IC 6. Because of this tilt, <u>the sun heats the northern and southern halves differently</u>.

P 7. <u>Rarely above the freezing point</u>, Mars's climate is colder than that of Earth.

DC 8. <u>Since Mars's surface apparently has polar caps</u>, some scientists believe that Mars contains water.

P 9. A reddish mineral called limonite is responsible <u>for Mars's surface color</u>.

IC 10. Because scientists are fascinated with the question of life on this planet, <u>space probes have explored Mars</u>.

Label each underlined group of words *P* (phrase), *IC* (independent clause), or *DC* (dependent clause).

_____ 1. The barracuda lives in saltwater seas, <u>where it is known for its destructive nature</u>.

_____ 2. The fish feeds <u>on both other fish and people</u>.

_____ 3. <u>Its extremely sharp teeth and aggressive habits</u> have earned the barracuda the title "tiger of the sea."

_____ 4. <u>Although there are twenty-one species of barracuda</u>, the great barracuda is the largest.

_____ 5. <u>This species can grow to be six feet long</u>!

_____ 6. The great barracuda lives in the Atlantic Ocean <u>with at least five other species</u>.

_____ 7. <u>Two other species live in the waters around Hawaii</u>; one species lives off the Pacific coast of the United States.

_____ 8. <u>Because barracuda most often live in shallow water</u>, they can be a menace to swimmers.

_____ 9. <u>Barracuda can also swim</u> far out into the ocean.

_____ 10. Interestingly, <u>this fierce animal resembles the common fresh-water pike</u>.

Simple Sentences

A **simple sentence** consists of one independent clause. All of the sentences you have studied so far in this book have been simple sentences. A simple sentence has only one subject and one predicate. However, either the subject or the predicate or both may be compound. All four of the examples are simple sentences even though some of them have compound parts.

William Carey obeyed God's Word.
He and his supporters formed England's first missionary society.
Carey traveled to India and ministered there.
Carey and his helpers learned the language and translated the Bible.

Compound Sentences

A **compound sentence** consists of two or more independent clauses. In other words, it is made of two or more simple sentences joined together by punctuation and sometimes a conjunction. Notice how the two simple sentences can be joined to form a compound sentence.

Compound comes from the Latin *companere,* meaning "to put together."

         S   **TrV**   **DO**

Simple: The English preachers rejected his idea.

         S   **TrV**   **DO**

Simple: Carey obeyed God's Word.

         S   **TrV**   **DO**   **S**

Compound: The English preachers rejected his idea, but Carey

         TrV   **DO**

         obeyed God's Word.

A compound sentence is always made up of at least two subject-predicate pairs. In addition, a compound sentence may have compound parts within it.

      S   **TrV**   **DO**   **S** **InV**

The missionary society supported William Carey, and he went
to India.

   S   **TrV**   **DO**   **S**   **S**   **TrV**   **DO**

Carey learned the language; he and his helpers translated the Bible.

These sentences are not incorrect sentences because they are joined correctly. Diagram a compound sentence in the same way that you would diagram two simple sentences; then join the two diagrams with a vertical dotted line (with a platform in the middle) from the verb of the first sentence to the verb of the second sentence.

Look at the diagram for this sentence: The missionary society supported William Carey, and he went to India.

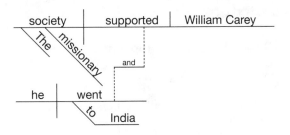

page 16

Comma splices

page 151

Conjunctions

page 291

Commas in a series

IN SUMMARY

A **simple sentence** consists of one independent clause.

A **compound sentence** consists of two or more independent
   clauses.

Label the sentences *S* (simple) or *Cd* (compound).

 1. Frozen foods stay fresh for long periods of time.

 2. Many cooks buy food in bulk and freeze part of it for later, or they make and freeze whole meals.

 3. Today, companies freeze a variety of food products. These products include pizza, juices, and vegetables.

S 4. In 1925 Clarence Birdseye first quick-froze vegetables and fish.

 5. The Postum Company bought Birdseye's patents, and the company began a frozen-food division in 1929.

 6. However, Birdseye's vision for frozen foods did not become a reality until the 1950s.

 7. In the 1950s freezers were more available to the average consumer; therefore, frozen food was used more widely in the home.

CD 8. Presently, most companies use liquid nitrogen for the quick-freeze process, but this method is expensive.

S 9. For safety, frozen food must be handled properly at home.

CD 10. Food poisoning can develop; cooks must cook the food quickly.

8-4 **REVIEW THE SKILL**

Label each sentence *S* (simple) or *Cd* (compound).

_____ 1. The psalms are poems of prayer and praise.

_____ 2. Asaph wrote ten psalms, and Solomon wrote Psalm 72 and Psalm 127.

_____ 3. The sons of Korah contributed Psalm 84, Psalm 85, and Psalm 87.

_____ 4. Moses wrote Psalm 90, but none of the others are his poetry.

_____ 5. David wrote Psalm 18; II Samuel 22 also includes this song of praise.

_____ 6. The psalms are of various lengths and about various topics.

_____ 7. Psalm 117 is the shortest psalm in the Bible; Psalm 119 is the longest.

_____ 8. The sections of Psalm 119 correspond to the letters of the ancient Hebrew alphabet.

_____ 9. Children often memorize Psalm 23, yet adults love this psalm too.

_____ 10. Many Christians choose a favorite psalm, but all the psalms give the readers a sense of God's wisdom, power, and love.

Complex Sentences

Like a compound sentence, a complex sentence consists of at least two clauses. However, a compound sentence contains two or more independent clauses whereas a **complex sentence** contains one independent clause and one or more dependent clauses.

            S   **TrV**   **DO**   **S**   **TrV**   **DO**
After the preachers rejected his idea, Carey explained his beliefs in a pamphlet.

The example is a complex sentence because it contains one independent clause *(Carey explained his beliefs in a pamphlet)* and one dependent clause *(After the preachers rejected his idea)*. Both clauses contain a subject and a predicate; the dependent clause also contains the subordinating word *after*.

Compound or Complex?

To determine whether a sentence is compound or complex, first find all the subjects and all the predicates. Then match the subjects to the predicates. Now you have found the clauses. Next, look for any subordinating words. If a clause contains a subordinating word, the clause is dependent. If it does not contain a subordinating word, the clause is independent. Now count the number of dependent and independent clauses in your sentence. If there are two independent clauses, the sentence is compound. If there are one or more dependent clauses and only one independent clause, the sentence is complex.

                           S   **TrV**   **DO**
Compound: The English preachers rejected his idea, but
          S   **TrV**   **DO**
          Carey obeyed God's Word.

                             S   **TrV**
Complex: Although the English preachers rejected his
    DO   **S**   **TrV**   **DO**
    idea, Carey obeyed God's Word.

Notice that the example labeled *compound* has two independent clauses joined by a comma and a coordinating conjunction. The example labeled *complex* has a dependent clause introduced by a subordinating word, and it has an independent clause. There is no coordinating conjunction joining the two clauses. The dependent clause may appear before the independent clause, after the independent clause, or within the independent clause.

Before: *Because Carey understood God's command,* he became a missionary to India.

After: The preachers realized their mistake *when they read Carey's pamphlet.*

Within: Carey's actions *while he was on the mission field* influenced many people.

page 295

Commas to separate

IN SUMMARY

A **complex sentence** consists of one independent clause with at least one dependent clause.

8-5   PRACTICE THE SKILL

A. Label the sentence patterns of all clauses as *S-InV, S-TrV-DO, S-TrV-IO-DO, S-LV-PN,* or *S-LV-PA.*
B. Place parentheses around any dependent clauses.
C. Label each sentence *S* (simple), *Cd* (compound), or *Cx* (complex).

_S___ 1. In the early 1800s mail delivery to California from east of the Mississippi River could take several weeks.

_Cx___ 2. Two Missouri businessmen devised a plan for faster mail service after they realized the need.

_Cd___ 3. The men bought four hundred horses and hired approximately eighty riders; this new business was the pony express.

_Cd___ 4. The express riders carried the mail for approximately two hundred miles a day, and they could deliver a letter to the West Coast in about ten days.

_Cd_   5. Although a rider traveled about seventy-five miles in a day, a horse traveled about ten to fifteen miles at a time.

_S_   6. The horses needed time for rest and preparation for the next trip.

_S_   7. The fastest trip between Missouri and California occurred when the express carried copies of a speech by President Abraham Lincoln.

_Cd_   8. During its two-year history the pony express continued day and night, and riders traveled in all kinds of weather.

_S_   9. Most riders carried both guns and knives for protection against attack.

_Cx_   10. Until the telegraph opened in October 1861, the pony express was the quickest method of message delivery.

8-6   REVIEW THE SKILL

Place parentheses around each dependent clause. Label each sentence _S_ (simple), _Cd_ (compound), or _Cx_ (complex).

_Cx_   1. During World War II, a group of Native Americans played an important role in the Pacific arena.

_S_   2. These Navajos received special training so that they could serve their country.

_Cd_   3. The code name for the Navajos was _Dineh_ or "The People"; the _Dineh_ coded and decoded critical messages between Marine Corps divisions.

_Cd_   4. The code included regular Navajo words and some made-up words using Navajo terms; for example, _Daghailchiih_, or "Mustache Smeller," became the code name for Adolf Hitler.

_Cx_   5. Although many Navajos volunteered for duty in 1939, the marines did not recruit them as Code Talkers until 1942.

_S_   6. At first some people believed that the Navajo code was too easy because the Code Talkers could decode so quickly.

_S_ 7. However, during its use the Navajo code was never cracked.

_CX_ 8. Because the code was never written down during the war, it was extremely difficult to decipher.

_S_ 9. Code Talkers served in Guadalcanal, Peleliu, Bougainville, Tarawa, Saipan, Okinawa, and Iwo Jima.

_CX_ 10. Since many Code Talkers did not discuss their experience, relatively few people know about their important contribution to the war effort.

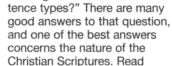

Learning Christianly

When writing for younger audiences, we often have to adjust our style. Normally, we like to use many compound and complex sentences. But children who are just learning to read find those types of sentence difficult to follow. For them to understand us, we should break up our compound and complex sentences into simple sentences. Learning this skill is very valuable for all writing. If a first grader can understand what you have written, certainly anyone who can read will understand you too. But perhaps you now have a troubling question facing you: "If the clearest sentence is a simple sentence, why bother learning about the other sentence types?" There are many good answers to that question, and one of the best answers concerns the nature of the Christian Scriptures. Read Ephesians 1:3-14 and see how many simple sentences you find.

8-7 USE THE SKILL

Combine each pair of sentences, using the word in parentheses.

1. Weather prediction has been attempted for thousands of years. People want to know the weather ahead of time. *(because)*

   _____

   _____

2. Weather forecasting existed many years ago. Prediction was based on the locations of the stars. *(when)*

   _____

   _____

3. Both the rain gauge and the weathervane had been invented by 50 B.C. Weather prediction was still unreliable. *(while)*

   _____

   _____

4. Scientists realized the importance of air pressure in weather forecasting. Many scientific inventions followed. *(after)*

   _____

   _____

5. Weather knowledge in the early 1800s could not be transmitted effectively. Storm reports usually arrived after the storm itself. *(since)*

   _____

   _____

6. Satellites take pictures of the earth. Meteorological centers receive these pictures. *(after)*

_____

_____

7. The stations transmit information to centers. Weather forecasts are prepared. *(where)*

_____

_____

8. The weather patterns follow the rules of physics. Mathematical calculations can help to predict the weather. *(because)*

_____

_____

9. The first successful computer-assisted weather forecast occurred in 1950. Scientists have improved the computer formulas for forecasting. *(since)*

_____

_____

10. Bjerknes developed an explanation for weather changes. His theory improved the accuracy of forecasting. *(when)*

_____

_____

 CUMULATIVE REVIEW

A. Label each underlined word *N* (noun), *P* (pronoun), *V* (verb), *Adj* (adjective), *Adv* (adverb), *Prep* (preposition), *Conj* (conjunction), or *Inter* (interjection).

B. Draw an arrow from each adjective or adverb to the word it modifies.

Have <u>you</u> ever been <u>out</u> <u>on</u> a lake and heard a <u>low</u>, haunting sound? You <u>probably</u> heard one of the <u>most</u> <u>interesting</u> birds in North America, <u>the</u> loon. Unfortunately, this <u>beautiful</u> bird <u>is</u> not as commonly seen as it once may have been. Are there any loons in Alaska? <u>Yes</u>, all <u>five</u> species of loons are present in Alaska. People like to watch the <u>loons</u> on lakes, <u>and</u> <u>most</u>

consider them <u>an</u> <u>important</u> part of the <u>Alaskan</u> wilderness. Some people mistake cormorants <u>or</u> other diving birds for loons. The five species living in Alaska <u>are</u> Common, Yellow-billed, Red-throated, Pacific, and Arctic. <u>Which</u> is most famous for its call? It is the Common loon. The Yellow-billed loon is <u>larger</u> than the Common. It is the largest of all North American diving birds. <u>One</u> who engages in loon watching must observe <u>them</u> <u>carefully</u>. If one gets too close, a loon may become <u>very</u> <u>nervous</u>. It will run and splash across the surface of the lake. <u>This</u> is called the "penguin dance." If one wants to hear the <u>eerie</u> calls of the loons, the best time is in the summer. Loons are usually quiet <u>in</u> winter.

≡SLIDING HOME

Isaac Bashevis Singer carefully uses simple, compound, and complex sentences in his story. When the idea is simple, the structure is simple: "The chimneys looked like pots." When the idea is more difficult, the structure is too: "Every month, the Lentshin letter carrier brought old Berl a money order and a letter that no one could read because many of the words were English." However, Singer uses more simple sentences than any other kind, perhaps to help us remember the simple life of Berl and Berlcha.

- *Look at paragraph two; find the fifth sentence. What kind of sentence structure does Singer use?*

- *What type of sentence structure does the first sentence in the passage have? Do you think it should be broken into two separate sentences rather than left as one? Why or why not?*

- *Find several examples of simple sentences.*

- *Look at the beginnings of the sentences. Do they all begin with subjects? Do you think that they should? How does a varied sentence structure make the passage better?*

Proverbs 25:21-22

21 If thine enemy be hungry, give him bread to eat; and if he be thirsty, give him water to drink:

22 For thou shalt heap coals of fire upon his head, and the Lord shall reward thee.

- *What are the two dependent clauses in verse 21? What is the subject of the two independent clauses in this verse?*

- *How are the two parts in verse 21 alike in structure?*

DRAMATIZING A SCENE

> I was in the Spirit on the Lord's day, and heard behind me a great voice, as of a trumpet, saying, I am Alpha and Omega, the first and the last: and, What thou seest, write in a book, and send it unto the seven churches. . . . And when I saw him, I fell at his feet as dead.
>
> *Revelation 1:10-11, 17*

Have you ever seen a play performed on stage? Many plays consist of several acts, each act having several scenes. There are many ways to define the term *scene*. In a general sense, a scene is simply a short section of a play, usually taking place in one location with one set of characters. When the location changes or new characters enter the action or a new idea is introduced, a new scene begins.

Your Turn

Choose a passage from a Bible account or from a book or a story that you like. Then write a dramatic scene for a play based on the excerpt that you chose. Put in stage directions wherever you can to keep the scene from becoming too still.

Planning

Choose a passage to adapt. Keep in mind that the text you choose should include some kind of conflict. Conflict in literature (including drama) is any kind of problem or disagreement. Sometimes the conflict is between two or more characters who have opposing views on an issue. Sometimes the conflict is within one character who must choose between two contrary courses of belief or action. Another type of conflict sets a character against a force greater than himself or herself; that force might be God or some manifestation of creation, such as nature.

One student was assigned by his teacher to select a passage from the book of Esther and to adapt it as a scene from a play. After reading the entire book, Tony chose a section that he found especially interesting and dramatic—the first ten verses of the sixth chapter of Esther. What is the conflict in this passage?

Determine your purpose. What lesson or message do you want your reader to learn from your scene? In his dramatic scene, Tony strives to reveal the character of both the king and Haman. To determine your purpose, read your passage several times. In addition to your text, you may need to read several verses or pages before and after your selection in order to get a more complete picture of the entire story. Tony read his chosen text several times; he also read previous verses that revealed more of Haman's character.

Develop your characters. At this point you need to identify the characters in your scene. Tony chose to develop two major characters: the king and Haman. Although the servant appears prominently at the beginning of the scene, the conflict of the scene does not involve him.

King	Haman	Servant
endured sleeplessness	angry	obedient
disturbed by injustice	sought to destroy Jews	
uninformed about his country's affairs	deceitful	
easily influenced	self-centered	

What kind of interaction do your characters have with each other? What part do they play in the scene? What do the characters need to do in the scene? Write a brief character sketch for each of the characters, describing both inward and outward characteristics.

Plan your scene. The text that you have chosen may provide descriptions that will help you plan your scene. These descriptions may be the physical appearance of the characters and the surroundings or the inner thinking of the characters. Tony chose to set the whole scene in the king's chamber because the Scripture says that the king could not sleep. The Bible does not describe the king's chamber, but Tony imagined that it would be grand and regal, with a lot of rich fabrics and gold and silver.

But this was not enough. In his first plan Tony did not include the part about Haman being there to ask the king to put Mordecai to death. After Tony thought about his ideas, he decided to include Haman talking to himself outside the door to the king's chamber. He decided to divide the stage so that one part would be the chamber and the other part would be the court outside the chamber.

Drafting

Designate a block of time to write. Your scene will flow more smoothly if you are able to write your first draft of the entire scene in one sitting. Do not be concerned at this point about errors. You will have the opportunity to evaluate your writing at a later time and to revise and proofread as necessary.

Develop the scene. Now you are ready to begin writing your scene. Begin by including any stage notes that will help set the scene. Tony's first stage note describes the physical appearance of the stage.

> [The scene opens in the king's chamber. There is a big pile of silk pillows and comforters where the king has been trying to get to sleep. There is a gold chair with footstool in the room. The king is sitting in the chair. There is a curtain that divides the king's room from the court. There are a pillar and a bench on that side of the stage.]

Begin writing your scene. After he wrote a stage note that helped him to imagine the setting for his scene, Tony began to write. Because he based his scene on a passage from the Bible, he used the information from the Book of Esther as his guide. In fact, Tony used the Bible's words as closely as he could.

Include dialogue between the characters to move the scene along. If necessary, use your characters' dialogue to give any background information that the audience might need to understand the scene better. At the beginning of Tony's scene, the servant reads from the book of records of the chronicles that tells of a plot to kill the king. The dialogue between the king and his servant reveals that nothing has been done for Mordecai, the man who warned the king of the plot.

If your dramatic scene comes from a Scripture passage, make the characters' words as close to the words of Scripture as possible. Compare Esther 6:2 with the servant's speech and Esther 6:9 with Haman's speech.

Esther 6:2	And it was found written, that Modecai had told of Bigthana and Teresh, two of the king's chamberlains, the keepers of the door, who sought to lay hand on the king Ahasuerus.
Servant	On the first day of the month, Bigthana and Teresh, two of the king's chamberlains, the keepers of the door, sought to lay hands on King Ahasuerus.
Esther 6:9	And let this apparel and horse be delivered to the hand of one of the king's most noble princes, that they may array the man withal whom the king delighteth to honour, and bring him on horseback through the street of the city, and proclaim before him, Thus shall it be done to the man whom the king delighteth to honour.
Haman	And let this apparel and horse be delivered to the hand of one of the king's most noble princes, that they may array the man withal whom the king delighteth to honor, and bring him on horseback through the streets of the city, and proclaim before him, "Thus shall it be done to the man whom the king delighteth to honor."

Indicate action through dialogue and stage notes. In a play both the dialogue and the characters' actions reveal the characters' motives and inner thoughts. Read the stage notes that Tony wrote to describe the actions and reactions of Haman. Which reveal to you more about Haman—the action or his dialogue?

[The scene opens in the king's chamber. There is a big pile of silk pillows and comforters where the king has been trying to get to sleep. There is a gold chair with footstool in the room. The king is sitting in the chair. There is a curtain that divides the king's room from the court. There are a pillar and a bench on that side of the stage.]

King:	Servant, come here.
Servant:	Your Majesty?
King:	I cannot sleep. Bring me the book of records of the chronicles and read them to me.
Servant:	[to the audience] If that don't put him to sleep, nothin' will! [turning to another servant] Go quickly and bring the book. [The other servant leaves, and the first servant turns to the king.] Do you wish anything to eat or drink, your Majesty?
King:	No, I want only to hear the book read.

[The other servant returns with book. The first servant starts to read.]

Servant: On the first day of the month, Bigthana and Teresh, two of the king's chamberlains, the keepers of the door, sought to lay hands on the king Ahasuerus.

King: Yes. I quite remember that incident. Those wicked men! But they have been punished. Read on.

Servant: The man who warned the king was Mordecai.

King: Ah, yes, Mordecai. A faithful man. What honor and dignity has been done to Mordecai for this?

Servant: [scanning over the page and then looking up] There is nothing done for him.

King: What? Nothing? This is wrong, I must think of something. Who is in the court? Go and see if any of my nobles are in the court.

[The king and the servant stay still. The lights go down on them. Haman comes into the court and begins to walk back and forth, talking to himself.]

Haman: That old Mordecai! I will not rest until he gets what he deserves! How he ruins my life! Surely the king will let me hang him!

[The lights come up on the other side of the stage, and the servant and the king begin to move again.]

King: Go, I say, and send me in a noble.

[The servant bows and goes out through the curtain. He sees Haman. He turns back in to the king.]

Servant: Behold, Haman standeth in the court.

King: Let him come in.

[The servant goes out into the court. Haman steps up to him.]

Servant: Lord Haman.

Haman: What is it?

Servant: The king wants you to go in and talk to him.

Haman: [Pushing past the servant, he goes to the king.] Your Majesty, you wanted to see me?

King: Yes. What shall be done unto the man whom the king delighteth to honor?

Haman: [smiling very big and sticking out his chest] Well, your Majesty, if it were up to me, I would say this. For the man whom the king delighteth to honor, let the royal apparel be brought which the king used to wear, and the horse that the king rides upon, and the crown royal which is set upon his head.

[The king nods. He gets up and goes to sit on the bed.]

Haman: And let this apparel and horse be delivered to the hand of one of the king's most noble princes, that they may array the man withal whom the king delighteth to honor, and bring him on horseback through the streets of the city, and proclaim before him, "Thus shall it be done to the man whom the king delighteth to honor."

King: Make haste, and take the apparel and the horse, as thou has said, and do even so to Mordecai the Jew, that sitteth at the king's gate. Let nothing fail of all that thou has said.

[Haman turns away from the king with a very sick look on his face. He starts to leave.]

King: That was a very good idea you had. I think I can sleep well now! [He lies down.]

Haman: Yes, your Majesty.

[Haman goes out into the court. He stamps his foot and shakes his fist. When the servant comes up to him, he pushes him out of the way and leaves the stage in a huff. Lights go out.]

Revising

Read through your scene out loud. As you read, ask yourself some questions. Does your scene flow smoothly? Does your scene reveal the conflict and the solution? Does the dialogue sound like real conversation? Are your characters convincing? If the answer to any of these questions is *no,* try to think of a solution to the problem.

Ask someone else to read your scene. Does your reader hesitate at any particular point in the scene? Does your reader misinterpret any part of the scene? When the reader has finished reading the scene, ask the reader to suggest changes that would make the scene more effective.

Make revisions for clarity. Implement the changes that you have determined will improve your scene.

Proofread your scene. Check for correctness of format, grammar, spelling, usage, and mechanics.

Publishing

Present your scene to your class or family and friends. In preparation for the presentation of your scene, invite interested friends to audition for the speaking parts. In addition to the speakers, you will also need people to work as a prop manager and a stage director.

Record your scene. Use a camera to record the performance while you present your scene to an audience. The recording could be a part of a permanent collection for your school, your class, or your family.

Grand Slam: Writing Across the Curriculum

During World War II, both sides used codes to keep communications secret—and both sides kept cracking the other side's codes. Then the Allies turned for help to the Navajo people. Known as Code Talkers, these soldiers used their native language to form a code that baffled the enemy. For example, the Navajo word for "owls" meant *bombers;* the Navajo word for "eggs" meant *bombs.* Nazi intelligence never cracked the Navajo code.

Try your hand at designing a code for secret communication. A code can be simple or complex. A simple code reverses the alphabet:

A B C D E F G H I J K L M N O P Q R S T U V W X Y Z
Z Y X W V U T S R Q P O N M L K J I H G F E D C B A

In this code, "Meet me for lunch" reads like this: "Nvvg nv uli ofmxs." You can also use symbols or numbers to replace letters.

After you have a code, choose your message. Write it in code and give the coded message to someone else to decipher or translate.

Only in English

Between Innings

Some things we say to each other would not make sense in any other language. We call these things *idioms*. You know what it means to have a frog in your throat. But translate that directly into French, and a French person might rush to save your life. To say the same thing, a French person would say he had *un chat à la gorge,* which means "a cat in the throat." Which do you think is a more accurate description of the problem?

In Germany, the English idiom "to chew someone out" is *jemandem den Kopf waschen*. Literally translated, the phrase means "to wash someone's head." If you think that phrase sounds funny, imagine how ours sounds to a German.

CHAPTER 9

SUBJECT-VERB AGREEMENT

In times and places where nails have been scarce or expensive, people have devised ways to build houses without them. Notice how the logs in the picture have interlocking notches to make them fit together. Some master builders were able to set logs so well that no chinking or filling was needed between them.

Good writers know a different kind of notching. One kind of "notching" in writing has to do with making the subject of the sentence fit the verb. If the subject and verb don't fit together, no amount of chinking will help.

Subject-Verb Agreement

ETYMOLOGY *Agreement* has its roots in Latin. The Latin prefix *ad-,* meaning *to,* was combined with a form of the Latin word *gratus,* meaning "pleasing." When two people agree, they are pleasing to one another. In subject-verb agreement, the subject and the verb are pleasing together.

Every verb must agree in **number** with its subject. In other words, a singular subject must have a singular verb, and a plural subject must have a plural verb. When the subject and the verb match in number, we say that they agree.

Singular: The boy *practices* basketball every day.
He *practices* basketball every day.

Plural: The boys *practice* basketball every day.
They *practice* basketball every day.

Notice that verbs form their plurals differently from nouns. A noun usually forms a plural by adding *s* or *es* (one boy, two boy*s*). A verb, however, usually forms a plural by dropping *s* or *es* (boy practice*s*, boys practice).

	Singular	Plural
Present	The boy *practices* every day.	The boys *practice* every day.
Past	The boy *practiced* every day.	The boys *practiced* every day.
Future	He will *practice* every day.	They will *practice* every day.

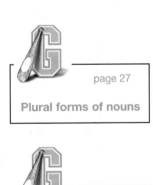
page 27
Plural forms of nouns

page 62
Present tense

Notice also that this change occurs only in the present tense. Past and future tense verbs do not show number.

page 51

Recognizing verbs

An exception to this rule for verbs is the verb *be*. The verb *be* is different from other verbs. To make *be* agree in number with the subject, you must know its forms.

Special Forms of the Verb *Be*				
	Present		Past	
	Singular	Plural	Singular	Plural
First-person pronouns	am	are	was	were
Second-person pronouns	are	are	were	were
Third-person pronouns and all nouns	is	are	was	were

All singular nouns and third-person singular pronouns *(it, he, she)* take *is* for the present tense and *was* for the past tense.

Present: That girl *is* a new student.
  She *is* my cousin.
Past: She *was* a student at Highland Christian in Asheville.
  Her father *was* a teacher there before they moved here.

All plural nouns, first-person and third-person plural pronouns *(we and they),* and the second-person pronoun *(you)* take *are* for present tense and *were* for past tense.

Present: The neighbors *are* here.
  They *are* the Kings.
  You *are* welcome to come too.
Past: Last week our teachers *were* at a conference.
  We *were* out of school for three days.
  They *were* learning more about teaching.
  You *were* out of school too, weren't you?

The first-person singular pronoun *(I)* takes *am* for present tense and *was* for past tense.

Present: I *am* glad to meet you.
Past: I *was* happy to hear you sing.

IN SUMMARY

In a sentence the subject and the verb must agree in **number.**

A singular subject must have a singular verb; a plural subject must have a plural verb.

The verb *be* has special singular and plural forms.

Label the subject S. Underline the verb form that agrees with the subject.

1. Ruth's story *(is, are)* a Bible story that ends happily.

2. Ruth *(decides, decide)* that she will remain with her mother-in-law, Naomi.

3. Ruth *(gathers, gather)* stalks of grain that have been dropped by reapers in a field.

4. One day Boaz *(sees, see)* Ruth in his field.

5. The reapers *(begins, begin)* to allow Ruth to gather whatever grain she needs.

6. The ladies *(rejoices, rejoice)* at their good fortune.

7. Boaz *(realizes, realize)* that he is in love with Ruth.

8. Desiring to marry Ruth, Boaz *(goes, go)* to make an agreement with Ruth's nearest kinsman.

9. The kinsman *(allows, allow)* the marriage.

10. In the end, Boaz *(marries, marry)* Ruth.

 **Learning Christianly**

Consistently choosing subjects and verbs that agree is the mark of a skilled writer. Many people, however, never achieve this skill because they are not convinced it is worth the effort. Why should no Christian think this way?

Label each subject _S_. Underline the verb form in parentheses that agrees with the subject.

1. The Lord _(requires, require)_ obedience from Christians.

2. Righteous people _(is, are)_ willing to be obedient.

3. Ron's sisters _(is, are)_ eager to learn verses about obedience.

4. They _(teaches, teach)_ Ron verses about obedience.

5. Their father _(talks, talk)_ about obedience in family devotions.

6. They _(was, were)_ sure that God would help them to be obedient.

7. God _(is, are)_ pleased to help them learn obedience.

8. When we _(is, are)_ obedient, we show our love for God.

9. Ron's mom _(quizzes, quiz)_ him on his verses once a week.

10. Last week she _(was, were)_ pleased when Ron recited every verse correctly.

Agreement with Indefinite Pronouns

page 93

Indefinite pronouns

page 200

Indefinite pronouns

Unlike many pronouns, indefinite pronouns do not have separate forms for subjective and objective case. They do, however, show number. Most indefinite pronouns are singular; some are plural; and some can be either singular or plural. An indefinite pronoun used as a subject must agree with the verb in the sentence.

Singular: Everyone _likes_ my mom's brownies.
Plural: Many _like_ her lemon pie even more.

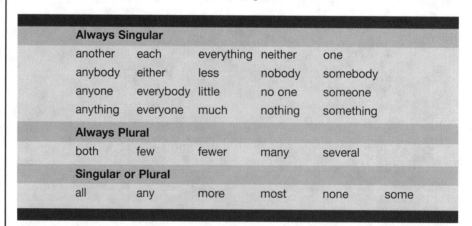

Always Singular					
another	each	everything	neither	one	
anybody	either	less	nobody	somebody	
anyone	everybody	little	no one	someone	
anything	everyone	much	nothing	something	
Always Plural					
both	few	fewer	many	several	
Singular or Plural					
all	any	more	most	none	some

Sometimes just knowing the meaning of an indefinite pronoun does not tell you whether the pronoun is singular or plural. In such cases you can tell whether the indefinite pronoun is singular or plural only by noticing the way it is used in the sentence.

Singular: All of the pie *is* gone.
Plural: All of the pieces *are* gone.

In the first example, *all* is singular (and takes the singular verb *is*) because it refers to just one thing—the pie. In the second example, however, *all* is plural (and takes the plural verb *are*) because it refers to several things—the pieces.

IN SUMMARY

Some indefinite pronouns are plural; some are singular; some can be either singular or plural.

An indefinite pronoun used as a subject must agree in number with its verb.

9-3 PRACTICE THE SKILL

Label the subject S. Underline the verb form that agrees with the subject.

1. Everyone in our astronomy class *(is, are)* eager to see the comet in March.

2. Many of the students *(is, are)* going to bring either binoculars or telescopes.

3. All of the students *(knows, know)* that seeing a comet is a unique experience. Natasha and Venika are especially excited about the comet.

4. Neither *(plans, plan)* to miss the comet.

5. Several students *(is, are)* interested in studying astronomy when they go to college.

6. No one *(complains, complain)* about the idea of coming to school at nighttime.

7. If someone *(brings, bring)* a pizza along, the trip will be even more enjoyable.

8. Many *(thinks, think)* that this trip will be fun and educational.

9. All of the comet *(is, are)* going to be clearly visible that night.

10. Most of the students *(has, have)* seen Halley's comet, but this is the first comet that I have ever seen.

REVIEW THE SKILL

Label each subject S. Underline the verb form in parentheses that agrees with the subject.

1. Everybody *(wants, want)* to look for seashells along the beach.

2. No one *(minds, mind)* getting up early in the morning to go looking for shells.

3. Few *(is, are)* interested in the clamshells that wash up on the shore in masses.

4. Fewer *(desires, desire)* getting stung by a jellyfish.

5. Somebody *(yells, yell)* in delight when he finds a big starfish.

6. At this beach, one *(does, do)* not need to go too far into the water to find shells.

7. Many *(finds, find)* beautiful shells at this beach.

8. Nobody *(likes, like)* to go away empty-handed.

9. All of the people *(was, were)* happy to find some seashells on the morning expedition.

10. Most *(likes, like)* the sand dollars and conch shells best.

Agreement with Compound Subjects

Making the verb agree with its subject can appear to be tricky if the subject is compound. However, the rules are actually very simple. If the two parts of the compound subject are joined by the conjunction *and,* the verb must be plural.

> **Plural:** Ruth *and* Esther *are* the two biblical books with a woman's name for a title.
> **Plural:** Montana *and* Wyoming *contain* parts of Yellowstone Park.

If the two parts of the compound subject are joined by the conjunction *or* or *nor,* the verb must agree with the subject closer to it.

> **Singular:** Hamburgers or *pizza is* on the menu tonight.
> **Plural:** Pizza or *hamburgers are* on the menu tonight.

If the compound subject joined by *or* or *nor* appears in a sentence with inverted order, the verb will still agree with the subject closer to it.

> **Singular:** *Is pizza* or hamburgers on the menu tonight?
> **Plural:** *Are hamburgers* or pizza on the menu tonight?

page 5

Finding subjects and predicates

page 151

Conjunctions

page 10

Subjects and predicates in inverted order

Compound subjects joined by *and* take a plural verb.

Compound subjects joined by *or* or *nor* take a verb that agrees in number with the subject closest to the verb.

 9-5 PRACTICE THE SKILL

Label the subject S. Underline the verb form that agrees with the subject.

1. Young Orville and Wilbur Wright often *(plays, play)* with toy helicopters.

2. The boys or their father *(visits, visit)* the library regularly to obtain books about flying.

3. A book by Otto Lilienthal or books by Octave Chanute *(is, are)* among their favorites.

4. Neither Wilbur nor Orville *(graduates, graduate)* formally from high school.

5. Their bicycle business or their small newspaper company *(takes, take)* most of their time.

6. However, both Wilbur and Orville *(wants, want)* to build gliders someday.

7. A front rudder or different angles for the glider's wings *(presents, present)* new possibilities for flight.

8. The sand dunes and the high wind *(makes, make)* Kitty Hawk, North Carolina, a perfect place for gliding.

9. Finally, in December of 1903, Orville and Wilbur separately *(flies, fly)* a machine-powered airplane for the first time.

10. The Wright Brothers' development of accurate air pressure tables or their unrelenting experimentation *(is, are)* their most important contribution to man's ability to fly.

Combine the two sentences, using a compound subject. Use the verb form that agrees with the subject of your sentence.

1. The crocodile is called a crocodilian.
   The alligator is called a crocodilian.

   The crocodile & alligator are called crocodilians.

2. The students are confused about the differences between alligators and crocodiles.
   The teacher is confused about the differences between alligators and crocodiles.

   _____

   _____

3. A crocodile lives at our local zoo.
   Two alligators live at our local zoo.

   Two alligators & a crocodile live at our local zoo.

4. Are the alligators' snouts pointy?
   Or is the crocodile's snout pointy?

   _____

   _____

5. Perhaps the alligators are more aggressive.
   Perhaps the crocodile is more aggressive.

   Perhaps the alligators or the crocodile is more aggressive.

6. The alligators have long bodies and short legs.
   The crocodile has a long body and short legs.

   _____

   _____

7. The crocodile has one tooth longer than the other teeth.
   The alligators have one tooth longer than the other teeth.

   _____

   _____

8. Is the crocodile's long tooth visible?
   Are the alligators' long teeth visible?

   _____

   _____

9. The alligator is similar to the crocodile.
   The crocodile is similar to the alligator.

   _____

   _____

10. Crocodiles lay eggs.
    Alligators lay eggs too.

    _____

    _____

Intervening Phrases, Predicate Nouns, and Inverted Order

Intervening Phrases

Sometimes we may lose track of which word in a sentence is the subject. For example, words that come between the subject and the verb may confuse us. Always find the true subject of the sentence in order to make the verb agree with it.

One common interrupter is a negative phrase. A negative phrase is a statement of contrast that often appears between the subject and the verb. The verb must agree in number with the subject, not the words in the negative phrase.

> The *racket,* not the tennis balls, *is* new.

The subject of this sentence is the singular noun *racket;* therefore, the verb must also be singular. The plural noun *balls* is part of the negative phrase; it is not the subject of the sentence.

Another common interrupter is a prepositional phrase. If a prepositional phrase comes between the subject and the verb, it does not affect the agreement of the subject and the verb. (Remember, though, that for some indefinite pronouns the prepositional phrase clarifies the agreement.)

> The two *books* on the shelf *show* pictures of Hawaii.
> The *pictures* in the first book *are* colorful.

The object of the preposition can never be the subject of the sentence. The verb must agree in number with the subject, not the object of the preposition.

page 144

Prepositional phrases

Predicate Noun of a Different Number

Sometimes the predicate noun and the subject do not have the same number; one is singular, and the other is plural. The verb must agree with the subject, not with the predicate noun.

His *donation* to the party *was* apples from the family orchard.

The verb *was* agrees with the singular subject *donation*. The number of the predicate noun *apples* does not change the agreement of the subject and the verb.

Inverted Order

Sometimes the verb comes before the subject in a sentence. When this happens we say that the subject is delayed. For example, the word *there* is almost never a subject, but it sometimes appears at the beginning of the sentence in the usual place of a subject. In these sentences the subject follows the verb, and the verb must agree with the subject, not with the word *there*.

Singular: There *is* one *earth*.
Plural: There *are* many other *planets*.

Remember that most interrogative sentences and some declarative sentences are written so that the verb comes before the subject. Be sure to find the subject of the sentence so that you can make the subject and verb agree.

Plural: Where *are* the *ingredients* for tonight's dinner?
Plural: On the counter *sit* the *groceries*.

page 55
Linking verbs and predicate nouns

page 10
Subjects and predicates in inverted order

IN SUMMARY

Negative phrases do not affect subject-verb agreement.

Prepositional phrases do not affect subject-verb agreement.

Predicate nouns do not affect subject-verb agreement.

Inverted sentence order does not affect subject-verb agreement.

9-7 PRACTICE THE SKILL

Label the subject S. Underline the verb form that agrees with the subject.

1. (*Is, Are*) the Ruiz family planning to go camping this summer?

2. There (*was, were*) the possibility that they were not going to go.

3. Marco and his brother, not the entire family, (*is, are*) going camping for a week.

4. Their idea of a good camping trip (*is, are*) a week in the mountains with few modern conveniences.

5. The maps on the table clearly (*shows, show*) the way the brothers will go to the campsite and various hiking trails throughout the park.

6. "Pietro, where *(is, are)* the sleeping bags?" Marco asked his brother.
  S

7. "There *(is, are)* sleeping bags in the attic," Pietro replied.
  S

8. The sleeping bags in the far corner of the attic *(belongs, belong)* to Marco and Pietro.
  S

9. Their mother's contribution to the preparations *(was, were)* two coolers of the boys' favorite foods and beverages.
  S

10. Their younger brother Felipe, not their sisters, *(wishes, wish)* that he could go camping too.
  S

9-8 REVIEW THE SKILL

Label each subject S. Underline the verb form in parentheses that agrees with the subject.

1. There *(is, are)* many different utensils for food.
  S

2. *(Is, Are)* you aware of some of them?
  S

3. Of course, the fork, not the hands, *(is, are)* most popular in North American culture.
  S

4. In some cultures, however, a person often *(eats, eat)* with his hands.
  S

5. The utensil of choice for many Asian people *(is, are)* the chopstick.
  S

6. A pair of chopsticks *(serves, serve)* well—if you know how to use chopsticks!
  S

7. For the inexperienced diner, the chopsticks, not the food, *(is, are)* the problem.
  S

8. Sometimes servers in an Oriental restaurant *(gives, give)* diners practice chopsticks.
  S

9. Into the air *(flies, fly)* bits of food.
  S

10. Remember, practice with the utensils *(makes, make)* perfect.
  S

A. Label the subject *S*.

B. Underline each verb.

C. If the subject and verb do not agree, write the correct verb form in the blank.

D. Write *C* if the sentence is correct. Be prepared to explain your answer.

_____C_____ 1. Angels have an important role in God's plan for humanity.

_____C_____ 2. Michael and Gabriel are the names of two specific angels.

_____has_____ 3. Michael, of all the angels, have the power of God against Satan and the fallen angels.

_____shows_____ 4. Everyone show interest in Michael's final victory over Satan and his fallen angels.

_____praise_____ 5. In the Book of Revelation, the angels often praises the Lord around His throne.

_____are_____ 6. There is several different terms for angels in the Bible.

_____have_____ 7. A few of Gabriel's jobs has been recorded in God's Word.

_____does_____ 8. As with all the angels, Gabriel do his jobs in obedience.

_____is_____ 9. Gabriel's announcement are good tidings to Zachariah and his wife, Elisabeth.

_____is_____ 10. The function of the angels are obedience to God.

TAKING NOTES

My son, keep my words, and lay up my commandments with thee. . . . Bind them upon thy fingers, write them upon the table of thine heart.
Proverbs 7:1, 3

Do these verses mean that someone took notes on a sermon like we do today? Not necessarily. However, we have a written record of the wisdom that Solomon gave. Solomon says that his sayings are for the good of the hearer and will profit the hearer spiritually and physically. Note taking helps the hearer focus on the sermon and enables the hearer to remember the ideas for later reflection and incorporation into his life. Solomon commands that the listener pay attention to the Holy Spirit–inspired words of Scripture.

Your Turn

Take notes on a Sunday morning or evening sermon.

Planning

Gather the necessary materials. Choose paper that is large enough to allow you to structure your notes effectively. A notebook provides a place to store your notes as well as a continuing record of what you are learning.

Prepare your heart. Don't fidget or daydream but focus on the sermon. Ponder what God will say to you through His Word and the preacher.

Listen attentively to the speaker. Be aware of content and organizational clues. Speakers often use cues to help their listeners follow the sermon.

- Transitions such as *next* or *finally*
- Enumerated points such as *first, second,* or *last*
- Alliterated main points
     God's Providence
     God's Presence
     God's Purpose
- Similar structures
     To bring men and women to Christ
     To conform us to the image of Christ
     To deliver us from our flesh
     To empower us to fulfill the ministry of Christ

Drafting

Record information about the sermon. On a new sheet of paper or in your notebook, write the speaker's name, date, text, title, or topic.

Write quickly. Try to record the ideas that the speaker gives rather than the actual words he uses. Taking notes is not the same as taking dictation.

Write down the skeleton of the sermon as a simple outline. Distinguish main points and subpoints. Use key words or phrases, not full sentences.

    I. Main point
       A. Subpoint
       B. Subpoint
   II. Main point

Write down ideas that are new to you or that apply to you in a specific way. Use key words that will help you to remember the important ideas.

Revising

Review your notes. While the message is still fresh in your mind, read your notes. Fill in any additional information that will clarify the sermon.

Make a clean copy of your notes to save. If your notes are messy from your effort to write quickly, copy them neatly onto a fresh sheet of paper.

Publishing

Exchange your notes with another student. Encourage him to comment on the content of your outline and on the notes you have taken.

Include your sermon notes in your writing folder. Use your notes to encourage you or to challenge you to search the Scriptures diligently.

CHAPTER 10

PRONOUN-ANTECEDENT AGREEMENT

D o you feel as if you are seeing double when you look at this photo? A reflection is produced when light waves are thrown back from a surface. Before mirrors were invented, people looked at their reflections in places like pools and polished metal.

Sometimes there are reflections in sentences as well. When a noun is replaced later in the sentence by a pronoun, that pronoun throws back meaning the way the surface of the water throws back the image of the trees. Writers are responsible to make pronoun "reflections" mirror the noun exactly.

Agreement with Personal Pronouns

Just as subjects and verbs agree in number, pronouns and their antecedents also agree in **number.** If the antecedent is a singular noun, the pronoun referring to it must also be singular. Pronouns, unlike verbs, often show gender. In other words, some pronouns are masculine, some are feminine, and some are neuter. Pronouns and their antecedents must agree in **gender** as well as number. If the antecedent is a masculine noun, the pronoun referring to it must also be masculine.

page 84

Pronouns and antecedents

page 86

Personal pronouns

ETYMOLOGY

The Latin prefix *ante* means "before," and the Latin verb *cedere* means "to go." The antecedent of a pronoun "goes before" it.

Where is *Javon? He* is late for class.

The pronoun *he* is replacing the noun *Javon.* The antecedent is a singular, masculine noun; therefore, the pronoun is also singular and masculine.

What should you do if the antecedent does not show gender? If the antecedent clearly refers to a person, use a singular, masculine pronoun.

A *student* should always bring *his* textbook to class.

Some nouns, especially those referring to animals, can be neuter, masculine, or feminine, depending on the context of the sentence. For example, is the noun *bear* masculine or feminine or both or neither? Notice how the gender of the pronoun changes in the following examples.

The *bear* slept in *its* den.
The *bear* protects *her* cubs.

The first sentence does not show gender. The author does not indicate whether the sleeping bear is female or male. The pronoun *her* in the second sentence, however, tells us that the bear is the cubs' mother. Always consider the meaning you are trying to convey with your sentence when choosing a pronoun to replace an antecedent. If the antecedent is compound, look at the conjunction joining the parts of the antecedent. If the nouns are joined by *and,* the pronoun must be plural. If the nouns are joined by *or* or *nor,* the pronoun must agree with whichever noun is closer to it.

Plural:	Brittany *and* Joseph welcomed *their* baby sister Erica.
Singular:	The monkeys *or* the *elephant* will appear in the center ring for *its* finale.
Plural:	The elephant *or* the *monkeys* will appear in the center ring for *their* finale.

Notice that the pronouns agree in both number and gender with their antecedents.

IN SUMMARY

Pronouns must always agree in **number** and in **gender** with their antecedents.

10-1 PRACTICE THE SKILL

Fill in each blank with the pronoun that agrees with its antecedent.

its 1. For over a thousand years, people have admired the cat for __?__ beauty and grace.

his 2. If a person killed a cat in ancient Egypt, that person had to pay with __?__ life.

their 3. The Greeks and Romans admired cats for __?__ ability to kill rodents.

his 4. In China or Japan, a writer often made the cat one of __?__ favorite subjects.

its 5. During the Middle Ages, people killed thousands of cats. They distrusted the cat because of __?__ association with evil.

their 6. The death of so many cats may have been an indirect cause of the Black Death, to which many people lost __?__ lives.

Learning Christianly

Have you ever wondered why we refer to God as "He"? We know that God is not human (Num. 23:19), so why would we use masculine pronouns when refering to Him? Read the following passages and see whether you can discern three good reasons: Isaiah 43:10; John 1:14, 8:28; Ephesians 5:22-23.

its   7. The disease caused _?_ victim's family and friends much sorrow.

its   8. The Black Death left _?_ impression on nearly everyone, rich or poor.

their   9. Cats caught the rodents that carried the Black Death. Slowly cats regained _?_ popularity.

their   10. Today, one cat or several cats can live happily and comfortably with _?_ owner.

10-2 REVIEW THE SKILL

Fill in each blank with a pronoun that agrees with its antecedent.

_____ 1. In 1775 Maria Theresa of Austria gave birth to _?_ fifteenth child, Maria Antonia.

_____ 2. Louis XV of France agreed to the marriage between Maria Antonia and _?_ son Louis.

_____ 3. Marie Antoinette and Louis became queen and king of France four years after _?_ wedding.

_____ 4. Marie Antoinette rarely allowed the serious affairs of court to enter _?_ mind.

_____ 5. New clothes or an expensive piece of jewelry often made _?_ appearance in Marie Antoinette's chambers.

_____ 6. Louis XVI soon proved inept in handling the serious financial problems of _?_ country.

_____ 7. On July 14, 1789, the French people led a revolt against _?_ government.

_____ 8. They made Louis XVI and Marie Antoinette _?_ prisoners.

_____ 9. Members of the aristocracy or any subject loyal to the monarchy could be sent to _?_ death instantly.

_____ 10. On October 16, 1793, Marie Antoinette died as _?_ husband had, on the guillotine.

page 93

Indefinite pronouns

page 186

Indefinite pronouns

Agreement with Indefinite Pronouns

Sometimes an indefinite pronoun is the antecedent of a personal pronoun. The personal pronoun must be singular if the indefinite pronoun it refers to is singular, or plural if the indefinite is plural. The personal pronoun always has the same number (singular or plural) as its antecedent.

Singular: *Each* has *his* bicycle.
Plural: *Both* have *their* bicycles.

If the indefinite pronoun is one that can be either singular or plural, look at the context of the sentence to determine its number. If the indefinite pronoun refers to only one thing, the personal pronoun should be singular. If the indefinite pronoun refers to more than one thing, the personal pronoun should be plural.

Singular: *Some* of the painting has lost *its* color.
Plural: *Some* of the paintings remain in *their* original frames.

Indefinite pronouns themselves do not show gender, but the context of the sentence may indicate a gender. Choose a personal pronoun that will agree with its indefinite pronoun antecedent in both number and gender.

Feminine: *One* of the girls has brought *her* textbook.
Neuter: *One* of the kittens has bent *its* whiskers.

What should you do if the context of the sentence does not indicate a specific gender but does clearly refer to people rather than animals or objects? If the indefinite pronoun is singular, use a singular, masculine pronoun. Do not use a plural personal pronoun to refer to a singular indefinite pronoun.

Wrong: *Everyone* clapped *their* hands at the end of the performance.
Right: *Everyone* clapped *his* hands at the end of the performance.

Refer to the chart of indefinite pronouns on page 186 in the subject-verb agreement chapter if you are unsure whether a certain indefinite pronoun is singular or plural.

IN SUMMARY

A personal pronoun that refers to an indefinite pronoun must agree in number with the indefinite pronoun.

A personal pronoun that refers to an indefinite pronoun must agree in gender with the context of the sentence.

Use the singular masculine pronoun to refer to an indefinite singular pronoun if the sentence does not indicate a specific gender.

Underline the indefinite pronoun. Underline the personal pronoun in parentheses that agrees with it.

1. <u>All</u> of the students like to play *(her, their)* favorite outdoor games on warm, sunny days.

2. <u>One</u> of the boys persuaded the others to help *(him, them)* start a softball game.

3. <u>Each</u> brought *(his, their)* own glove.

4. <u>Several</u> of the girls decided to begin *(her, their)* own softball game.

5. <u>Either</u> the boys or the girls could have the field for *(his, their)* game.

6. <u>Some</u> of the boys suggested that the girls join *(him, them)*.

7. <u>Most</u> of the girls decided that *(she, they)* would challenge the boys.

8. <u>Someone</u> on the boys' team thought that *(his, their)* team had won.

9. <u>All</u> of the girls agreed that the victory was *(hers, theirs)*.

10. At the end of the game, <u>everyone</u> agreed that *(he, they)* had enjoyed playing the game.

Underline the indefinite pronoun. Underline the personal pronoun in parentheses that agrees with it.

1. In the Middle Ages <u>many</u> of the boys followed (*his,* <u>*their*</u>) fathers' examples and became knights.

2. Aspiring to be a knight, <u>each</u> began (<u>*his*</u> *their*) training at age seven.

3. <u>All</u> started (*its* <u>*their*</u>) training by serving noblemen as pages.

4. No <u>one</u> serious about becoming a knight took (*its,* <u>*his*</u>) training lightly.

5. <u>Each</u> of the dubbing ceremonies was recognized for (<u>*its*</u> *their*) importance.

6. <u>Many</u> of the young men spent the night before (*his* <u>*their*</u>) dubbing ceremonies in prayer at the church.

7. To become a knight, <u>someone</u> swore allegiance to (*its* <u>*his*</u>) king, country, and the church.

8. <u>Some</u> of the knights lost (*his,* <u>*their*</u>) lives in battle.

9. As a knight, <u>one</u> had (<u>*his*</u> *their*) own coat of arms, which helped identify him on the battleground.

10. <u>Most</u> of the knights believed (*his,* <u>*their*</u>) participation in the Crusades, also called the Holy Wars, pleased God.

Fill in the blank with the appropriate pronoun.

_____ 1. Coffee is one of the world's most popular beverages, and the United States consumes more of _?_ than does any other country.

_____ 2. Brazil and Colombia are known for _?_ high production of coffee beans.

_____ 3. A legend says that anyone who eats coffee berries or leaves can keep _?_ awake.

_____ 4. In Arabia some used coffee as a medicine, probably because the drink made _?_ feel more alert.

_____ 5. Coffee berries grow best in a tropical climate, where most are handpicked by the people who grow _?_.

_____ 6. First, workers pick berries from coffee plants; then machines separate the berries' pulp from _?_ seeds.

_____ 7. Once machines discard the outer layers and keep the seeds, the workers are ready to roast _?_.

_____ 8. The beans are roasted for sixteen to seventeen minutes, during which time _?_ will reach approximately nine hundred degrees.

_____ 9. A vacuum tin or paper bags of coffee beans will be sent to stores where grocers will put _?_ on the shelf.

_____ 10. Shoppers buy coffee beans or preground coffee and brew _?_ at home.

Most of the sentences in the short story below contain errors in subject-verb agreement or pronoun-antecedent agreement. Correct the eleven errors.

No one fully understand the truth about the Trojan War. Much has been written about the conflict, but some of the facts is obscured. Sometimes the legends are true; sometimes it is false. The facts and legends seem to say this: for ten years the Greek army attacks the city of Troy but cannot conquer them. Neither the Greek army nor the Trojans is willing to give in. Each side claims various victories for themselves. In one battle the Trojans receive aid from the Ethiopians and the Amazons. Finally the Greeks devise a plan to defeat its enemies. They build a giant wooden horse and place it outside the walls of the city of Troy. Inside the horse sit part of the Greek army. Believing that the horse will bring protection, the Trojans pull them inside the city. During the night Odysseus and the Greek army emerges from the horse and conquers the sleeping city. Troy is burned, and the Greeks are victorious. To this day the term *Trojan horse* means something or someone used to deceive or sabotage an enemy.

_____

_____

_____

_____

_____

_____

_____

_____

_____

_____

DEFINING TERMS

Now faith is the substance of things hoped for, the evidence of things not seen.
Hebrews 11:1

"How do you spell —— ?" "Look it up in the dictionary!" This scenario is familiar to most of us. An entry in a dictionary offers much more than just the spelling of a word and the appropriate definitions, however. Among other things you can also find

- etymologies or the backgrounds of words.
  (The term southpaw *comes from the practice in baseball of arranging the diamond with the batter facing east to avoid the afternoon sun. A left-handed pitcher facing west would therefore have his pitching arm toward the south of the diamond.)*

- pronunciation guides.
  (Lou Gehrig's name is pronounced gêr ́ ĭg, with the e *like* pet *and the* i *like* pit*.)*

- biographical information.
  (Billy Sunday was originally a professional baseball player [1883-91] who began preaching in 1896 and became a Presbyterian minister in 1903.)

- geographic location.
  (Cooperstown is a residential village of east central New York west-south-west of Schenectady. The National Baseball Hall of Fame is located there.)

- illustrations of selected entries.
  (The dictionary has a photo of Babe Ruth taken in the 1930s as well as a photo of an aerial view of a baseball diamond.)

Your Turn

Write a creative definition that goes beyond the dictionary; expand your thinking to other associations of the word you chose to define.

Planning

Determine which word to define. Choose one of the following terms: loyalty, writer, baseball, or family.

Begin with the dictionary. Look up the meaning of the word. Then write the definition of your word on a piece of paper.

Consider both the denotative and connotative meanings of the word. The denotative meaning is the exact meaning found in the dictionary. The connotative meaning is the dictionary meaning along with emotional meanings associated with it.

Expand your thinking to other associations of the word. At this point, write down the connotative meanings of the word. For example, consider the word *hope.* If you look up *hope* in the dictionary, you will probably find a definition that includes the idea of fulfilled expectations. But hope is not always as certain as the dictionary implies. We are all familiar with this idea: we hope that it won't rain out the ball game; we hope there will be ice cream for dessert; we hope that we will get what we want for our birthdays. These connotations imply a type of wishful thinking. A really good definition of *hope* would include both the denotative meaning of the word and its associated, or connotative, meanings.

Include the *who, what,* and *why* of the word. The answers to these questions will be part of a complete definition. For example "Who uses this term?" and "Why is it an important word?"

Drafting

Develop your definition of the word. Incorporate ideas from the dictionary definition as well as the connotative ideas that you have found.

Put your definition into standard definition format. Remember that the correct pattern is subject, linking verb, and then predicate noun or predicate adjective. Be careful to use good grammar. A good definition of *hope* might be this:

> A hope is a wish that may or may not carry expectations. It all depends on the source of hope. If someone hopes for something that God has promised, he fully expects it to happen. If someone bases his wish on luck or chance, his hope carries little comfort. Therefore, it is important for the Christian to hope for things that God approves or promises. Then his course will be nearer to trusting than to gambling.

Revising

Reread your definition. Determine whether there are ways to improve or clarify your ideas. Did you include both denotative and connotative ideas? Did you answer all the *who, what,* and *why* questions? If not, revise now.

Check your definition for precision. Is your choice of words exact? Is your definition clear? Does your definition convey the meaning that you intended for it to convey?

Proofread for correctness. Be sure that your sentence structure is accurate and clear. Check your definition for correct spelling and punctuation too.

Publishing

Display your definition. Post your definition as part of a class bulletin board. Be prepared to respond to any comments from your peers regarding your definition.

Make a mini-dictionary. Arrange the definitions that your class has written alphabetically. Then publish the definitions as a booklet.

Shades of Gray

"When *I* use a word, . . . it means just what I choose it to mean—neither more nor less." Do you agree with this opinion? Or do we all have to agree on what words mean?

Notice the difference between these two statements: *The Eagles won their game last night. The Eagles triumphed in their game last night.* In the dictionary, *win* and *triumph* mean the same thing: to gain a victory. But these two words have different *connotations.* Which one sounds bigger? Which one sounds better? A triumph seems more dramatic and important than a win.

A connotation is a meaning in addition to the dictionary meaning. What would you think if someone described you as dressing *simply?* You would probably consider that remark a compliment. But what if he said you dressed *plainly?* Not as good, right? Both words mean that the style of dress is uncomplicated and uncluttered, but the first has a much more positive connotation.

To write clearly, you must be aware not only of the dictionary meanings of your words but also of the connotations of your words. Otherwise, you might seem as self-centered as the speaker quoted in the first paragraph. The speaker was Humpty Dumpty in *Alice's Adventures in Wonderland*—and we all know what happened to him.

CHAPTER 11

PRONOUN USAGE

Yarn made by beginning spinners is often lumpy and so thin in places it is likely to break. Experienced spinners make yarn that is even and smooth. The reason for the difference is that experienced spinners know how to keep the right degree of tension between the wool they hold and the yarn being wound by the wheel.

Writers spin words into sentences, controlling the thread of thought. Careless writers can make lumps in their sentences. For example, "David told John that he thought his bike was stolen." The lump in that sentence is that we don't know whose bike was stolen. The antecedent of *his* could be either David or John. The thread of thought breaks.

Using Subjective and Objective Case Pronouns Correctly

Singular

	Subjective Case	Objective Case	Possessive Case
First Person	I	me	my, mine
Second Person	you	you	your, yours
Third Person			
neuter	it	it	its
masculine	he	him	his
feminine	she	her	her, hers

Plural

	Subjective Case	Objective Case	Possessive Case
First Person	we	us	our, ours
Second Person	you	you	your, yours
Third Person	they	them	their, theirs

page 86

Personal pronouns

The chart shows the four characteristics of all personal pronouns: person, number, gender, and case. This unit will teach you how to use the different forms of these pronouns correctly.

Using Subjective Case Correctly

Pronouns that are subjects and predicate nouns must be in the **subjective case.**

> **Subject:** *Wendell Willkie* fought against the New Deal.
>
> **S   InV**
> *He* fought against the New Deal.

Predicate Noun: In 1940 the candidates for president were *Willkie* and Roosevelt.

S   LV PN

In 1940 the candidates for president were *he* and

PN

Roosevelt.

In informal speech this rule is not always followed. The most common change is saying "It's me" for "It is I." Because "It's me" has become so common, usage experts tell us that "It's me" is acceptable to most people in informal speech. "It is I" would be the best usage for, say, a secretary who speaks with strangers. You should use it in writing and in formal speech. Notice a similar problem that can be easily avoided: when a telephone caller asks to speak with Rachel, should Rachel answer "This is she" or "This is her"? She could avoid the problem entirely by answering, "This is Rachel."

It is "I."

Compound Subjects and Predicate Nouns

Use the same rules for compound subjects and predicate nouns as you use for single subjects and predicate nouns.

Single:	*I* invited her to the recital.
Compound:	*He and I* invited her to the recital.

If you are unsure which pronoun case to use in a compound, try dropping the other half of the compound. The correct choice will usually be clear.

Original:	Sean and *(I, me)* invited her to the recital.
Subjective:	*I* invited her to the recital.
Objective:	*Me* invited her to the recital.
Correct Choice:	*Sean and I* invited her to the recital.

Using Objective Case Correctly

Pronouns that are direct objects, indirect objects, and objects of prepositions must be in the objective case.

Direct Object: Franklin Delano Roosevelt defeated *Willkie*.

S   TrV   DO

Franklin Delano Roosevelt defeated *him*.

Indirect Object: The voters gave *Roosevelt* the presidency.

S   TrV IO   DO

The voters gave *him* the presidency.

Object of Preposition: The loss was a disappointment to *Willkie*.

S LV   PN   OP

The loss was a disappointment to *him*.

Compound Objects

Use the same rules for compound objects as you use for single objects.

Single:	I invited *her* to the recital.
Compound:	I invited *Juan and her* to the recital.

Learning Christianly

In the middle of a course like this, you may start to wonder how practical grammar really is. Sure, excellent grammar will allow you to be a better writer, and that is important. But have you ever thought about how grammar is useful in other ways? How would pursuing excellent grammar help you to be a better reader?

If you are unsure which pronoun case to use in a compound, try dropping the other half of the compound. The correct choice will usually be clear.

Original: I invited Juan and *(she, her)* to the recital.
Subjective: I invited *she* to the recital.
Objective: I invited *her* to the recital.
Correct Choice: I invited *Juan and her* to the recital.

IN SUMMARY

Subjective case pronouns work as subjects and predicate nouns in sentences.

Objective case pronouns work as direct objects, indirect objects, and objects of prepositions in sentences.

11-1 PRACTICE THE SKILL

In the first blank label the function of each underlined noun S (subject), DO (direct object), IO (indirect object), PN (predicate noun), or OP (object of the preposition). Fill in the second blank with the correct pronoun to replace the underlined noun.

_____ _____ 1. We read about <u>Babe</u>.

_____ _____ 2. Her name was Mildred Didrikson Zaharias. <u>Babe</u> is best known as Babe Didrikson.

_____ _____ 3. One of the most versatile women athletes ever was <u>Babe</u>.

_____ _____ 4. When Babe was young, <u>Babe</u> ran errands in the neighborhood.

_____ _____ 5. This gave <u>Babe</u> good training.

_____ _____ 6. Her mother could call <u>Babe</u>, and she would come in a flash.

_____ _____ 7. During high school <u>Babe</u> wanted to play basketball, but the coach thought that Babe was too short.

_____ _____ 8. Babe's hard work eventually brought <u>Babe</u> success as one of the best players in the state.

_____ _____ 9. In 1932, the National Women's Track and Field Championship was awarded to her team. The team was made up of <u>Babe</u> alone.

_____ _____ 10. Later that year the spectators watched <u>Babe</u> as she won two gold medals and broke four world records at the 1932 Los Angeles Olympics.

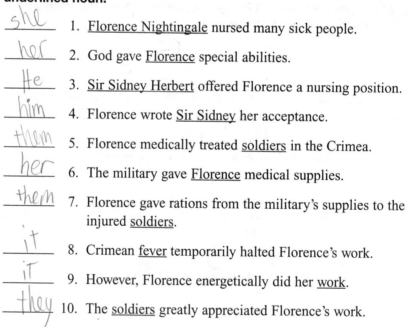

11-2 REVIEW THE SKILL

Above each underlined noun, label its function _S_ (subject), _DO_ (direct object), _IO_ (indirect object), _PN_ (predicate noun), or _OP_ (object of the preposition). Fill in each blank with the correct pronoun to replace the underlined noun.

she 1. <u>Florence Nightingale</u> nursed many sick people.

her 2. God gave <u>Florence</u> special abilities.

_He_ 3. <u>Sir Sidney Herbert</u> offered Florence a nursing position.

him 4. Florence wrote <u>Sir Sidney</u> her acceptance.

them 5. Florence medically treated <u>soldiers</u> in the Crimea.

her 6. The military gave <u>Florence</u> medical supplies.

them 7. Florence gave rations from the military's supplies to the injured <u>soldiers</u>.

_it_ 8. Crimean <u>fever</u> temporarily halted Florence's work.

_it_ 9. However, Florence energetically did her <u>work</u>.

they 10. The <u>soldiers</u> greatly appreciated Florence's work.

Underline the correct pronoun. Fill in the blank with the function of the pronoun: _S_ (subject), _DO_ (direct object), _IO_ (indirect object), _PN_ (predicate noun), or _OP_ (object of the preposition).

_Me_   1. Oren's parents have invited Oren, Donald, Jennifer, and (me, I) to their home in Colorado this summer.

_I_   2. Jennifer and (me, I) will go to Pikes Peak while we are in Colorado.

him   3. Oren and Donald have been to the top of Pikes Peak twice. Oren told us that his father had given Donald and (he, him) two of his horses for their trip to the top.

_me_   4. When we arrived at Oren's parents' house, Oren's father lent Oren, Jennifer, Donald, and (me, I) four horses.

_me_   5. Oren's father gave the calmest horses to Jennifer and (me, I) because neither of us had ever ridden a horse before.

_____ 6. Oren and Donald led the way up the mountain. Oren and (he, him) told us a little of the history of Pikes Peak.

_____ 7. Oren gave some interesting details about the history of Pikes Peak. Since everything he said was new to us, the most enthralled ones were Jennifer and (I, me).

_____ 8. Pike had led an expedition to explore Pikes Peak in 1806. Lack of supplies forced (he, him) and his men to end the expedition.

_____ 9. In 1820 Stephen Long led an expedition to the top of the 14,110-foot-high mountain. The first people ever to go to the top were (him, he) and his exploring party.

_____ 10. Everyone enjoyed the ride to the top of Pikes Peak. Information about the history interested Jennifer and (me, I) greatly.

11-4 REVIEW THE SKILL

Underline the correct pronoun. Fill in the blank with the function of the pronoun: *S* (subject), *DO* (direct object), *IO* (indirect object), *PN* (predicate noun), or *OP* (object of the preposition).

_____ 1. Nichole's mother remarked to Shandra and *(her, she),* "Mrs. Harris is ill."

_____ 2. Shandra told Mrs. Harris, "Nichole and *(I, me)* want to help you with your household chores."

_____ 3. Mrs. Harris gratefully accepted the offer from Nichole and *(she, her).*

_____ 4. Shandra's brother Jason said that he would help too. *(Him, He)* and his friend Dean would do the yard work.

_____ 5. Shandra said to Nichole, "Jason and Dean will do the yard work. Mrs. Harris has given you and *(me, I)* housework."

_____ 6. While Jason and Dean did the yard work, Shandra and Nichole stayed busy. *(She, Her)* and Nichole cleaned the kitchen, living room, dining room, and bathroom that afternoon.

_____ 7. Dean brought a bouquet inside. "Give these to Mrs. Harris," he said. "They are from Jason and *(me, I).*"

_____ 8. Shandra put the flowers into a vase, and *(she, her)* and Nichole took them into Mrs. Harris's room.

_____ 9. After she had thanked Mrs. Harris for the invitation, Nichole said to her, "Shandra, Jason, Dean, and *(me, I)* were happy to help you with your work."

_____ 10. Nichole told her mother, "Mrs. Harris said she will invite Jason, Dean, Shandra, and *(me, I)* over to dinner some night in appreciation for our work."

Using *We* and *Us* Correctly

Problems with pronoun case sometimes occur when the pronouns *we* and *us* are used with a noun. Be careful to use the subjective case pronoun *we* for subjects and the objective case pronoun *us* for objects.

> *We* classmates gave our teacher a surprise birthday party.

> She sent a thank-you note to each of *us* students.

Notice that the noun does not affect the case of the pronoun. In the first sentence, the pronoun is the subject; therefore, the subjective case *we* is the correct choice. The pronoun in the second sentence is the object of the preposition *of;* the objective case pronoun *us* is the correct choice.

Using *Who* and *Whom* Correctly

The interrogative pronouns *who* and *whom* are often confused. Use the subjective case pronoun *who* for subjects and use the objective case pronoun *whom* for objects.

page 89

Interrogative pronouns

Subject:	*Who* wrote the editorial in this week's school newspaper?
Direct Object:	*Whom* did you interview?
Object of Preposition:	About *whom* did you write?

If you are not sure whether the pronoun in an interrogative sentence should be subjective or objective, try rearranging the order of the sentence. You will usually be able to see the sentence pattern clearly.

You did interview *whom.*
You did write about *whom.*

IN SUMMARY

Use the subjective case pronouns *we* and *who* for subjects and the objective case pronouns *us* and *whom* for objects.

11-5 PRACTICE THE SKILL

Underline the correct pronoun.

1. *(We, Us)* have just finished reading Sir Arthur Conan Doyle's short story "The Speckled Band."

2. *(Whom, Who)* is the detective in the story?

3. Sherlock Holmes's powers of deduction amazed *(us, we)* readers.

4. Holmes knew the solution before *(us, we)* could figure it out.

5. *(Who, Whom)* would have thought of using a snake to commit murder?

6. It really did not surprise *(us, we)* too much when we learned the guilty person's name.

7. *(We, Us)* thought it was exciting when Holmes drove the snake back up the bell rope.

8. *(Who, Whom)* did the angry snake bite instead of the intended victim?

9. According to *(us, we)*, the guilty person deserved his punishment.

10. *(We, Us)* students enjoyed the story so much that our teacher has told us that we will read "The Blue Carbuncle," another Sherlock Holmes story.

11-6 REVIEW THE SKILL

Underline the correct pronouns.

1. *(We, Us)* memorized the entire book of I John.

2. *(Whom, Who)* gave you the assignment?

3. Mr. Rathburn assigned the project to *(us, we)* quiz team members.

4. Mark said to Peter and me, "*(We, Us)* already know some of the verses."

5. *(Us, We)* all spent one hour every day on our project.

6. Mark and I read the verses and put them into a logbook. *(We, Us)* recorded our progress in it daily.

7. *(Whom, Who)* does not think I John is worth the effort?

8. To *(whom, who)* did you recite your verses?

9. Mr. Rathburn said that he was pleased with *(us, we)* for our efforts.

10. *(We, Us)* quizzers learned much from doing this project.

page 310

Apostrophe

Problem Pronouns

Possessive Pronouns and Contractions

Some possessive pronouns and contractions are homonym pairs. Homonyms are words that sound the same (and may or may not have the same spelling) but mean different things. Be careful to spell the possessive personal pronouns correctly—without apostrophes.

Your/you're

Your is a possessive pronoun.
   Don't forget *your* camera.

You're is a contraction of *you are*.
   You're going to see Old Faithful.

Its/it's

Its is a possessive pronoun.
   Its stream shoots nearly two hundred feet into the air.

It's is a contraction of *it is*.
   It's a geyser that erupts about once every hour.

Their/they're

Their is a possessive pronoun.
>My aunt and uncle saw it, but *their* pictures are not as colorful as the one on the post card.

They're is a contraction of *they are.*
>*They're* on the desk with the post cards from my grandparents.

Theirs/there's

Theirs is a possessive pronoun.
>My snapshots are with *theirs.*

There's is a contraction of *there is.*
>*There's* Aunt Lora by Old Faithful.

Whose/who's

Whose is a possessive pronoun.
>*Whose* snapshot is the best?

Who's is a contraction of *who is.*
>*Who's* standing behind Aunt Lora in this picture?

page 89

Interrogative pronouns

Courtesy Order

When you use personal pronouns in pairs, put the one referring to yourself last.
>Helen wrote to him and me.

Always mention the person you are speaking to first in any personal pronoun pair.
>You and I will answer.

>I will give the stamps to you and him.

page 86

Personal pronouns

In Summary

Do not confuse possessive pronouns with similar-sounding contractions; possessive pronouns do not contain apostrophes.

When using personal pronoun pairs, always mention the person spoken to first and yourself last.

11-7 PRACTICE THE SKILL

Correct any pronoun or contraction error by underlining the incorrect pronoun and writing the correct word above it. Write *C* in the margin beside any sentence that is correct.

1. I and you are going to play chess.

2. It's not hard to learn to play chess.

3. I am one who's experience in chess has taught me to plan out a strategy before moving one piece.

4. Whose moving a piece first in this game?

5. Since you're pieces are light-colored, you will go first.

6. Guard the king and queen carefully! Their the most valuable pieces.

7. The queen is valuable because of it's ability to move as far as it can in any direction.

8. Your not allowed to put your king in danger.

9. If your king is captured, you lose the game.

10. Theirs a draw when a game ends with neither player winning.

11-8 REVIEW THE SKILL

Correct any pronoun error by underlining the incorrect pronoun and writing the correct one in the blank. Write *C* if the sentence is correct.

_____ 1. The teacher gave the assignment to write a report on Vikings to me and you.

_____ 2. The Viking men were large, and they're facial expressions were fierce.

_____ 3. When the Vikings raided villages, they sometimes made the citizens their prisoners.

_____ 4. Its important to know, however, that some Vikings did other things besides raid villages.

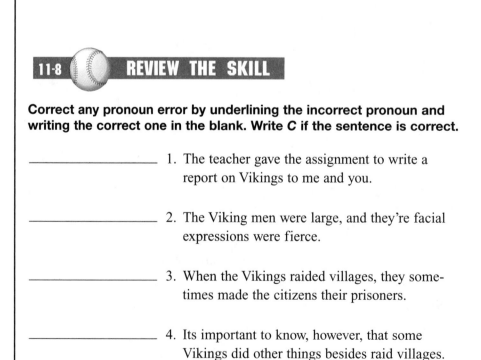

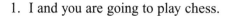

_____ 5. Many Vikings spent part of they're time farming or doing other skills, such as woodworking and metalworking.

_____ 6. Some Vikings became famous for their explorations.

_____ 7. Whose the Viking who discovered Greenland?

_____ 8. Eric the Red gave the island the name Greenland in the hope that its name would attract settlers.

_____ 9. Eric the Red is also the Viking who's son Leif sailed to North America to explore new territories.

_____ 10. Archaeologists have learned much about the Vikings, but undoubtedly theirs more waiting to be discovered.

Reflexive and Intensive Pronouns

Be careful to use reflexive and intensive pronouns correctly. Never use a reflexive or intensive pronoun in place of a personal pronoun. Remember that reflexive pronouns always refer to the same person or thing as the subject. Therefore, you cannot use a reflexive pronoun as a direct object, an indirect object, or an object of the preposition unless it refers to the subject. Never use an intensive pronoun unless there is another noun or pronoun for it to intensify. Use a personal pronoun instead.

page 91

Reflexive and Intensive pronouns

ETYMOLOGY

Reflexive is from a Latin word meaning "to reflect." A reflexive pronoun "reflects" another noun in the sentence.

Intensive comes from a Latin root meaning "to stretch out," that is, "to extend." An intensive pronoun "extends," or gives emphasis to, another word in the sentence.

> **Wrong:** They presented the award to Trudi and *myself.*
> **Right:** They presented the award to Trudi and *me.*

The pronoun *myself* is incorrect because it does not refer to the subject *they.* The personal pronoun *me* is correct.

> **Wrong:** Trudi and *myself* thought Mikail deserved it more.
> **Right:** Trudi and *I* thought Mikail deserved it more.

The pronoun *myself* is incorrect because it does not refer to any other word in the sentence. The personal pronoun *I* is correctly used as the subject.

Never use the nonstandard forms *hisself* or *theirselves*. Instead use *himself* or *themselves*.

Wrong: Alex only drew attention to *hisself* by shouting.
Right: Alex only drew attention to *himself* by shouting.

Wrong: They built the house *theirselves*.
Right: They built the house *themselves*.

IN SUMMARY

Never use a reflexive or intensive pronoun in place of a personal pronoun.

Avoid the nonstandard forms *hisself* and *theirselves*.

11-9 PRACTICE THE SKILL

Underline the correct pronoun.

1. Janelle and *(I, myself)* wanted to visit Zoo Atlanta.

2. Joel *(himself, hisself)* had been to the zoo five times already.

3. Dad asked Joel, "Why don't you go with your sisters rather than letting them go by *(theirselves, themselves)*?"

4. Joel decided to go with Janelle and *(myself, me)*.

5. Janelle *(herself, herselves)* enjoyed taking pictures of the animals.

6. Joel bought ice cream for *(himself, hisself)*.

7. He also bought ice cream for Janelle and *(myself, me)*.

8. Joel did not want to see the reptiles, so Janelle and I went by *(ourself, ourselves)*.

9. *(I, Myself)* appreciated the good day I was able to spend with my brother and sister.

10. Later, Joel *(himself, hisself)* admitted that he had really enjoyed his sixth visit to the zoo because he was with his sisters.

Fill in the blank with an appropriate reflexive or intensive pronoun.

_____ 1. Kris and I worked on the project __?__ .

_____ 2. Weston wanted to do the project by __?__ .

_____ 3. Alicia and Kerri finished their project by __?__ .

_____ 4. Weston __?__ was the last one to finish.

_____ 5. I __?__ thought that teamwork made the job easier.

_____ 6. We __?__ did a very good job on our project.

_____ 7. Kris __?__ was surprised that we worked so well together.

_____ 8. We were pleased with __?__ for all our hard work.

_____ 9. Weston decided to help __?__ next time by working with a friend.

_____ 10. Kris and I told him that we would help him __?__ .

Clear Pronoun Reference

Every pronoun must have an antecedent. We say that a pronoun refers to its antecedent. The antecedent of a pronoun is the noun that the pronoun replaces; the antecedent usually precedes the pronoun.

> Judy likes dogs, but she is allergic to cats.

In some poorly written sentences the antecedent of a pronoun is unclear.

> Leroy saw Sung Soo when he was mowing the lawn.

In this sentence it is unclear who mowed the lawn. We cannot tell for sure what the antecedent of the pronoun *he* is. Does *he* refer to Leroy or to Sung Soo? Sentences with unclear pronoun references need to be revised to clarify the antecedents of the pronouns. If we assume that Leroy was mowing the lawn, there are at least three revisions that make the antecedent clear. Sometimes we replace the pronoun with a noun.

> Leroy saw Sung Soo when Leroy was mowing the lawn.

page 84

Pronouns and Antecedents

Because this kind of revision often sounds awkward, we usually rearrange the parts of the sentence; sometimes we rewrite the sentence completely.

> When Leroy was mowing the lawn, he saw Sung Soo.
> Leroy, who was mowing the lawn, saw Sung Soo.

Some pronoun reference problems are caused not by too many possible antecedents but by no possible antecedent.

> Rosanna visited the Alamo. They have a historical museum there.

The word *they* has no clear antecedent in this sentence. You can correct this problem by rewriting the sentence to get rid of the unnecessary pronoun.

> Rosanna visited the historical museum at the Alamo.
> The Alamo, which Rosanna visited, has a historical museum.

IN SUMMARY

Every pronoun must have a single, clear **antecedent**.

11-11 **PRACTICE THE SKILL**

Revise each of the following sentences to make the pronoun reference clear.

1. Bonnie and Diane studied for her Bible test.

   _____

   _____

2. Bonnie told Diane that she needed to do well on this test.

   _____

   _____

3. Diane and Bonnie agreed that she needed the most help with the Old Testament material.

   _____

   _____

4. Diane told Bonnie that she was having trouble understanding the Minor Prophets. They studied for many hours.

_____

_____

5. On the morning of the test, Diane and Bonnie prayed that she would do well.

_____

_____

6. Diane and Bonnie were happy about the results of her test.

_____

_____

7. Bonnie and Diane agreed that reviewing the test material together helped her remember things.

_____

_____

8. Diane reminded Bonnie that praying before the test had undoubtedly helped her too.

_____

_____

9. Bonnie told Diane that she wanted to go out to eat to celebrate.

_____

_____

10. Diane took Bonnie to Pavlov's Pizza Palace. They have pizza with jalapeño peppers there.

_____

_____

Learning Christianly

Has anyone ever knocked on your door and tried to sell something to your parents? You may even remember someone who came to your door and spoke with very poor grammar. You probably felt sorry for him, that he hadn't had more opportunity to learn good grammar. But his difficulties with the English language might also make you more hesitant to take him and what he is selling seriously. Christians are called to go into all the world and share the gospel of Christ with others (Matt. 28:19-20). How would the skills of good writing and grammar help you in this calling?

Rewrite each sentence to make the pronoun reference clear.

1. Malissa told Meghan that she was going to Charleston in a few weeks.

   _____

   _____

2. Malissa wanted to go to Charleston Place. They have a hotel on the upper level of the building and some exclusive shops on the lower level.

   _____

   _____

3. Meghan heard Malissa's vacation plans while she was waiting for the program to begin.

   _____

   _____

4. Meghan and Malissa agreed that she should take some time to see some of the beautiful houses near the Battery.

   _____

   _____

5. Malissa said that she might take a stroll along one of the beaches. They have some beautiful seashells there.

   _____

   _____

6. Malissa told Meghan that she was also going to visit Fort Sumter.

   _____

   _____

7. While she was in Charleston, Malissa visited The Oceania Restaurant. They serve excellent seafood there.

   _____

   _____

8. Later Malissa and Meghan looked at her pictures from Charleston.

_____

_____

9. Both of them laughed when they saw the picture of her falling into the ocean.

_____

_____

10. Meghan and Malissa both knew that she had had a wonderful vacation.

_____

_____

11-13   USE THE SKILL

Correct any pronoun error by underlining the incorrect pronoun and by writing the correct one above it. Write _C_ beside any sentence that is correct.

1. Louis Joliet and Jacques Marquette were explorers who's discoveries were important to the settlement of the American frontier.

2. Louis Joliet hisself was a fur trader living in New France (now Canada) when his government chose them to lead an important expedition.

3. Him and Marquette were to explore the upper Mississippi River.

4. He attempted to find a Mississippi River route to the Pacific Ocean for the New French government.

5. They're voyage began in 1673 at Lake Michigan and continued through the area that is now Wisconsin.

6. Soon the two explorers realized that the river flowed south, not west; he guessed that it flowed to the Gulf of Mexico instead.

7. Although their known for the Mississippi River exploration, Joliet and Marquette were not able to complete the expedition by himself.

8. The Indians and Spaniards among who the men traveled were hostile.

9. Alone on the return trip to New France, Joliet lost all the maps and other records when their canoe tipped over.

10. Amazingly, his knowledge allowed the explorer themselves to reconstruct some maps from memory.

Locate and correct the thirteen errors in the paragraph: subject-verb agreement errors, pronoun-antecedent agreement problems, and pronoun usage problems.

Seoul are one of the largest cities in the world. Seoul has many modern buildings yet contain some ancient palaces. Yi Songgye founded it in memory of his ancestors. He built hisself the Chongmyo Royal Shrine. One of the ancient buildings in Seoul are the Changdok Palace. They keeps it well preserved. Most of the people in Seoul lives near the Palace. Their is also sports facilities in Seoul. The Koreans used Olympic Park for the 1988 Seoul Olympics. They also provide theirselves with entertainment from theaters and musical performances. Their love of them result in many theatrical companies within the city limits of Seoul. Through much development, Seoul itselves has changed dramatically within the past few decades.

_____

_____

_____

_____

_____

_____

_____

_____

_____

_____

_____

_____

_____

_____

And Moses sent them to spy out the land of Canaan, and said unto them, Get
you up this way southward, and go up into the mountain: And see the land, what
it is; and the people that dwelleth therein, whether they be strong or weak.
Numbers 13:17-18

"The shortest distance between two points is a straight line." How often
have you heard that statement? Or how about this common expression: "It's
about fifteen miles as the crow flies." "As the crow flies"—if only it were
that easy to get from Point A to Point Z without going over, through, and
around Points B-Y! Unfortunately, when it comes to destinations, they often
lie over bridges, through intersections, and around corners. Look at this set
of directions. How effective is it?

> I declare to my nephew, Guido Spada, my sole heir, that I have
> buried in a place which he has visited with me, namely, in the caves
> of the little island of Monte Cristo, everything I possess in ingots,
> gold, money and jewels, that I alone know of the existence of this
> treasure, and that he will find it by lifting the twentieth rock in a
> straight line from the small creek to the east. Two openings have
> been made in these caves; the treasure is in the furthest corner of
> the second one.
>
> *The Count of Monte Cristo* by Alexandre Dumas

Giving directions is an important skill. While sometimes the conse-
quences of poor directions are no more serious than a missed turn, at other
times major damage can result from inaccurate or incomplete directions.
Giving precise directions will bring about the desired result: the arrival at
the correct destination with a minimum of fuss.

Your Turn

Write out directions from your house to another specified location.

Planning

Select a location. Think about places that you frequent often such as your
church, your school, your grandparents' home, or the local grocery store
where your family shops. Be sure that your choice is a location that is familiar to you.

Make a list of streets and landmarks. Do not pay attention at this point to
the exact order or importance of streets or landmarks that you can think of
between your house and the location that you have chosen. Rather, randomly
write any of these that come to your mind.

Look over your entries and determine those that are most important.
You will need to delete unnecessary information. Including too much information or too many landmarks can distract the person following the directions. Choose only those that clarify your route.

Arrange these ideas in proper order. When telling a friend how to get
from here to there, it is best to begin *here* and work your way to *there*. After
you have presented a step in the directions, going back to fill in something
that you forgot only confuses the reader and results in inaccurate directions.

Drafting

Write a draft of your directions. Pretend that you are going from your home to your destination. As you write your draft, make sure that your directions follow a pattern similar to "First you turn onto Street A and go two blocks before you turn left. Then you proceed to the statue in the middle of the square."

Avoid including unnecessary details. Describing too many landmarks on the way to the destination can cause the person following your directions to be distracted and to miss a turn. Choose a few distinctive landmarks that are large or obvious; they are easy to notice and they allow the follower to concentrate on the directions themselves, not the scenery.

Give accurate, complete directions. Your directions will not get the desired result if you count on your follower to read your mind. Remember that the reason for the directions is to help the other person on an unfamiliar trail. Caesar Spada's directions to his nephew, Guido, certainly seem precise. Notice the detail of the "twentieth rock" and the "straight line from the small creek to the east." Remember though that no two people understand things exactly the same. Using the detail of "the second [cave]" could present problems. Does one count from right to left or from left to right? Would the numbering of the caves be affected by the way one approached them? In the story the Count has no trouble retrieving the treasure, but in real life, directions like "It's the third exit from the end" are hard to follow. The goal is to arrive at the destination with as little lost time and effort as possible, not to drive to the end and then to backtrack three exits!

Revising

Read through your directions. In each step of the directions, consider whether or not you have been clear in your landmarks, street signs, and left or right turns. Do the steps of the directions follow in a logical order?

Exchange directions with a peer. Encourage your peer to identify parts of the directions that are not clear or accurate.

Revise and proofread for correctness. Incorporate any suggestions or corrections that your reader has given you. Then proofread your directions for correct grammar, spelling, and mechanics. Make a clean copy of your assignment.

Publishing

Publish a directions guide. As a class project, publish a guide to local places. Include each class member's assignment in the directions guide.

Read your directions for your family. Ask your parents to listen to your directions. Encourage them to comment on the exactness of your route.

Pinch Hitter: Critical Thinking

"The facts are the same in every case, Inspector. No locks were picked, no windows were broken or left open, no doors were forced open, no possible way to gain unlawful entry without detection, and yet it was done." Officer Bell ran his fingers through his hair. His widened eyes and disheveled hair were difficult to ignore.

Inspector Jameson stroked his chin.

"Five burglaries this month and no clues, no fingerprints, no suspects, not one shred of evidence," said Bell. "These have to be inside jobs! The only possible way to enter these homes is with keys. It has to be!"

"These burglaries are connected, Bell," said Inspector Jameson. "The facts we have tell us that. Look at this chart I've been constructing." Inspector Jameson stood up. "I still say someone outside is doing this. Let's go back to those houses, Bell. Perhaps the obvious has been overlooked. I'll meet you downstairs. You'll—ah—need to comb your hair before we go anywhere."

Reinspection of the homes brought no new leads. The doors and windows of all the houses were as they should be. The only marks anywhere were a few scratches on the inside handles of the doors and a smudge on the wall alongside two of the doors. Jameson pointed out the scratches to Officer Bell.

"The scratches are only on the inside," Bell said. "You said someone on the outside came in, not vice versa. Besides, they are small. Nothing out of the ordinary about a scuffed door handle or a smudge."

The Inspector said, "Let's see how long these marks have been here. Mr. Cohn, could you step over here?"

Mr. Cohn, the owner of the home, approached the Inspector and Officer Bell. The Inspector asked, "Mr. Cohn, would your dog have barked at an intruder or scratched the door?"

"Oh, he wasn't our dog. He was a lost dog we took in. He just appeared in our yard one day and was such a nice dog we decided to keep him till we could find his owner. My wife liked the dog because he was so quiet and knew so many commands and tricks. As for the scratches, I had never noticed the scratches before. I couldn't tell you whether they are recent or not."

"I remember liking that dog," said Officer Bell. "I saw him when we came after the burglary. He's a big golden retriever, isn't he? Really well behaved and gentle. I can't imagine him going after anyone. Where is he now?" Bell was a soft touch for dogs and cats.

"Oh, he's back where he came from. His owner placed an ad in the newspaper. We called him yesterday. He was a nice guy and glad to have the dog back. The dog was glad too. He whined and jumped like a puppy when the guy came to get him."

Later that day, the Inspector and Officer Bell continued discussing the difficulties of the burglaries. The Inspector looked over his chart again. "No evidence of entry, no fingerprints, no witnesses. All we do have are five burglaries and maybe some scratches on the inside of the houses. How was it done? I wonder if anyone else had a dog. Did we find that out? Did anyone hear any barking? Someone might have looked to see a dog barking and seen something we could use."

"I'll call the other homeowners," said Bell. Later he reported to the Inspector. "This is odd, Inspector. I was able to reach three other homeowners. Mr. Spanner and Mr. Gibson had each found a lost retriever a few days before the burglaries and were trying to find the owners just like Mr. Cohn. Mr. Reame also had a dog that disappeared during the burglary, but didn't want to mention it before because his kids had found the dog in their yard and wanted to keep it. The family thought the dog would come back later, but it hasn't. How about that, Inspector. Curious, isn't it?"

Inspector Jameson didn't hear Officer Bell's question. He was busy looking through the newspaper.

1. *Why did Inspector Jameson think, by looking at his chart, that all the burglaries were connected?*

2. *If the Inspector had added a column to his chart headed "Dogs," which houses would get a check mark?*

3. *If you were Inspector Jameson, where would you be looking in the* Chicester Times? *What would you be looking for? Whom could you call for a possible lead on solving this case?*

INSIDE:
Robberies Increase
Details on B1

Chicester Times

Golf Tournament begins today.

Thursday, June 15   Chicester County

Local School Named Best in County

by Bruce Ulmer
Times Staff Writer

Yesterday afternoon Mayor Price announced that Central High School has been named the best school in Ada County. At a news conference Price said, "This unique high school is superior in all aspects of education and administration."

The mayor cited Central's dedicated faculty as a primary factor in the school's success.

Price also mentioned the degree of student involvement at Central. Each school surveyed has strong extracurricular programs in sports, music, and debate. Central High School also features a school newspaper, a student writer's guild, and a popular drama club.

Price presented Jeanne Travois, principal of Central High School, a certificate with this inscription: "The Annual School Excellence Award of Ada County is hereby presented to Central High School for its superior standards in both academics and administration."

Chicester Times
104 Watson St.
Chicester
Publisher - Al Ross
City Editor - Frank Cook
Classified Ads - Jane Dyes
Call 555-0318

Today's weather forecast: Warm and windy. High near 80°F with 20 percent chance of rain.

Jack Mason described his grief at seeing the Logan Station burn. "The station has always been a sort of tourist attraction for visitors passing through this community."

Logan Corner Railroad Station was established in 1855 by Mr. Michael Williams. Mr. Williams, a man of much influence in the state house, persuaded his colleagues of the benefits of a station in Logan. Many famous persons passed through Logan Station throughout the years, including Abraham Lincoln.

"When my great-great grandfather passed on," explained Williams, "the state house decided that it would be better for the railroad to run through Millrock, which was a larger town nearby. The town has lost a priceless treasure."

Inside Chicester Times

Arts	B2
Business	A3
Classified Ads	
Auctions	D1
Lost/Found	D2
Rentals	D1
News	B1
Sports	C1
Weather	D4
World News	A1

Fire Destroys Historical Site

Early Tuesday morning the Logan Corner Railroad Station burned to the ground. Alerted by a smoke alarm, Hazel Williams crawled to the nearest exit and used a pay phone to call 911. Williams has been a live-in resident of the historical site for nearly fifty years.

Firefighters battled the blaze for nearly four hours but were unable to save the railroad station building. Firefighter

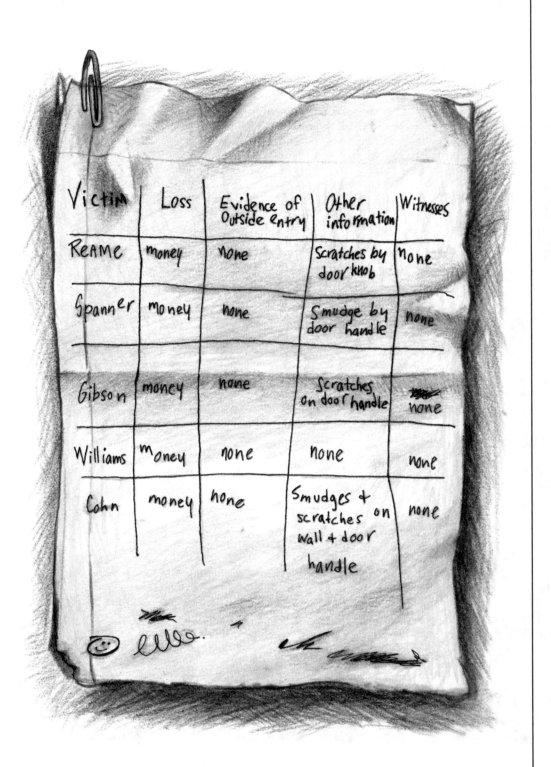

Victim	Loss	Evidence of Outside entry	Other information	Witnesses
Reame	money	none	Scratches by door knob	none
Spanner	money	none	Smudge by door handle	none
Gibson	money	none	Scratches on door handle	none
Williams	money	none	none	none
Cohn	money	none	Smudges & scratches on wall & door handle	none

CHAPTER 12

USING ADJECTIVES AND ADVERBS CORRECTLY

Do you know someone who talks very little? Is he thought of as having good sense? Alexander Pope wrote, "Words are like leaves; and where they most abound, much fruit of sense beneath is rarely found."

Sprinkling many adjectives and adverbs into your sentences will not make them more effective or even more pleasing. The extra words only clutter the text, making it less meaningful and definitely less memorable. Good writers know how to use adjectives and adverbs correctly—and sparingly—to allow more light to fall on meaning.

Adjective or Adverb?

Adjectives and adverbs sometimes confuse people. Because both are modifiers, some writers incorrectly use an adjective when they should use an adverb, or they use an adverb where an adjective should be used. In order to choose the correct modifier, you must know what type of word you are modifying. Carefully analyze your sentences to determine whether an adjective or adverb is needed. Remember to use adjectives, not adverbs, to modify nouns and pronouns. Use adverbs, not adjectives, to modify verbs, adjectives, and other adverbs.

page 55

Linking verbs

page 102

Adjectives

Adjective: Today's temperature is (normal, normally).

S ↗ LV ↘ PA
Today's temperature is normal.

Adverb: The temperature is (normal, normally) warm.

S ↗ LV ↘ PA
The temperature is normally warm.

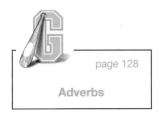

page 128

Adverbs

Notice that both sentences follow the sentence pattern S-LV-PA. In the first sentence the adjective *normal* is necessary to complete the sentence pattern. Also, the adjective modifies the subject *temperature,* a noun. In the second sentence the adverb *normally* is the correct choice because it answers the question "to what extent?" about the adjective *warm.*

The words *good* and *well* are especially confusing to some people. Remember that *good* is an adjective and that *well* is an adverb.

Wrong: Her performance was well.

S ↗ LV ↘ PA
Right: Her performance was good.

The adjective *good* is correct in this example. Because it follows the linking verb *was,* we know it is a predicate adjective that modifies the subject (a noun). The adverb *well* is incorrect because an adverb cannot modify a noun.

Wrong: Lila played good at the music contest.

S   InV
Right: Lila played well at the music contest.

In this example, the adverb *well* is correct because the verb *played* is the word being modified. *Well* answers the question "how?" about the verb. The adjective *good* is incorrect because an adjective cannot modify a verb.

The words *real* and *really* can also be confusing. The two words are not interchangeable in formal speech or writing. *Real* is an adjective that means "true or genuine." *Really* is an adverb that means "truly."

IN SUMMARY

Use adjectives to modify nouns or pronouns.
Use adverbs to modify verbs, adjectives, or other adverbs.

12-1 PRACTICE THE SKILL

In the first blank, label the underlined word *Adj* (adjective) or *Adv* (adverb). In the second blank, write the words modified.

_____ _____ 1. In a marathon the runners do not begin too <u>fast</u>.

_____ _____ 2. The key is a <u>fast</u> finish.

_____ _____ 3. My shoe hung <u>loose</u>.

_____ _____ 4. I tripped on a <u>loose</u> rock.

_____ _____ 5. I leaned against the <u>nearest</u> tree and fixed my shoe.

_____ _____ 6. The other runners came <u>nearer</u>.

_____ _____ 7. As I turned the corner, the others again fell <u>back</u>.

_____ _____ 8. I came into the <u>back</u> entry of the stands and crossed the finish line first.

_____ _____ 9. The runner from France finished <u>later</u> than I.

_____ _____ 10. The <u>later</u> response of the newspaper reporters gave our trainers the credit for our excellent running times.

Fill in each blank with an appropriate adjective or adverb. Avoid the use of *very*.

_____ 1. The students were _?_ excited.

_____ 2. The school gym was decorated _?_ with streamers and banners.

_____ 3. _?_ balloons formed an arch over the doorway.

_____ 4. A _?_ table in the center of the room held colas, sloppy joes, and chips.

_____ 5. Everyone thought that the decorations for the pep rally had been designed _?_.

_____ 6. The students were _?_ for the pep rally to begin.

_____ 7. The coach and the team led cheers _?_.

_____ 8. No one saw the _?_ dog enter the gym.

_____ 9. The dog ran _?_ to the food table.

_____ 10. What happened next was _?_! "Oh, well," said the student body president, "at least the brownies were saved!"

12-3 **PRACTICE THE SKILL**

Underline the correct modifier.

1. Edgar Allan Poe's mystery and suspense stories are written *(good, well)*.

2. Even today, Poe's works remain *(enjoyable, enjoyably)* for old and young readers.

3. Poe was born on January 19, 1809, to actress Elizabeth Poe. Elizabeth's performances on the stage were done *(brilliant, brilliantly)*.

4. When Poe was two years old, his mother became ill and *(eventual, eventually)* died. A rich merchant named John Allan took Poe into his home.

5. Poe's behavior toward Allan was not *(good, well)*, however.

6. In 1827 Poe had a small volume of poetry published *(private, privately)*. His writing career had begun.

7. Poe later married Virginia Clemm; he spoke *(fond, fondly)* of her.

8. Many of the circumstances surrounding Poe's life were not *(good, well)*.

9. Rufus Griswold, Poe's biographer, did not like Poe, and the biography he wrote was *(terrible, terribly)* distorted.

10. On October 8, 1849, Poe died in Washington Hospital. The cause of his death remains *(mysterious, mysteriously)* to this day.

 12-4 REVIEW THE SKILL

Underline the correct modifier. Be able to give a reason for your answer.

1. Tom, your first sermon was *(good, well)*.

2. You spoke *(good, well)* all the way through it.

3. David was feeling *(bad, badly)*, so he couldn't come.

4. I understood your main points. They were *(clear, clearly)*.

5. Pastor Grant *(real, really)* appreciated your help.

6. The sound system crackled *(bad, badly)* at one point.

7. Despite that problem, even the smallest children listened *(good, well)*.

8. Your little brother whispered *(loud, loudly)* that you are a real preacher now.

9. Your sincerity was very *(evident, evidently)*.

10. It was obvious that you studied *(hard, hardly)* for the sermon.

 **Learning Christianly**

Learning how to use adjectives and adverbs correctly can be challenging, and this challenge reminds us that becoming skilled at writing and grammar does not come naturally. Why do you think that learning to communicate well in this world does not come naturally to us?

Double Negatives

In some languages, adding more negative words to a sentence just makes the negative stronger. But in the standard English of today only one negative is used. Using another negative word along with the adverb *not* is an error in usage called a **double negative**. One of the negative words should be eliminated.

Negative comes from a Latin root that means "to say no."

> **Wrong:** I do*n't* have *nothing.*
> **Right:** I do*n't* have anything.
> I do *not* have anything.
> I have *nothing.*

page 128

Adverbs

> When a sentence with the word *some* is made negative, *some* is replaced with *any.*
>
> Examples:
> 1. Norman bought *some* ice cream.
>   Norman didn't buy *any* ice cream.
> 2. We have *some* new books.
>   We don't have *any* new books.

Adjectives and Adverbs in Comparisons

Many adjectives and adverbs have comparative and superlative forms. Be careful to use these forms correctly. Use the **positive form** when you are describing only one thing or action. Use the **comparative form** *(er* or *more)* when you are comparing two things or actions. Use the **superlative form** *(est* or *most)* when you are comparing three or more things.

> **Comparative:** Paco is older than his friend Kai.
> **Superlative:** He is not the oldest boy in his class, however.
> **Comparative:** We often eat lasagna, but we eat spaghetti more often.
> **Superlative:** We eat pizza most often.

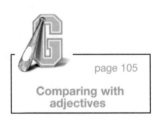

page 105

Comparing with adjectives

Be sure to avoid **double comparisons.** A double comparison is a usage error similar to a double negative. You can correct the error by eliminating one of the comparative or superlative words.

> **Wrong:** Is the cheetah the *most fastest* animal on earth?
> **Right:** Is the cheetah the *fastest* animal on earth?

page 134

Comparing with adverbs

Do not use another negative word with the adverb *not*.

Use the **comparative form** of a modifier to describe two things or actions.

Use the **superlative form** of a modifier to describe three or more things or actions.

Do not use *more* or *most* with a modifier that ends in *er* or *est*.

12-5 PRACTICE THE SKILL

Underline the correct modifier.

1. Jerry doesn't know *(nothing, anything)* about computers.

2. Jayne, however, thinks that using a computer is *(more better, better)* than using a typewriter.

3. Computers are often *(quieter, more quieter)* than typewriters.

4. A regular typewriter cannot do *(no, any)* graphics.

5. Because a computer usually has a spell checker, it is *(more helpful, helpful)* to poor spellers than a standard typewriter.

6. Jayne says that one cannot store *(no, any)* information in a standard typewriter.

7. Jerry and Jayne took a computer class together. Jerry said that Jayne did better because she is *(more smarter, smarter)* than he is.

8. Of all the students in the computer class, Jayne was in the computer lab *(more frequently, most frequently)*.

9. The time she spent in the lab was worthwhile. Jayne did not have *(any, no)* mistakes on her homework assignments.

10. Jayne thought that the computer class was the *(more beneficial, most beneficial)* of all her classes for that semester.

Underline the correct modifier. Be able to give a reason for your answer.

1. I think that I did *(well, good)* on my literature test.

2. I studied for this test *(most diligently, more diligently)* than I did for the first test.

3. I did not waste *(no, any)* time in beginning to study for the test.

4. I *(most often, more often)* study in the library.

5. It is a good idea to begin studying for a test *(most immediately, immediately)*.

6. *(Often, Oftener)* my mom wants me to study right when I get home from school.

7. I eat a snack in the kitchen since I am not allowed *(no, any)* food in my bedroom.

8. Mom rarely says that she doesn't have *(anything, nothing)* for my afternoon snack.

9. My *(favorite, most favorite)* snack is hot cookies.

10. Mom makes the *(best, bestest)* milk-chocolate cookies ever!

Cross out any incorrect adjective or adverb. Write the correct word above it.

1. Of all the structures in the world, the Eiffel Tower may be the most famousest.

2. It is situated beautiful against the Paris skyline.

3. The tower's builder, Alexandre Gustave Eiffel, did a well job.

4. At 984 feet, the Eiffel Tower stood more taller than any other structure in Paris at the time.

5. The tower contained 12,000 metal parts, and each part was numbered separate for easy assembly.

6. The tower was planned real well; most of the 2.5 million rivets were installed ahead of time.

7. Because of good prior planning, the project proceeded smooth, and not no one was killed in the building process.

8. The tower was completed relatively quick—in just twenty-six and a half months.

9. The tower's builder also designed many other structures good; the framework for the Statue of Liberty is another of his most great creations.

10. Because it is so well built, the Eiffel Tower moves only minimal, even in hurricane-force winds.

Locate and correct the twenty-four errors in the paragraph: subject-verb agreement errors, pronoun-antecedent agreement problems, pronoun usage problems, and adjective/adverb usage problems.

Dolphins are close associated with whales and porpoises. Dolphins has lungs, so it must surface regular to breathe air. A dolphin grasps it's prey with a beaklike snout with as many as two hundred cone-shaped teeth. Dolphins swallows they're prey of fish and squid whole. Dolphins often travels in groups, and it plays and hunts food together. Its sense of hearing is sophisticated. They also communicates among itself. Dolphins uses different sounds to mean different things. The entire surface of its bodies have a keen sense of touch. Their vision are good, but he has no sense of smell. All of their senses functions above and below the water. The chief enemy of dolphins are sharks. The killer whale, a kind of dolphin, and the bottle-nosed dolphin is the dolphins most frequently trained for aquariums and zoos. They shows the most apparent friendliness toward people.

_____

_____

_____

_____

_____

_____

_____

_____

_____

_____

_____

Explaining the Rules of a Game or Sport

> Therefore all things whatsoever ye would that men should do to you, do ye even so to them.
>
> *Matthew 7:12*

What happens when your friends talk you into playing a game that you don't really understand? It is frustrating at first, isn't it? You wish someone had taken the time to explain *beforehand* that those blank tiles could stand for any letter or that you should have saved your *z* tile for the triple letter score space on the board. Becoming skilled at explaining the rules of a game will enhance both your enjoyment of games and your friends' enjoyment of those games.

Your Turn

Write an overview and directions for a simple game such as Hangman or Ticktacktoe.

Planning

Choose a game that you know how to play. Be sure that you understand the game and directions well. How can you hope to explain what you do not know? Let's consider the game of Draw Two.

Determine what information is necessary and what can be picked up as the game is actually played. Stick to the necessary information. Do not overload the reader with more information than he needs. Some things about a game are learned best by doing them.

> In the game of Draw Two, experience will teach the player the best strategy for building words that contain a large number of points. (Each letter tile includes a number representing its point value.) Using words that contain many vowels will often restrict his ability to make other words later on.

Define any unfamiliar terms. Most games have their own language. These terms may be familiar to you but will be unclear to someone who does not know the game.

> The terms used in Draw Two are common ones: *tile* is the only new term, and it refers to the individual letter pieces from the Scrabble game.

Use comparisons to familiar games if possible. These details give the reader a reference point.

> Discussing Draw Two in the context of the familiar game of Scrabble makes the new game easier to understand. The goal, rules, and scoring of Draw Two are all similar to Scrabble.

Drafting

Organize your instructions logically. Do not assume that the other person knows what you know or can figure out what you mean. In fact, you will often be better off to assume that the reader knows little if anything about the game.

Be clear and precise. As with any explanation, the goal is to be understood by the other party. Often one aspect of the game depends on another, so understanding the game as a whole is impossible if one part remains unclear.

Give an overview of the game. An overview is often helpful since it allows the reader to have a context for the details that you will give him. Include the goal of the game and any materials needed.

> Draw Two is a word game similar to Scrabble. Using the Scrabble tiles, each player will construct his own crossword-shaped puzzle similar to the one large puzzle made in a regular Scrabble game. Scoring for the games uses the same principles as the Scrabble game.

Write your directions. Cover the entire game in a logical fashion. The best approach is to explain the game chronologically, from start to finish. Look at the directions for the Draw Two game.

> Lay all the tiles from any Scrabble game face down in the middle of the playing surface. Have each player draw seven tiles and turn them over in front of him. When everyone has his tiles, play begins. Each player creates his own crossword-puzzle shape as in a regular Scrabble game, trying to use all his tiles. As in Scrabble, using a letter both horizontally and vertically will result in a higher score since the letter then counts twice.

> As soon as one player uses all seven of his tiles in proper form, he shouts, "Draw Two," and all the players must then draw two tiles from the pile regardless of the number of tiles they still have to use from the first draw. Play continues until all the tiles have been drawn from the pile and a player has used all his tiles.

> If necessary, a player may rearrange any or all of his puzzle at any time in the game. If at any time no player is able to use all his tiles, the players may agree to draw two tiles each from the pile.

> When the game ends, count the number of points earned by each player. The easiest way to tally each player's score is to count all horizontal words and then all vertical words. Subtract any unused tiles from each player's score. The game continues until a player reaches a predetermined number of points, such as five hundred.

Demonstrate any part of the game that you can. Examples help us to learn more easily. Lay out a sample of your puzzle before play actually begins to help the reader visualize his goal. Notice the example of the Draw Two puzzle.

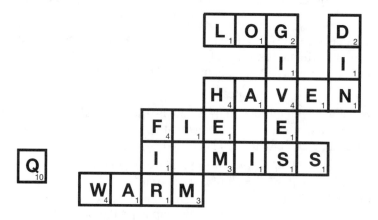

Scoring the sample puzzle will help as well.

Horizontal score: 42

Vertical score: 27

Total: 69

Unused Q: -10

Total   59

Playing a practice round of the game, if possible, will also help the players understand the game without the pressure of competition. A visual demonstration can be worth a thousand words of explanation.

Revising

Look carefully at your directions. Did you identify your game in the opening sentence of the directions? Do your instructions follow a logical pattern? Have you defined any terms that are unfamiliar to the reader? If you find any problems, rework those steps in your explanation of the game.

Proofread your directions. After you have incorporated revisions and changes in your directions, check your work for errors in grammar, spelling, and mechanics.

Make a clean copy of your assignment. Incorporate any corrections that you identified in the proofreading stage. Make your final copy.

Publishing

Exchange directions with a classmate and play that person's game. Play the game exactly according to the directions written by the other person. Evaluate the directions for the game as you play.

Publish a book of games. Compile the directions for each student's game into a booklet. This booklet can be a source for many hours of enjoyable activity.

Would that title mean saying something two times or three? The real answer is three. When you restate something, you are saying the same thing twice. When you add the word *again,* then, that would make three times. If you were meaning only two times, then *restating again* is a *redundancy.*

How are the following phrases redundancies?
- nine A.M. in the morning
- unfilled vacancy
- a good improvement
- the honest truth
- a terrible disaster
- a free gift
- the exact same thing

You create a redundancy when you use unnecessary words.

Redundancies make your writing difficult to follow and hard to understand. Try to eliminate them totally and completely from whatever you write or author.

Between Innings

Grand Slam: Writing Across the Curriculum

Below are the words from a famous hymn that we often sing. Because the words are so familiar to us, we may not think about their meaning. Read through a few of the lines from the song.

> Long may our land be bright
> With freedom's holy light;
> Protect us by Thy might,
> Great God, our king!

What do these lines mean to you? Think about two words from these lines: "freedom" and "protect." Write about what freedom means to you or what you may see is happening to freedom in America at this time.

CHAPTER 13

USING TROUBLESOME WORDS CORRECTLY

"The difference between the *almost*-right word and the *right* word is really a large matter—it's the difference between the lightning bug and the lightning." Mark Twain made this statement in a letter to a friend.

What words would you say are lightning bugs? Which are lightning? Many times the answers depend on the effect you want your writing to produce. Writers who produce "lightning" know how to choose the most striking words and how to keep the troublesome words in a jar.

Using Troublesome Words Correctly

Pairs of words that have similar spellings or pronunciations are often confused and used incorrectly. Often these words have similar meanings as well, making their correct use even more difficult. The following list gives definitions and examples for some commonly confused words.

Troublesome Verbs

There are three pairs of verbs that are to many people especially confusing. The confusion most often comes from mistaking a transitive verb for an intransitive verb. Knowing the principal parts of these verbs will help you to use them correctly.

page 53

Transitive and
Intransitive verbs

Lie/lay

When the verb *lie* means "to recline," it never has a direct object. It is an intransitive verb, used only in the S-InV sentence pattern.

                S InV
lie: Every day now, I **lie** on the sofa.

              S InV
lay: Yesterday I **lay** on the sofa.

           S   InV
lain: I **had lain** on the sofa for half an hour when you called.

The verb *lay* means "to put or place." It is a transitive verb; therefore, it takes a direct object.

S TrV   DO

lay: Every day now, I **lay** the book on the table.

S TrV   DO

laid: Yesterday I **laid** the book on the table.

S TrV   DO

laid: I **had laid** the book on the table before you came.

Rise/raise

The verb *rise* means "to go up." It is an intransitive verb.

S   InV

rise: The balloon **rises** gracefully.

S InV

rose: It **rose** yesterday.

S   InV

risen: It **has risen** before.

The verb *raise* means "to make something go up." It is a transitive verb.

(Aux) S TrV   DO

raise: Does she **raise** violets?

S   TrV   DO

raised: She **raised** roses for many years.

S   TrV   DO

raised: She **has raised** other plants also.

Sit/set

The verb *sit* means "to be in a seated position." It is an intransitive verb.

S InV

sit: Every day now, I **sit** at the piano.

S InV

sat: Yesterday I **sat** at the piano.

S InV

sat: I **had sat** at the piano for more than an hour without playing the same song twice.

The verb *set* means "to put or place." It is a transitive verb.

S TrV   DO   DO

set: Every day now, I **set** the cup and saucer on the shelf.

S TrV   DO   DO

set: Yesterday I **set** the cup and saucer on the shelf.

S TrV   DO   DO

set: I **had set** the cup and saucer on the shelf, but they fell off.

Underline the correct verb.

1. This morning I *(rose, raised)* at six o'clock.

2. I usually *(lay, lie)* in bed for a few minutes, but this morning I got out of bed right away.

3. I *(rose, raised)* the window and was glad to see that it was not raining. The first day of our vacation was starting out well.

4. I took my suitcase outside and *(sat, set)* it beside the car.

5. My cat *(lay, laid)* on the sofa and watched us getting ready to leave. She looked worried.

6. I *(lay, laid)* my jacket beside her, and she curled up inside it.

7. My dad *(set, sat)* the last of the suitcases inside the trunk of the car.

8. My sister Leissa and I were going to *(set, sit)* on the back seat of the car.

9. Earlier, I *(had lain, had laid)* a book on the back seat. I can usually read in a car.

10. The sun *(had raised, had risen)* by the time we left for our trip to Quebec.

11. By the time we arrived in Quebec, Leissa and I were tired. We *(had sat, had set)* in the car for ten hours.

12. In the hotel room, we *(set, sat)* the suitcases down on the floor by the closet door.

13. I *(laid, lay)* down on one of the beds and took an hour-long nap.

14. While I was sleeping, the rest of the family visited Aunt Meg. She is a horticulturist who likes to *(raise, rise)* unusual plants in her garden.

15. When Leissa and my parents returned to the hotel, the sun had already *(set, sat)*. Everyone was happy, and I knew that I was going to enjoy my first trip to Quebec.

Learning Christianly

While struggling to learn the difference between *lie* and *lay* or *sit* and *set*, some students complain that they are working to learn something that doesn't matter very much. "Everyone I know talks this way. Why learn something that nobody else finds important?" If a friend of yours asked you that question, how would you respond? Remember to "think Christianly."

**Circle each incorrect verb and write the correct verb on the blank.
Write *C* if the sentence is correct.**

_____ 1. On warm summer evenings, my grandfather and I liked to set for hours on the back porch.

_____ 2. The roses my grandfather had carefully risen looked beautiful in the moon's silver light.

_____ 3. On many evenings my grandmother would come out and sit down two tall glasses of cool, freshly squeezed lemonade.

_____ 4. Sometimes I would walk out onto the lawn. There I would lie flat on my back and look up at the stars.

_____ 5. Often my grandfather would raise from his chair and walk out to where I was lying. He told me the names of some of the constellations.

_____ 6. In the distance I could see the chicken coop. My grandmother had risen chickens for many years.

_____ 7. On evenings that my grandmother joined us, my grandfather would raise from his chair, go out into the yard, and cut off a rose from one of the bushes. He would place it in Grandmother's lap.

_____ 8. Now I am older, and I watch my own children lying on the lawn where I had laid.

_____ 9. Now I sit and show my children some of the same constellations my grandfather showed me.

_____ 10. Other times, though, I remain on the porch and allow myself to lie aside the cares of the day and to think back to the quiet, peaceful summer evenings with my grandfather and grandmother.

Other Troublesome Words

Some words have a pronunciation, spelling, or meaning that is similar enough to another word to cause confusion. Other troublesome words are nonstandard forms or misspellings of other words. Be sure that you can use these words correctly.

page 111

Articles

a/an: *A* is used only before words that begin with a consonant sound.
An is used before words beginning with a vowel sound.

She lit **a** candle.
She searched with **an** anxious heart.

accept/except: *Accept* is a verb that means "to receive"; it is never a preposition.
Except is a preposition that means "not including."

All of the winners **except** one will **accept** their prizes at the awards ceremony.

ain't: *Ain't* is a nonstandard contraction for *am not.* Replace *ain't* with *am not, is not, are not, have not, has not,* or an accepted contraction, such as *isn't, aren't, haven't,* or *hasn't.*

Wrong: I **ain't** going to the parade tomorrow.
Right: I **am not** going to the parade tomorrow.

alot/a lot: *Alot* is not a word; it is a misspelling of *a lot.*

Wrong: She has **alot** of snacks left over from last night's party.
Right: She has **a lot** of snacks left over from last night's party.

alright/all right: *Alright* is not a word; it is a misspelling of *all right.*

Wrong: Yes, he fell; but he is **alright.**
Right: Yes, he fell; but he is **all right.**

between/among: *Between* is a preposition generally used when comparing just two items or people.
Among is a preposition used when comparing three or more items or people.

He divided the money **between** the two boys.
The students in the class divided the work **among** themselves.

Underline the correct word.

1. Lady Ellesdayle decided to hold *(a, an)* party.

2. The daughters of her poor neighbors eagerly *(accepted, excepted)* the invitation that Lady Ellesdayle had kindly extended to them.

3. All of the daughters were going *(accept, except)* Margaret, who was too young to attend a party.

4. Margaret pouted and said, "It *(ain't, is not)* fair that I cannot go to the party."

5. Camisha and Elizabeth hoped that their Sunday dresses would be *(alright, all right)* to wear.

6. Camisha, Elizabeth, and Mary each wished that she could have a new dress, but they knew that their parents did not have *(alot, a lot)* of money.

7. To decorate their dresses, the three girls divided some late roses *(among, between)* themselves.

8. Lady Ellesdayle was *(an, a)* elegant lady. She looked beautiful in her blue satin gown.

9. Lady Ellesdayle smiled when she saw the girls. "Thank you for *(excepting, accepting)* my invitation," she said. "I have been wanting to meet my new neighbors."

10. After the party, Lady Ellesdayle allowed the girls to take some leftover cake home with them. As the girls divided the cake *(among, between)* themselves, Camisha said, "I don't think Lady Ellesdayle is snooty at all. She is the nicest person I've ever met."

Circle any incorrect word and write the correct word in the blank.
Write C if the sentence is correct.

_____ 1. In 1957 the Soviet Union launched a unmanned satellite into space.

_____ 2. One month later the space dog Laika received a lot of attention for being the first living creature in orbit.

_____ 3. Soon the United States sent _Explorer I_ into space, and the race among the two nations to send a man into space was on.

_____ 4. Unfortunately, the Americans ain't the ones who won the race.

_____ 5. A cosmonaut named Yuri Gagarin returned to earth alright after orbiting the earth once.

_____ 6. Alan Shepard Jr. excepted the role of being the first American in space.

_____ 7. Shepard was chosen from between his many peers as an aircraft readiness officer for the Atlantic naval fleet.

_____ 8. Alot of people don't realize that Shepard didn't orbit the earth on his first mission.

_____ 9. _Friendship 7_ was manned by astronaut John Glenn, who later became an senator.

_____ 10. From 1969 to 1972, every Apollo mission except _Apollo 13_ (which made an emergency return to earth) landed on the moon.

Homonyms

Homonyms are words that sound the same and may or may not have the same spelling. Many homonyms make confusing pairs of words.

**capital/capitol/
Capitol:** A *capital* is a town or city that is a center of government. A *capitol* is the building in which a state legislature meets. The *Capitol* is the building in Washington, D.C., in which the U.S. Congress meets.

Did you know that St. Paul is the **capital** of Minnesota? Cass Gilbert designed the **capitol** with its large marble dome.
He also designed the Supreme Court Building near the **Capitol** in Washington, D.C.

desert/dessert: *Desert* can be used as a noun to mean "a wasteland" or as a verb to mean "abandon." *Dessert* is a noun indicating a dish, usually sweet, served as the last course of a meal.

Have you ever visited the Mojave **Desert?**
Only a coward would **desert** his comrades in battle.
Chocolate ice cream is my favorite **dessert.**

pain/pane: A *pain* is an unpleasant physical sensation. A *pane* is a piece of glass used in a door or window.

The **pain** in his side could be a symptom of appendicitis.
The softball broke the upper **pane** of the neighbor's front window.

pray/prey: *Pray* is a verb that means "to make an earnest request." *Prey* can be used as a verb to mean "to hunt" or "to victimize" or as a noun to mean "an animal that is hunted" or "a victim."

Hannah **prayed** for a son from the Lord.
Con artists often **prey** on elderly people living alone.
The lion devoured its **prey.**

**principal/
principle:** *Principal* can be used as a noun to mean "a person who holds the highest rank" or as an adjective to mean "main or most important." *Principle* is always a noun that means "a basic truth or guiding policy."

Does the **principal** hire the new teachers?
Who has the **principal** role in this year's school play?
Do you understand the **principles** of geometry?

profit/prophet: *Profit* can be used as a verb to mean "to benefit or earn" or as a noun to mean "a gain or income." *Prophet* is a noun that means "a predictor" or "the interpreter through whom God speaks."

Mark will **profit** from this computer instruction.
She deposited the **profits** from the bake sale in the school's account.
Elijah thought that he was the only **prophet** of the true God.

 PRACTICE THE SKILL

Underline the correct word.

1. Our seventh-grade class has been studying about Pennsylvania. This spring we went to Harrisburg, the *(capitol, capital, Capitol)* of Pennsylvania.

2. The *(capital, capitol, Capitol)* was modeled after the Paris Opera House.

3. The *(principal, principle)* thing people remember about Pennsylvania is that it was in Philadelphia that the United States Constitution was adopted.

4. It was also in Philadelphia that the Continental Congress met to lay down the *(principles, principals)* of government.

5. Benjamin Franklin, who suggested that Congress *(prey, pray)* before each session, lived in Pennsylvania.

6. In Philadelphia, Robert Green invented a popular *(desert, dessert)*, the ice-cream soda.

7. The *(panes, pains)* in the windows of your house may have come from Pittsburgh, Pennsylvania. One of the world's largest glass manufacturers is based there.

8. The third day of our trip, our *(principal, principle)* took us to Gettysburg, where Abraham Lincoln delivered his famous Gettysburg Address.

9. I must admit that I did *(profit, prophet)* from our trip to Pennsylvania.

10. Next year when we study United States government, we will visit the *(capital, capitol, Capitol)* in Washington, D.C.

**Circle any incorrect word and write the correct word in the blank.
Write *C* if the sentence is correct.**

_____ 1. In October, Martine and her family visited Denver. Denver is the Capitol of Colorado.

_____ 2. Elijah Myers and Frank Edbrook were the two architects who designed the capital with its gold-plated dome.

_____ 3. Martine learned that there are two senators and six representatives from Colorado serving at the Capitol in Washington, D.C.

_____ 4. After the tour, the family went to see a Denver Broncos game. Martine did not know much about football, but she did prophet from her parents' explanations during the game.

_____ 5. One of the players broke his leg during the game. He looked as if he was in a lot of pane.

_____ 6. After the game, Martine and her family went to Brown's Palace to get something to eat. Over dessert, they talked about other places to see in Denver.

_____ 7. Martine's mother, an artist, thought that the Museum of Western Art would be the principle place to see.

_____ 8. Martine and her brother, however, did not think that they would profit from such a trip.

_____ 9. The family decided to go to the Museum of Western Art and to the United States Mint. They thought that it would be interesting to learn the principals of moneymaking at the mint.

_____ 10. The family enjoyed their trip to Denver. Before leaving to go home, they preyed for safety in traveling.

More Homonyms and Troublesome Words

role/roll: *Role* is a noun that means "a part or position that an individual plays." *Roll* can be used as a noun to mean "a register or list" or "a portion of bread" or as a verb to mean "to turn over."

He is playing the title **role** in the production of *Hamlet*.
Is your name on my class **roll?**
Roll the bowling ball toward the pins.

stationary/ stationery: *Stationary* is an adjective that means "unmoving." *Stationery* is a noun that means "writing paper."

The large saw at the mill is fastened to a **stationary** stand.
My aunt sent me a letter on beautiful blue **stationery.**

than/then: *Than* is a conjunction used to introduce the second part of a comparison. *Then* is an adverb usually indicating time.

Is Anna older **than** Alison?
Hit the ball and **then** run around the bases.

to/two/too: *To* is a preposition often indicating direction. *Two* is a number word often used as an adjective. *Too* is an adverb that means "also" or "very."

Are you going **to** the store?
Yes, I need **two** onions for this recipe.
Please buy me a banana **too.**
You can't have **too** much fruit in your diet.

wear/where: *Wear* is a verb that means "to have on" or "to damage." *Where* is an adverb indicating place or position.

Did your **wear** your coat?
Long use will **wear** out these shoes.
Where is the library?

were/we're: *Were* is the third-person plural form of the past tense of the verb *be*. *We're* is a contraction of *we are*.

We **were** late for school yesterday.
We're not going to be late today, however.

Underline the correct word.

1. *(Were, We're)* going to put on a production of William Shakespeare's *Macbeth*.

2. Hovsep, who does well in all his speech classes, is playing the leading *(role, roll)*.

3. Candyce printed announcements on good quality *(stationary, stationery)* and posted them in public buildings in the neighborhood.

4. On the evening before opening night, we will have a dress rehearsal and *(than, then)* go to the director's house for fellowship and light refreshments.

5. *(To, Two, Too)* other students and I are working on the stage crew.

6. The Playhouse is the place *(wear, where)* we will be performing the play.

7. Roberto said that he was coming to see the play. Jenni said she was coming *(to, two, too)*.

8. The actors and actresses will *(where, wear)* Shakespearian costumes.

9. We *(were, we're)* pleased with the performance of the cast in past years.

10. I think this play will be better *(than, then)* last year's.

William Shakespeare, Macbeth, *Bob Jones University Classic Players*

Circle any incorrect word and write the correct word on the blank. Write *C* if the sentence is correct.

_____ 1. The editor-in-chief of the Stone Valley Christian School yearbook sent banquet invitations on pale blue stationary.

_____ 2. Debbie decided to go, and Kuri said that she would go two.

_____ 3. Kuri asked Debbie, "Should I wear my blue dress or my green dress?"

_____ 4. Debbie said, "I think your green dress is prettier then your blue one."

_____ 5. The Greene Room was wear the banquet was to be held.

_____ 6. There were assigned tables at the banquet. Debbie whispered to Kuri, "Were sitting at Jack's table!"

_____ 7. Kuri was so nervous about sitting next to the editor-in-chief that she dropped a roll into her soup.

_____ 8. After almost everyone had finished eating, Jack went up too the platform and began giving out awards for the exceptional jobs done by members of the yearbook staff.

_____ 9. Toward the end of the awards ceremony, Jack paused; than he smiled at Kuri. "And in recognition of her hours of hard work, the 'Best Staff Member of the Year' award is presented to Kuri Carrington."

_____ 10. The to girls were excited about Kuri's award and could not wait to tell everyone they knew.

Fill in each blank with the correct word from the chapter. Use the clues given in parentheses.

_____ 1. Detective Piers Templeton _?_ quietly at his desk and listened as his client Majel Flemming told her story. *(to be in a seated position)*

_____ 2. Majel said that she had _?_ the emerald ring on the dresser. When she awoke from her nap, the ring was gone. *(to put or place)*

_____ 3. The emerald ring was worth _?_ of money. *(much)*

_____ 4. Majel wanted Piers to discover who _?_ the twelve guests had stolen the ring. *(comparing three or more people or objects)*

_____ 5. Although Majel did not have the money to pay his fee, Piers decided that he would not _?_ his client. *(abandon)*

_____ 6. Piers went _?_ the house where the theft had taken place and began to investigate. *(indicates direction)*

_____ 7. Piers asked each of the guests, "_?_ were you yesterday about four o'clock in the afternoon?" *(indicates place or position)*

_____ 8. Majel's room was dark when Piers entered. He _?_ a blind to let in some light. *(make something go up)*

_____ 9. Piers looked carefully at the crumpled pieces of paper in the trash can. There was a letter written on _?_ that had an insurance company's letterhead. *(writing paper)*

_____ 10. Piers discovered that Majel would actually _?_ from the theft. The insurance company would pay $500,000 in case of theft. *(to benefit)*

_____ 11. Piers also knew that all of the other guests' alibis
_?_ backed up by irrefutable evidence. *(plural form of the past tense of* be*)*

_____ 12. Piers now knew who had stolen the ring and why. The _?_ thing was to prove that he was right. *(main or most important)*

_____ 13. As he walked in the garden, Piers noticed that some of the soil had been disturbed. There was a small indentation in the soil _?_ two rosebushes. *(comparing two items or people)*

_____ 14. Piers came into the room where Majel was waiting for him and _?_ a small object on the table. It was a soil-encrusted emerald ring. *(to put or place)*

_____ 15. As the police arrested her, Majel learned an important _?_. It never pays to tell a lie. *(basic truth or guiding policy)*

Locate and correct the fifteen errors in the paragraph: subject-verb agreement errors, pronoun-antecedent agreement problems, pronoun usage problems, adjective/adverb usage problems, and errors involving troublesome words.

Cheetahs live mainly in the grassy areas of Africa and are the faster of all animals in short distances. Cheetahs hunt during the day rather then at night. They prefer small pray, such as an young antelope. Cheetahs lay in tall grass and pounce upon they're prey. Alot of times an hyena, leopard, or lion steal the cheetahs' food. The cheetahs' slender bodies and extreme long legs helps them move rapid. They have brownish yellow coats with black spots accept on the throat and underparts. These parts are white. Today, the number of cheetahs are declining; it is hunted for their pelts, and farmland has taken over their habitat.

_____

_____

_____

_____

_____

_____

_____

_____

_____

_____

_____

_____

_____

_____

ANSWERING ESSAY QUESTIONS

Seest thou a man that is hasty in his words? there is more hope of a fool than of him.

Proverbs 29:20

Writing an in-class essay by itself or as part of a test need not be difficult. Think of the steps that a cook would follow in making a fruit pie. Simply make the crusts and then add the filling. Rather than being intimidated by an essay question, you can concentrate on what you know if you use this strategy. Consider the recipe for an in-class essay "pie."

2 crusts, bottom and top:	Topic sentence and summary sentence
Sliced apples or other fruit:	Specific facts
Sugar and flour (for the goo):	Transitions and stylistic aids

Your Turn

Write a one-paragraph in-class essay on one of the following topics:

- Describe your favorite vacation.
- Compare football and soccer.
- Contrast summer and winter or spring and fall.
- Explain why the chapel time at your school is important.

Planning

Analyze the assignment. When you are given a question to answer, read it carefully and make sure that you know what it is asking. Focus on the key terms in the questions, such as describe or explain, compare or contrast. These terms will determine the type of filling your pie needs.

Craft a preliminary topic sentence. The foundation, or "bottom crust," of your essay will be your topic sentence. Use the key words from the assigned topic or the essay question itself and create a statement (rather than a question) to guide you as you plan your answer. During the drafting stage you will refine this statement as a proper topic sentence.

Compile the content of your essay. The content of your essay is the filling of your in-class essay pie. Jot down ideas that you may want to include in your answer. Avoid generalities and be specific. For example, if you are asked to describe your favorite African animal, do not merely say that the cheetah has spots. A leopard also has spots. Tell your reader that although a cheetah has spots as a leopard does, someone can tell the two apart by the dark lines under the cheetah's eyes that make him look at though he has been crying. Details help to fulfill the requirements of the term *describe*. Then consider the ideas that you have written down. If any points do not directly answer the question, delete them.

Drafting

Begin with your topic sentence. The first sentence of your answer should state your main idea clearly. Refine your preliminary topic sentence from the planning stage. If you are given just a topic in class, create a specific topic sentence that indicates what your focus will be. For example, if you are asked to write an in-class essay about dogs, your topic sentence might be "Dogs make great helpers." If the test question asks you to "Describe the

Learning Christianly

Why are writing and grammar taught in the same textbook? Is it just an attempt to combine two topics into one course, like combining physical education and math into one class? Or is there a better reason? Given your familiarity with both writing and grammar, consider the following statement and respond to it: "Learning about grammar doesn't make a student a more effective writer."

process of making a peanut butter and jelly sandwich," your topic sentence might be "Making a peanut butter and jelly sandwich is a simple process." Notice how much of the question appears in the topic sentence.

Develop your supporting sentences. Craft supporting sentences from the details that you recorded earlier. A thorough essay will have at least three complete sentences as filling between the bottom and top crusts. For the topic sentence "Dogs make great helpers," you could give several examples of ways dogs help people. Some dogs help the disabled, some help with work like herding sheep, some help police officers track criminals, and some help the government to stop drug smuggling.

Organize your supporting details. Just as a recipe has a logical order for mixing the ingredients, so your essay should move logically from one idea to another. After you determine the best order for your support, create that "sugary goo" that holds your facts together by using transitions between sentences. Transitions do not need to be complex; use words like *first, next,* and *last* to give a sense of progression to your essay.

End with a restatement of the topic sentence. Like a double-crust pie, a well-written essay also has a "top crust" that concludes the essay by restating the main point. This last sentence of the essay should not repeat the topic sentence exactly. Its purpose is to recap the main idea of the paragraph and to give the reader a sense of completion. Notice the topic sentence, supporting sentences, and restatement in this example paragraph for the following assignment: Explain why baby-sitting is a good job.

> Baby-sitting is a great job. First, it is a good way to earn money. Second, baby-sitting has more variety than most other jobs. You can play outside, eat an ice-cream cone, make fun crafts, or learn a new game all in a few hours. Finally, baby-sitting is an excellent way to learn responsibility. Baby-sitting is one of the best ways to earn money for interesting work and to learn important lessons at the same time.

Revising

Evaluate your paragraph. Did you respond to the essay question? Does your topic sentence guide the paragraph? Did you cover all the points that you intended to cover? Check your facts. Have you been accurate? Do you need more details? Does your concluding sentence restate the main point? If you follow the recipe—understand the question, create a topic sentence, organize your support, write an orderly paragraph, and reinforce your idea— you will have a blue-ribbon essay.

Save some time to proofread. Even if you spend most of your time on planning and drafting instead of revising, be sure to allow enough time to proofread for correct grammar, spelling, and punctuation.

Publishing

Post your essay on a bulletin board. After your paragraph has been evaluated, you may wish to incorporate your teacher's suggestions and then to make a clean copy for display on the classroom bulletin board.

Include your essay in your writing folder. Keep a copy of your answer and your teacher's comments. Review them periodically to understand how to write a more effective essay answer in the future.

Between Innings

When we call an object by the name of something different from itself as a means of comparison, we use a metaphor. For example, you call the device attached to your computer a *mouse*. It's not really a rodent. In fact, it's quite different. But it is similar enough for almost anyone to see the connection.

Sometimes metaphors have been used for so long that we no longer recognize the original connection of unlike things. We hardly stop to think that *table leg* is a metaphor. People in the late 1800s did, however. They even sometimes went so far as to cover the legs with skirts for modesty's sake.

It can be fun to bring an overused metaphor to life again, to make the comparison stand out. What metaphor is at work in the phrase *book jacket?* A publisher putting out a book on formalwear might revive the metaphor with a clever cover.

Grand Slam: Writing Across the Curriculum

To prepare a travel brochure to a real or an imaginary place, fold a white piece of paper ($8\frac{1}{2}$" x 11") in half. Write a real or imaginary place name on the front of the paper. You may wish to use special lettering and to decorate the page with images that would possibly be seen in the place.

Next, open the page to its full size. Look for various pictures to represent the best features of the place and attach them to the inside of the folder. Write a brief description under the pictures to "sell" the idea of taking a trip to your real or imaginary place.

On the back of the folded paper, give information about the climate in the area. State information about what kind of clothing is needed and what kinds of accommodations are available. Give any other information that you believe a person would need in order to have an enjoyable visit. Write a memorable slogan to summarize the reasons someone would choose this place as the ideal vacation spot.

CHAPTER 14

CAPITALIZATION

The photographer took advantage of the setting sun when this photograph was taken. What does the light draw your attention to? It draws your eyes through the cemetery to the church steeple and then up to the brilliantly lit cross. The highest point in the picture is highlighted for visual emphasis.

Language has means of emphasis as well. In English, certain words are capitalized to emphasize their importance. Capitalizing a word is like shining a light on it.

Capitalization

In general, the rule is that we capitalize proper nouns and their abbreviations but that we do not capitalize common nouns. The problem comes when we must decide which nouns are common and which are proper. The rules of capitalization below can help you decide.

page 35

Identifying common and proper nouns

Proper Nouns: People and Places

Names and initials

> **D**ee Anne **D**aly, John **A**. Holmes Jr.

Capitalize words for family relationships when they are used as proper nouns.

> I asked **D**ad for a bicycle for my birthday.

If a word for a family relationship is modified by an adjective, it is not being used as a proper noun and should not be capitalized.

> Do you think your **m**other can fix the sewing machine?
> My favorite **a**unt is Aunt **M**argie.

Personal titles used with a name

> **P**resident Lincoln, **Q**ueen Elizabeth I, **D**r. Ricardo Sanchez, Caren Smith, Ph.**D**.

> (*But:* Do not capitalize titles used in place of a person's name. *The council president wrote a letter to the mayor of the city.*)

Specific geographic names

Countries and continents

> **Z**imbabwe, **A**frica

Cities and states

> Tempe, Arizona

Streets and roads

> Continental Drive, West Maple Avenue (*But:* the road)

Recreational areas

> Superior National Forest, Sea World, Rice Park (*But:* the park)

Bodies of water

> Hudson Bay, Nile River, Pacific Ocean (*But:* the river)

Geographic Features

> Old Faithful, Rocky Mountains, Gobi Desert (*But:* the desert)

Sections of the country or world

> the Panhandle, the Far East

>> (*But:* Do not capitalize direction words when they refer only to the compass directions. *Fred went east on Route 52. Fred lives in the East.*)

Heavenly bodies

> Saturn, the Whirlpool Galaxy, Orion

>> (*But:* Capitalize the words *earth, sun,* and *moon* only when they appear with a list of other heavenly bodies. Never capitalize *earth* when it is preceded by *the.*
>> *Venus, Earth,* and *Mars are closer to the Sun than Jupiter, Saturn,* and *Pluto.*
>> *The moon is shining brightly tonight.*
>> "*The earth is the Lord's, and the fulness thereof; the world, and they that dwell therein*" [*Ps. 24:1*]).

14-1 PRACTICE THE SKILL

Cross out each capitalization error. Write the correction above it.

1. This past summer, Derek's only cousin, jean-paul Fourier, came to visit him.

2. Jean-Paul had come all the way from belgium to visit Anthony.

3. Derek's favorite uncle, Richard fourier, is a neurosurgeon in europe.

4. Derek asked his Dad whether he and Jean-Paul could visit atlanta on a weekend.

5. Derek's father replied, "Yes, and your mother wants to take a family trip to callaway gardens while Jean-Paul is here."

6. While they were in Atlanta, Derek and Jean-Paul went to a planetarium showing. The show focused on mars.

7. Later the boys went to some of the shops on peachtree street.

8. On the way back to the hotel, the boys got lost. They had gone North instead of South on the Street.

9. During the last week of Jean-Paul's vacation, he went with Derek's family to a popular vacation spot near Pine Mountain. While they were there, the family had a picnic by the Lake.

10. After his vacation was over, Jean-Paul told Derek that he had really enjoyed his first trip to the south.

14-2 REVIEW THE SKILL

Cross out any capitalization error. Write the correction above it.

1. Mother's sister, aunt mackenzie leigh, has seen many natural wonders.

2. The grand canyon is a massive rock canyon in Arizona.

3. This Canyon contains huge mesas and valleys.

4. Paricutin, one of the world's youngest volcanoes, is located in mexico city, mexico.

5. The Great barrier reef in queensland, australia, protects the coral sea from invaders.

6. Mt. everest is located in the himalayan mountain range.

7. My Aunt also visited victoria falls in Zimbabwe.

8. In scandinavia, she viewed the Aurora borealis, also known as the northern lights.

9. She has seen many spectacular wonders in the east.

10. Her favorite vacation spot is asia minor, where alexander the great ruled.

Other Proper Nouns

Certain religious terms

Names of religions whether true or false

Christianity, **B**uddhism

All nouns and pronouns referring to the one true God

If you pray to **G**od, **H**e will hear you.

(*But:* Do not capitalize words referring to mythological gods other than their proper names: *The month of June is named for the Roman **g**oddess **J**uno*.)

The words *Holy Bible* or *Bible* and the parts of the Bible and the names of sacred writings of other religions

Gospels, **N**ew **T**estament, **D**euteronomy, **K**oran

Names of large constructions

Buildings and structures

Empire **S**tate **B**uilding, the **G**reat **W**all

Monuments

Vietnam **V**eterans **M**emorial

Aircraft and spacecraft

*S*pirit of *S*t. *L*ouis, *D*iscovery (*But:* **a**irplane, **s**pace shuttle)

Ships

Constitution, Titanic

Trains

the *New Orleans*

Names of organizations and businesses as well as their abbreviations

Businesses

Sears, **GE**, **P**eter's **G**rill

Learning Christianly

Have you ever wondered why we capitalize God's name and any other nouns or pronouns referring to Him? Christians are in a perfect position to explain why we capitalize any name referring to God. Given what you know about God from your study of the Bible, why is it appropriate to capitalize His names?

Brand names of business products

> Ford Mustang, Kleenex (*But:* a Ford car, facial tissue)

Political parties

> Republican Party, GOP

Governmental departments

> Department of Education, EPA

Schools

> Hampton Christian Academy, Winthrop College, UCLA

Clubs

> 4-H Club, Science Club, the Girl Scouts

Members of most organizations

> a Girl Scout, a Democrat

Programs

> Operation Safety

Nationalities, races, languages, and flags

Nationalities

> Koreans, Australians

Races and Ethnic Groups

> Caucasian, Hispanic

Languages

> Latin, American Sign Language

Flags

> the Union Jack, Old Glory

Calendar items

Months

> December

Days

> Sunday

Holidays

> Labor Day

A.D. and B.C.

Notice that *B.C.* (before Christ) properly follows the year and that *A.D.* (*anno domini,* "in the year of the Lord") properly comes before the year.

Socrates died in 399 B.C.
Leif Ericson sailed to Newfoundland about A.D. 1002.

(*But:* Do not capitalize the seasons. *My favorite season is autumn.*)

Historical and special events, documents, and periods

Historical events

Battle of **G**ettysburg, **W**ar of 1812

Special events

Olympics, **W**inter **C**arnival, **A**wards **B**anquet

Documents

Declaration of **I**ndependence, **T**reaty of **P**aris

Periods

Industrial **R**evolution, **M**iddle **A**ges

14-3 **PRACTICE THE SKILL**

Cross out each capitalization error. Write the correction above it.

1. Leia and laura decided to visit washington, d.c., on their vacation.

2. They flew from honolulu, hawaii, on an Airplane. They knew that going by plane would be faster than going by ship, although riding on the ocean liner u.s.s. *emerald* did look like a lot of fun.

3. One of the first places the girls visited was the capitol. While they were there, they visited leia's Cousin, Kumiko Noguchi, who works as an aide to one of the Senators.

4. The girls later went to see the lincoln memorial. A picture of this memorial is stamped on the back of the united states penny, and if one looks carefully enough, one can see the statue of abraham lincoln etched on the coin.

5. Laura and Leia took a stroll down pennsylvania avenue. They wanted to take a tour of the white house.

6. The girls did not see the president or his family while they toured the white house.

7. One of the last places that laura and leia visited was the smithsonian institution's National Museum of natural history. There they saw many fascinating things, such as the beautiful Hope Diamond.

8. Before going home, the girls visited the national zoo. They saw many unusual animals there, including a white tiger.

9. The girls enjoyed their trip, but they were sad when they realized that few of the people involved in the government are christians.

10. They decided to pray each day that god would send more christians into the government and that other government officials would accept christ as their savior.

14-4 **REVIEW THE SKILL**

Cross out any capitalization error. Write the correction above it.

1. This summer a group of us from sonshine christian academy went to france on a mission trip.

2. Most of us were members of the french club, but some were non-members who had studied french in school.

3. Part of our ministry involved handing out French bibles and tracts to the people we met on the Street.

4. Another part of our ministry was opération enfant, a program in which we invited children to bible club.

5. Although many of the french people are catholics, we met people of other religions while we were there.

6. We saw god working in the hearts of many unsaved people, and we led several to christ.

7. We spent one saturday sightseeing in paris. I asked someone to take a picture of us standing in front of the eiffel tower.

8. We also rode the train à grande vitesse, or tgv, a fast-moving train. It was an exhilarating experience.

9. I am interested in the french revolution and was able to find out many interesting things about the revolution while we were in france.

10. Early in october, dr. bernson, our school's administrator, asked several of us to give testimonies of how god had blessed in our ministry in france.

14-5 REVIEW THE SKILL

Cross out any capitalization error. Write the correction above it.

1. christopher columbus was born in the early Autumn of a.d. 1451.

2. Columbus believed that he could reach asia by sailing West across the atlantic ocean.

3. He appealed to Spain's king ferdinand and queen Isabella to give him financial support for the journey.

4. When columbus announced that he planned to use whatever money he gained to recapture Jerusalem from the muslims, he gained the support of many jews, including those who had converted to christianity.

5. Finally, on August 3, 1492, columbus and his crew sailed westward on three ships, the *niña*, the *Pinta*, and the *santa maria*.

6. Columbus had few navigational instruments. He knew how to measure the latitude by the north star, however.

7. On October 12, one of the crew members spotted land. Columbus believed they had reached the islands of the east indies.

8. Columbus called the inhabitants of the islands indians. He did not know he had landed on islands in the caribbean sea.

9. The new world he had discovered was named after another man, amerigo vespucci.

10. Today, however, Americans remember columbus and his discovery every October with a holiday called columbus day.

More Proper Nouns: Titles

Capitalize the first and last words in a title as well as all other important words. Do not capitalize an article, a coordinating conjunction, or a preposition of fewer than five letters unless it is the first or last word in the title.

Newspapers

> *Los Angeles Times*

Literary works

> "**Old China**," *The Scarlet Letter*

Works of art

> *The Thinker*

Musical compositions

> "Nothing **Between My** Soul and the Savior," Handel's *Messiah*

Magazines

> *Reader's Digest*

Television and radio programs

> *Wall Street Week in Review*
> *Morning News Notebook*

Plays

> *Hamlet, The Importance of Being Earnest*

Specific courses of study

> Algebra II, **H**istory 101
> (*But:* His best subject is **a**lgebra. Do you have your **h**istory book?)

14-6 PRACTICE THE SKILL

Cross out each capitalization error. Write the correction above it.

1. Several students from our school class hiked to basin lake.

2. They climbed to the top of twin mountain, the one featured on the front cover of *mountaineer monthly*.

3. A few of the students tried to find some leaves for their science 101 project.

4. Others chose to sit on the edge the of lake and sing hymns such as "this is my father's world."

5. An article appeared in the school newspaper, the *banner*, about their hike in the mountains and their enjoyment of creation.

6. Instead of going to the mountains, some other students purchased tickets to the play *a christmas carol*.

7. The students were excited because they had studied charles dickens's novel in english class.

8. After the play they went to cannini's pizzeria for dinner.

9. Someone picked up a copy of the *evening independent* to read the comics for the day.

10. The newspaper also had a review of the previous night's performance of a christmas carol as well as the symphony orchestra's performance of beethoven's *ninth symphony*.

14-7 REVIEW THE SKILL

Cross out any capitalization error. Write the correction above it.

1. The *literary scholar*, a monthly publication produced by danfield university, has articles of interest for all english students.

2. In its may issue, the *literary scholar* stated that the television show *masterpiece theater* was showing a series based on some of nathaniel hawthorne's short stories.

3. The stories include "ethan brand," "The minister's black veil," and "rappaccini's daughter."

4. The *literary scholar* had a special article on a composer who wrote a song based on "Rappaccini's Daughter." The name of the piece is "beatrice, or the ill-fated lady."

5. At the end of the television series, there will be a two-part dramatization of *the house of the seven gables.*

6. The instructor in our Literature class encouraged us to watch the series.

7. Since nathaniel Hawthorne is one of my favorite writers, I plan to record the entire series on videotape.

8. Our instructor, dr. James Westcott, wrote his doctoral dissertation about Nathaniel Hawthorne.

9. In the Spring semester, Dr. westcott will be teaching an entire class on hawthorne.

10. I am sure that the Course will be very interesting and informative.

Proper Adjectives and Other Words

Proper adjectives

> (*But:* Do not capitalize a word modified by a proper adjective unless the two together form a proper name. *The British Isles are home to many people who are not British citizens.*)

The word *I*

> Breanna and **I** will make the decorations.

First words

In a sentence

> **T**he man said that his favorite poet is Lewis Carroll.

In a line of dialogue

> Then he said, "**H**is best poems are very entertaining."

In a line of poetry

> 'Twas brillig, and the slithy toves
> **D**id gyre and gimble in the wabe:
> **A**ll mimsy were the borogoves,
> **A**nd the mome raths outgrabe.

page 116

Proper adjectives

Certain parts of a letter

The first word and all nouns in the greeting

Dear **A**leta and **F**amily,

The first word in the complimentary closing

Yours truly,

14-8 PRACTICE THE SKILL

Cross out each capitalization error. Write the correction above it.

dear emily and family,

i arrived in london on saturday. all went well except that I had a little trouble with my luggage, which got rerouted to a different plane. The people at the airport were very helpful, though. I guess that british citizens are not so arrogant as we might think. tomorrow I am going to Cumbria, where the english poet william wordsworth grew up. several scenes from Wordsworth's famous poem *The prelude* are set in the area. the first few lines of the poem are

Oh there is blessing in this gentle breeze,
A visitant that while it fans my cheek
Doth seem half-conscious of the joy it brings.

Our cousin matthew said, "some of William Wordsworth's poetry is beautiful." I am planning to travel to stratford-upon-avon also. since I took a special interest in shakespeare while I was a student at yates college, i want to spend some extra time there. At the end of the summer i will return to london to do some leisurely shopping. i hope all is well. I look forward to visiting you this christmas up in frigid new england!

love,

janet

Cross out any capitalization error. Write the correction above it.

dear aletheia,

i could hardly believe it when I saw on the calendar that it is november 7 and i had forgotten your birthday! I hope that it was wonderful. this time of the semester is really busy here at college, so it is no wonder that time is seeming to go by so quickly! In a few weeks I will be taking final exams. the only one that I am really concerned about is my history of world civilizations exam.

I just finished writing a paper about edgar allan poe's poem "the raven." It is a fascinating poem. you may have heard it. The first lines are

> once upon a midnight dreary,
> while i pondered, weak and weary,

poe's poetry and stories are interesting. i remember that you read "the tell-tale Heart" at your recital.

I would write more, but some friends and i are going to the westmoreland mall tonight. Tell mom and dad that I said hello. See you in spokane in a few weeks!

> love,
>
> zoe

Common Nouns Not Capitalized

Some common nouns are often mistakenly capitalized as proper nouns. Do not capitalize common nouns.

Common names of flowers, trees, animals, and birds

> **d**aisies, **o**aks, **c**ollies, **p**arakeets
> (*But*: **A**merican **B**eauty **r**ose, **N**orway **s**pruce, **I**rish **s**etter)

Games, foods, and musical instruments that are not brand names

> **f**ootball, **p**izza, **f**lute
> (*But*: **M**onopoly, **T**otino's **p**izza, **S**teinway **p**iano)

Members of a class or a group that is not a proper name or title

We have fifty seniors this year.
A gaggle of geese flew above us.

14-10 **PRACTICE THE SKILL**

Cross out each capitalization error. Write the correction above it.

A new Group of Students enters senior high school each year. Although some Freshmen struggle with this transition, many enjoy the new opportunities offered. As the school year progresses, Students adjust to tougher academic requirements and find time for Extracurricular activities. The more active students may play on the Basketball team or join a musical Ensemble, while other students may choose to take private Piano lessons, help the Senior class, or work on the Newspaper. Other students may decide to work in the science lab and grow idaho potatoes, beans, or carrot tops. Most students will find some enjoyable activity when they get to Senior High.

14-11 **REVIEW THE SKILL**

Cross out any capitalization error. Write the correction above it.

1. The state of Pennsylvania is located in the middle atlantic region of the country and has various Seasonal attractions.

2. In Winter, a person may wish to visit the pennsylvania farm show, which is held annually in the capital city of Harrisburg; but in summer, a person may wish to visit Harrisburg's surrounding towns and cities.

3. One such town is Hershey, where the aroma from the chocolate factory invites vacationers to enter such restaurants as friendly's and hershey pantry.

4. Some companies that make chocolate get their cocoa beans from various countries on the south american continent.

5. Visitors to the city of philadelphia learn much about American History.

6. Germantown, which is part of Philadelphia, was founded in the late 1600s after people of german heritage arrived in 1683 on the ship *concord*.

7. Benjamin Franklin, who was from Philadelphia, is well known for his books *The Autobiography of benjamin franklin* and *The way to wealth*.

8. Near Philadelphia is longwood gardens, which has one of the most magnificent horticultural displays in the world. There one may see beautiful flowers and shrubs such as the rose of sharon.

9. The capital city, Harrisburg, sits on the banks of the Susquehanna river, which flows into the chesapeake bay.

10. Harrisburg contains places of historical interest, such as the john harris mansion and the william penn memorial museum.

 **14-12 USE THE SKILL**

Cross out each capitalization error. Write the correction above it.

1. In 1852, a group of Pioneers from illinois founded a town that they named Seattle. The town was named after chief seattle, leader of the suquamish and duwamish tribes.

2. today, seattle is the largest city in Washington. It is also the transportation center of the pacific northwest.

3. The City is bordered on the West by Puget sound and on the east by lake Washington.

4. Since World war II, manufacturing has been a major source of seattle's economy. The boeing company is one of the largest aircraft manufacturers in the united states.

5. The well-known producer of video games, nintendo, also bases itself near Seattle. Betty MacDonald, the author of *The egg and i*, lived there too.

6. One of the largest buildings on the west coast is located in this city. It is the seventy-six-story columbia seafirst center.

7. Another famous landmark is the 605-foot-high Space needle.

8. The kingdome, a dome-shaped stadium, was in downtown seattle. The Seattle Seahawks, a professional football team, played there until 1999.

9. Also impressive is the Seattle public library, which has about two million books and operates twenty branches.

10. For a quiet afternoon, one might visit one of the city's three hundred Parks. woodland park has an amusement area, gardens, and a zoo.

14-13 CUMULATIVE REVIEW

Locate and correct the twenty-five errors in the paragraph: subject-verb agreement errors, pronoun-antecedent agreement problems, pronoun usage problems, adjective/adverb usage problems, errors involving troublesome words, and capitalization errors.

The Allies surround the germans until their troops lie stationery and cut off from its supplies. Even though Hitler do not rise the flag of surrender, alot of soldiers dessert rather than fall pray to the Allied guns. May 7, 1945, signify the end of world war II when the Germans sign a unconditionally peace treaty with the allied forces. Because Hitler killed hisself on April 30, General Alfred Jodl signs the treaty for Germany. After six years of pane and suffering, Germany final surrender in Rheims, France. On May 8, Russia requires an second surrender ceremony in Berlin, the capitol of Germany. Most countries, accept those in the Axis powers, calls this day Victory in europe (VE) Day. Around the world, people honor the soldiers who fought good for so many years.

WRITING A BIOGRAPHICAL SKETCH

Josiah was eight years old when he began to reign, and he reigned thirty and one years in Jerusalem. . . . And he did that which was right in the sight of the Lord, and walked in all the way of David his father, and turned not aside to the right hand or to the left.

II Kings 22:1-2

Biography: What does this word mean? According to its roots, *bio* has to do with life (as seen in words like *biology)* and *graph* has to do with writing (as in *calligraphy).* A biography then is the writing down of a person's life. If you look in a library, you will find biographies of all sizes, some as long as six volumes, such as Carl Sandburg's biography of Abraham Lincoln. Obviously, you do not want to write a six-volume biography, nor does your teacher wish to grade it!

So what is a biographical sketch? Just as an artist's small drawing has all the elements of the finished painting to give an idea of the finished work, so a biographical sketch has the elements of biography, but on a smaller scale. The Scriptures give us many biographical sketches. In II Kings 22, for example, just two verses reveal many important facts about King Josiah.

Your Turn

Interview a person whom you admire, such as a parent, a grandparent, a friend, a missionary, or a neighbor. Write a three-paragraph biographical sketch of the person. Include your interview notes with the finished sketch.

Planning

Read some sample biographical sketches. The encyclopedia contains many biographical sketches, and your literature book probably contains a brief biographical sketch about each author. The newspaper obituaries also often contain a type of biographical sketch.

Choose a person to interview. Think of someone that you wish others could know about. You may already know whom you want to interview. If you are not sure, take some time to think about someone whom you admire or respect, someone who has influenced your life, or someone that you particularly like. Primary sources of information are the person himself or people who knew him well. You can usually gather accurate information from these primary sources. Secondary sources—people who knew the people who knew the subject—are often unreliable. Your better choice, therefore, is to choose a subject with whom you can talk in person or by phone or can correspond with. If your subject is someone who has passed away, make sure his acquaintances are people you can contact directly.

Decide what information you want to find out about your subject. First, since you are writing only a short sketch, you must decide what is important; obviously, it would be impossible for you to include every detail of your subject's life. So if the subject is well known, you might focus on how he became well known. For example, Carl Sandburg's wife, Lillian, besides being the wife of that famous poet and biographer and the sister of Edward Steichen, a well-known photographer, was also remarkable in her own right for her business of raising goats. A biographical sketch would mention her important relationships and her personal accomplishments.

Formulate questions that you want to ask. Think of yourself as a journalist: many of the questions that a journalist asks are the questions that you should ask as well.

- **Who:** Find out the subject's full name (ask how to spell it even if you think you know; the spelling of names is notoriously unpredictable). Find out who his parents are and what they do for a living. Find out about his family. Does he have brothers and sisters? Is he married? Does he have children?
- **What:** Ask what the subject does for a living. Find out what he does that is not so well known as well as what he is better known for. What are his goals in life? Remember that the purpose of a biographical sketch is not only to present information in a logical manner but also to educate the reader, so share the little-known facts that you learn through your interview.
- **Where:** Find out the geographical facts associated with the subject. Where was he born? Where has he lived? Where has he traveled?
- **When:** Find out the chronological facts associated with the subject. When was he born? When was he married? When did he begin his career? When did he die?
- **Why:** Find out why the subject chose his career. Why does he think his job is important or worthwhile? Why is he important or interesting?

Include both open-ended and closed-ended questions in your interview. Open-ended questions generate more detailed answers, elicit opinions, allow explanations, provide quotable material, and use *what* and *why*. You might, for example, ask "What do you like about your job?" or "What was your childhood like?" Closed-ended questions elicit facts, provide specific answers (usually one-word answers) and use *when* and *where*. Examples of closed-ended questions are "Where do you work?" and "When were you born?"

Conduct your interview. As you conduct the interview, remember your manners.

1. Respect the time of the one you are interviewing: be on time and stay within the time limits.

2. Write out questions ahead of time, leaving room on your paper after each question to write the answer. Bring a pen to take notes. If possible, bring an audio recorder as well. Taking notes by hand as well as by recorder will eliminate the frustration of losing the entire interview if the recorder does not work.

3. Respect the subject's privacy. If your great-aunt does not want to tell you the year she was born, don't pester her about it!

4. Make sure that you understand the answers to your questions. Clarify any unusual terms that the subject uses and spell them correctly.

5. Make arrangements to contact the subject again in case you need to clarify your notes or have forgotten to ask a question. You might ask, "May I call you again if I have any questions as I write my sketch?" Most subjects will be happy to talk with you again if the need arises.

6. Thank the subject for his time and help. You will want to do so first at the time of the interview and then again a little later by means of a thank-you note.

Drafting

Organize your notes. Chronological order is often effective. For example, you might begin with family background or the person's early life, then move to his preparation (schooling), and then discuss to his career. Topical organization is another way to prepare your sketch. You might write about the person's family background, then his career, and then interesting facts about him or significant quotations from the interview.

Be factual. Remember that a biographical sketch must be accurate. You are reporting the facts about the subject's life; you are not giving your opinions about that person.

Begin writing. Take a close look at the method of organization you have chosen. Set aside a block of time so that you can write without stopping. Follow the organization of your notes.

Revising

Read over what you have written. Have you answered the important *wh* questions about the person your interviewed? Is the organization of your paragraphs clear? Have you been factual in your writing?

Think about the beginning and ending of your sketch. Do the opening sentences catch the reader's attention? Have you used descriptive words that portray your subject clearly? Does the ending of your sketch sum up what you want to say about your subject? Is your reader left with any unanswered questions?

Make a clean copy. Incorporate any changes that you feel are necessary to improve your sketch. Proofread for correctness in grammar, spelling, and mechanics. Then write or print a clean copy to give to your teacher.

Publishing

Send a copy of your sketch to the person you interviewed. Your subject would probably like to know what you have said about him.

Share your sketch with people who know your subject. Friends, relatives, or classmates who know the person you wrote about might enjoy reading your sketch.

Read your sketch orally in class. Your teacher may set aside a class period in order to have an oral portrait gallery. Be prepared to read your sketch as part of the gallery presentation.

CHAPTER 15

PUNCTUATION

A pulley is a machine made of a rope and a wheel. It helps you lift things too heavy for you to lift by yourself. Pulling down on the rope on one side of the pulley will cause the rope on the other side to lift an object. The pulley changes the direction of the force of your pull.

Punctuation marks function something like pulleys. They can change the direction of your sentences. They also make sentences easier to read. Here's one example: "I have to hang up now. A friend just drove over Grandma." This is a terrible tragedy—but only of punctuation. Compare the correctly punctuated sentence: "I have to hang up now. A friend just drove over, Grandma." Good writers realize that proper punctuation, like a pulley, gives sentences a lift.

End Marks

Period

Use a period at the end of a declarative sentence.

> I spoke to Carlyle yesterday.

Use a period at the end of an indirect question.

> He asked me what I said.

Use a period at the end of an imperative sentence that does not express strong emotion.

> Please close the window.

Question Mark

Use a question mark at the end of an interrogative sentence.

> "Who is like unto thee, O Lord, among the gods?" (Exod. 15:11)

Exclamation Point

Use an exclamation point (sometimes called an exclamation mark) at the end of an exclamatory sentence.

> We won the championship game!

Use an exclamation point at the end of an imperative sentence that expresses strong emotion.

> Stop teasing your sister!

Use an exclamation point after an interjection that expresses strong emotion.

> Ouch! I stubbed my toe.

page 3

Sentence types

page 155

Interjections

Insert the correct end mark in each of the following sentences.

1. Has your class learned about the Plymouth Colony, Craig

2. The Pilgrims landed at Cape Cod Bay

3. This area was originally named Plimouth

4. Boy, did they miss their destination of Virginia

5. It took sixty-five days to sail from England to the New World

6. What a trip

7. Before they landed, the leaders composed the Mayflower Compact

8. When did the Pilgrims meet Squanto

9. Yuck! They prepared eel for their first Thanksgiving in 1621

10. Read the next chapter by tomorrow

Label each sentence as declarative, imperative, interrogative, or exclamatory. Add the correct end mark to each sentence.

_____ 1. Have you ever heard the story of Paul Revere

_____ 2. General Gage moved his British troops to Boston in 1774

_____ 3. The British decided to destroy the American patriots' ammunition

_____ 4. How would the patriots know when the British were coming

_____ 5. One patriot would signal by hanging lanterns in the church

_____ 6. Look at the two lanterns

_____ 7. They will be here soon

_____ 8. Tell Paul Revere to warn the people

_____ 9. The British are coming

_____ 10. Because of Paul Revere's warning, the patriots were ready for the British when they arrived in the morning

Other Uses for the Period

A period usually follows an initial or each letter of an abbreviation.

> D. L. Moody (Dwight Lyman)
> Washington, D.C. (District of Columbia)
> M.Ed. (masters in education)

In recent years periods have been left out of some common abbreviations.

> USMC (United States Marine Corps)
> NASA (National Aeronautics and Space Administration)

A period follows the numbers and letters of an outline.

> I. First main idea
>   A. Supporting idea
>   B. Supporting idea
>   1. Supporting detail
>   2. Supporting detail
> II. Second main idea
> III. Third main idea

A period follows the numbers or letters in a list.

> 1. eggs
> 2. bread
> 3. milk
> 4. cheese

A period is used as a decimal point.

> $3.54
> 98.6°F
> 10.5%

Insert any missing periods, question marks, exclamation points, or decimal points in the following sentences.

1. Give me that book on astronauts

2. Did you know that Sally K Ride was the first female U S astronaut in space

3. Sally Ride was born in Los Angeles, California, in 1951

4. Amazing She earned a PhD from Stanford University in physics

5. Did you know that she flew aboard the *Challenger* and the *Discovery* for NASA

6. Wow What an exciting job

7. Have you read her book *To Space and Back*

8. Dr Ride gives an accurate, yet humorous, account of life aboard a space shuttle

9. She dedicated her book to the memory of the astronauts aboard the *Challenger*

10. Can you imagine The *Challenger* had been in the air for only 73 seconds or 12167 minutes before it exploded

Insert any missing periods, question marks, exclamation points, or decimal points.

1. George Washington Carver (or G W.) was born a slave

2. Mrs. Carver taught George how to work in the kitchen and the laundry room

3. Boy Did he ever have a secret touch with plants

4. He received a B S in agriculture from Iowa State College

5. George made many items from peanuts:

   a   axle grease

   b   coffee

   c   face powder

   d   milk.

6. Amazing Who would imagine so many things from a peanut

7. Didn't Carver teach at Booker T Washington's Tuskegee Institute

8. Yes, Thomas A Edison even offered Carver a salary of $175,000 00

9. Did you know that Carver was also a talented painter

10. Carver preferred to work where he could help people

Comma

Commas in a Series

Use a comma to separate three or more items in a series.

> Matthew, Mark, Luke, and John are the four Gospels.
> (*But:* Ruth and Esther are the only books of the Bible named for women.)
> The class read the novel, researched the author, and wrote a report.
> (*But:* The class studied the poem and memorized it.)

A comma sometimes separates two adjectives that modify the same noun. If you can reverse the order of the adjectives or replace the comma with the word *and* without changing the meaning, use a comma.

> A warm, gentle breeze blew off the gulf.
> A gentle, warm breeze blew off the gulf.
> A warm and gentle breeze blew off the gulf.
> (*But:* The new music teacher plays the clarinet.)

Use a comma to separate the first independent clause from the conjunction in a compound sentence. (*Do not use a comma before a conjunction that joins a compound predicate.*)

> The wind is blowing, and the air is cool.
> (*But:* The rain is falling heavily and flooding the streets.)

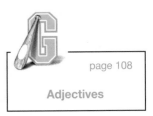

page 108

Adjectives

page 16

Comma splices and
Fused sentences

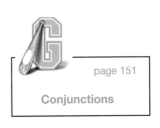

page 151

Conjunctions

page 166

Compound sentences

Insert any missing commas and circle any unnecessary commas in the following sentences. Write *C* to the left of the number if the sentence is correct.

1. Francis Scott Key worked as a prominent lawyer, served as Attorney General, and spoke as an opponent to slavery.

2. Key's strong, confident, and persuasive manner, made him an obvious choice to help Dr. William Beanes.

3. During the night the British soldiers awakened, arrested, and imprisoned Dr. Beanes.

4. Key, and John Skinner boarded the British ship and requested the release of Dr. Beanes.

5. President Madison's letter for release, Key's persuasive speech, and British soldiers' letters convinced the British to give Dr. Beanes freedom. C

6. The British made Dr. Beanes, Francis Key, and John Skinner wait to leave until after the British attack upon Fort McHenry.

7. Key scribbled the words to "The Star-Spangled Banner" as he witnessed the forceful, British onslaught of cannons upon the fort.

8. The fort withstood the attack, and the flag waved in the air. C

9. Francis Scott Key's strong national pride and relief at this comforting, stirring sight resulted in America's national anthem. C

10. The flag flies twenty-four hours a day at Fort McHenry, Key's birthplace, and Key's gravesite.

Insert any missing commas and circle any unnecessary commas in the following sentences. Write C to the left of the number if the sentence is correct.

1. Many, loyal Englishmen opposed the ascension of a foreign Scottish ruler to their throne after Elizabeth's death.

2. James Stuart reigned on the English throne, and the Scottish throne until his death in 1625.

3. The weak, unattractive, and frail Charles became king after his father's death.

4. Historians depict James as greatly immoral, but they describe Charles as quite chaste and ethical.

5. Charles was not impressive to his parents, the Parliament, or the rest of England. C

6. He did finally develop a strong bond with the Duke of Buckingham. C

7. Charles's reign included wars within his country, with France, and with Spain.

8. Charles brought a moral, spiritual, and cultural influence to the court. C

9. He purchased many paintings by Mytens, Van Dyck, and Rubens.

10. The English people never favored Charles, and eventually beheaded him.

Combine each pair of sentences into one sentence. Portions of most of the sentences have been underlined to help you. Be sure to use correct punctuation.

1. Nicaragua lies <u>south of Honduras</u> and <u>north of Costa Rica</u>. Nicaragua lies <u>between the Pacific and Atlantic Oceans.</u>

   _____

   _____

2. <u>The Pacific Lowlands</u> is one of the three geographic regions in Nicaragua. <u>The Central Highlands</u> and <u>the Mosquito Coast</u> are also geographic regions in Nicaragua.

   _____

   _____

3. The <u>beautiful</u> city of Managua is the capital of Nicaragua. The <u>growing</u> city of Managua is the capital of Nicaragua.

   _____

   _____

4. Nicaraguans grow <u>bananas</u> and <u>rice</u>. Nicaraguans grow <u>sugar cane</u> too.

   Nicaraguans grow bananas, rice, and sugar cane.

5. Nicaraguans <u>believe in a male dominant society</u>. The Nicaraguans <u>elected Violeta de Barrios Chamorro as president in 1990</u>.

   Nicaraguans believe in a male dominant society, but they elected Violeta de Barrios Chamorro as president in 1990.

6. The terrain of Nicaragua includes <u>mountains, valleys, and grasslands</u>. There are <u>rain forests</u> in Nicaragua also.

   The terrain of Nicaragua includes mountains, valleys, grasslands, and rain forests.

7. Because of the tropical climate, each year Nicaragua has <u>about sixty inches of rain</u>. Nicaragua has an <u>average temperature of about 80°F</u>.

   _____

   _____

8. Children are required to attend school in Nicaragua until the age of twelve. Many children do not have schools to attend.

_____

_____

9. Granada and León are large cities in Nicaragua. Jinotepe is also a large city in Nicaragua.

_____

_____

10. Most of the people in Nicaragua speak Spanish and farm to earn a living. Most claim Roman Catholicism as their religion.

_____

_____

Commas to Separate

A comma sometimes separates introductory words from the rest of the sentence.

> First, I want to tell you about mainland China.
> However, my slides are of only Taiwan and Hong Kong.

Use a comma to separate an introductory dependent clause from the independent clause in a complex sentence.

> Although the sun is shining, clouds are gathering on the horizon.

Use a comma or a pair of commas to separate a noun of direct address (a noun that names the person being spoken to) from the rest of the sentence.

> Luis, where is your coat?
> Where is your coat, Luis?
> Where, Luis, is your coat?

A comma or a pair of commas sometimes separates an interrupting phrase that could be left out of the sentence.

> Neil Armstrong was an American astronaut, as you know.
> He was, in fact, the first person to walk on the moon.

A comma sometimes separates an interjection from the rest of the sentence.

> Yes, I know the answer.
> Open your book to page 79, please.

page 169

Complex sentences

page 155

Interjections

Insert any missing commas and circle any unnecessary commas. Write C to the left of the number if the sentence is correct.

1. Though not as famous as their fathers, White House children have made their own marks in history.

2. For example, John Quincy Adams became the sixth president in 1825.

3. Esther Cleveland, interestingly enough, was the only child born in the White House.

4. Maria Monroe, on the other hand, receives special honor as the first to have her wedding in the White House.

5. Martin Van Buren's son married the niece of Washington Irving. C

6. In some cases, however, the grandchildren of the presidents lived in the White House.

7. Unfortunately, the White House had not yet been built when George Washington's grandchildren and great-grandchildren lived with him during his presidency.

8. Mary Custis, who was George Washington's great-granddaughter, married Robert E. Lee.

9. The marriage of Julie Nixon and David Eisenhower joined‚ two former White House children.

10. Furthermore‚ President Eisenhower named Camp David, a presidential retreat in Maryland‚ after his grandson David.

15-9 REVIEW THE SKILL

Insert any missing commas and circle any unnecessary commas. Write C to the left of the number if the sentence is correct.

1. Have you ever gone ice skating‚ Bob?

2. Well‚ we should go to a skating rink sometime soon.

3. Even though most of the skilled skaters started young, people of all ages can learn. C

4. Some kids‚ however, start when they are two‚ or three years old.

5. Standing, walking‚ and stopping are some of the basic skills in skating.

6. After mastering these skills, skating backwards‚ some say, is not very difficult.

7. Ice skating‚ with the invention of indoor skating rinks, can be enjoyed all year long.

8. To create a smooth surface Frank Zamboni invented the Zamboni. This machine resurfaces the ice. C

9. Even though a Zamboni costs up to $50,000‚ it can last ten, twenty‚ and even thirty years.

10. I would love to drive a Zamboni sometime, but I will probably never get a chance. C

Commas with Quotations, Dates, and Addresses
Commas in Letters

In a written dialogue a comma separates the direct quotation from the rest of the sentence.

> Magda asked, "What is the reference for the verse that says that all have sinned?"
> "It's Romans 3:23," Mr. Cooper replied.
> "Which verse," Jaime asked, "teaches us to obey our parents?"

In a date a comma separates the day from the year.

> May 11, 1858

A comma also follows a date within a sentence when the year is also given.

> She was born March 2, 1969, in Baltimore.
> (*But:* She was born March 2 in Baltimore.)

In an address a comma separates the city from the state or country.

> New Brighton, Minnesota
> Tokyo, Japan

A comma also follows a state or country when the city is also named within a sentence.

> Oslo, Norway, is his favorite European city.
> They went to Seattle, Washington, for their vacation this summer.
> (*But:* They went to Seattle for their vacation this summer.
> They went to Washington for their vacation this summer.)

A comma does not separate the state from the ZIP code in an address.

> Mr. Brad Abercrombie
> 2 Audley Lane
> Chapel Hill, North Carolina 27514

Use a comma after the greeting of a friendly letter and the closing of all letters.

> Dear Ronda,
> Sincerely yours,

Insert any missing commas and circle any unnecessary commas in the following letter.

628 West Main Avenue

Fredericksburg, OH, 44627

June 15, 2000

Dear Tim,

Thanks for writing me back. It sounds like you are learning a lot about living in Africa. My teacher told us that on May 31, 1961, South Africa became a republic. I would like to learn more about this country.

People at church miss you. They ask me to tell them how you are doing. Mrs. West, asked, "Have you heard from Tim yet?" "Yes," I said, "I get a letter from him every month." I told her all about the elephants you saw on the reserve.

I cannot wait to see you in August. (Don't forget that August, 27 is my birthday!) Mom said we would be able to pick you up at the airport.

I hope you will write to me soon. I will be in Austin, Texas, during the month of July. You can send a letter to me at 4523 Sullivan Lane, Austin, TX 43211-4567.

Please write soon!
Your friend,

Kristen

Kristen

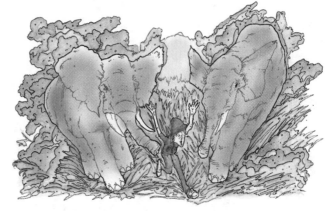

Insert any missing commas and circle any unnecessary commas.

B.P. 252

Koussui, Cameroon

West Africa

July, 11, 2000

Dear Kristen,

Thank you for your friendly, informative letter. It is always good to hear from the USA.

I read the biographies of C. T. Studd, David Livingstone, and Mary Slessor, and learned much from their experiences. In 1841, David Livingstone became a missionary to Africa. When Mary Slessor heard that Livingstone had died, she told her mother, "I want to offer myself as a missionary." Within two years, Mary was in Africa.

I plan to arrive in Boston on August 12. First, I want to eat a hamburger! After that, I would like to visit our friends from church. I look forward to seeing you.

In Him,

Tim

Tim

Semicolon

A semicolon sometimes separates two independent clauses in a compound sentence.

> Ravi cooked the meal and set the table; his sister washed the dishes.

Colon

Use a colon to separate the chapter from the verse in a Bible reference.

> Isaiah 40:8

Use a colon to separate the hour from the minutes in a statement of time.

> 9:45 A.M.

Use a colon after the greeting of a business letter.

> Dear Mr. Noguchi:

Use a colon to introduce a list after an independent clause.

> You must assemble these ingredients for lemonade: lemons, sugar, and water.

page 166

Compound sentences

 **15-12 PRACTICE THE SKILL**

Insert any missing semicolons or colons in the following sentences. Write C to the left of the number if the sentence is correct.

1. Joseph was a wise leader he saved Egypt as well as other countries from starvation.

2. Joseph's story begins in Genesis 37 1.

3. Joseph's responsibilities included the following assisting the pharaoh, collecting 20 percent of the surplus grain, and storing the grain for the time of famine.

4. Joseph was prepared to be a good administrator he had learned necessary skills by being a faithful slave and prisoner in Egypt.

5. When the years of famine came, the country was adequately prepared.

6. All the people came to Joseph for food he was prepared to help them.

7. Joseph sold the grain to the people and saved them from starvation.

8. Not only the Egyptians were saved by Joseph's foresight other people suffering from the famine came to Egypt to see Joseph.

9. One group of visitors came to buy food, and Joseph realized that they were his brothers.

10. Joseph's wisdom helped many people he saved his own family from starvation.

15-13 REVIEW THE SKILL

Combine the following sentences using either a comma and conjunction, a semicolon, or a colon.

1. General Thomas "Stonewall" Jackson graduated from West Point. He was one of America's greatest military leaders.

   _____

   _____

2. Jackson demonstrated admirable character qualities. He demonstrated loyalty, dependability, and courage.

   _____

   _____

3. Jackson wanted to keep the Union together. He fought for the Confederacy in the Civil War.

   _____

   _____

4. Jackson was a religious man. He became a Christian when he was a young man.

   _____

   _____

5. He loved the Scriptures. He read his Bible frequently.

   _____

   _____

6. He showed his concern for his troops in several ways. He read the Scriptures to them, preached to them, and prayed for them.

   _____

   _____

7. He seemed to fear nothing in battle. He had great fear and respect for God.

   _____

   _____

8. Jackson was involved in numerous battles. He was involved in Bull Run, Richmond, and Antietam.

   _____

   _____

9. In the First Battle of Bull Run, Jackson and his troops stood firm. Another general cried, "There is Jackson standing like a stone wall."

   _____

   _____

10. Stonewall Jackson died on May 10, 1863. Both the North and the South mourned his death.

    _____

    _____

Insert any missing semicolons or colons in the following sentences. Circle any unnecessary semicolons, colons, commas, end marks, or decimal points.

November 9, 2000

Grace Flanders

5703 Washburn Road

Vassar, MI 48768

Dear Miss Flanders

Thank you, Miss Flanders, for the article you submitted entitled "Holiday Helpers." We are happy to inform you that "Holiday Helpers" will be featured in the December issue of *Your Voice.*

For the use of your article, we would like to present you with a free issue of *Your Voice.* In addition, you may choose one of these three books for only $5.00 *Writing as a Craft, The English Manual for the Writer,* or the *Oxford English Dictionary.*

Your Voice would also like to invite you personally to be a guest at our next writers' banquet. The banquet will be held at Helena Hotel in Helena, Montana. Our theme verse for this year's banquet is I Corinthians 1440. The banquet will begin at 700 P.M. on the night of January 15, 2001. At 800 P.M. we will gather in the conference room for a fascinating workshop on the topic "Organizing Your Written Work." You may attend a second workshop the following morning, before you leave.

We encourage you to continue to submit articles for publication. These are the topics for the month of January: add-on bedrooms, children's sports, and health food.

Once again, thank you for writing. We hope to hear from you again.

Sincerely,

Betsy Kingston

Editor of *Your Voice*

Quotation Marks

Use quotation marks to show words taken from another source.

> John Donne wrote the words "No man is an island."

Use quotation marks to show the words of the speakers in a dialogue.

> "David, did you play miniature golf Saturday?" Tana asked.
> "Yes, but I didn't see you," David answered.
> "I was there with my friend Ann."
> "Oh, I remember her."

Quotation marks are not used with indirect quotations.

> David said that he remembered Ann.

Follow these rules for using other punctuation with quotation marks:

- Always place periods and commas before the quotation marks.

  > He said, "I remember her."
  > David thought for a moment. "I remember her," he said.

- Place question marks and exclamation points either before or after closing quotation marks, according to the meaning of the sentence. If the entire sentence is a question or an exclamation, place the question mark or exclamation point after the quotation marks.

  > Did you hear David say "I remember her"?
  > I can't believe you've never read "Birches"!

- If only the quotation is a question or an exclamation, place the question mark or exclamation point before the quotation marks.

  > Lane asked, "Do you smell smoke?"
  > "The house is on fire!" he exclaimed.

- Notice that no period or comma follows a question mark or an exclamation point.

Quotation marks are placed around the following kinds of titles.

short stories:	"Rikki-Tikki-Tavi"
chapters:	"Father Speaks"
short poems:	"Paul Revere's Ride"
essays:	"Our Blessed Land"
periodical articles:	"What It's Like When You Can't Read or Write"
songs:	"When I Survey the Wondrous Cross"
television or radio episodes:	"Charlie Coulson: Drummer Boy"

A. Insert any missing quotation marks.
B. Circle any misplaced quotation marks.
C. Write C if the sentence is correct.

1. When asked if he could tell a sinner how to get to heaven, Dr. Walter Wilson would reply, Yes, that is my principal business in life.

2. One time, Dr. Wilson was to board a train on June 28; however, because he had not received his ticket, he could not board the train until July 3.

3. A woman on the train saw Dr. Wilson reading his Bible and asked, "May I sit with you?

4. When Dr. Wilson looked up to see a woman dressed in mourning clothes, what do you think he said but "Certainly?"

5. "Is there something I can help you with"? Dr. Wilson asked.

6. The woman asked him, "Can you help me find Jesus?"

7. Let's see what God has to say", replied Dr. Wilson.

8. After reading verses from God's Word and praying, the woman exclaimed, "I know now that my Savior has taken away my sins!

9. The woman told Dr. Wilson, I had planned to board this train on June 26, but my sister became ill, and my trip was delayed until July 3.

10. Dr. Wilson prayed, "Thank you, God, for showing me the reason for the delay.

15-16 REVIEW THE SKILL

A. Insert any missing quotation marks.
B. Circle any misplaced quotation marks.
C. Write *C* if the sentence is correct.

1. Rachel looked at her new baby sister through the nursery window and exclaimed, "She's beautiful"!

2. The doctor told Rachel's mother ", She has a collapsed lung; we will watch her for a few days."

3. Every day, Rachel visited her mother in the hospital and asked, May I hold Hannah?

4. Her mother replied, She must grow stronger lungs first; then we may hold her.

5. The doctor told Rachel's mother that Hannah must stay in the hospital one more night.

6. What else could Rachel and her mother do but pray, "God, please help Hannah's lungs?"

7. The next morning, the doctor told Rachel's mother, "Hannah may go home today.

8. "Yea!" Rachel shouted.

9. Rachel asked her mother, "May I hold Hannah today"?

10. "Yes, today you may hold Hannah", replied Rachel's mother.

Underlining for Italics

In handwritten or typed papers, the following items are underlined. In printed books they are in italics.

Words and letters being discussed

How many i's are in the word <u>impossibility</u>?
How many *i*'s are in the word *impossibility*?

Names of large vehicles

ships:	*Mayflower*
planes:	*Spruce Goose*
trains:	*Orient Express*
spacecraft:	*Apollo 11*

Titles of long works

books:	*Caddie Woodlawn*
magazines:	*U.S. News & World Report*
newspapers:	*New York Times*
	(The word *the* is not part of a newspaper title.)
musical compositions:	Mendelssohn's *Elijah*
television or radio series:	*Miracles*
plays:	*Romeo and Juliet*

Names of works of art

paintings:	*American Gothic*
sculptures:	*Spoonbridge and Cherry*

15-17 PRACTICE THE SKILL

A. **Insert any missing quotation marks.**

B. **Underline any words that should be in italics.**

C. **Circle any unnecessary quotation marks or incorrectly italicized words.**

D. **Write *C* if the sentence is correct.**

1. "Webster's New World Dictionary" defines an aircraft carrier as "a warship that carries airplanes."

2. In 1922 the first U.S. aircraft carrier was commissioned. It was named the Langley and could accommodate about thirty-five aircraft.

3. David Brown's book, "Aircraft Carriers," reports that the Saratoga, a carrier similar to the Langley, could carry up to ninety aircraft.

4. The article Wheels over Water appeared in a 1939 edition of the "Reader's Digest." This article tells the story of a fighter plane's attempting to land aboard the Lexington during a storm.

5. During the early 1940s, informative articles about aircraft carriers appeared in other leading magazines, such as "Popular Science," "Popular Mechanics," and "Life."

USS *Langley* in May 1928

15-18 | REVIEW THE SKILL

A. **Insert any missing quotation marks.**

B. **Underline any words that should be in italics.**

C. **Circle any unnecessary quotation marks or incorrectly italicized words.**

D. **Write *C* if the sentence is correct.**

1. Many people associate Beverly Cleary's name with a character in her books, Ramona Quimby.

2. However, Ramona was only briefly mentioned in Cleary's first book, Henry Huggins.

3. In the final chapter of her autobiography, My Own Two Feet, Cleary tells of her efforts at writing a book. The chapter is called A House, a Cat, a Letter.

4. "Henry Huggins" began as a short story entitled Spareribs and Henry.

5. Someone encouraged her to add more short stories to "Spareribs and Henry to make one book-length story.

6. One story Cleary added, entitled *The Green Christmas,* was a new version of a short story she had written in high school.

7. Cleary finished her manuscript and sent "Spareribs and Henry," the book, to her publisher.

8. Before her manuscript could be published, Cleary had to change the title from Spareribs and Henry to "Henry Huggins."

9. Other books by Cleary include "Ramona and Her Father," "Ramona Quimby, Age 8," and "Ramona the Brave."

10. Cleary's mother encouraged her to write her stories by saying, Make it funny.

page 128

Adverbs

page 216

Possessive pronouns
and contractions

page 30

Forms of nouns

Apostrophe

Use an apostrophe to show the omission of letters or numbers.

Contractions: I + have = I've
                could + not = couldn't
        Dates: 1929 = '29

Use an apostrophe to show the plurals of letters being discussed.

the *d,* the *d*'s

Use an apostrophe to form the possessive of nouns.

- To form the singular possessive, add *'s* to the singular form of the noun.

  man—man's   The man's hat blew into the water.
  lady—lady's   Kevin turned to speak to the lady's daughter.
  Gladys—Gladys's Gladys's glasses lay on the windowsill.

- Traditionally, only an apostrophe is added to the proper names *Jesus* and *Moses.*

  Moses—Moses'   God turned Moses' rod into a snake.
  Jesus—Jesus'   Was Bartholomew one of Jesus' disciples?

- If a plural ends with an *s,* add only an apostrophe to make it possessive.

  ladies—ladies' The ladies' luncheon will be held at Turner's Restaurant.

- If a plural does not end with an *s,* add an *'s*

  men—men's   Does your church sponsor a men's softball team?

15-19   **PRACTICE THE SKILL**

Correct the following sentences by inserting apostrophes.

1. Havent you heard of the loyalty of Mordecai?

2. He overheard the terrible plan of the kings guards.

3. Mordecai warned King Ahasuerus of the mens intent to kill him.

4. How many *u*s are in Ahasuerus?

5. Mordecai worshipped only God; he wouldnt bow down to Haman.

6. Hamans pride was injured, and he made plans to kill Mordecai.

7. One night the king couldnt sleep, so he had his book of records read to him.

8. The servants read the record of how Mordecai had saved Ahasueruss life.

9. The king decided that some reward should be given for Mordecais act of loyalty.

10. Haman had to lead Mordecai through all the citys streets and proclaim honor for Mordecai.

REVIEW THE SKILL

Underline each word that contains an apostrophe error and then rewrite the word correctly in the blank. If the sentence contains no errors, write _C_ in the blank.

_____ 1. Hiram Revels was Congress' first black member.

_____ 2. He was born in 1822 and became a member of the Senate in '70.

_____ 3. Revels did'nt serve only as a senator.

_____ 4. He pastored and taught in several churches in the North and Midwest.

_____ 5. He cared for the former slaves's physical and spiritual needs.

_____ 6. He later became the president of Mississippis' Alcorn College.

_____ 7. As secretary of state in Mississippi, he was still involved in the nations politics.

_____ 8. In 75' he wrote a letter to President Grant expressing his disappointment with the corrupt government in Mississippi.

_____ 9. He claimed that the government leaders shouldv'e been more honest and benevolent.

_____ 10. Revels wouldn't quit preaching; he continued his ministry until his death in 1901.

Hyphen

Use a hyphen to divide words at the end of a line. (Divide words only between syllables; never divide a one-syllable word.)

Leave at least two letters and a hyphen on the first line.

> **Wrong:** Three maidens tell Hercules not to be a-
> stonished at anything the old man says.

> **Right:** Nathaniel Hawthorne tells the story of an ad-
> venturous quest for three golden apples.

Put at least three letters on the next line.

> **Wrong:** The maidens tell Hercules to hold the craft-
> y man until he tells him the way to Atlas.

> **Right:** The old man could change from one physi-
> cal form into another.

Leave the hyphen on the first line; do not carry it to the second line.

> **Wrong:** The giant will not hold the sky on his shoul
> -ders again, but Hercules tricks him.

> **Right:** Hercules holds up the sky while the enor-
> mous Atlas picks the apples.

Use a hyphen between the words of multiword numbers up to ninety-nine.

> Twenty-four members of the youth group attended the meeting.

Use a hyphen between the two parts of a fraction that is written out.

> They make up more than three-fourths of our class.

Use a hyphen to show the omission of a connecting word.

> Your assignment is to read pages 21-25.
> The revival services are May 17-23 this year.

15-21   PRACTICE THE SKILL

Insert any missing apostrophes and hyphens in the following sentences. Circle any wrong items. Write *C* if the sentence is correct.

1. Louisa May Alcott lived from 183288 and wrote mainly childrens liter- ature.

2. Her familys move from Philadelphia to Boston occurred during her childhood.

3. Her fathers trip to Europe inspired plans for a large farm.

4. Mrs. Alcotts desire was for her four daughters happiness.

5. Louisa and her sisters often heard stories of Jesus' life and of Moses life.

6. The Alcotts' friends and neighbors included Ralph Waldo Emerson, Nathaniel Hawthorne, and Henry David Thoreau.

7. Louisa's first book, *Flower Fables,* was published when she was twenty two years old and was written for Emerson's daughter Ellen.

8. Louisa was a Civil War nurse from 1862-63 in Washington, D.C.

9. Louisa's most famous book is *Little Women,* which she wrote when she was thirty five years old.

10. *Little Women*'s characters also appear in the book *Little Men*. These books represent two thirds of the books about the March family.

15-22 REVIEW THE SKILL

Insert any missing apostrophes or hyphens. Write *C* if the sentence is correct.

1. Did you know that Queen Victorias reign over Great Britain lasted sixty three years?

2. The other British monarchs reigns have not been as long as hers.

3. Victoria ruled during the years 1837 1901.

4. Many historians call this time the Victorian Age.

5. Her reign is famous for the expansion of Britains properties in other parts of the world.

6. The British Empire included one fourth of the worlds land and population.

7. Charles Dickens was one of Britains celebrities during the Victorian Age.

8. Have you ever read Dickenss novel *Nicholas Nickleby*?

9. Queen Victorias family included five daughters and four sons.

10. The queens eldest son became King Edward VII after his mothers death in 01.

Learning Christianly

Have you ever read a fascinating story? Or have you ever heard someone read a poem that captured your imagination? One of the wonderful things about mastering a language is that it allows us to read and write beautiful things. Read Galatians 5:14. How can you love your neighbor better because of your access to some of the more beautiful things in our language?

15-23 **USE THE SKILL**

A. Insert any missing punctuation marks: end marks, commas, semicolons, colons, quotation marks, apostrophes, and hyphens.
B. Underline any words that should be written in italics.
C. Circle any misplaced punctuation marks.

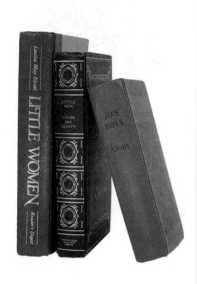

Louisa May Alcott wrote a series of books based on her own familys experiences. This series included the following titles Little Women Little Men and Jo's Boys Alcott used her own life as a model for Jo the main character in all three of these books. "Little Women" was written when Louisa was thirty five years old; and tells the antics of Jo and her three sisters Meg, Beth and Amy. The sisters' many mishaps draw them closer and teach them important lessons about life.

Jos story continues in Little Men. The book chronicles the lives of Jo and her husband the couple runs a boarding school. Imagine living with twelve boys Further "adventures" at the boys school continue in the final-book, Jo's Boys.

15-24 **CUMULATIVE REVIEW**

Locate and correct the fifteen errors in the paragraph: troublesome words, capitalization, and punctuation.

Somehow the fledgling United States of America had to pay for the Revolutionary War. However, without the power of taxation their were few ways for the colonists to rise money. Congress had decided in 1775 to issue a new, kind of Money. Soon Congress had distributed so many new bills that they we're almost worthless. Congress could not prophet from this valueless money. Individual state's contributed money but they could not give to much. Some wealthy, american colonists lent money to the government with the agreement that the loan would be paid back in full. Finally it was gifts from other countries like Spain, France, and the netherlands that rescued the young Nation.

CRAFTING A LETTER TO THE EDITOR

But sanctify the Lord God in your hearts: and be ready always to give an answer to every man that asketh you a reason of the hope that is in you with meekness and fear.

I Peter 3:15

Persuasion focuses on changing a person's thinking, choices, and behavior. A major indication that a person has been persuaded is his behavior. Successful persuasion results in someone's changing his actions. Wrong actions are often the result of negative or dishonest persuasion.

In a letter to the editor, the writer uses persuasion to sway others to take action on a certain issue. A letter to the editor is a response to an editor's opinion on the editorial page, an article published in the paper, or a topic of significance in the community. These letters are published on the editorial page of newspapers and magazines. If your school has a school newspaper, look to see whether it includes any letters.

Your Turn

Write a persuasive letter to the editor. Remember to suit the topic of the letter to the audience. (The readers of *USA Today,* for example, are not interested in the poor garbage pickup in your neighborhood.)

Planning

Choose an issue. Read a newspaper or a news magazine, listen to the news on the radio, or talk with a friend. Do you have strong emotional reactions to something that you read or heard? Perhaps you have strong feelings about several issues. As you consider a possible issue, you may find that your letter will be more successful if you choose a local issue.

Freewrite for several minutes. Write down everything you currently know about the issue. Then examine your notes. Are your ideas based on facts? Are there examples or expert opinions that support your ideas?

Identify your purpose. Based upon the ideas that you have written, what do you hope to accomplish with your letter? Do you want to argue your opinion in a way that will cause people to change their minds? Or do you want to persuade people to follow a course of action?

Many writers use emotion to persuade their readers. However, emotional appeal by itself is not often effective. Many persuasive writers use argumentation to present their viewpoint. Argumentation focuses solely on changing someone's mind about an issue, whereas persuasion tries to change not only someone's thinking but also his choices and behavior. When argumentation and persuasion are combined, the writer has a powerful tool at his disposal.

Drafting

Write an introduction. Use an introductory sentence or paragraph to identify who you are and why you are qualified to write your letter. Many letters to the editor come from doctors, preachers, professors, or other trained individuals. In their letters they state that they have had years of training in a particular field, and they may describe some of their experiences. This background information, called credentials, helps prove that the writer possesses enough knowledge to write about the subject. As a student, your credentials will probably not be your education or your job. Students' credentials could include a class project, a trip, or a special interest.

Support your opinions. Keep your letter simple. Use details to explain why you believe your position is the right one. Read the two example letters written by seventh-grade students about a topic that they believed was significant to the community.

Dear Mr. Editor,

I am Juan in the seventh grade at Oak Park School. I think the park's courts need another basketball hoop. I don't like shooting baskets with a bunch of other boys all the time. Some boys play rough, and kids get pushed around. I think the city needs to help kids play better ball by adding another hoop.

Juan

Dear Editor:

My name is Santiago. I am a seventh grader at Oak Park School. One of my hobbies is playing basketball, and I hope to play for Oak Park this year. In fact, I practice shooting baskets every day after school at Rigley Park on Hastings Road.

I like Rigley Park a lot except that it is always crowded in the afternoon. I counted thirty-five people on the courts the other day. Later that day a player was knocked to the ground while he was trying to rebound a ball. He went to the hospital because he broke his elbow.

I think the city should add another court or another basketball hoop to the park. An additional hoop would relieve crowded conditions and would help prevent injuries caused by overcrowding.

Sincerely,

Santiago Carlton

Which letter do you believe would be published by the newspaper? Which letter do you believe would cause the city to add another basketball court? Santiago used details so that his readers would know which city park he was talking about. He also used specific examples about what happens because of insufficient space. In addition, Santiago tells why he is qualified to write about his topic, and his grammar skills are much better than Juan's.

Incorporate common arguments that are used as tools to persuade.

- **Simile:** a comparison that uses *like* or *as.* A letter to the editor urging people to vote in an upcoming election might include the following simile: "People who don't vote but then complain about the results of elections are like people who won't help make supper but then complain about the meal."

- **Metaphor:** a comparison that does not use *like* or *as*. "Our city taxes are a burden that is too heavy to carry any more" is a metaphorical comparison.

- **Testimonial:** information about the writer's credentials or personal experience. Testimonial is one way to prove that you are qualified to write about a topic. Santiago's statement "I practice shooting baskets every day after school at Rigley Park on Hastings Road" lets the reader see that Santiago has personally experienced the problem at the park.

- **Bandwagon:** device that urges people to become a part of a group. This device is often used in advertising and can be easily misused, so be careful if you include it. A statement such as "Everyone who thinks carefully about this problem will have to agree with me" is a band-wagon statement—but it may not actually be true! (Other people might think long and hard about a situation and come to a conclusion different from yours.) If you've ever said something such as "But Mom, everyone else is going!" you have used a bandwagon appeal. Did it work?

Write a conclusion. End your letter with your most important thought or recommendation. In the last paragraph of his letter, Santiago presents what he thinks the city should do. His concluding paragraph leaves the reader with the main reason for his letter.

Keep your letter simple. Write clear, grammatically correct sentences. Because the editor may need to shorten your letter for publication, make your letter brief and well organized.

Use correct form for your letter. Begin your letter with "Dear Editor." Be sure to close your letter with your full name and address. Newspapers and magazines automatically reject letters that are anonymous.

Revising

Evaluate your argument or ask a peer to evaluate it. Have you stated your opinion clearly? Have you used facts to support your argument? Did you include examples to prove your point? Is your letter convincing?

Proofread for correctness. Make sure that your letter is error free. Be alert for errors in grammar, spelling, and mechanics. You do not want to risk having your letter rejected because of careless mistakes.

Publishing

Send your letter for publication. If you have responded to a magazine article, send your letter to the magazine that published the article. If you addressed a local issue, submit your letter to the local newspaper.

Post your letter on a classroom bulletin board. If you are responding to an article from a magazine, your may wish to attach the article to your letter. Your readers will have a clearer point of reference to evaluate your letter. You might also include a comment sheet for readers' responses.

Include your letter in your writing folder. Include the article in your folder as well as your letter if you are responding to an article.

CHAPTER 16

SPELLING

Does the pattern on these roofs remind you of anything? A reptile, perhaps? A diamondback rattler, to be specific? Writers notice patterns and use them to make unusual comparisons. But not all patterns are as easy to see. Sometimes it takes years for people to recognize a pattern of thought.

Patterns are at work, even in the words we use. These patterns help us make general rules for spelling English words. In a brief condemnation of a borough of New York City, Ogden Nash plays with a spelling pattern: "The Bronx? No, thonx!"

Spelling Hints

Spell by syllables.

Pronouncing distinctly each syllable of a long word will often help you spell correctly. Thinking about prefixes, suffixes, and other word parts can be helpful.

un + necessary	unnecessary
dis + appoint	disappoint
under + age	underage
mis + spell	misspell
personal + ly	personally
gentle + ness	gentleness

Suffix comes from two Latin words that mean "to fasten under." Today *suffix* is used only for something added at the end of a word.

Look up the spellings of doubtful words.

Use your dictionary to look up the spellings of words with confusing spellings. Even if you do not know how to spell the word, you should be able to make a reasonable guess about its spelling. Use the guide words to help you find it in the dictionary.

Keep a list of words that are problems for you.

A word should go on your list when you find that you have misspelled it.

Look for possible groupings among your problem words.

If you find a group of similar words, try to figure out or find a rule for that group. For instance, if you have problems with *ie* and *ei,* study that rule and write those words correctly.

Study your list of problem words systematically.

Begin by writing a word several times, concentrating on its appearance and its sound. Repeat this procedure on three or four different days within

page 337

Finding the word

the next week. Then have someone quiz you on that word. If you can write the word correctly and without hesitation, transfer it to your "learned" list. If a problem or a doubt remains, keep working on the word.

page 28

Spelling the plurals of nouns

page 51

Recognizing verbs

Rules for Spelling Singular Present-Tense Verbs and the Plural Forms of Nouns

If the word ends in *ch, sh, s, x,* or *z,* add *es.*

march	marches
push	pushes
genius	geniuses
tax	taxes
buzz	buzzes

If the word ends in a consonant followed by *y,* change the final *y* to *i* and add *es.*

poppy	poppies
pony	ponies
rally	rallies
deny	denies

If the word ends in a vowel followed by *y,* add *s.*

key	keys
toy	toys

If the word ends in *f* or *fe,* consult your dictionary. For most, add *s;* for others, change the *f* to *v* and add *es.*

roof	roofs
safe	safes
leaf	leaves
shelf	shelves

If the word ends in *o,* consult your dictionary. For most, add *es;* for others add *s.*

tomato	tomatoes
echo	echoes
solo	solos
photo	photos

Add *s* to most other words.

look	looks
bug	bugs
menu	menus
bone	bones

Some nouns have irregular plural forms. Consult your dictionary for nouns with irregular plurals.

ox	oxen
goose	geese
deer	deer

A. Underline any misspelled word.
B. Write the word correctly in the blank.
C. Write *C* if the sentence is correct.

_____ 1. Seals are marine animals that have bodys shaped like torpedos.

_____ 2. A seal eats a variety of fishs. It also preyes on squid and shrimp.

_____ 3. Because they have sharp pointed tooths with no flat surfaces, seals cannot chew their food. They either grasp and tear it or swallow it whole.

_____ 4. Every spring, seals go to breeding grounds called rookerys.

_____ 5. The mother seals' babys are born at the rookery.

_____ 6. Seals have few enemies other than hunters.

_____ 7. Some people hold strong believes that some seals should be protected because their species are becoming extinct. These people oppose hunting seals for any reason.

_____ 8. Sharkes, killer whales, and polar bears are among the seal's natural enemies.

_____ 9. Seals defend themselfs in the water by diving deeper or by swimming between rocks. On land, they have little chance of escaping an enemy.

_____ 10. Sometimes people get an opportunity to watch certain types of seals swim near beachs.

A. Underline any misspelled word.

B. Write the word correctly in the blank.

C. Write *C* if the sentence is correct.

_____ 1. We spent five dayes at our grandparents' farm last summer.

_____ 2. Our grandparents live in a white farmhouse. Their front walk is lined with short, fat bushs.

_____ 3. One day my sister Sachi and I picked tomatos from the garden and put them into wooden boxs.

_____ 4. Another time, we walked to the country store. My foots were sore because I was not used to walking so much.

_____ 5. Every time our grandparents go to the store, Grandpa carrys most of the grocerys.

_____ 6. Grandma knites well. She often makes hand-knit things and gives them as giftes.

_____ 7. In the spring I like to visit the farm to see the adorable newborn calfs.

_____ 8. Sachi would rather see the sheep and lambs.

_____ 9. I remember the time that Grandma gave Sachi and me two of Lady's puppies.

_____ 10. Grandpa and Grandma told our parents that they are happy to have their grandchilds visit them at the farm.

Rules for Spelling with *ie* and *ei*

When the sound is "long *e*," put *i* before *e* except after *c*.

i before *e*	except after *c*
shriek	ceiling
shield	receipt
grieve	conceit

(*But: caffeine, leisure, protein, seize, sheik, weird. Either* and *neither*, in their more common American pronunciation, are also exceptions to this rule.)

When the sound is "long *a*," put *e* before *i*.

freight   vein   weight

 **16-3   PRACTICE THE SKILL**

A. **Underline any misspelled word.**
B. **Write the word correctly in the blank.**
C. **Write *C* if the sentence is correct.**

_____ 1. I beleive that winter is a beautiful season, especially when there is a lot of snow.

_____ 2. It is fun to take a ride in a horse-drawn sliegh on a wintry afternoon.

_____ 3. Our nieghbors, the Sandersons, have a horse, and they often let us borrow it and their sleigh for a ride.

_____ 4. One day we received an invitation to go with them on a ride through the countryside.

_____ 5. My neice and I were the only ones who could go.

_____ 6. Renee, who is eight years old, enjoyed the ride immensely.

_____ 7. I also enjoyed the liesurely time with the Sandersons.

_____ 8. Niether Renee nor I complained about the cold weather.

_____ 9. I cannot concieve of a more relaxing way to enjoy the beauty of the winter scenery.

_____ 10. Some people are greived to see winter arrive, but Renee and I look forward to it.

 **Learning Christianly**

Why is learning to spell in English difficult for some people? There are many answers to that often-asked question because many different factors have caused this difficulty. One factor is the presence of many loanwords. An English loanword is a word that English speakers take from another language and use as though it were English. Over the past three or four centuries, English has picked up many loanwords, each reflecting its own language's system of spelling. So if you ever get frustrated trying spell *chassis, clique, chutzpah,* or *fjord,* you can blame French, Yiddish, or Norwegian. But if you think about why English has so many loanwords, you begin to realize that our difficulty in learning to spell could actually be a blessing in disguise. Can you figure out what that blessing is?

A. Underline any misspelled word.
B. Write the word correctly in the blank.
C. Write *C* if the sentence is correct.

_____ 1. The Bible teaches that anyone can recieve Christ as his Savior.

_____ 2. An atheist is someone who thinks that there is no God. He does not think there is such a thing as the gift of salvation.

_____ 3. Unfortunately, many people are decieved into beleiving that they do not need God.

_____ 4. The old fiend, Satan, is the one who tells people these lies.

_____ 5. Some people think that they can get to heaven through their own acheivements.

_____ 6. The only way to get to heaven is to yeild to the fact that you are a sinner and accept Christ as your Savior.

_____ 7. Christians ought to tell others about the gift of salvation. They can begin by telling family members and neighbors.

_____ 8. The need for people to become saved weighs so heavily on the hearts of some Christians that they devote their lives to full-time mission work.

_____ 9. It is encouraging when Christians eagerly sieze the opportunity to witness to an unsaved person.

_____ 10. The cheif thing that God wants Christians to accomplish on earth is to tell others about Him.

Rules for Adding Suffixes

Doubling a final consonant

If a one-syllable word ends with a single consonant preceded by a single vowel, double the final consonant before adding a suffix beginning with a vowel.

      snob   snobbery

If a multisyllabic word with its main accent on the final syllable ends with a single consonant preceded by a single vowel, double the final consonant before adding a suffix beginning with a vowel.

      occur   occurring

If a word ends with a single consonant preceded by a double vowel, do not double the final consonant before adding a suffix.

      droop   drooped
      greet   greeter

Changing final *y* to *i*

Change final *y* to *i* before adding a suffix if a consonant precedes the *y*.

      baby   babied
      plenty   plentiful
      sixty   sixtieth

However, if the suffix itself begins with *i,* do not change final *y* to *i.*

      cry   crying
      carry   carrying

Dropping final silent *e*

Drop the final silent *e* preceded by a consonant before adding a suffix beginning with a vowel.

      hope   hoping
      like   likable
      use   using

(*But: noticeable, courageous*)

Keep the final silent *e* before adding a suffix beginning with a consonant.

      hope   hopeless
      like   likely
      use   useful

(*But: truly, argument, judgment*)

Learning Christianly

Have you ever seen a lawyer on television presenting a case on behalf of his client? Or have you ever heard a politician promising to represent others in getting a law changed or improving conditions in a certain area of town? If so, you have seen people pleading the cause of others in order to improve their lives. How will improving your writing and grammar skills allow you to show your love to your neighbor in this way?

page 62

Past tense

16-5 ⚾ PRACTICE THE SKILL

Add the suffixes to the following words by writing the word correctly in the blank.

_____ 1. clue + less   _____ 9. drag + ing

_____ 2. trade + ed   _____ 10. bare + ly

_____ 3. beauty + ful   _____ 11. hoot + ed

_____ 4. meet + ing   _____ 12. hungry + ly

_____ 5. slip + er   _____ 13. come + ing

_____ 6. forty + eth   _____ 14. hug + ed

_____ 7. adore + able   _____ 15. try + ing

_____ 8. happy + ly

16-6 ⚾ USE THE SKILL

A.   Underline any misspelled word.
B.   Write the word correctly in the blank.
C.   Write _C_ if the sentence is correct.

_____ 1. Marcus and Olivia helped celebrate their grandmother's ninetyeth birthday this year.

_____ 2. Marcus, who has an engaging personality, was
the host of the party.

_____ 3. The room was decorated prettyly with green and
maroon balloons and crepe paper.

_____ 4. Olivia and her sister Georgina used most of the
precedeing week to bake their grandmother's
favorite desserts.

_____ 5. Marcus and some of the other relatives spent the
day before the party setting up chairs and tables.

_____ 6. All during the week, everyone made sure that Grandmother was not spiing on them.

_____ 7. Grandmother was curious, so it was likly she would be tempted to spy.

_____ 8. On the day of the party, everyone clapped when Grandmother came into the living room.

_____ 9. While the guests were eatting, Marcus and Olivia told stories about their childhood visits to Grandmother's house.

_____ 10. Toward the end of the party, Grandmother unwrapped a large present. Her eyes sparkled when she saw a beautiful cuckoo clock.

16-7 REVIEW THE SKILL

Fill in each blank with the letter of the misspelled word. You may use your dictionary for help.

_____ 1. a. recieve
      b. naming
      c. churches
      d. feet

_____ 2. a. crying
      b. tomatoes
      c. monkies
      d. yield

_____ 3. a. artful
      b. deceive
      c. babies
      d. brushs

_____ 4. a. wives
      b. mooses
      c. foxes
      d. cats

_____ 5. a. sleigh
      b. potatos
      c. occurring
      d. buzzes

_____ 6. a. huged
      b. crosses
      c. chief
      d. donkeys

_____ 7. a. nameless
      b. pianos
      c. likelihood
      d. wiegh

_____ 8. a. moose
      b. dogs
      c. makeing
      d. halves

_____ 9. a. knifes
      b. dresses
      c. fishes
      d. pizzas

_____ 10. a. lookking
      b. vein
      c. fiftieth
      d. marries

Locate and correct the twenty errors in the paragraph: troublesome words, capitalization, punctuation, spelling, subject-verb agreement, and adjective and adverb usage.

Many folkes prefer hot cereal too cold cereal especially in the Winter. Either the low temperatures or the frozen precipitation make a bowl of hot cereal "inviting." Of course, babys eat alot of cooked cereal since its more soft for there tender gums and is alright for young Digestive Tracts. Some hot cerealses requires fifteen minutes of cooking time, others' need only three minutes. still others are made instantly with boiling water. Accept when one has much time, instant cereals are oftener the best option.

_____

_____

_____

_____

_____

_____

_____

_____

_____

_____

_____

_____

_____

_____

_____

_____

EVALUATING A SCIENCE FAIR PROJECT REPORT

And this I pray, that your love may abound yet more and more in knowledge
and in all judgment; That ye may approve things that are excellent.
Philippians 1:9-10

Have you ever heard someone say "It was as interesting as seeing the
sap rise"? This expression indicates irony; the speaker sounds as though he
is saying that something is interesting, but he is really saying that whatever
activity he is describing is as boring as one could imagine. Yet, *is* this activity
boring? Sap's rising is a scientific process. The sample science fair project
and report below demonstrates how interesting this process really is.

Your Turn

Read the science fair project report at the end of this section and evaluate
it as though you were a science fair judge. Use the following information
about science fair projects and reports as your guide. Then write a paragraph
that summarizes your evaluation.

Planning

**Understand the correct contents and format of a science fair project
report.** The information below describes a typical science fair project and
the elements that make up the science fair project report.

First, a scientist (or a student in a science class) asks himself a question.
For example, you may wonder whether nourishment from a
plant's roots reaches all the way to the top of the stem or just to the
root system or leaves. More specifically, if you put a white carnation
into a glass of water tinted with food coloring, will the tinted
water color the white petals of the flower, or will it merely travel in
the stem and leaves? This sort of question is what scientists call the
hypothesis.

After forming a hypothesis, a scientist designs an experiment to
prove or disprove his idea. To test the plant nourishment question,
you could perform this experiment: Trim the end of the flower stem
with a sharp knife and place the stem into the colored water.
Observe the petals at regular intervals and keep a log of your observations—write
down what you see and when you see it. Make drawings
or photographs of the progress of the experiment. Describe in
detail the amount of color in the petals, if any.

Finally, the scientist will report on his findings. The report should
be able to stand alone as an explanation for the project and be complete
enough to allow another person to repeat the experiment by
following the same procedures. Although the requirements for science
fair project reports vary from location to location, the following
guidelines are generally accepted.

Title Page

The title should be a complete sentence or the statement of the science
project's purpose. It should, however, suggest the topic of the
experiment and cause the reader to turn the page and read about
your experiment. Make the page attractive by using an appropriate
font and color. For this experiment, a good title might be "Turning
Blue in the Face: The Path of Sap in a Flower."

Table of Contents

The table of contents lists the items in the report and the pages on which they begin. Do not list the title page or the table of contents page itself.

Abstract

The abstract is the first item in the report. Think of it as a one-page summary of the entire project. All of the vital information about the project should appear on the abstract page. First, list the project title (from the title page); then state the purpose of your project. The statement of purpose is exactly what it sounds like: state what you hope to prove by your experiment. Next, state the hypothesis, which is the statement of the project question, followed by a brief description of the procedure and the results. Because it is an overview of the entire project, this page of the report is quite possibly the most important one of all.

Introduction

The introduction, next in the report, contains your statement of purpose and any background information about the project, such as how you became interested in the idea or what made you come up with your hypothesis. List any books you read or experiments done by others that prompted you to do your project.

Materials and Methods

Then comes the actual description of the experiment in the experiment and data section. Remember that someone should be able to follow this description and repeat your project. First write out the purpose of the experiment—what you hope to accomplish. Follow that statement with a list of the materials you used (and the amount needed of each) in the experiment. For the sake of those who may repeat your experiment, be complete. Finish the section with an explanation of the procedures. Be detailed with the steps you took to test your hypothesis. Your log will be vital here. Be sure to include all the measurements and data from your experiments. Arrange the information neatly and clearly, using graphs and charts. If you have a large amount of data, you may put the majority of it in an appendix at the end of the report and merely summarize the data in this section of the report.

Results and Discussion

The results and discussion section is a short (about one page) summary of what you learned. State the hypothesis again and then state whether you were able to prove or disprove it by your experiments. If this experiment has made you curious about other possible experiments, you may list these possibilities here.

Sources

On this page list all of the information about any written materials that you read or interviews that you did as part of the experiment or in preparation for it. Use proper bibliography page form.

Acknowledgments

Acknowledgments are a list of those who helped you and how they did so. Although you should have done the majority of the science project yourself, you may have received some assistance. If your relatives helped, it is not necessary to give their names; you may say, "Thanks to my mother, who typed my report."

A good science fair project takes much work. But keep in mind that the qualities of a good scientist are precision, accuracy, and completeness. Attention to these details will give a project and report the credibility it needs to be a winner.

Preview the report. Before you read the report thoroughly, check to see that all the necessary elements are present. Has the writer presented both problems in his findings as well as successes? Has he included a log of results? Are there sources and acknowledgments for his work? Does the report follow the correct form?

Read the report. As you read, take notes. Has the writer developed a hypothesis? Does he include the necessary materials for the experiment? Does the experiment prove or disprove the hypothesis? Does he use clear scientific language to express his findings? Does the report present accurate, well-documented information? Does it follow a logical order?

Evaluate the writer's style. Did the writer get your attention with the beginning of his report? Does he present his material in a convincing way? You may want to use the categories of *purpose, organization, vocabulary,* and *details* to organize your notes.

Drafting

Begin with a topic sentence that will give direction to your paragraph. State your overall evaluation in a simple, direct topic sentence. The rest of the paragraph will explain the reasons for your overall evaluation.

Support your topic sentence. Let the organization of your notes be your guide as you write your paragraph. Each sentence in your paragraph should help to support the overall evaluation in your topic sentence by giving further details. Include the reasons for the evaluations that you give.

Use proper tone as you write. The tone of your writing reveals your attitude toward the subject and the writer. Keep in mind why you are writing the evaluation—you are a judge. The tone of your evaluation should be confident and courteous.

Revising

Take a fresh look at your paragraph. Reviewing your paragraph at a later time will help you to identify problems. Does the paragraph meet the expectations of the assignment? Is the evaluation clear and easy to follow?

Incorporate additions and revisions. Rewrite your paragraph, including any changes or additions that you decide are necessary.

Proofread your paragraph for correct grammar, spelling, and mechanics. Try reading the paragraph backwards, one word at a time.

Make a clean copy of your paragraph. Incorporate any additional corrections that you marked on your paragraph as you proofread.

Publishing

Share your evaluation with a peer. No two people have the same observations and evaluations. Make notes for yourself regarding the difference between your observations and your peer's.

Get an expert opinion. If possible, ask a science teacher to read your evaluation and to write comments about your paragraph. Include these comments with your evaluation in your writing folder.

Table of Contents

Abstract

The purpose of this project was to demonstrate that nutrients reach the petals of a flower, not merely the stem and leaves. The experiment measured the progress of colored water up the stem of a white carnation and into the petals. I noted the amount of color present in the petals at set intervals.

The resulting patterns of blue seen on the petals of the carnation confirmed my hypothesis that water travels throughout the entire flower, not just through the stem and leaves. These results cause me to wonder whether nutrients cause the opening of the flower head. It is common scientific fact that sap rises throughout a plant's stem and carries nutrients with it to the leaves and stem, but what is the effect of this transportation system on a flower blossom?

Introduction

It is common knowledge that plants need water and other nutrients to grow. But exactly where in a plant are these nutrients found? It is logical to assume that they are found in the roots of the plant and probable to assume that they are found in the stems and leaves as well. Scientists have determined that sap (the liquid nutrients that travel upward from the roots of a plant) is found in the stems and leaves of a plant, but what about the petals? Since most flowers' blooms do not last a long time before dying, are nutrients found in the petals at all? Is the lack of nutrients responsible for the dying of the flower blossoms?

Before I could determine whether nutrients cause the opening of a flower head, I had first to determine whether a simple liquid such as water makes its way to the flower petals. To discover this, I placed a white carnation in colored water and charted the progress of the color in the petals.

My curiosity about this process resulted in this project to demonstrate that nutrients do indeed travel throughout a plant. My hypothesis is that water will travel from the bottom of a flower stem to the top, throughout the entire plant.

Materials and Methods

a white miniature carnation
a vase with water
dark food coloring (blue)

To determine whether nutrients will flow through a stem to the petals of a flower

1. Make a solution of the food coloring and water. I used 6 drops of blue food coloring in $\frac{1}{4}$ cup water since I used 1 white miniature carnation.

2. Trim the end of the carnation stem using a sharp knife. Cut at an angle to give the stem a maximum absorption surface.

3. Place the stem into the colored water.

4. Observe the carnation periodically and record any change in the petal color.

Results and Discussion

As it was stated in my hypothesis, I believe that sap flows through the entire plant: roots, stem, leaves, and flower petals. I believe that the nutrients contained in the sap and transported from the roots of a plant are responsible for the actual opening of a plant's blossoms. While this experiment did not confirm the second part of the hypothesis, it did answer the preliminary question of whether nutrients found in roots, stems, and leaves are present in the flower petals as well.

The experimental data showed that the colored water at the base of the carnation stem did travel up the stem and into the flower petals. This progress was fairly easy to chart by using colored water that contrasted with the flower petals. As the tinted water entered the white petals, they turned blue.

This experiment has prompted other questions about the progress of nutrients in a plant and various factors that affect that progress. Future experiments could explore the effect of freshness of the flower on the progress of the colored water. Is the progress of the colored water faster if the flower is cut and placed into the water immediately? Is the progress of the water affected by the degree to which the flower bud is closed? Are the results different with different flowers? Do the petals gradually lose their ability to transport water, and is that what causes them to die?

Sources

Hargis, Grace Collins. *Writing from Research for Christian Schools.* Greenville, S.C.: Bob Jones University Press, 1998.

"Sap." *1997 Grolier Multimedia Encyclopedia.* CD-ROM. Danbury, Conn.: Grolier, 1997.

Acknowledgments

I would like to thank my sister Eileen for her help in thinking of an idea for this project. I would also like to thank my science teacher, Mr. Howell, for his help, and my mom for buying the carnation for me.

Science Project Log

Saturday

8:10   Put 6 drops of blue food coloring into ¼ cup water. Cut the stem of a miniature white carnation and placed it into the colored water.

9:10   No change in petal color (I wonder whether roses work better?)

10:10   No change in petal color (Does the freshness of the flower change the speed of absorption?)

12:10   Bare traces of blue on outer edge of outer petals; center petals the same

1:10   More blue on outer petals; none on center yet

5:10   More blue on outer petals; center ones still white

Sunday

8:10   Outer petals still absorbing blue; center petals beginning to turn slightly

1:10   Center petals still hardly affected

4:10   Outer edges of outer petals quite blue; center still little affected

Monday

7:30   Little change from yesterday

Tuesday

7:15   No change from yesterday

Wednesday

7:10   No change from yesterday

Thursday

7:10   Carnation stem broken at level of the jar top; no noticeable difference from Friday's observation. Broken carnation allowed a glimpse of the underside of the flower bloom; significant veining with blue; I should have checked the progress of the water on the underside as well as on the top.

Modifications (to be made if experiment repeated)

1. Check progress of color on the underside of petals as well as on the top.
2. Try experiment with other flowers, such as roses.
3. Try experiment with buds that were cut more recently.

Observations

1. Notched edges of the petals had the most color.
2. Outer petals were affected more than inner petals.

CHAPTER 17

DICTIONARY SKILLS

A **dictionary** is the most common tool used for learning about words and languages. The dictionary gives a word's spelling, syllabification, pronunciation, definitions, different forms, parts of speech, synonyms or antonyms, and capitalization. The information in a good dictionary is reliable because it comes from the speech and the writing that is most often accepted by educated people. Many dictionaries also list abbreviations, geographic names, and biographical names; they may even include a brief history of the English language or a handbook of style and usage. Notes and guides in your dictionary can help you understand the content of the dictionary. To use your dictionary in the right way, you will want to become familiar with all such helps.

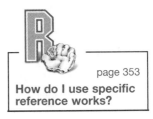

page 353

How do I use specific reference works?

Finding the Word

At the top of each dictionary page you will find two words in large dark print. These **guide word**s tell you the first and last word defined on that page. Any word that alphabetically comes between those two words can also be found on that page. Using the guide words will save you much time when trying to find a particular word.

The **entry** is the word being defined (usually printed in bold type) and all the information about that particular word. Look here for the proper spelling of a word. Most dictionaries will also list other forms of the word. For example, an entry for a noun will list the noun's plural form; an entry for a verb will list the verb's principal parts. Remember that the entry word itself is always the base form of the word.

page 39

Compound nouns

17-1 PRACTICE THE SKILL

Underline the entry words that would appear on a dictionary page with the guide words *pledge / plesiosaur.*

1. Pleiades

2. Plexiglas

3. plenary

4. plenty

5. pleurisy

Zag·ros Mountains (zăg′rəs). A range of W Iran forming the W and S borders of the central Iranian plateau and rising to 4,550.6 m (14,920 ft).

Za·har·i·as (zə-hăr′ē-əs), **Mildred Ella Didrikson.** See Mildred Ella **Didrikson.**

zai·bat·su (zī′băt-sōō′) *n., pl.* **zaibatsu. 1.** A powerful family-controlled commercial combine of Japan. **2.** A Japanese conglomerate or cartel. [J. : *zai,* wealth (< Chin. *cái* + *batsu,* powerful person or family (< Chin. *fá).]*

zaire (zī′ir, zä-ir′) *n.* See table at **currency.** [Port., the Congo River < Kongo *n-zadi,* large river.]

Zaire (zī′ir, zä-ir′). Formerly (1885–1908) **Con·go Free State** (kŏng′gō) and (1908–60) **Bel·gian Congo** (bĕl′jən) and (1960–71) **Congo.** A country of central Africa astride the equator; achieved full independence from Belgium in 1960. Cap. Kinshasa. Pop. 29,671,407. — **Za·ir′e·an, Za·ir′i·an** *adj. & n.*

Zaire River. See **Congo River.**

za·kat (zə-kät′) *n.* The alms tax required of all Muslims by the shari‘a.

Za·ma (zā′mə, zä′mä). An ancient town of N Africa SW of Carthage in present-day N Tunisia; site of the Roman defeat of Hannibal, which ended the Second Punic War (202 B.C.).

Zam·be·zi (zăm-bē′zē). A river of central and S Africa rising in NW Zambia and flowing c. 2,735 km (1,700 mi) to the Mozambique Channel.

Zam·bi·a (zăm′bē-ə). A country of S-central Africa; gained independence from Great Britain in 1964. Cap. Lusaka. Pop. 5,661,801. — **Zam′bi·an** *adj. & n.*

za·mi·a (zā′mē-ə) *n.* Any of various chiefly tropical American cycads of the genus *Zamia,* having a thick trunk, palmlike terminal leaves, and seeds borne in woody cones. [NLat. *Zamia,* genus name < misreading of *(nucēs) azāniae,* pine cone (nuts), prob. < Gk. *azainein,* to dry up < *azein,* to dry. See **as-*.**]

zam·in·dar also **zem·in·dar** (zăm′ən-där′, zĕm′-, zə-mĕn-där′) *n.* **1.** An official in precolonial India assigned to collect the land taxes of his district. **2.** A landholder in British colonial India responsible for collecting and paying to the government the taxes on the land under his jurisdiction. [Hindi *zamīndār* < Pers. : *zamin,* earth; see **dhghem-*** + *-dār,* -holder; see **dher-*.**]

zan·der (zăn′dər) *n., pl.* **zander** or **-ders.** A common European pikeperch (*Stizostedion lucioperca*) valued as a food fish. [Ger. < LGer. *Sander.*]

Zanes·ville (zānz′vĭl′). A city of E-central Ohio E of Columbus; a former state cap. (1810–12). Pop. 26,778.

Zan·gwill (zăng′gwĭl′, -wĭl′), **Israel.** 1864–1926. British writer whose works include *Children of the Ghetto* (1892).

za·ny (zā′nē) *n., pl.* **-nies. 1.** A comic performer who assists or imitates a clown, acrobat, or mountebank. **2.** A comical person given to extravagant or outlandish behavior. — *adj.* **-ni·er, -ni·est. 1.** Ludicrously comical; clownish. **2.** Comical because of incongruity or strangeness; bizarre. [Fr. *zani* < Ital. dial. *zanni* < *Zanni,* var. of Ital. *Gianni,* nickname for *Giovanni,* John, the name of servants who act as clowns in commedia dell'arte.] — **za′ni·ly** *adv.* — **za′ni·ness** *n.*

Zan·zi·bar (zăn′zə-bär′). **1.** A region of E Africa, comprising **Zanzibar Island** and several adjacent islands; became an independent sultanate in 1963 and in 1964 joined Tanganyika to form Tanzania. **2.** A city of Tanzania on the W coast of Zanzibar I.; founded in the 16th cent. Pop. 110,699.

zap (zăp) *Slang.* — *v.* **zapped, zap·ping, zaps.** — *tr.* **1.a.** To destroy or kill with a burst of gunfire, flame, or electric current. **b.** To kill or destroy as if by shooting. **c.** To strike suddenly and forcefully as if with a projectile or weapon. **d.** To expose to radiation; irradiate. **2.** To attack (an enemy) with heavy firepower; strafe or bombard. **3.** To use a remote control device to switch (channels on a television) or to turn off (a television set). — *intr.* To move swiftly; zoom. — *n.* Something that imparts excitement or great interest. — *interj.* **1.** Used to imitate a sound made by a gun when fired. **2.** Used to indicate a sudden occurrence. [Imit.]

Za·pa·ta (zə-pä′tə, sä-pä′tä), **Emiliano.** 1879?–1919. Mexican revolutionary who led an agrarian revolt (1910–1919).

za·pa·te·a·do (zä′pə-tā-ä′dō, thä′pä-tä-ä′thô, sä′-) *n., pl.* **-dos.** A Spanish flamenco dance in which the performer stamps and taps rhythmically with the heels. [Sp. < *zapatear,* to tap with the shoe < *zapato,* shoe.]

Za·po·pan (zä′pō-pän′, sä′pô-). A city of SW Mexico W of Guadalajara. Pop. 345,390.

Za·po·ro·zhe (zä′pə-rô′zhə, zə-pə-rô′zhyĕ). Formerly **A·lek·san·drovsk** (ăl′ĭk-sän′drəfsk, ä-lĭk-sän′-). A city of S Ukraine W of Donetsk; founded 1770. Pop. 852,000.

Za·po·tec (zä′pə-tĕk′, sä′pô-) *n., pl.* **Zapotec** or **-tecs. 1.a.** A member of a Mesoamerican Indian people of southern Mexico, whose civilization reached its height around A.D. 300–900. **b.** A modern-day descendant of this people. **2.** Any of a group of related languages spoken in southern Mexico. [Sp. *Zapoteco* < Nahuatl *tzapotēcah,* pl. of *tzapotēcatl,* person from Tzapotlan < *Tzapotlān,* place name : *tzapotl,* sapodilla + *tlān,* place.] — **Za′po·tec′** *adj.*

zap·py (zăp′ē) *adj.* **-pi·er, -pi·est.** *Slang.* Lively.

Za·ra·go·za (zăr′ə-gō′zə, thä′rä-gô′thä). See **Saragossa.**

Zar·a·thu·stra (zăr′ə-thōō′strə). See **Zoroaster.**

za·re·ba also **za·ree·ba** (zə-rē′bə) *n.* **1.** An enclosure of bushes or stakes protecting a campsite or village in northeast Africa. **2.** A campsite or village protected by such an enclosure. [Ar. *zarībah,* pen for cattle.]

zarf (zärf) *n.* A chalicelike holder for a hot coffee cup, typically made of ornamented metal, used in the Middle East. [Ar. *zarf,* container.]

zas·tru·ga (ză-strōō′gə, zä-) *n.* Var. of **sastruga.**

z-ax·is (zē′ăk′sĭs) *n., pl.* **z-ax·es** (zē′ak′sēz). *Math.* One of three axes in a three-dimensional Cartesian coordinate system.

za·yin (zä′yĭn) *n.* The seventh letter of the Hebrew alphabet. [Heb. < Aram.]

Zc *abbr. Bible.* Zechariah.

zeal (zēl) *n.* Enthusiastic devotion to a cause, an ideal, or a goal and tireless diligence in its furtherance. [ME *zele* < OFr. *zel* < LLat. *zēlus* < Gk. *zēlos.*]

Zea·land (zē′lənd). See **Sjaelland.**

zeal·ot (zĕl′ət) *n.* **1.a.** One who is zealous, esp. excessively so. **b.** A fanatically committed person. **2. Zealot.** A member of a Jewish movement of the first century A.D. that fought against Roman rule in Palestine as incompatible with strict monotheism. [ME *zelote* < Lat. *zēlōtēs* < Gk. < *zēlos,* zeal.]

zeal·ot·ry (zĕl′ə-trē) *n.* Excessive zeal; fanaticism.

zeal·ous (zĕl′əs) *adj.* Filled with or motivated by zeal; fervent. — **zeal′ous·ly** *adv.* — **zeal′ous·ness** *n.*

ze·a·tin (zē′ə-tĭn) *n.* A cytokinin originally isolated from young corn kernels. [NLat. *Zea,* corn genus; see **ZEIN** + -IN.]

ze·bec or **ze·beck** (zē′bĕk′) *n. Naut.* Var. of **xebec.**

Zeb·e·dee (zĕb′ĭ-dē′). In the Bible, a fisherman whose sons James and John became disciples of Jesus.

ze·bra (zē′brə) *n.* Any of several swift, wild, horselike African mammals of the genus *Equus,* having distinctive overall markings of alternating white and black or brown stripes. [Ital. < OPort. *zevro, zevra,* wild ass.] — **ze′brine′** (zē′brīne′) *adj.*

zebra crossing *n. Chiefly British.* A pedestrian crosswalk.

zebra finch *n.* A small Australian bird (*Poephila guttata*) having black and white markings and popular as a cage bird.

zebra fish *n.* A small freshwater tropical fish (*Brachydanio rerio*) of India having horizontal dark blue and silvery stripes.

ze·bra·wood (zē′brə-wŏŏd′) *n.* **1.** Any of several African or tropical American trees having striped wood. **2.** The wood of any of these trees, used in cabinetmaking.

ze·bu (zē′bōō, -byōō) *n.* A domesticated ox (*Bos indicus*) of Asia and eastern Africa having a prominent hump on the back and a large dewlap. [Fr. *zébu.*]

Zeb·u·lon also **Zeb·u·lun** (zĕb′yə-lən). In the Bible, a son of Jacob and Leah and the forebear of one of the tribes of Israel.

zec·chi·no (zĕ-kē′nō) also **zec·chin** or **zech·in** (zĕk′ĭn) *n., pl.* **-ni** (-nē) or **-nos** also **-chins** or **-ins.** See **sequin** 2. [Ital. See SEQUIN.]

Zech·a·ri·ah[1] (zĕk′ə-rī′ə) *n. Bible.* **1.** A Hebrew prophet of the 6th cent. B.C. **2.** See table at **Bible.** [Heb. *Zĕkaryāh : zekar,* remembrance + *Yāh,* God.]

Zech·a·ri·ah[2] (zĕk′ə-rī′ə). See **Zacharias.**

zed (zĕd) *n. Chiefly British.* The letter *z.* [ME < OFr. *zede* < LLat. *zēta,* zeta < Gk. See ZETA.]

Zed·e·ki·ah (zĕd′ĭ-kī′ə). 6th cent. B.C. The last king of Judah (597–586 B.C.), who led an unsuccessful uprising (588–586) against Nebuchadnezzar II and was sent to captivity in Babylon.

zed·o·ar·y (zĕd′ō-ĕr′ē) *n., pl.* **-ies. 1.** An Indian plant (*Curcuma zedoaria*) having yellow flowers and starchy tuberous rhizomes. **2.** The dried rhizomes of this plant, used as a condiment and in perfumes, medicines, and cosmetics. [ME *zeduarie* < Med.Lat. *zeduāria* < Ar. *zadwār* < Pers.]

zee (zē) *n.* The letter *z.*

Zee·land (zē′lənd, zā′länt). A historical region of SW Netherlands bordering on Belgium and the North Sea; part of Holland after the 10th cent.

Zee·man (zē′män), **Pieter.** 1865–1943. Dutch physicist who shared a 1902 Nobel Prize.

Zeeman effect *n.* The splitting of single spectral lines of an emission spectrum into three or more polarized components when the radiation source is in a magnetic field.

ze·in (zē′ĭn) *n.* A prolamine protein derived from corn, used in the manufacture of various plastics, coatings, and lacquers. [NLat. *Zea,* corn genus (< Lat. *zēa,* emmer < Gk. *zeia,* one-seeded wheat, barley; see **yewo-***) + -IN.]

Zeist (zīst). A city of central Netherlands E of Utrecht. Pop. 60,478.

Zeit·geist (tsīt′gīst′, zīt′-) *n.* The spirit of the time; the taste and outlook characteristic of a period or generation. [Ger. : *Zeit,* time (< MHGer. *zīt* < OHGer.; see **dā-***) + *Geist,* spirit; see POLTERGEIST.]

zem·in·dar (zăm′ən-där′, zĕm′-, zə-mĕn-där′) *n.* Var. of **zamindar.**

zemst·vo (zĕmst′vō, zyĕm′stvə) *n., pl.* **-vos.** An elective council responsible for the local administration of a provincial dis-

Zambia

ă pat	oi boy
ā pay	ou out
âr care	ŏŏ took
ä father	ōō boot
ĕ pet	ŭ cut
ē be	ûr urge
ĭ pit	th thin
ī pie	*th* this
îr pier	hw which
ŏ pot	zh vision
ō toe	ə about,
ô paw	item

Stress marks:
′ (primary);
′ (secondary), as in
dictionary (dĭk′shə-nĕr′ē)

PRACTICE THE SKILL

Using the sample guide words, write the number of the page on which you would find each entry word.

lesson/level   780
lever/liberal   781
Liberia/licorice 782

_____ 1. liberty   _____ 6. license

_____ 2. library   _____ 7. levee

_____ 3. letter   _____ 8. Leuctra

_____ 4. libel   _____ 9. lichen

_____ 5. levy   _____10. liar

PRACTICE THE SKILL

Using the sample dictionary page on page 338, answer each question.

_____ 1. What is the plural form of *z-axis?*

_____ 2. What is the alternate spelling of *zamindar?*

_____ 3. What is the plural form of *zedoary?*

_____ 4. What is the correct spelling of the adjective form of *zebra?*

_____ 5. What is the correct spelling of the word that means "a domesticated ox"?
     a. zeebu   c. zeboo
     b. zebu   d. zebyu

Pronouncing the Word

Most dictionaries show the entry word's **syllabification** by placing dots between each syllable. Recognizing syllable divisions will help you learn to pronounce words that appear difficult at first glance; a syllable of few letters is much easier to pronounce than a word of fifteen letters. Syllable divisions will also help your spelling. When you can hear the sound of the individual syllables, you will be less likely to leave out letters or even entire syllables when you spell the word.

Immediately after the entry word will be its **pronunciation;** this is a respelling that shows you how to pronounce the word correctly. Some of the symbols used in the respelling may be unfamiliar to you. Near the front of the dictionary and at the bottom of each page, a **pronunciation guide** lists the symbols used in that dictionary to represent sounds. Refer to the pronunciation guide when you are unsure how to read the entry word's respelling. The respelling usually shows syllable divisions by placing hyphens or other marks between each syllable. An accent mark indicates which syllables will be emphasized, or stressed, when pronounced. Some words may have more than one accent mark if more than one syllable is pronounced with stress. The largest accent mark indicates the strongest stress in a word.

page 62

Principal parts of verbs

17-4 PRACTICE THE SKILL

Using the sample dictionary page, fill in each blank with the number of syllables in the word. Underline the syllable that is stressed most strongly.

_____ 1. Zambezi

_____ 2. zayin

_____ 3. Zechariah

_____ 4. zein

_____ 5. Zeist

17-5 PRACTICE THE SKILL

Using the sample dictionary page, draw a vertical line between the syllables of each word. If the word has only one syllable, do not draw a vertical line.

1. zaibatsu

2. zander

3. zeal

4. zeatin

5. zedoary

Using the sample dictionary page, answer the following questions.

_____ 1. How do the two pronunciations of *zebu* differ?
   a. The *z* is pronounced differently.
   b. The *b* is pronounced differently.
   c. The *u* is pronounced differently.
   d. All of the above.

_____ 2. How do the two pronunciations of *Zapotec* differ?
   a. The *z* is pronounced differently.
   b. The *o* is pronounced differently.
   c. Both of the above.
   d. None of the above.

_____ 3. How do the two pronunciations of *Zeeland* differ?
   a. The *e* is pronounced differently.
   b. The *a* is pronounced differently.
   c. The *d* is pronounced differently.
   d. All of the above.

_____ 4. How do the two pronunciations of *Zeitgeist* differ?
   a. The *z* is pronounced differently.
   b. The *z* and the *t* are pronounced differently.
   c. The *t* and the *g* are pronounced differently.
   d. None of the above.

_____ 5. How do the two pronunciations of *zaire* differ?
   a. The *z* is pronounced differently.
   b. The *r* is pronounced differently.
   c. The *e* is pronounced differently.
   d. None of the above.

Using the Word

Most dictionaries will also include a **function label** to indicate the entry word's part of speech. Many words can function as more than one part of speech. For example, the word *walk* would have function labels for noun and verb.

Next you will find the **definition** or meaning of the word; some words may have several definitions. Be sure that you choose the one that best fits the meaning of what you are reading or writing. Always read all the definitions and then decide. Some dictionaries also list **synonyms** (words with the same or similar meaning) of the entry word.

After the definition in most dictionaries (but before the definition in some) is the **etymology**, or the word's history. Knowing the history of a word can sometimes help you to understand why that word is spelled a certain way or how the word came to have several different meanings.

Learning Christianly

Learning to use the dictionary is a basic skill in learning to do research of all kinds. Many people do not like to research subjects that they do not find to be interesting. However, many Christians have devoted their lives to research, and they believe that Psalm 24:1 gives them good reason for doing so. Read this verse and see whether you can determine how it applies to research.

page 386

Precise words

17-7 **PRACTICE THE SKILL**

Using the sample definitions, write the number of the definition that corresponds to the use of this entry word from the *American Heritage College Dictionary*.

chute (sho͞ot) *n.* 1. An inclined trough, passage, or channel through or down which things may pass. 2. A waterfall or rapid. 3. A parachute, such as one for pilots or skydivers.

_____ 1. The machine includes a chute that delivers the parts to the assembler.

_____ 2. Did his chute catch on the tree or the telephone pole?

_____ 3. The chute flows into Lake Superior.

_____ 4. The logs were sent to the mill by way of a wooden chute.

_____ 5. We visited the chute on the Cascade River last summer.

Using the sample dictionary page, answer the following questions.

_____ 1. What is the adverb form of the word *zany?*

_____ 2. From what language does the word *zed* originally come?

_____ 3. What is the meaning of the Persian word from which we get the word *zamindar?*

_____ 4. What part(s) of speech is the word *zap?*

_____ 5. What is the Latin form of the word from which we get the word *zealot?*

CHAPTER 18

LIBRARY SKILLS

What Can I Find in the Library?

Libraries today are not only places for quiet research and study but also exciting centers of activity. Modern libraries contain much more than books. You can often find magazines, newspapers, audio cassettes, videocassettes, and puppets. You can attend classes, listen to lectures, or view displays on interesting topics. Many large public libraries offer free computer access to the Internet. Going to the library is a helpful and enjoyable way to learn. Today's libraries provide a broad selection of information and tools for you to use. Before you can use these tools, however, you need to know where to find them.

Libraries usually are divided into several sections. Sometimes these sections are separate rooms in the library building. Sometimes the sections are an area of shelves set apart from the other shelves. Each section contains a different type of library material.

Books, of course, are still the main feature of most libraries. In fact, our word *library* comes from the Latin word *liber,* which means *book.* Librarians arrange books on shelves called stacks. These stacks usually take up the most space in any library.

Book grew out of an Old English word for "beech," a kind of wood. *Book* comes from the old practice of carving letters into wood.

The **periodical** section contains materials published at regular intervals, such as monthly magazines or daily newspapers. Because they are published regularly, periodicals are an excellent source for current information about a wide variety of topics.

The **reference** section contains materials that do not circulate. In other words, they cannot be checked out of the library. They remain in the library where they will always be available to everyone. Many libraries reserve an entire room for reference materials. A capital letter *R* or the abbreviation *REF* on a book's spine indicates that the book belongs in the reference section.

Many libraries now have a separate section for **audio-visual** materials. These materials may include audio cassettes, videocassettes, works of art such as paintings and sculptures, or even puppets and games for young children. Some libraries have equipment for using the audio-visual materials right there in the library; others allow you to check out the materials for home use. The letters *AV* usually refer to the audio-visual collection.

Most libraries place the books written for **children** and **young adults** in a separate area of the library. This area usually contains both circulating and reference books and may even have its own periodical section and audio-visual materials. The capital letters *J* (for juvenile) or *YA* (for young adult) on a book's spine indicate that the book belongs to this section of the library.

Learning Christianly

Mankind's study and research of the world is as old as mankind itself. In ancient times one of the most accomplished researchers was King Solomon. The wisdom and knowledge of this king of Israel was like no other, and his wisdom was not limited to strictly moral matters (I Kings 4:30-33). In Proverbs 2:1-5 Solomon talks about some of the basics of the right kind of wisdom and knowledge. What does he emphasize in these verses?

How Are the Books Arranged?

All books fall into one of two categories: fiction or nonfiction. **Fiction** books, although sometimes based on facts, tell about events from an author's imagination. Regardless of its topic, a fiction book is arranged on the shelf alphabetically by the author's last name. If two authors share the same last name, their books are arranged alphabetically by the authors' first names. If a library has more than one book by the same author, the author's books are arranged alphabetically according to the first words of the titles (not including *A, An,* or *The*). The list below shows the order in which these books would appear on a library shelf.

> *Jane Eyre* by Charlotte Brontë
> *Wuthering Heights* by Emily Brontë
> *The Deerslayer* by James Fenimore Cooper
> *The Mystery of Edwin Drood* by Charles Dickens
> *Oliver Twist* by Charles Dickens
> *A Tale of Two Cities* by Charles Dickens

ETYMOLOGY The word *fiction* comes from the Middle English word *ficcion,* "invention," and the older Latin source *fictus,* "formed, molded." Fiction is writing that has been formed or invented by its writer.

Some libraries separate the **mystery fiction** and **science fiction** books from the other fiction books. These libraries will have shelves marked *mystery fiction* or *science fiction* where those books can be found. In addition, the book spines will usually be marked with the letters *MYS* for mystery fiction or *SCI* for science fiction.

Nonfiction books present facts on almost every subject. Books about airplanes, livestock, mythology, poetry, and government are examples of nonfiction books. Most libraries use the **Dewey Decimal System** to arrange nonfiction books. The arranging is called "decimal" because many of the numbers have decimal points. The numbers are found on the spine of each book, along with the author and the title.

Melvil Dewey developed this system to bring together all the different books on one subject rather than having them scattered throughout the library. He divided knowledge into ten subject categories. To these categories he assigned numbers.

000-099   Generalities (including encyclopedias and general reference works)

100-199   Philosophy and psychology

200-299   Religion (including mythology)

300-399   Social sciences (including government, education, and etiquette)

400-499   Language

500-599   Natural sciences and mathematics (including chemistry and biology)

600-699   Technology (including occupations and professions)

700-799   The arts (including sports)

800-899   Literature and rhetoric (including short stories and plays)

900-999   Geography and history (including travel and biography)

A **biography** is a book written by one person about another person's life; an **autobiography** is a book about the author's own life. Many libraries separate the biographies and autobiographies from the other nonfiction books and shelve them in a separate area of the stacks. A capital *B* or the Dewey Decimal number *920* or *921* on the spine of a book indicates that the book is a biography or an autobiography. Biographies and autobiographies are arranged alphabetically by the last name of the subject, not the author. For example, a biography about the missionary Adoniram Judson would be shelved with other biographies under *J* for Judson.

Some large libraries use the **Library of Congress System** instead of the Dewey Decimal System. The Library of Congress System uses letters and numbers instead of numbers only and has twenty-one subject categories instead of ten. For example, in one library the book *Birds' Eggs* may have the Dewey Decimal number 598.233 and the Library of Congress call number QL 675.W32. Be sure you understand the system that your library uses.

18-1   PRACTICE THE SKILL

Number the titles and authors of the following fiction books in the order in which they would appear on the fiction shelves of a library.

_____ Norton Juster, *The Phantom Tollbooth*

_____ Rosemary Sutcliff, *Simon*

_____ Stephen W. Meader, *Clear for Action*

_____ Jim Kjelgaard, *Big Red*

_____ Betsy Byars, *The Summer of the Swans*

_____ Geoffrey Trease, *Web of Traitors*

_____ Sheila Burnford, *The Incredible Journey*

_____ Will James, *Smoky*

_____ Stephen W. Meader, *Boy with a Pack*

_____ Rosemary Sutcliff, *The Silver Branch*

Using the Dewey Decimal chart on pages 346-47, write the numbers for the correct category of each of the following books.

_____ 1. *Janice VanCleave's Geometry for Every Kid*

_____ 2. *Encyclopaedia Britannica*

_____ 3. *The Winter Olympics*

_____ 4. *Myths and Legends of the Ancient Near East*

_____ 5. *Perfect Pigs: An Introduction to Manners*

_____ 6. *Aesop's Fables*

_____ 7. *Clara Barton: Soldier of Mercy*

_____ 8. *The Guinness Book of World Records*

_____ 9. *How We Choose a President*

_____10. *Favorite Operas*

_____11. *Careers in Horticultural Science*

_____12. *The Essence of Ancient Philosophy*

_____13. *Everyday Life in Ancient Crete*

_____14. *Indian Signals and Sign Language*

_____15. *The Internal Combustion Engine*

How Are the Books Labeled?

Every book in the library will have a label on the spine of the book. For a nonfiction book, this label contains the book's **call number.** The call number is the Dewey Decimal number with the first letter of the author's last name under it. Sometimes the label will also contain a **section letter** (such as *R*) if the book belongs in a separate section of the library (such as reference). Fiction books usually do not have call numbers. A fiction book is labeled with the first few letters of the author's last name and the capital letter *F*. The label may also include a section letter if the book belongs in a special section, such as *MYS* (mystery) or *YA* (young adult).

The call number or letters that appear on a book's spine will also appear on the **catalog entry.** Traditionally, libraries used **card catalogs** as tools to help people find the books they wanted. Today, many libraries have converted their card catalogs to on-line **computer catalogs.** Both types of catalogs contain the same information in approximately the same format. Computer catalogs, however, offer the user more ways to search for information.

How Do I Use the Card Catalog?

A card catalog is a cabinet with small drawers, usually located near the library entrance. Here, cards contain information on each book in the library. The three types of cards in the card catalog are the author card, the title card, and the subject card. These cards are usually alphabetized all together (not separated into three groups) in the drawers. Each card has a different top line: the author card starts with the author; the title card starts with the book's title; and the subject card starts with the subject of the book. Each card will include the title, the author, the place of publication, the date of publication, the publisher, the number of pages, and the call number (for a nonfiction book).

To use the card catalog you need to know the author or the title or the subject of the book you want. Perhaps you want a book by a particular author, but you are not sure of the title. Find the author card, which is filed alphabetically according to the author's last name. If there is more than one author with that same last name, the cards under that last name will be arranged alphabetically by the first names. For example, under *Brontë,* the name *Brontë, Anne,* would come before *Brontë, Charlotte.* Both fiction and nonfiction books have author cards.

Title cards are placed alphabetically in the drawers according to the first word in the title (again, not including *A, An,* and *The*). There are title cards for both fiction and nonfiction books.

If you do not know the titles or authors of nonfiction books on a subject that interests you, look for subject cards in the card catalog. There may be more than one subject card for some books. Subjects include noteworthy people, geographic locations, languages, countries, and other topics of interest.

When you find the card for the book you want, first write down the call number from the upper left-hand corner of the card (for a nonfiction book); then copy the name of the author and the title of the book. With this information you can ask for the book or go to the shelf and get it yourself.

How Do I Use the Computer Catalog?

Instead of individual filing cards, a computer catalog contains electronic records for each book. Each record includes the same information you would find on an author, title, or subject card in the card catalog. In fact, a computer catalog may contain more information than a card catalog. For instance, some computer-catalog records include a summary of the book. The summary can help you decide whether the book will be helpful to you. In addition, most computer catalogs also contain information about each book's status. In other words, the computer catalog can tell you if a book is available or is already checked out. If the book is already checked out, the catalog may tell you when it is due to be returned.

Using the computer catalog is similar to using the card catalog. First, you need to know the author or the title or the subject of the book you want to find. Next, type the information you know into the computer, according to the instructions on the screen. The computer will begin to search for the book you need by comparing the words you typed to the information in its database. When it finds a match, the computer screen will display the record for that book. If the information you typed was not specific enough, the computer screen will display a list for you to choose from. For instance, if you type the subject rather than the title, the screen will list several books about that subject. To see the record for an individual book, simply type the number displayed next to that title on the list.

The computer catalog at one library may be somewhat different from the computer catalog at another library. Be sure to ask the librarian for help if you do not know how to use your library's computer catalog.

date of publication	
publisher	
city of publication	

MATERIAL: Book

CALL NUMBER: J 973.099 Blue

AUTHOR: Blue, Rose.

TITLE: The White House kids / Rose Blue and Corinne J. Naden.

PUBLICATION: Brookfield, Conn.: Millbrook Press, c1995.

DESCRIPTION: 96 p.: ill. (some col.); 24 cm.

NOTES: Includes bibliographical references (p. 93) and index.

number of pages

contains illustrations
(some in color)

height of book's spine

SUBJECT: Children of presidents—United States—History—Juvenile literature.

SUBJECT: Children of presidents.

SUBJECT: Presidents—Family.

SUBJECT: White House (Washington, D.C.).

MATERIAL: Book
CALL NUMBER: 598.233 Walters
AUTHOR: Walters, Michael
TITLE: Birds' eggs / Michael Walters; photography by Harry Taylor.
EDITION: 1st American ed.
PUBLICATION: London; New York: Dorling Kindersley, 1994.
DESCRIPTION: 256 p.: col. ill.: 22 cm.
SERIES: Eyewitness handbooks
NOTES: Includes index.
SUBJECT: Birds—Eggs.

Using the catalog entry above, answer the following questions.

_____ 1. Who is the author of *Birds' Eggs*?

_____ 2. How many pages are in *Birds' Eggs*?

_____ 3. Who is the photographer whose work appears in *Birds' Eggs*?

_____ 4. *Bird's Eggs* is part of what series?

_____ 5. What company published *Birds' Eggs*?

18-4 PRACTICE THE SKILL

A. Choose five topics from the list below.

B. Use your library's card catalog or computer catalog to find one book on each topic.

C. List the title, author, and call number for each book you choose.

1. Church history _____

   _____

2. Holidays _____

   _____

3. Ethics _____

   _____

4. Zoology _____

   _____

5. Old English _____

   _____

6. Classical music _____

   _____

7. Tokyo _____

   _____

8. Dairy farming _____

   _____

9. Journalism _____

   _____

10. Greek drama _____

   _____

How Do I Use Specific Reference Works?

Dictionaries

All dictionaries are pretty much alike, right? Actually, there are many different types, and you need to be acquainted with each one. An **unabridged dictionary** gives the most complete list of words and definitions. Although an abridged dictionary, or **desk dictionary**, is not as complete as the unabridged dictionary, it contains most of the words that you will need for your own reading and writing. Some desk dictionaries are designed for junior high students.

Abridge comes from the Latin word for "abbreviate," which means "to shorten."

A **foreign language dictionary** lists the words of another language and gives their meanings in English. Many foreign language dictionaries have two sections, one listing English words with their foreign language counterparts and the other listing words from a foreign language with their English translations.

Other dictionaries define special terms or provide information not found in a regular dictionary. A **dictionary of synonyms**, or **thesaurus**, gives words with similar meanings; some also give **antonyms**, words with opposite meanings. A **biographical dictionary** gives information on important people from the past and the present. A **geographic dictionary**, or **gazetteer**, lists places and their locations. It provides not only a correct pronunciation of the name of a place but also a description of its geographic features (such as rivers or mountains) and other helpful information (such as population).

Encyclopedias

Encyclopedias contain articles on almost every imaginable subject. These articles are arranged alphabetically. The volumes of an encyclopedia are usually labeled with one or more letters as well as with a numeral.

Find the article you need with the help of guide words at the top of each page. These words tell you the topic of the first article on each page, somewhat like the guide words that help you find words in a dictionary.

Check also in the index to find the pages where articles on your topic appear. Some sets of encyclopedias have an index in each volume, while others have a special volume (usually the last volume) that is the index for the entire set.

Investigate other references on the same topic when the encyclopedia gives them. They help you find articles with important additional information. These additional references, called cross-references, are often listed at the end of the article under a heading such as "See also."

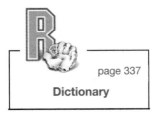

page 337
Dictionary

Almanacs

An **almanac** supplements the encyclopedia by giving more current information. An almanac includes tables of weights and measures, lists of sports statistics, names of award winners, information about government agencies and programs, summaries of recent events, and other miscellaneous facts. Most almanacs are published every year. You can find the information you need by looking in the almanac's index. An almanac's index may appear at the front, like a table of contents, instead of at the back, where most indexes appear.

Atlases

An **atlas** is a collection of maps. It can provide some of the same information as a geographic dictionary. Some atlases contain only political maps, which show political divisions such as countries, states, or cities. Other atlases include topographical maps, which show geographic features such as mountain ranges and bodies of water. The most commonly used atlases contain road maps, which show the roads connecting various cities. Some atlases also include information about populations, crops, weather, and similar facts. Every atlas has an index that lists the page number where you can find the map you need.

Books of Quotations

A **book of quotations**, such as Bartlett's *Familiar Quotations,* allows you to find a quotation by looking up its author, first line, or subject. Most books of quotations also list each quotation's original source and date.

Concordances

The Bible **concordance** gives key words from the Bible with lists of verses where the key words appear. When you can remember only part of a verse, look up an important word from the verse, a key word, in the concordance's alphabetical list.

For example, if you remember reading a verse that says something about temptation being common to man, you can look up *temptation* and find I Corinthians 10:13 as well as other verses listed under that topic. If the particular passage you want is not listed, try another key word. Not all key words or passages will be given in every concordance.

Some concordances are available in software form for use on computers. These products make searching the Scriptures even easier. For example, finding all the occurrences of the phrase "son of God" in a printed concordance would be time consuming, and you might miss references. But in a software version it can take less than a second.

Readers' Guide to Periodical Literature

The **Readers' Guide to Periodical Literature** is the most commonly used periodical index. In the same way that the card catalog or computer catalog can help you find a specific book, the *Readers' Guide* can help you find a specific periodical article. It lists articles from approximately two hundred fifty magazines by subject and by author. Each entry will tell you the article's subject, its title, its author, the magazine in which it appears, the issue number or date of the magazine, and the page numbers where you can find that particular article.

beginning page number

FARGO (N.D.)

subject heading

includes illustrations

Flooded Red River ruins crops. K. Johnston. il *Midwesterner* no15 p28-9+ My 1997

indicates article continues on other pages

date

article title

author

magazine title

issue number

18·5 PRACTICE THE SKILL

Identify the type of reference tool you would use to find the answer to each question: desk dictionary, foreign language dictionary, thesaurus, biographical dictionary, geographic dictionary, encyclopedia, almanac, atlas, book of quotations, concordance, or *Readers' Guide to Periodical Literature*.

_____ 1. What baseball team won the 1956 World Series?

_____ 2. From what language does the English word *fantastic* originate?

_____ 3. Which of the fifty states have cities named Maplewood?

_____ 4. Which spacecraft was launched on November 3, 1973?

_____ 5. How many verses in Proverbs include the word *believe?*

_____ 6. What is an antonym for *resolution?*

_____ 7. Who discovered uranium?

_____ 8. Who said "A good book is the best of friends"?

_____ 9. What is the Portuguese word for *cow?*

_____ 10. Where did soccer originate?

_____ 11. Which magazines published articles about Hale-Bopp in April 1997?

_____ 12. What is the average yearly rainfall in Sri Lanka?

_____ 13. In which verse does the apostle Paul mention "a thorn in the flesh"?

_____ 14. John Chapman is better known today by what nickname?

_____ 15. What are some breeds of horses?

 **18-6** **PRACTICE THE SKILL**

CRUISING

Barging your way through Europe: river barge cruises. T. Innes. il
World Traveler no79 p12+ O 1998

Use the entry from the *Readers' Guide to Periodical Literature* to answer each question.

1. Who is the author of the article?_____

_____

2. Is the article illustrated? How do you know?_____

_____

3. What is the title of the article?_____

_____

4. In which issue of the magazine did this article appear?_____

_____

5. Is there more than one page for the article? How do you know?_____

_____

Techno-Talk

Between Innings

A headline in an Internet trade publication declared that "Firewall Can Now Block Spam." To people not familiar with computer talk, this says that walls used to prevent fires from spreading between apartments can also keep out canned pork. But to people in the computer industry, it means there is a software program that can filter out unwanted e-mail.

We call words that are used only by people in certain fields *jargon*. To the outsider, jargon is almost impossible to understand. Christians use jargon too. How might this sound to someone who has never heard the gospel: "I covet your prayers as I go on visitation; pray that I will be a good testimony"?

The words *covet, visitation,* and *testimony* mean different things outside the Christian context. Jargon is language that excludes those not in the group. Christians should take care not to use words that confuse those who most need to understand.

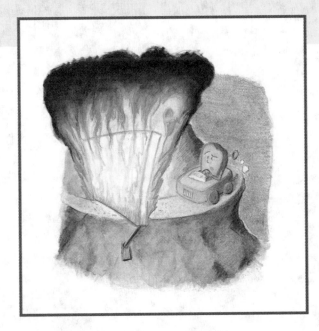

CHAPTER 19

STUDY SKILLS

Developing an Interest

Do you ever have problems concentrating on what a teacher is saying because you are not interested in the subject? You are interested in certain subjects because God has given you these interests; therefore, you achieve good grades more easily in some classes than in others. However, you are not doomed to be bored or to achieve a lower grade if you are not interested in a certain subject (such as science or math). Interest can be developed.

Each class has something new or interesting. Look for one fact that can be useful or interesting to you. There are many ways to focus your attention and to discover interesting information.

1. Sit in your chair as if you are interested. Do not slouch.

2. Keep your eyes focused on your teacher to help you concentrate better.

3. Listen (or read) to learn. Try to learn while you are listening to the teacher or doing your class work. The more you learn in class, the less time you will have to spend studying outside class.

4. Write (or mark) important points. If the teacher or textbook emphasizes a point, write it down.

5. Practice guessing. Think ahead. What will the teacher or the book state next? Were you correct? If you were not, why not?

6. Connect the information that you are learning. How does what you are now learning relate to what you learned yesterday or in another class?

7. Ask questions, especially about information that you do not understand. If you are shy, write your questions down and then ask at least one question in each class until you become more confident.

Using the Parts of a Book

If you understand the parts of a book, you can find information in it quickly. Not all books have all of these parts, nor are they arranged in the same order in all books.

Every book begins with a **title page,** which gives the title of the book, the name of the author, the name of the publisher, and the place of publication. On the back of this page is the **copyright page,** which gives the year the book was copyrighted. *Copyright* is the legal right to that book; no one can reprint any part of it without permission.

A **table of contents** gives the chapter or unit divisions with page numbers in numerical order. A **list of illustrations** is similar to a table of contents; it tells where the pictures are in the text.

Some books also include **acknowledgments,** the names of people the author or editor wants to thank, and an **introduction** or **preface**, an explanation of the purpose of the book.

The major part of every book is the **text**. In both fiction and nonfiction books, the text is usually divided into units, sections, or chapters.

Other pages of information come after the text in many nonfiction books. The **bibliography** lists either the books that the author used in writing the text or the titles of some other books about the same subject.

An **appendix** includes extra helps, such as charts, diagrams, long lists, and notes of explanation. One kind of appendix is a **glossary,** which gives the definitions of special vocabulary used in the text. Many textbooks have glossaries and other appendixes.

An **index** is an alphabetical listing of key words and phrases with all the page numbers where they appear in the text. Sometimes the index will also list the page numbers for the illustrations.

You may notice that fiction books usually have only a title page, a table of contents, and a text. The main purpose of fiction is usually to entertain, not to inform; therefore, the other parts are not necessary.

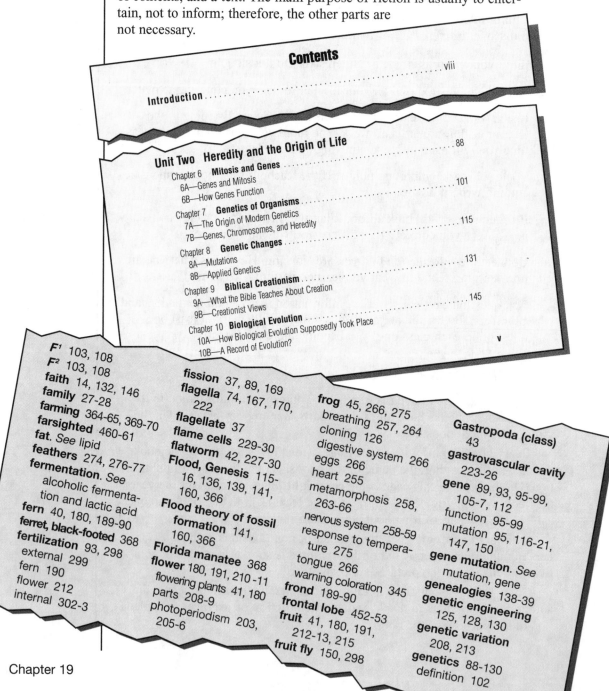

Use the sample table of contents and index to find the answer to each question. Fill in each blank with the letter of the correct answer.

_____ 1. In which chapter would you find the theory of fossil formation after the Flood?
a. 7
b. 8
c. 9

_____ 2. Which page would tell about the black-footed ferret?
a. 189
b. 229
c. 368

_____ 3. Which chapter contains information on genetic engineering?
a. 6
b. 7
c. 8

_____ 4. Which page would tell about parts of a flower?
a. 203
b. 208
c. 210

_____ 5. Fission is discussed in chapter
a. 6.
b. 7.
c. 8.

_____ 6. Genealogies can be found in the same chapter as
a. farming.
b. the Flood.
c. genetic engineering.

_____ 7. Which page would help you learn about flame cells?
a. 227
b. 229
c. 231

_____ 8. Which chapter includes Bible teaching about Creation?
a. 7
b. 8
c. 9

_____ 9. Genetics is discussed in all these chapter parts except
a. 7A.
b. 8B.
c. 9B.

_____ 10. The definition of genetics is discussed in the same chapter as
a. F^2.
b. fern fertilization.
c. the function of genes.

19-2 PRACTICE THE SKILL

Fill in each blank with the letter of the correct book section that would give you the information requested. Letters may be used more than once.

A. title page
B. copyright page
C. table of contents
D. text
E. bibliography
F. appendix
G. glossary
H. index

_____ 1. the place of the book's publication

_____ 2. the definition of a math term in the math text

_____ 3. the main portion of the book

_____ 4. a list of the chapter titles

_____ 5. a special chart

_____ 6. the name of the book

_____ 7. the order of the textbook's main ideas

_____ 8. the books that the author used when writing the text

_____ 9. the pages on which a certain term is used

_____ 10. the year the book was published

Reading Textbooks

In elementary school, your textbooks were filled with stories. Even your science and history textbooks were written to sound like stories. You have probably discovered that in junior high most of your textbooks are not written as stories. Therefore, you need to learn how to use different kinds of reading skills.

When you receive a new textbook, take a few minutes to see where you are headed. Survey your textbook by looking over the table of contents. The table of contents will tell you two important things: the major topics in the textbook and the logical organization the author uses to discuss those topics.

Textbook authors almost always organize their topics by units and chapters. For example, this textbook has three units: grammar, usage, and reference. Each unit is divided into chapters. In this book, the reference unit contains four chapters: Dictionary Skills, Library Skills, Study Skills (the chapter you are reading now), and Composition Skills.

Each chapter may be further divided into sections. This chapter has large bold headings and small bold headings. Each heading tells you which part of the topic will be discussed. The rest of the information is in regular paragraphs. Read each paragraph looking for the one topic in that paragraph. Once you have found that topic, look further to see what in-depth information the paragraph includes about the topic. Also notice the pictures and illustrations. They are there to help you better understand what is being taught. Actually, reading a textbook can be easier than reading a novel because you have all these wonderful clues to help you along.

Improving Your Study Time

The purpose of studying is to learn the information. You might be surprised to discover that the students who make the best grades are not necessarily the most intelligent students in the class. They are usually the ones who have figured out the best methods of study.

Be prepared for every class period. Come to class with your textbook. Check before you get to class to be certain that you have everything (pen, paper, text, etc.) that you will need for that class. Take time every day

1. to write down each homework assignment in an assignment booklet.

2. to put each paper where it belongs.

3. to take home every book you need.

4. to have every book, paper, and other study tool before you begin your homework.

You may think that some homework or tests are beyond your ability. With the help of the Lord and with some organization, however, you can conquer many difficulties.

Scheduling Your Study Time

Life in junior high is very busy. Therefore, you need to use a schedule to make the best use of your study time.

First, you should develop a priority schedule. To create priorities means to "establish by order of importance or urgency" (from *The American Heritage College Dictionary*). Once a month you should take at least five minutes to think ahead. Think about the activities scheduled for that month: church activities, sports practice, jobs at home, due dates for school assignments. Write these events on a calendar. Then you will know what days you already have things planned if another activity comes up. If you know your schedule in advance, you can plan to work ahead on school projects.

Second, you should have a detailed homework schedule. An assignment notebook is a must. It is wise to write "to do" lists, because the average person's mind is crowded with too much information to remember everything that occurs. That is why even many adults have appointment books.

Write down every assignment as soon as the teacher gives it to you. If you have no homework in a certain class on one day, write the word *none* for this class in your assignment notebook. If you do not write anything, you might think that you have homework but forgot to write it down.

When your teacher assigns a long-term project, mark the due date on your calendar. Then plan a schedule for completing the assignment one part at a time. Give yourself a due date for each part of the project and mark these dates on your calendar. This strategy reminds you to continue working on the project until it is finished.

Learning Christianly

Studying is not easy but it is rewarding. Proverbs 25:2 is a great verse proving that a Christian can get excited about studying for Christian reasons. Read this verse for yourself and see what you think.

Third, you should have a daily study schedule. You need to have a plan for your after-school study time. This plan must include the "when," "where," and "how" of study.

When: Your study time is limited. Your choices are right after school or between supper and bedtime. Do not wait until the next morning to do your homework. Between getting dressed and eating breakfast, you will not have enough time to study.

Where: Establish one place to study—your bedroom, the kitchen, the living room, or a special study room. Choose a place where you can be comfortable, but not so comfortable that you are tempted to fall asleep. If you have just one study place, your mind will become conditioned to study in that place.

How: Which subject do you study first and which last? Determine which subject is your most difficult. Then decide whether to study that subject first or last. Do you retain more information when you study your hardest subject first? Or do you remember best what you study last?

Once you have determined the order of your study, decide approximately how long the homework for each class usually takes. Of course, some evenings the timing will vary. You should always set aside some time to review. These review sessions save study time later by allowing the information to become more firmly rooted in your long-term memory.

Using Profitable Memory Techniques

Once you have completed your daily reading assignments and your written homework assignments, the only type of assignment left to do is studying for those quizzes and tests. What you study includes the information from class and the information in your textbook. Here are some techniques to improve your memory.

1. Determine to remember. In other words, pay attention as you study. Do not be mentally lazy.

2. Ask yourself questions about your notes and answer them aloud.

3. Make flash cards from note cards. Write the question on one side and the answer on the other side.

4. Create your own written quizzes. Put your quiz aside for a day or two. Then return to the quiz and try to answer the questions. The questions you cannot correctly answer are the ones to restudy.

5. Have a friend or family member quiz you orally.

6. Think of some picture which you can associate with the fact you are studying. For example, you have read that China throughout most of its history has had a policy of isolationism. (It discourages the influence of non-Chinese peoples and cultures.) You know about the Great Wall of China. You could think of China as enclosed by a huge wall keeping out everyone who does not already live in China. This strategy can help you remember China's isolationist policy.

7. Cluster the information you are learning. If your history teacher gives you a list of names to learn for the final exam, learn them by category groups: the names of Chinese rulers, the names of Japanese rulers, and so on.

8. Use mnemonic [nĭ-mŏn´-ĭk] devices to help you remember.

   a. Create rhymes.

> Predicate nouns, the subject rename.
> To do their jobs, linking verbs they claim.

   b. Create acronyms and acrostics. An acronym is a word in which each letter stands for another word. An acrostic is a word in which each letter stands for a phrase or a sentence. Here is an example of an acronym:

> To remember the names of the great lakes (Superior, Huron, Michigan, Erie, Ontario), take their first letters *(S, H, M, E, O)* and rearrange them into a single word: *HOMES*.

Improving Your Reading Comprehension

Your school career involves much reading. Although you do not always know the meaning of every word you read, you do not always have time to stop reading and to search for the meaning of each unfamiliar word. How can you discover the meanings of these words while you continue to read your assignments? You can "read around" the word itself, or you can analyze the parts of the word. You may not discover the word's exact dictionary definition, but you will know enough of the meaning to understand the concept being taught.

Definitions

Look for a definition. Sometimes the text gives a definition with the word. In this example, what does *joual* mean?

> The Canadian Indian spoke *joual* to the missionaries, a dialect of Canadian French using nonstandard grammar and English vocabulary.

Restatements

Look for a restatement. If the text does not give a definition of the word, look for extra information after the word that may explain the word's meaning.

> The *edentate* man, who found it impossible to eat anything requiring chewing, settled for some rice pudding and hot coffee.

What does *edentate* mean? The sentence explains that chewing is difficult for the man. You can probably guess that *edentate* means "lacking teeth."

Examples

Look for an example. The extra details in the rest of the sentence help you guess the meaning of the word you do not know.

> The *recalcitrant* young man resisted his teacher's authority and refused to apologize.

What does *recalcitrant* mean? The sentence gives two examples of the young man's attitude and behavior. From the context, you can determine that *recalcitrant* means "stubborn and defiant."

Write the definitions of the words in italics. Use contextual clues to determine the definitions.

1. The knight's *vambrace,* the piece of armor protecting his arm from the wrist to the elbow, was damaged during the battle.

   _____

2. The *deluge* last night caused the river and the sewers to overflow this morning.

   _____

3. The *jovial* man, who was never in a bad mood, laughed heartily at his guest's joke.

   _____

4. Mother said I must have been starving since I left only a *scintilla* of mashed potatoes in the bowl.

   _____

5. The teacher told the students to *cogitate,* think very carefully, before they answered the next question.

   _____

Word Parts

Look at the parts of the word. If you know the meaning of part of the word, you may be able to determine what the entire word means. Listed below are several prefixes, suffixes, and root words and their meanings.

- Prefixes

   A **prefix** is added to the beginning of a word.

Prefix	Meaning	Example
ante-	before	antecedent
e-/ex-	out, from	emit, exhale
in-	not	insane
inter-	between, among	interstate
intra-	within	intramural
per-	through	permit
super-	above normal	supervise

- Suffixes

  A **suffix** is added to the end of a word.

Suffix	Meaning	Example
-ion	action/condition	exception
-ous	having/possessing	spacious

- Roots

  A **root** is the main part of a word. Some roots can act alone as words without any prefixes or suffixes attached.

Root	Meaning	Example
ced/cede	to move, to yield	concede
cept	take	except
flu	flow	fluid
leg/lect	read, choose	illegible
mit/mis	send	permission
urb	city	suburban
vide/vise	see	supervise

19-4 PRACTICE THE SKILL

Using the definitions of the prefixes, suffixes, and root words given above, guess the definitions for the words given below. Even if you do not know the entire definition, give the part that you do know.

1. vision _____

2. superscript _____

3. perception _____

4. flume _____

5. indestructible _____

6. interurban _____

7. exclude _____

8. antechamber _____

9. neglect _____

10. gracious _____

Taking Tests

While part of your grade depends on how well you do on your homework and quizzes, another part of it depends on how well you do on your tests. Taking good notes, doing your homework, and studying your notes and homework weekly will help you to do better on your tests than you will do if you wait until the night before the test to begin studying. The more often you review, the more information your memory will retain.

How to Take Classroom Tests

1. Look over the test to discover what types of questions there are and to see how many questions you have to answer.

2. Read the directions to each section carefully.

3. Work through the entire test in one of two ways.

   a. Start at the beginning and keep going. Answer all those questions that you know and those that you are 50 percent to 75 percent certain of. Mark somehow those that you do not know or that you need to spend more time thinking about (circle the number, place a check beside the number, etc.). Come back to those later.

   b. Choose the most difficult section of the test and do it first. Be certain, however, not to spend too much time on that one section, or you will not have enough time to complete the easier sections. (Again, mark the questions with which you are having problems and come back to those later.) (Note: Be aware that sometimes information given in another question on the test may provide you with just the clue you need to answer one of the questions that you do not know the answer to.)

4. Try to answer all the questions, even if you have to guess at some.

5. Think before you write. It is always better to write a little about what you do know than to write a lot about what you do not know.

6. Write neatly. Correct answers will not count if the teacher cannot read what you have written.

How to Answer Objective Test Questions

Multiple Choice

1. Read the question carefully. Try to think of the answer before you look at the choices.

2. Read all the choices carefully. Ignore those that you know are wrong. (You might want to cross them out.)

3. Choose the best answer from the choices that are left.

Example: _d_   During World War II, what country controlled most of the activity in the Pacific Ocean?
    a. Germany
    b. China
    c. England
    d. Japan

Matching

1. Read all the questions carefully. Try to think of the correct answer for each question before you look at the choices.

2. Match the questions and answers that you know are correct.

3. From the choices remaining, choose the best answer for each question.

Example: A. Aleksandr Solzhenitsyn
    B. Elizabeth II
    C. Pablo Picasso
    D. Marie Curie
    E. Franklin Pierce

_E_   1. American president

_C_   2. Spanish artist

_A_   3. Russian writer

_B_   4. English queen

_D_   5. French scientist

True/False

1. Read each item carefully. If any word in the item is false, the entire item is false.

2. Look for words such as *always, never,* or *only;* these words often signal a false item.

Example:

false   Adverbs modify only verbs.

(Adverbs modify verbs, but they also modify adjectives and other adverbs. The word *only* makes this statement false.)

Short Answer

1. Answer accurately and completely those questions you know.

2. If you do not know the answer, guess as well as you can. You may get partial credit for your answer.

Example:

_____ *May* _____   1. Mother's Day in the United States is observed in what month?

_____ *November* _____   2. Thanksgiving in the United States is observed in what month?

_____ *June* _____   3. Flag Day in the United States is observed in what month?

How to Take Standardized Tests

According to your school's schedule, you will take standardized tests periodically. If you are familiar with the types of questions usually included on a standardized test, you will have a better chance of doing well on it.

Reading Comprehension

The reading comprehension section tests your ability to analyze a written passage. The questions may ask about the main ideas, details, or meaning of the passage. You may have to evaluate information or draw conclusions. Use these strategies for this part of the test.

1. Briefly look at the questions.

2. Read the paragraph and answer the questions you definitely know.

3. Then read the other questions carefully; eliminate the choices that you know are incorrect.

4. Choose the most logical answer from the choices remaining.

Example: One by one the French posts began falling to the British. Late in 1758 a British force ousted the French from Fort Duquesne. The British rebuilt the badly damaged fort and renamed it Fort Pitt.

    _C_   In this paragraph the word *posts* means
      A. wooden supports
      B. mail deliveries
      C. military bases
      D. assigned positions

The paragraph has no information leading the reader to think that *wooden supports* or *mail deliveries* would be the correct choice. *Assigned positions* would come closer, but the contextual clues should signal that *military bases* is the best answer.

Vocabulary

The vocabulary section tests your knowledge of common English words. This section may include two types of questions. One type gives you part of a sentence or an entire sentence with a word in bold print. You choose from a list of choices the word that best matches the meaning of the word in bold print. Use your knowledge of contextual clues to help you choose an answer.

Example: _C_   The boat moved into the **harbor.**
        A. island
        B. outlet
        C. sheltered body of water
        D. water

Another type of question may list several sentences, all including the same underlined word. You choose from the list of choices the sentence in which the word has the same meaning as in the original sentence.

Example: _B_   The senator will take a <u>stand</u> for what he believes.
        A. Please <u>stand</u> for the doxology.
        B. Our pastor's <u>stand</u> is the same as our family's.
        C. I could <u>stand</u> having some breakfast.
        D. The bookcase will <u>stand</u> six feet high.

In the original sentence, *stand* means "a position one is prepared to uphold." *Stand* in the first choice means "to rise to an upright position." In the second choice, *stand* means "a position one is prepared to uphold." In the third choice, *stand* means "to benefit from." *Stand* in the fourth choice means "to measure to a specified height." The correct answer is the second choice.

Grammar, Usage, and Mechanics

Some standardized tests combine questions about grammar, usage, and mechanics in one section. Other standardized tests include several separate sections of questions. The questions may appear in several different formats. The test may show a sentence with several words underlined and labeled. Then you choose the word that contains an error. If the sentence is correct, choose the "no error" option.

Example: _A_   Sheila, our <u>Dog,</u> <u>climbs</u> the steps <u>carefully</u>. <u>No error</u>
                A   B   C   D
The correct choice is *A* because the word *dog* should not be capitalized.

Another type of question may show you a sentence with part of the sentence underlined. You then choose one of several possible replacements for the underlined part. If the underlined part is correct, choose the answer that indicates no change is necessary.

Example: _B_   One of my dogs <u>is missing their</u> collar.
        A. are missing their
        B. is missing its
        C. are missing its
        D. (correct as is)

The correct choice is *B* because the pronoun *its* agrees with its singular antecedent *One* and the verb *is* agrees with the singular subject *One*.

Some standardized tests have separate sections for mechanics (capitalization and punctuation). The question may divide one sentence into several parts. Each part is listed separately. You choose the part that contains an error. If the sentence is correct, choose the answer that indicates no change is necessary.

Example: _D_ A. Candy went to the store
              B. and bought a collar
              C. for her dog.
              D. (no error)

Because each section of the sentence is correct, the correct answer is *D (no error)*.

19-5   PRACTICE THE SKILL

Reading Comprehension

When the United States entered the nineteenth century, it was a quiet land with family farms, small villages, and a few small cities on the Atlantic coastline. By the end of the century, however, crowded cities, busy factories, and mechanized farms stretched across the country. At the dawn of the twentieth century, the United States was on its way to becoming the greatest industrial nation in the world.

_____ 1. The topic of the above paragraph is
    A. American farming methods.
    B. villages and cities in the United States.
    C. the twentieth century.
    D. the industrialization of the United States.

Vocabulary

_____ 2. Settlers used wagons to carry their supplies over the narrow <u>isthmus</u> that separated the two large lakes.
    A. steel bridge
    B. strip of land
    C. mountain passage
    D. river

_____ 3. Kris received an autographed <u>copy</u> of his sister's novel.
    A. Amber tried to <u>copy</u> Ryan's actions.
    B. Pablo wrote the <u>copy</u> for the newspaper advertisement.
    C. The teacher wanted me to print another <u>copy</u> of my report.
    D. Biographical <u>copy</u> for people can be found in an encyclopedia.

Grammar, Usage, and Mechanics

_____ 4. Sarah, <u>who</u> wears <u>the</u> uniform, <u>ride</u> her bicycle. <u>No error</u>
                        A   B   C   D

_____ 5. Everyone <u>clapped their hands</u> as Danika walked off stage.
- A. clapped their hand
- B. clapped his hands
- C. clapped its hand
- D. (correct as is)

_____ 6. A. David said to
- B. his Father,
- C. "Where is Aunt Beth?"
- D. (no error)

CHAPTER 20

COMPOSITION SKILLS:
THE WRITER'S TOOLBOX

What Is a Paragraph?

You are reading a paragraph right now. A **paragraph** consists of a group of sentences related closely to one main idea. The main idea of the paragraph is usually stated in the **topic sentence.** As you write, you indent each new paragraph to show that you are introducing another idea or point.

Besides the topic sentence, paragraphs contain **supporting sentences.** These sentences may use details, examples, illustrations, or other methods to support the topic sentence.

A **concluding sentence** joins all the ideas together so that the paragraph will be complete. Many concluding sentences restate the idea in the topic sentence.

Caring for Your Cat

Every cat owner is responsible to provide for three basic survival needs of his pet. The first need is food; any cat will die without food, of course. Another need is fresh water. A cat's water dish should be rinsed and refilled at least once a day. Finally, every cat (whether it lives indoors or out) needs a warm, dry place to sleep. Providing for these simple needs for his pet is the duty of a dependable cat owner.

Topic Sentence

Supporting Sentences

Concluding Sentence

Planning

How Do I Choose a Topic?

Before you begin to write, you must choose a **topic**. Some people have trouble thinking of anything to write about; other people have so many ideas that they have trouble choosing just one. Choose a topic that interests you. If you are interested in your topic, your reader will be more interested in what you have to say. Here are some methods you can use to find topic ideas.

- **Individual techniques**

Make a list

Recall and list events, experiences, and memories from the past that you could write about. To jog your memory you may want to

- Read journal or diary entries.
- Look at personal photos or scrapbooks.
- Observe objects or scenes that you enjoy.
- Make a map of your neighborhood or home.

Various descriptions of the writing process name different numbers of steps. Some list as many as six steps; some list as few as three. You may have used a five-step writing process in which the revising stage is divided into two separate steps called revising and proofreading. The system you will use in this text names four steps in writing process: planning, drafting, revising, and publishing.

Ask yourself questions

Here are some questions to get you started. You may be able to think of more questions that will lead you to a topic.

- What are my favorite pastimes? Why?
- Whom could I pattern my life after? Why?
- What is a book I have enjoyed? Why?
- What is my best (or most difficult) subject? Why?
- What is the funniest thing that ever happened to me?

• Group techniques

Use brainstorming

Brainstorming is a useful tool for a group of students to use together. One student begins by stating a subject. Then the others list everything they can about that subject.

- Work in a small group of students.
- Bring up a subject in which you are interested.
- Start commenting on the subject.

Look at the example of a list from a brainstorming session. Notice that the students start with one word and end with many possibilities.

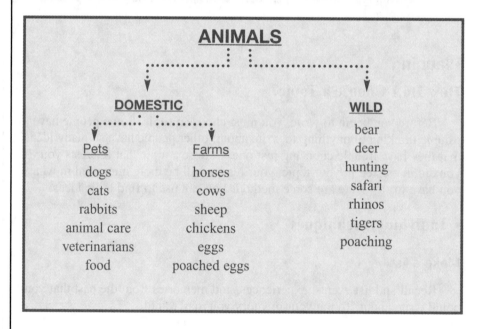

Work in pairs

Talk with another student about a topic you think you may use. Allow him to ask you questions about the topic in order to spark some creative ideas in your mind. Take notes as your partner asks you questions.

How Do I Narrow My Topic?

After you choose your topic, you may need to narrow it. For example, the topic "domestic" is too broad for a paragraph. One might think of household chores, tamed pets, or servants. The topic "cat" is also too broad because there are many different types of cats. Of course, some topics are too narrow. The topic "my cat's left ear" would be difficult to develop into an entire paragraph.

If you have chosen a broad topic, think of specific things about your topic that you could develop into a paragraph. One good topic idea from the brainstorming example is caring for a cat's basic needs. This topic combines the broad topic "cats" with the specific idea of "animal care."

How Do I Gather Information?

Now that you have decided on a topic, you need to gather information about your topic. List everything you already know about your topic. You can use the same methods for gathering information that you used to choose a topic: listing, asking questions, brainstorming, and working in pairs. Look at the example: this student gathers information on the topic "my favorite activity" by asking questions.

1. What is my favorite activity?
   <u>playing soccer</u>

2. When did I first try this activity?
   <u>My friend Joe brought his new soccer ball to my house, and we started kicking it around the yard.</u>

3. Did I enjoy the activity the first time I tried it?
   <u>Yes, although my aim wasn't very good yet.</u>

4. Why do I enjoy this activity?
   <u>I like to run, and it's fun to see my skills improve. I also like working together as a team with the other players.</u>

5. What is the most fun I have had with this activity?
   <u>The time our team won the city championship was really exciting.</u>

Does this student have enough information to write a good paragraph? If he is writing about his personal experience, he probably has enough information.

If you still need more information, you may want to research your topic. You could look for facts in books and periodicals from the library. Or you could interview someone you know who is an expert on your topic. If you use any information from a source, be sure to tell where you found the information.

Learning Christianly

Writing from research is an important skill that Christians need to acquire. Many Christians, however, think that acquiring this ability is a waste of time. The verse they tend to quote is Ecclesiastes 12:12. Read this verse in context. How would you respond to someone who thinks the verse is telling Christians to stop reading and writing?

Considering Audience and Determining Purpose

After you decide on a topic and gather information, you must decide what information to include in your paragraph. How do you choose the information to include? Considering your audience and determining your purpose will help you decide your focus.

When you write, you are writing to a person and for a purpose. Perhaps you are writing a thank-you note to a friend, a science report for your teacher, or a book report to persuade another student to read the book.

The **audience** is the person or group to whom you are writing. Knowing your audience will help you choose effective words and structure as you write. For example, a letter to a friend would be worded differently from a science report for your teacher.

The **purpose** is the reason for your writing. Your purpose may be to describe, inform, persuade, or entertain. The reason to write your friend could be to inform him about what has been going on in your life, while the purpose for the science report would be to explain the procedure and outcome of an experiment or to persuade your audience that one detergent is better than another.

As you plan your paragraph, ask yourself these questions:

- Who is my audience? (fellow students? the editor of the local newspaper?)

- What is my purpose? (to persuade someone to do something? to describe an experience I had?)

- What information does my audience already know about my topic?

- What about my topic will interest my audience?

Be sure to include in your paragraph information that will interest your audience and help you to achieve your purpose.

Look again at the example in the previous section. What information should the writer include in his paragraph if his purpose is to entertain his teacher? Would he include different information if his purpose is to persuade another student to play soccer?

If the writer wants to persuade another student to play soccer, he would include the information from questions three, four, and five. He would emphasize the fun and excitement of playing soccer with other students.

Read the following student paragraph and answer the questions at the end.

Do we have to tear down the old department store building? It seems it could be put to another use. The students of Red Mill need a recreation center. It would give them a place to go that is safe and keep them off the streets after school. Parents would know where their children are. It would make money and be cheaper than building a new building. Please consider this proposal before it is too late.

_____ 1. What is the purpose of this paragraph?

_____ 2. Who is the intended audience for this paragraph?

_____ 3. What other audience might be interested in this information?

Drafting

Writing a Topic Sentence

Now that you have chosen a topic, narrowed your subject, determined your purpose, and identified your audience, you are ready to write your paragraph. First, write your topic sentence. The topic sentence states the main idea of the paragraph. Look at this example.

Great Faith

Many Old Testament characters had great faith. Noah had enough faith in God to build an ark on dry ground. Abraham's strong faith enabled him to present his son Isaac as a sacrifice. Only because he believed in God's care could Moses give up his riches in Pharaoh's house to suffer with God's people. These people are given as examples to us so that we might become more faithful.

If someone asked you right now what the example paragraph is about, what would you say? You would probably say something like "Old Testament characters who had great faith." And you would be correct. If you said only "Old Testament men" or "faith," you would not be entirely accurate. The paragraph tells about Old Testament men, but it more specifically tells how they demonstrated their strong faith in God.

You could answer that question with the first sentence of the paragraph: "Many Old Testament characters had great faith." The first sentence is the topic sentence of the paragraph. It tells you both the subject and what will be said about the subject.

The topic sentence is usually, but not always, the first sentence in a paragraph. Because it introduces the topic, it is often helpful to the writer as well as to the reader if it does come first.

20-2 PRACTICE THE SKILL

Write a good topic sentence for the following paragraph. The sentence should both tell the subject of the paragraph and indicate what will be said about the topic.

Miriam bravely went to Pharaoh's daughter in order to protect Moses. Esther, the beautiful queen of Ahasuerus, risked her life to save the Jewish people from Haman's scheme. Perhaps not as well known, but just as brave, was Jael, who killed an enemy of God's people. These women had the courage to do what had to be done.

_____

_____

Esther before Ahasuerus by Claude Vignon,
From The Bob Jones University Collection

Developing the Supporting Sentences

Now that you have a topic sentence, you need sentences to support your topic. Your supporting sentences use the information that you gathered in the planning stage. Remember your audience and purpose: what kind of support will help you reach your goal?

Paragraph Development

Kind	Definition	Example
Fact	A statement that can be proved	The moon travels around the earth as the earth revolves around the sun.
Example	An instance or event that occurred	Moonrise is that time of the appearance of the moon above the eastern horizon.
Statistic	A fact expressed in numbers	The average period of the moon's revolution around the earth is 29 days, 12 hours, 44 minutes.
Incident/ anecdote	Brief personal account that illustrates the point	Last night the moon looked beautiful through the trees behind our house.
Sensory details	The use of sense words—taste, touch, smell, etc.	When the moon is full, it looks more like a spongy ball than a piece of cheese.
Reasons	Explanation of a truth	We distinguish between a calendar month and lunar month because the two time intervals are not exactly the same.

Look again at the example paragraph about Old Testament characters who had great faith. Notice that all the sentences coming after the topic sentence support it by giving examples about the topic. Noah, Abraham, and Moses are specific examples of Old Testament characters who had great faith. An effective paragraph needs both a clear topic sentence and specific supporting sentences.

Organizing the Supporting Sentences

Now that you have your details, you need to think about the best way to organize the information. As you look at your information, think about the different ways in which you could put your paragraph together. Keep your audience and your purpose in mind. Choose the organizational method that best helps you reach your goals.

Paragraph Organization		
Method	**Definition**	**Good places to use**
Chronological order	A presentation of events in the order of their occurrence	Stories, history, biography, news reports, processes, or instructions
Spatial order	A description according to how something is arranged	Description of a place or an object
Order of importance	A move from least important to most important or vice versa	Persuasive writing, description

Notice how the different organizational methods are used to achieve different purposes in these examples.

Chronological Order

As Easy as Pie

Pie crust is easy to make. First measure flour, salt, and shortening into a bowl. Then use a pastry cutter to mix the ingredients until the dough resembles small peas. Next add one tablespoon of ice water at a time to the mixture until the dough can be gathered into a ball. Finally, pat the ball into a flattened disk and put it into the refrigerator to cool. Anyone can prepare this simple food in minutes.

The writer uses the words *first, then, next,* and *finally* to show the order of the steps to make pie crust. Using words like these helps your reader to understand clearly the process you are describing.

Spatial Order

What words indicate that this paragraph's development is spatial?

A Home Away from Home

The guest room at my aunt's house is a pleasant place to stay. A comfortable bed stands to the right of the door. In the corner is a small nightstand with a good reading lamp and a loud alarm clock. The next wall has a window with heavy curtains. On the wall across from the bed, a bureau with a mirror above it stands next to a desk and chair. The fourth wall contains a large closet with folding doors. A guest will enjoy his stay at my aunt's house.

Expressions such as *in the corner* and *across from the bed* help the reader picture the room being described. Notice that the writer begins to the right of the door and describes everything in order. Do not describe things randomly; your reader will have difficulty picturing the room.

Order of Importance

What words let the reader know what is of most importance and what is of least importance?

The Importance of a Good Vocabulary

Every student should try to increase his vocabulary. First, a good vocabulary helps the student understand what he reads. Second, a good vocabulary can help a student improve his grades. Most importantly, a good vocabulary allows the student to communicate more effectively with other people. Every student will benefit from improving his vocabulary.

The words *most importantly* signal the most important support for the thesis. Notice that the writer places the most important idea last. Last is the most effective position because people usually remember best what they read last.

Coming to a Conclusion

A good paragraph usually contains a good conclusion. As you end your paragraph, you want your audience to have a sense of closure—bringing your discussion to an end. There are several ways to conclude. One common method is to summarize your main idea. However, you could also give a solution to a problem or even ask your audience a question. The purpose of your paragraph will help determine how you end your paragraph.

Look at the example paragraphs in the previous section. Each of the paragraphs uses the summary method to conclude. Compare the first sentence (the thesis) in each paragraph to the last sentence (the conclusion). Notice that the writer uses the same idea stated in different words.

Now look at the following example. Which method does this writer use to conclude the paragraph?

A Useful Tree

The tree in the empty lot on Elm Street should not be cut down. It is not in anyone's way. It does not interfere with power lines. It gives extra shade to the houses on either side of the empty lot. And who knows how much the next person who buys the lot might wish he had a tree were the tree to be cut down?

The writer uses a question to conclude the paragraph. The question draws the reader into the discussion and leaves him thinking about the writer's thesis.

Choosing a Title

After you have finished writing your paragraph, you need to choose a title for your work. Choosing a title is important. The title tells the reader what you are about to discuss. A good title also captures the reader's attention. For example, "Dogs" is not a good title. It is too broad; it does not let the reader know anything about the paragraph's specific topic. A better title is "Dogs Are My Favorite Pets" or "Why Do Dogs Make the Best Pets?" Both of these titles let the audience know the paragraph's topic. The second title even indicates that the paragraph may give reasons that dogs make good pets. The second title also grabs the reader's attention by asking a question. Choose a title for your paragraph that interests your readers and indicates your topic.

Revising

No one writes a perfect paper on the first try. No experienced writer skips the process of revision, nor should you. Revision is the way you improve whatever you are writing at the time, and it will gradually help you produce better first drafts too.

Revising for Ideas

Revision of the first draft should always be *re-vision*—seeing the material again. That is, you look at the rough draft again to see whether you have said what you wanted to say and to see how you can improve the saying of it. You may want to take the following steps as you revise.

1. After you have written your first draft, put it aside for a while. Come back to it later. The lapse of time helps you see your draft more objectively, as other people will see it. You will be better able to notice problems in your paragraph.

2. Look for ways to improve your rough draft. Use your pencil to mark changes you want to make. You may circle words you want to change, cross out unrelated sentences, draw arrows to indicate you want to move a word to another position, insert a caret where you want to add a word, or make other changes.

3. Read your paper aloud. Just hearing the words will give you a better insight into how you used your words.

The chart summarizes specific areas you need to consider as you revise your paragraph: clarity of purpose, audience interest, unity of ideas, coherence, and emphasis.

Potential Problems	Solutions
Is my purpose clear in my topic sentence? (My topic sentence should clearly state my purpose for my audience.)	Be more specific; zero in on one idea.
Is my paragraph interesting to my audience? (Let one or more friends read it and give you their reactions.)	Try writing an alternate beginning. Use an interesting fact, question, or anecdote to get your audience interested.
Is my paragraph unified? (Every sentence in the paragraph should relate to the topic sentence.)	Leave out any sentence that does not belong or rewrite the sentence to make it pertinent to the topic.
Is my paragraph coherent? Do my sentences "stick together" well? (The relationships between ideas should be clear and logical.)	Use clear transitional words (*now, then, next, because, in addition, also*). You may need to link some sentences with connecting words.
Does my audience know what I am emphasizing? (The best way to show emphasis is by position.)	Put the most important point of a paragraph at the beginning or at the end.

Look at this example of a student's revision for ideas.

How Rabbits Grow

~~Cats are very clever in the way they hunt mice, chipmunks, and rabbits. Some rabbits are domesticated, but most live in~~ Rabbits grow in distinct stages. ~~the wild.~~ (When they get older, they have thick fur.) Baby rabbits drink only their mothers' milk. Because of their constantly growing teeth, adult rabbits must gnaw on harder food like pellets or vegetables. If you want to learn more about how rabbits ~~or cats~~ develop, go to your local library.

Sentence one has nothing to do with the rest of the paragraph. Sentence two introduces the subject of domesticated and wild rabbits, but the rest of the paragraph discusses how rabbits grow. The writer deleted both sentences and wrote a new topic sentence to introduce the topic of a growing rabbit.

Sentences three, four, and five discuss the stages of rabbit growth. However, sentence three discusses an adult rabbit, sentence four discusses a baby rabbit, and sentence five bounces back to the characteristics of an adult rabbit. The writer fixed this problem by putting the stages in chronological order.

Sentence six mentions cats, which are not discussed in the paragraph. The writer deleted the phrase "or cats" from the concluding sentence.

Revising for Style

After you revise for ideas, look at your paragraph again to revise for style.

Precise Words

As you revise, correct the inaccurate or imprecise words. Precise words help you to get your message across to your reader clearly. Use precise nouns and verbs. Some words may be general (like *state* or *said*) and some words may be specific (like *North Carolina* or *shouted*). A thesaurus may help you find the specific word you need.

Showing, not Telling

Have you ever heard the expression "Don't tell me; show me"? Your paragraph will be more effective if you show, not just tell, your idea. Use words that refer to the senses—taste, hear, touch, smell, see—to show your audience what you are describing. Do not rely on adjectives and adverbs alone; try to use precise nouns and verbs too.

Notice the details in the following examples. Which example shows the reader its topic?

1. The meal was delicious.

2. Steam rose from the huge turkey. When the host began to carve, the tender meat fell away from his knife. Each juicy slice gleamed in the candlelight. The spicy aroma of the herb dressing teased each hungry guest.

The second example successfully shows the reader the delicious meal. The writer appeals to the reader's senses with precise words: *tender, juicy, gleamed, spicy,* and *aroma.*

 **PRACTICE THE SKILL**

20-3

Rewrite the passage to make it more precise. Show the reader what is happening.

The next morning we started for the lake. We arrived at the dock after traveling through fog. We rented a boat and waited until the fog lifted and then started out. We cast our lines. A fish struck mine and after a fierce battle, I landed him.

_____

_____

_____

_____

_____

_____

_____

_____

_____

_____

_____

_____

_____

Proofreading

Proofreading your paper is just as important as revising. Make sure that you made no errors as you wrote your final draft. Mistakes can occur accidentally as you rewrite or type your paper, but you need to find and correct them. Even if someone else types your paper, you are still responsible for any errors.

Good proofreading takes practice, but you can learn to do it well. The most important principle is this: do not expect to find every error (or every kind of error) in a single reading. Read in different ways to find different things.

Use these tactics to proofread your paragraph:

- Slow down by using a blank sheet of paper to cover the part you have not yet read.

- Read the paper aloud. You may hear an error that you did not see when you read the paper silently.

- Look at the words in reverse order; begin reading at the end of the paper and work toward the beginning. This tactic will force you to look at each word individually for spelling or capitalization errors.

Potential Problems	Solutions
Grammar	
Do I have any fragments or run-on sentences?	Figure out what is missing with a fragment and complete the sentence. Divide the run-on sentence and punctuate it correctly.
Usage	
Do my subjects and verbs agree and do my pronouns and antecedents agree?	Put a singular subject with a singular verb. Follow the correct rules for pronoun/antecedent agreement. Check the rules in Chapter 9 and Chapter 10.
Punctuation	
Have I omitted any punctuation marks or used any marks incorrectly? Have I used the correct end punctuation or omitted any end punctuation?	Read each sentence carefully. Check the rules in Chapter 15.
Capitalization	
Does every sentence begin with a capital letter? Are all proper nouns capitalized?	Look for specific places, people, events, and objects. Check each sentence.
Spelling	
Have I misspelled any words?	Look deliberately at every word.

Finally, you may want to read the paper through more quickly a few times, looking each time for some particular problem area that has been difficult for you in the past. For instance, it is fairly easy to spot comma problems when you read looking only for commas.

Careful proofreading does take some time. It is only a little more time, however, compared to the time you have already invested in your paragraph. And it can make an important difference in people's impression of your work.

Publishing

Publishing your paper simply means that you are sharing it with someone else. You could publish your paper a number of ways:

- Send it to your local newspaper.

- Put together a class literary collection.

- Use your work for programs (Parent Teacher Fellowships, holiday programs).

- Read your work over the school's public address system.

- Share it with your English class.

- Read your work to someone at home.

- Mail it to a friend or relative.

Writing Folders

After you finish your final draft, you may want to put it in a folder or notebook. By the end of the year, you would have a collection of your work. You could include your rough drafts and final papers or just the final papers. You and your teacher may find these folders helpful because the folder allows you, your parents, and your teacher to see your progress over the weeks, semester, or year. The folder also can help you see mistakes you have made in the past so that you will not make them again.

Chapter 1: Sentences

Sentence Types and Punctuation

Identify each sentence as declarative, interrogative, imperative, or exclamatory. Write in the blank the letter that corresponds to the correct answer. Then supply the correct punctuation mark at the end of the sentence.

A. declarative
B. interrogative
C. imperative
D. exclamatory

_____ 1. Have you heard of Sergeant Alvin York

_____ 2. He fought in World War I

_____ 3. His bravery was incredible

_____ 4. Did you know he won the Congressional Medal of Honor

_____ 5. Read on to learn about his heroic exploits

Simple Subjects

Find the simple or compound subject in each sentence. Write in the blank the letter that corresponds to the correct answer.

_____ 6. Sergeant York and many other men formed a special nationwide division of soldiers.
A. Sergeant
B. Sergeant York
C. Sergeant York, men

_____ 7. At first York had requested his removal from the draft lists.
A. At
B. York
C. removal

_____ 8. Can you imagine the loss to the American troops?
A. Can, imagine
B. you
C. loss

_____ 9. Fortunately, someone in Washington denied his request.
A. Fortunately
B. someone
C. someone, Washington

_____ 10. Superiors and comrades were surely glad for York's presence on the battlefield.
  A. Superiors
  B. Superiors, comrades
  C. York's

Simple Predicates

Find the simple or compound predicate in each sentence. Write in the blank the letter that corresponds to the correct answer.

_____ 11. York's fame rests primarily on his actions in the Argonne Forest.
  A. fame
  B. rests
  C. primarily

_____ 12. Early one morning York and his unit made and executed plans for a charge up a hill.
  A. York, unit
  B. made, executed
  C. charge, hill

_____ 13. There was extremely stiff resistance from the enemy.
  A. was
  B. extremely
  C. resistance

_____ 14. What would you have done?
  A. would
  B. would have done
  C. have done

_____ 15. York's unit found an empty trench and sneaked behind enemy lines.
  A. found
  B. sneaked
  C. found, sneaked

Correct Sentence Structure

Identify each group of words as a correct sentence, fragment, comma splice, or fused sentence. Write in the blank the letter that corresponds to the correct answer.

  A. correct sentence
  B. fragment
  C. comma splice
  D. fused sentence

_____ 16. The unit saw two German stretcher bearers, York and his men followed the Germans to their headquarters.

_____ 17. Although the soldiers at the headquarters surrendered to York and his men.

_____ 18. More Germans with machine guns joined the fight.

_____ 19. York stood and fired against the Germans until his rifle became too hot, he next fought six men with bayonets single-handedly and killed all of them with a .45.

_____ 20. The remaining German gunners surrendered York and his men returned to their camp with 132 prisoners.

Correcting Sentence Structure

Correct the sentences above for which you chose letters *B, C,* or *D.* If the sentence is correct as it is, write *correct* in the blank.

21. _____

_____

22. _____

_____

23. _____

_____

24. _____

_____

25. _____

_____

Chapter 2: Nouns

Identifying Nouns

Questions 1-5: Underline each common noun once and each proper noun twice in the following paragraph.

Hair used to be a symbol of nationality. A Muslim wore a turban. In China the men shaved the front part of the head and tied the back. In Africa the women dyed their hair with red earth and grease. In America Aztecs showed many conquests by a ridge at the scalp.

Forms of Nouns

Identify the form of each italicized noun. Write in the blank the letter that corresponds to the correct answer.

        A. singular
        B. singular possessive
        C. plural
        D. plural possessive

_____ 6. *Women's* hair in the medieval era was very long.

_____ 7. *Egyptians* wore wigs to protect their heads from the hot sun.

_____ 8. An Inca chief wore a *headband* wrapped around his head five times.

_____ 9. A *girl's* hairstyle indicated whether she was married.

_____ 10. In the eighteenth century, women wore their hair over wire *cages*.

Forming Possessive Nouns

Identify the correct possessive form of each phrase. Write in the blank the letter that corresponds to the correct answer.

_____ 11. the color of the hair
        A. hairs color
        B. hairs' color
        C. hair's color

_____ 12. the arrangements of the hairdressers
        A. hairdressers arrangements
        B. hairdressers' arrangements
        C. hairdresser's arrangements

_____ 13. the brightness of the ribbons
        A. the ribbons brightness
        B. the ribbons' brightness
        C. the ribbon's brightness

_____ 14. the fullness of the wig
       A. the wigs fullness
       B. the wigs' fullness
       C. the wig's fullness

_____ 15. the length of the mustache
       A. the mustaches length
       B. the mustaches' length
       C. the mustache's length

Count and Noncount Nouns

Questions 16-20: Look at the italicized common nouns in the following paragraph. Underline the count nouns. Double underline the noncount nouns.

Proper hair care is essential to any *hairstyle*. Shampoos help keep hair very healthy. Egg shampoos add extra sheen to hair. Lemon *shampoos* cut out extra oils. Washing hair with just *water* does not thoroughly clean the hair. Hair should be cleaned at least once every other *day*. Hairdressers help to clean and trim hair. Some people find *enjoyment* in going to the hairdresser each week.

Compound Nouns

Write *Cpd* (compound) in the blank if the italicized noun is a compound noun. Leave the blank empty if the italicized noun is not a compound noun.

_____ 21. Egyptian *noblemen* shaved their hair close for coolness and cleanliness.

_____ 22. Even in ancient times, public *barbershops* were common.

_____ 23. Jewels and ornamental *hairpins* provided extra beauty.

_____ 24. Some cultures used *horsehair* in making wigs.

_____ 25. Hair fashion changes from *generation* to generation.

Chapter 3: Verbs

Simple Predicates

Find the simple predicate in each sentence. Write in the blank the letter that corresponds to the correct answer.

_____ 1. Trees grow nearly everywhere on the earth's surface.
    A. grow
    B. nearly
    C. surface

_____ 2. Literally thousands of varieties exist.
    A. thousands
    B. varieties
    C. exist

_____ 3. Except in extreme cold or extreme dryness, trees can thrive anywhere.
    A. can
    B. thrive
    C. can thrive

_____ 4. Size, longevity, and leaf type are distinctions of different tree types.
    A. are
    B. are distinctions
    C. types

_____ 5. Despite their differences, all trees share many characteristics.
    A. Despite
    B. share
    C. characteristics

Action and Linking Verbs

Identify each italicized verb as action or linking. Write in the blank the letter that corresponds to the correct answer.

    A. action
    B. linking

_____ 6. A tree surgeon *treats* wood and bark injuries in trees.

_____ 7. Water and minerals *move* most quickly up and down in a tree.

_____ 8. Side-to-side movement of water in the tree *is* somewhat slow.

_____ 9. Therefore, the tree surgeon *must shape* any cuts into the tree to provide for the best healing.

_____ 10. The repairs sometimes *appear* strange after the tree surgeon finishes.

Sentence Patterns: S-InV, S-TrV-DO, and S-TrV-IO-DO

Identify the sentence pattern for each sentence. Write in the blank the letter that corresponds to the correct answer.

      A. S-InV
      B. S-TrV-DO
      C. S-TrV-IO-DO

_____ 11. The tree surgeon first cuts the dead bark away from the live tissue.

_____ 12. He then paints the tree tissue with an orange shellac.

_____ 13. Later the tree surgeon gives the tree a coat of another type of paint.

_____ 14. The bark grows over the wound in about six months.

_____ 15. Sometimes paint must be reapplied to the wound.

Sentence Patterns: S-LV-PN and S-LV-PA

Identify the sentence pattern for each sentence. Write in the blank the letter that corresponds to the correct answer.

      A. S-LV-PN
      B. S-LV-PA

_____ 16. Bark injury is the least difficult type of injury.

_____ 17. An injury to the tree cavity is more dangerous.

_____ 18. A diseased tree may appear fine outwardly.

_____ 19. The tree could be quite sick inside.

_____ 20. The two types of treatment for diseased trees are closed-cavity and open-cavity surgery.

Verb Forms

Identify the correct verb form to complete each sentence. Write in the blank to the left of the sentence the letter that corresponds to the correct answer.

_____ 21. Last week a tree surgeon __?__ on a tree in our back yard.
      A. operates
      B. operated
      C. had operated

_____ 22. Every day for two weeks the tree __?__ many leaves.
      A. has lost
      B. will have lost
      C. loses

_____ 23. On any job this tree surgeon always __?__ in the early morning.
      A. will work
      B. had worked
      C. works

_____ 24. On our tree the surgeon used cement; before this job he _?_ an asphalt-dust
mixture.
A. uses
B. had used
C. will use

_____ 25. He _?_ cement to all of his jobs from now on.
A. applied
B. will apply
C. will have applied

Chapter 4: Pronouns

Pronoun Identification
Choose the correct pronoun to replace the italicized word or phrase. Write the correct answer in the blank.

_____ 1. Jonathan Swift published *Jonathan Swift's* well-known <u>Gulliver's Travels</u> in 1726.

_____ 2. *The book* tells the story of Lemuel Gulliver.

_____ 3. *Gulliver* is an English doctor who has amazing adventures.

_____ 4. Gulliver likes being at home with *Gulliver's wife* and their children.

_____ 5. But Gulliver's medical practice proves unprofitable, so Gulliver decides to sail as surgeon with *the crew of the <u>Antelope</u>.*

Pronoun Antecedent
Identify the antecedent of each italicized pronoun. Write in the blank the letter that corresponds to the correct answer.

_____ 6. During the voyage the ship runs into a storm, and *it* splits apart on a rock.
A. voyage
B. ship
C. storm

_____ 7. Gulliver escapes into a boat with five other men, but *he* alone survives.
A. Gulliver
B. boat
C. men

_____ 8. Having reached land and rested for several hours, Gulliver awakens to find his arms and legs tied to *their* positions on the ground and little people crawling on him.
A. hours
B. arms and legs
C. people

_____ 9. He has unknowingly reached the island of Lilliput, and one of *its* important officials greets him from a specially-built platform a foot and a half off the ground.
A. island
B. officials
C. platform

_____ 10. The official and his people provide Gulliver with food—so tiny that he can eat three loaves of bread in one mouthful—but not at first with *his* freedom.
  A. official
  B. people
  C. Gulliver

Pronoun Identification

Identify each italicized pronoun as personal, demonstrative, interrogative, or indefinite. Write in the blank the letter that corresponds to the correct answer.

  A. personal
  B. interrogative
  C. demonstrative
  D. indefinite

_____ 11. Eventually allowed to roam freely through the land, Gulliver receives permission to visit the capital city with its large wall and great palace.

_____ 12. Later *someone* from the government explains an important national controversy to him.

_____ 13. *Which* is the proper end of an egg to crack, the big or the little one?

_____ 14. *That* is the question that had divided Lilliputians and helped stir up war with the neighboring island of Blefuscu.

_____ 15. Feeling responsibility to *many* of the Lilliputians, Gulliver is persuaded to fight for them by walking off with a good part of the Blefuscans' fleet.

Pronoun Identification

Identify each italicized pronoun as reflexive, intensive, demonstrative, or indefinite. Write in the blank the letter that corresponds to the correct answer.

  A. reflexive
  B. intensive
  C. demonstrative
  D. indefinite

_____ 16. Gulliver's adventures do not end in the land of the little Lilliputians, however; he *himself* is the midget at his next stop.

_____ 17. *This* is Brobdingnag, the land of the giants.

_____ 18. Almost *everyone* is as much bigger than Gulliver as he is than the Lilliputians.

_____ 19. Here Gulliver discovers for *himself* what it is like to be held in someone's hand or to be shocked at someone's appetite.

_____ 20. Through his adventures with bigger and smaller peoples, Gulliver sees the foolishness of pride for *anyone*.

Chapter 5: Adjectives

Identifying Adjectives
Questions 1-10: Underline each adjective in the following paragraph and draw an arrow to the word it modifies.

Antarctica is an icy continent. Most plants cannot survive in the dry climate.

The coldest temperature ever recorded (-128.6°F) was in Antarctica. Severe winds

also help explain why Antarctica is not an inviting place to live.

Comparing with Adjectives
Identify the correct form of the adjective in parentheses for each sentence. Write in the blank the letter that corresponds to the correct answer.

_____ 11. In 1911, Roald Amundsen and Robert Scott began a *(famous, positive)* race to
reach the South Pole first.
A. famous
B. more famous
C. most famous

_____ 12. Scott's motor sleds travelled slowly in the snow, but Amundsen used much *(fast, comparative)* Eskimo dogs.
A. fast
B. more fast
C. faster

_____ 13. Amundsen travelled the shortest but *(unfamiliar, superlative)* route.
A. more unfamiliar
B. most unfamiliar
C. most unfamiliarest

_____ 14. Amundsen had a *(good, comparative)* plan and reached the South Pole several
weeks before Scott's team arrived.
A. gooder
B. better
C. more good

_____ 15. The *(dangerous, superlative)* part of trip was getting home. Amundsen's team
arrived safely, but Scott and his five men died in Antarctica.
A. most dangerous
B. more dangerous
C. more dangerest

Common and Proper Adjectives

Underline the common adjectives once and the proper adjectives twice in the following sentences.

16. Before Antarctica had ever been seen, Greek scholars speculated that there could be a continent at the bottom of the earth.

17. Nathaniel Brown, an American sealer, was one of the first men to see the southern continent.

18. The same year, a member of the British navy, Captain Edward Bransfield, may have seen Antarctica.

19. The stormy Antarctic waters are very dangerous for sailors.

20. Many animals live in the waters, including whales and Adélie penguins.

Adjectives, Nouns, Independent Possessives

Identify each italicized word as an adjective, noun, or independent possessive. Write in the blank the letter that corresponds to the correct answer.

      A. adjective
      B. noun
      C. independent possessive

_____ 21. Most of Antarctica is covered with ice. The *thickest* ice is 15,700 feet deep.

_____ 22. Scientists from several different countries have *research* stations in Antarctica.

_____ 23. Scientists have learned more about the history of the earth through their *research* in Antarctica.

_____ 24. Many other scientists have interesting jobs, but *theirs* is certainly one of the most complex and difficult.

_____ 25. Because of *their* studies, many facts have been discovered about the ozone layer.

Chapter 6: Adverbs

Identifying Adverbs
Questions 1-7: Underline each adverb in the following paragraph.

During sleep the eyes usually close and the body remains fairly still. In contrast, the brain is not still; it is rather active. Scientists have documented two types of sleep that take place in the brain: nonrapid eye movement (NREM) and rapid eye movement (REM). Approximately every ninety minutes the body changes from one type of sleep to the other. These two types are entirely different from each other, yet both are quite necessary for the body's proper function.

Modifiers
Identify the type of word that each italicized adverb modifies. Write in the blank the letter that corresponds to the correct answer.

        A. verb
        B. adverb
        C. adjective

_____ 8. Several factors *definitely* influence sleep patterns.

_____ 9. Scientists have learned several *remarkably* interesting facts.

_____ 10. *Not* surprisingly, a lack of sleep makes someone more sleepy.

_____ 11. Boredom *also* contributes to sleepiness.

_____ 12. By contrast, new situations and worry *sometimes* prevent sleep.

_____ 13. Other factors which influence the *exceedingly* delicate sleep process are noise and warmth.

_____ 14. Even outside barometric pressure can be a *somewhat* important influence on sleep.

_____ 15. Time of day is *very* definitely the most important factor in sleep.

_____ 16. Travelers to other time zones *normally* feel sleepy during the same time they would in their home time zone.

_____ 17. Full adjustment to a new time zone often takes *almost* ten days.

Positive, Comparative, and Superlative Adverbs

Identify the correct form of the adverb in parentheses for each sentence. Write in the blank the correct answer.

_____ 18. The average adult *(often, superlative)* needs between seven and eight hours of sleep per night.

_____ 19. However, some adults perform *(well, superlative)* with as little as three hours of sleep.

_____ 20. Babies and young children *(likely, superlative)* require more sleep than adults.

_____ 21. Lack of sleep can be *(extremely, positive)* harmful.

_____ 22. People who lose just one night's sleep *(frequently, superlative)* suffer very little except tiredness.

_____ 23. After two and a half days with no sleep, a person's behavior may become *(noticeably, comparative)* bizarre.

_____ 24. Some people suffering from extreme lack of sleep may even experience *(frighteningly, positive)* real hallucinations.

_____ 25. Sleep deprivation also causes memory problems and generally makes a person perform *(badly, comparative)* on even a daily task.

Chapter 7: Prepositions, Conjunctions, and Interjections

Adjectival and Adverbial Prepositional Phrases

Underline each prepositional phrase and circle the object of the preposition. Identify each phrase as adjectival or adverbial. Write in the blank the letter that corresponds to the correct answer.

A. adjectival prepositional phrase
B. adverbial prepositional phrase

_____ 1. Time is an indispensable part of our lives.

_____ 2. Our daily schedules revolve around time.

_____ 3. You eat lunch at noon.

_____ 4. Then you have a three o'clock appointment with your dentist.

_____ 5. You finish the day with an eight o'clock play performance.

_____ 6. Each activity is regulated by time.

_____ 7. Change is an important indicator of time's passage.

_____ 8. Regular changes help divide time into units.

_____ 9. The earth's rotation on its axis gives us days.

_____ 10. Its revolution around the sun gives us years.

Prepositions and Adverbs

Identify each italicized word as a preposition or an adverb. Write in the blank the letter that corresponds to the correct answer.

A. preposition
B. adverb

_____ 11. Hours, minutes, and seconds likely came *through* the Babylonians.

_____ 12. Looking *up* at the sky, they divided a day into 24 parts, 12 for darkness and 12 for light.

_____ 13. In addition, they split a circle into 360 parts, each of which was later further split *into* 60 smaller parts.

_____ 14. Hours came *about* by the divisions of the day, and minutes and seconds by the divisions of the circle.

_____ 15. Hours, minutes, and seconds came together *in* one timepiece with the refinement of the clock.

Conjunctions

Circle the conjunction in each sentence. Determine which parts of the sentence the conjunction joins. Write in the blank the letter that corresponds to the correct answer.

_____ 16. A clock in Hong Kong and a clock in Bermuda are not set at exactly the same time.
A. subjects
B. predicates
C. direct objects

_____ 17. If they were, noon would be in the middle of the day in one place but in the middle of the night in the other.
A. subjects
B. prepositional phrases
C. indirect objects

_____ 18. Instead, clocks in each location register noon approximately in the middle of the day and midnight approximately in the middle of the night.
A. direct objects
B. objects of the preposition
C. indirect objects

_____ 19. Two methods of time measurement are local time zones and standard time zones.
A. subjects
B. predicate nouns
C. direct objects

_____ 20. Local time depends entirely on the position of the sun overhead and differs from location to location.
A. direct objects
B. subjects
C. predicates

_____ 21. Standard time zones establish identical times throughout given regions and create less confusion for travelers.
A. subjects
B. predicates
C. objects of the preposition

_____ 22. The world is divided into twenty-three full time zones and two half time zones.
A. prepositional phrases
B. objects of the preposition
C. predicates

_____ 23. Measurement of time and measurement of distance start with the prime meridian of Greenwich, England.
A. subjects
B. predicates
C. direct objects

_____ 24. Time moves forward one hour for each new time zone to the east but moves backward one hour for each zone to the west.
   A. subjects
   B. predicates
   C. indirect objects

_____ 25. The International Date Line, an imaginary line, separates the time zones and signals a change in day.
   A. predicates
   B. direct objects
   C. prepositional phrases

Conjunctions and Interjections

Identify each italicized word as a conjunction or an interjection. Write in the blank the letter that corresponds to the correct answer.

   A. conjunction
   B. interjection

_____ 26. Time is obviously important to man, *but* does God care about it?

_____ 27. *Yes,* the Bible contains many references to the concept.

_____ 28. *Really?* Where?

_____ 29. *Well,* Hosea 10:12 warns the Israelites that it is time to seek the Lord.

_____ 30. Romans 13:11 speaks of a time to wake to action, *and* Ephesians 5:16 commands all believers to make wise use of their time.

Chapter 8: Clause Structure

Clauses and Phrases

Identify each underlined group of words as a phrase, an independent clause, or a dependent clause. Write in the blank the letter that corresponds to the correct answer.

A. phrase
B. independent clause
C. dependent clause

DC   1. <u>There are fifty-three different countries in the continent of Africa</u>, where the people and their cultures differ widely.

P   2. Africa is <u>the third largest continent in the world</u>.

IC   3. <u>A large part of the land is covered with tropical rain forests</u>, and animals such as gorillas and crocodiles live there.

DC   4. Egypt is in the northeastern part of Africa, <u>where the Nile flows south to north</u>.

IC   5. <u>It is the longest river in the world</u>; along its banks great civilizations have risen.

IC   6. <u>The Nile is over four thousand miles long</u>.

DC   7. Much of the land is covered by the Sahara, <u>which is the largest desert in the world</u>.

DC   8. <u>Elephants and lions, two fascinating animals</u>, live in the grasslands of Africa.

DC   9. <u>Although hunters have threatened the existence of several species</u>, fascinating wildlife is still abundant in Africa.

DC   10. Mt. Kilimanjaro, <u>the highest mountain in Africa</u>, is 19,340 feet high.

Simple and Compound Sentences

Identify each sentence as simple or compound. Write in the blank the letter that corresponds to the correct answer.

A. simple sentence
B. compound sentence

C   11. An abundance of precious metals, including gold and diamonds, are found in Africa, but most of the people who live there are not wealthy.

S   12. Farmers without modern farming tools cannot make the best use of their land.

S   13. The poor people sometimes suffer from severe famines.

C   14. The medical conditions in rural Africa are very poor, and many people die of various African diseases.

S   15. The general life expectancy for Africans is only about fifty-four years.

Simple, Compound, and Complex Sentences

Identify each sentence as simple, compound, or complex. Write in the blank the letter that corresponds to the correct answer.

        A. simple sentence
        B. compound sentence
        C. complex sentence

_C_ 16. Africa is a continent of many different ethnic groups, where religious and political unity is difficult.

_A_ 17. The various tribes of Africa speak innumerable languages and dialects.

_C_ 18. Since communication is vital to business, many Africans speak English as a second language.

_C_ 19. Although most Africans in the cities wear Western dress, many still prefer the traditional robes and head coverings.

_A_ 20. Numerous people in northern Africa share the Arabic language, but the languages in southern Africa are as diverse as the people.

_A_ 21. The governments of Africa have improved their educational systems.

_B_ 22. The literacy rate is quite low; fewer than half of the people can read and write.

_S_ 23. Since the 1940s, many more Africans have attended colleges in their own countries.

_S_ 24. Rice, bread, fruits, and vegetables are the main elements of the African diet.

_S_ 25. While conditions have improved in Africa, malnutrition, lack of education, and disease are still significant problems for the continent.

Chapter 9: Subject-Verb Agreement

Agreement
Questions 1-5: Find the errors in agreement in the following paragraph. Rewrite the paragraph correctly in the space provided.

How aware is you of the rules of etiquette? For many years Emily Post were the authority on etiquette, and copies of her book was on the shelves of all well-bred families. Some rules of etiquette has changed drastically since Post's book first came out in 1922; however, basic good manners is timeless. What are your thoughts on the following social customs of 1937?

_____

_____

_____

_____

_____

_____

Agreement with Indefinite Pronouns
Underline the verb in parentheses that agrees with the subject of the sentence.

6. Few (*disagrees, disagree*) with Post's comments on conversation.

7. Anyone (*is, are*) capable of carrying on a conversation with a little effort.

8. All of the guidelines (*boils, boil*) down to thinking before you speak.

9. Nobody (*likes, like*) a bragger, so do not talk too much about yourself.

10. Most of the conversation problem (*is, are*) solved by the participants' resolve to be thoughtful speakers and interested listeners.

Agreement with Compound Subjects
Underline the verb in parentheses that agrees with the subject of the sentence.

11. Men and women (*has, have*) whole chapters devoted to their dress.

12. In 1937 hats and gloves (*was, were*) mandatory in many cases for a lady in public.

13. His nails or his haircut (*was, were*) evidence of a gentleman.

14. Carelessly tossed clothes or an unworn shoe without a shoetree (*was, were*) not appropriate.

15. A college student or other young men (*was, were*) warned not to coordinate outfits too noticeably, though they might safely match golf stockings with sweaters and ties.

Intervening Phrases, Predicate Nouns, and Inverted Order

Circle the subject of each sentence. Underline the verb in parentheses that agrees with the subject.

16. Table manners (*is, are*) an especially important part of etiquette.

17. (*Is, Are*) each utensil used properly at your table?

18. The fork and the spoon, never the knife, (*is, are*) the utensils that should enter your mouth.

19. The tines of a fork (*faces, face*) up for everything that does not involve cutting.

20. There (*is, are*) different ways of using a spoon, depending on the food.

21. Soup, but not ice cream and cereal, (*requires, require*) a scooping movement away from yourself and a sipping from the side of your spoon.

22. There (*is, are*) almost no situation in which fingers are appropriately used for messy foods.

23. Despite this precaution, a finger bowl, in addition to a napkin, (*completes, complete*) each guest's place at the home of a good hostess.

24. (*Has, Have*) you ever removed food from your mouth? Do not!

25. Finally, the chewer with his mouth open and the talker with his mouth full (*is, are*) never in good taste.

Chapter 10: Pronoun-Antecedent Agreement

Agreement with Personal Pronouns
Fill in each blank with a pronoun that agrees with its antecedent.

his 1. Henry Ford is known throughout the world by _?_ association with the automobile.

its 2. Ford's hometown of Dearborn, Michigan, bears many marks of _?_ famous citizen.

their 3. Undoubtedly, many residents and _?_ guests have visited Greenfield Village and the Henry Ford Museum, showcases of history and technology established by Ford.

his 4. Both places are excellent spots for a teacher to take _?_ class on a field trip.

his 5. Does the teacher or the children learn the most from _?_ study of Ford's story?

its 6. Henry Ford devoted much energy to the development of the automobile, although he was not _?_ original creator.

his 7. Ford built _?_ first car in 1896 and established the Ford Motor Company in 1903.

its 8. These events were crucial in _?_ impact on Ford's future.

their 9. Ford and other company executives wanted _?_ product to be well built but affordable.

his 10. With the Model T, the common man had found _?_ car.

Agreement with Indefinite Pronouns
Identify the pronoun that agrees with the antecedent. Write in the blank the letter that corresponds to the correct answer.

his 11. Few could part with enough of _?_ money to buy a Model T at the original price of $850.
   A. his
   B. her
   C. their

_a_____ 12. No one can run a successful business if _?_ product is too expensive.
A. his
B. her
C. their

_a_____ 13. Most of the extra expense of the product was due to _?_ high cost of production.
A. its
B. his
C. their

_a_____ 14. Therefore, everyone in leadership contributed _?_ ideas for the best way to lower that cost.
A. his
B. her
C. their

_b_____ 15. With the introduction of the assembly line, every department shortened _?_ production time.
A. his
B. its
C. their

_b_____ 16. With everybody focusing on _?_ one task as parts moved along a conveyor belt, much less labor was required.
A. her
B. his
C. their

_b_____ 17. Anything requiring less labor can have _?_ price lowered.
A. his
B. its
C. their

_c_____ 18. In addition, many of the cars' parts became cheaper when _?_ suppliers were replaced with in-house producers.
A. her
B. its
C. their

_a_____ 19. Finally, each of the major market regions received _?_ own plant where parts could be sent for assembly, cutting down on shipping costs.
A. its
B. his
C. their

_c_____ 20. With all of these improvements, most of the nation's workers could afford cars for _?_ families by 1924, when the price had fallen to $290.
A. his
B. its
C. their

Chapter 11: Pronoun Usage

Subjective, Objective, and Possessive Cases
For each sentence, underline the correct pronoun in parentheses.

1. Robert E. Lee is remembered in the Hall of Fame for Great Americans because of *(him, his)* contribution to America.

2. Zach and *(I, me)* visited the Hall of Fame at New York University.

3. The hostess was pleased to give Zach and *(I, me)* a tour of the museum.

4. We saw the bust of Robert E. Lee, and Zach read its inscription to *(I, me)*.

5. I listened to *(he, him)* as he read, "Duty then is the sublimest word in our language."

6. Even when his responsibilities were small and insignificant, Robert E. Lee took care to fulfill *(they, them)* completely.

7. His superiors were always assured that *(he, him)* would complete his assignments.

8. Robert E. Lee's commitment to duty made him a successful general in the Civil War and an excellent example for *(we, us)*.

We, Us, Who, and *Whom*
Choose the correct pronoun to complete the sentence. Write in the blank the letter that corresponds to the correct answer.

    A. we
    B. us
    C. who
    D. whom

_____ 9. _?_ students studied famous Americans in our history class.

_____ 10. _?_ was the most famous general in the Confederate army?

_____ 11. Our teacher told _?_ students to look for the answer in our history books.

_____ 12. At Appomattox Court House, General Lee surrendered to _?_ ?

_____ 13. Ulysses S. Grant, _?_ was very generous and kind to the general, accepted Lee's surrender.

Problem Pronouns

Choose the correct pronoun to complete the sentence. Write in the blank the letter that corresponds to the correct answer.

_____b_____ 14. Have you read __?__ assignment about the Civil War?
        A. you're
        B. your

_____a_____ 15. __?__ quite long, so I began reading it yesterday.
        A. It's
        B. Its

_____a_____ 16. Some other students finished __?__ last night.
        A. theirs
        B. there's

_____b_____ 17. They wanted to finish early; __?__ going to the basketball game tonight.
        A. their
        B. they're

_____a_____ 18. All of the students __?__ assignments are complete will probably be going to the game tonight.
        A. whose
        B. who's

Clear Pronoun Reference

Identify each sentence as having correct or incorrect pronoun reference. Write in the blank the letter that corresponds to the correct answer. If you choose B, rewrite the sentence correctly in the space provided.

        A. correct sentence
        B. incorrect pronoun reference

_____ 19. Diannah and Hannah traveled to Gettysburg, Pennsylvania. They have a lot of Civil War memorabilia there.

_____

_____

_____ 20. Diannah told Hannah that she loved to visit Civil War sites.

_____

_____

_____ 21. The girls read about the famous battle at Gettysburg, and they learned that it was the turning point of the Civil War.

_____

_____

_____ 22. The Confederate army met the Union army at Gettysburg in 1863. On July 3 they attempted to gain control of Cemetery Ridge.

_____

_____

_____ 23. The Confederates fought valiantly, but after a fierce battle, the Union army had prevented their advance.

_____

_____

_____ 24. The day after the battle, General Lee decided that they would begin a retreat.

_____

_____

_____ 25. The Union army wanted to pursue the Confederates, but they safely returned to Virginia.

_____

_____

Chapter 12: Using Adjectives and Adverbs Correctly

Adjective or Adverb

Choose the correct word to complete the sentence. Write in the blank the letter that corresponds to the correct answer.

_____ 1. Over nineteen million people live in the _?_ populated metropolitan area of Mexico City.
    A. heavy
    B. heavily

_____ 2. Many people have moved to the city _?_ , and there has been an incredible growth in population.
    A. quick
    B. quickly

_____ 3. Because of the increased population, finding _?_ housing for everyone is difficult.
    A. sufficient
    B. sufficiently

_____ 4. Many middle-class residents have _?_ jobs and enjoy more modern homes.
    A. good
    B. well

_____ 5. Crime is a _?_ problem in Mexico City, and alcohol and drug abuse only complicate the problem.
    A. real
    B. really

_____ 6. Because the city is in a valley, pollution is not blown away _?_ .
    A. easy
    B. easily

_____ 7. The government has enforced _?_ strict laws regarding pollution to help alleviate the problem.
    A. real
    B. really

_____ 8. Because streets in Mexico City are very crowded, people travel _?_ by bus.
    A. most
    B. mostly

_____ 9. The city contains a _?_ and sophisticated subway system.
    A. fast
    B. fastly

_____ 10. Mexico City is the home of El Palacio de Bellas Artes, a __?__ center for the performing arts.
   A. cultural
   B. culturally

Adjective and Adverb Modifiers

Label the italicized word *adj* (adjective) or *adv* (adverb) by writing the correct abbreviation in the blank.

_____ 11. The Monument to Independence stands *high* in Mexico City at an intersection on the *Paseo de la Reforma*.

_____ 12. The city contains very old Spanish buildings along with *high,* modern structures.

_____ 13. Because of crowded traffic conditions, the cars often move *slowly.*

_____ 14. The buses often are *slower* than the subways.

_____ 15. During congested times, taking a car might be the *slowest* way to travel.

Double Negatives and Comparisons

Write in the blank the correct form of the word in parentheses.

_____ 16. Mexico City is one of the __?__ cities in the world. *(developed)*

_____ 17. Some residences are __?__ than others. *(luxurious)*

_____ 18. Poorer residents frequently do not have __?__ good jobs or homes. *(any)*

_____ 19. For buildings, cement is used __?__ than wood. *(often)*

_____ 20. Of all the museums in Mexico City, the National Museum of Anthropology is the __?__ . *(fine)*

Chapter 13: Using Troublesome Words Correctly

Troublesome Verbs

Choose the correct verb to complete the sentence. Write in the blank the letter that corresponds to the correct answer.

_____ 1. Some items are used all the time while others mostly _?_ around.
   A. sit
   B. set

_____ 2. Money _?_ to the top of the list of items used often, for few things are used more.
   A. rises
   B. raises

_____ 3. Just think of how many times you _?_ money down for purchases.
   A. lie
   B. lay

_____ 4. Or perhaps you prefer to _?_ your money aside in a bank account to earn interest.
   A. sit
   B. set

_____ 5. In that case the bank _?_ money for itself by lending out what you have deposited.
   A. rises
   B. raises

_____ 6. Either way, your money does not _?_ idle but is constantly moving from person to person.
   A. lie
   B. lay

_____ 7. Money rarely _?_ in one place for any length of time.
   A. sits
   B. sets

_____ 8. So what _?_ behind the desirability of money?
   A. lies
   B. lays

_____ 9. We _?_ money to obtain things that we do not have but either need or want.
   A. rise
   B. raise

_____ 10. With all of our needs and desires, it is no wonder that money rarely _?_ still.
   A. sits
   B. sets

Other Troublesome Words and Homonyms

Choose the correct word to complete the sentence. Write in the blank the letter that corresponds to the correct answer.

_____ 11. There has always been a need _?_ the peoples of the world to find a way of getting what they want.
A. between
B. among

_____ 12. The _?_ method in early days was barter, the trading of one item for another.
A. principal
B. principle

_____ 13. Barter might still be used today in a country _?_ most people are farmers or the currency has become worthless.
A. wear
B. where

_____ 14. The problem with barter, though, is that you must find someone who has what you want and is willing to _?_ what you have.
A. accept
B. except

_____ 15. In addition, although barter is _?_ when it is the only option, it lacks certain qualities of money.
A. alright
B. all right

_____ 16. For one thing, the value of items traded does not remain _?_ but varies.
A. stationary
B. stationery

_____ 17. Also a cow, for instance, could cause _?_ of trouble for the trader who must travel far away to make his purchase.
A. alot
B. a lot

_____ 18. Finally, it _?_ very easy to divide a cow if the item the trader wants is not worth the entire animal.
A. ain't
B. isn't

_____ 19. To solve the problems posed by barter, metal coins and eventually pieces of paper _?_ introduced as units of money.
A. were
B. we're

_____ 20. Originally paper notes were just signs that their holders had coins deposited at a bank, but later the paper took on the _?_ of money itself.
A. role
B. roll

Chapter 14: Capitalization

People and Places
Questions 1-5: Circle the capitalization errors in the following paragraph.

Empress Catherine II, also known as Catherine the great, was one of russia's most intense rulers. Ironically, Catherine was not even a Russian. She was a German. She involved Russia in many wars that led to possession of the Crimea and access to the Black sea. Catherine lived many years in St. Petersburg because she hated moscow. Catherine enjoyed the title Little mother.

Other Proper Nouns
Identify the word that is an example of a capitalization error. Write in the blank the letter that corresponds to the correct answer.

_____ 6. Catherine the Great once said, "my heart cannot be happy, even for an hour without love."
A. Great
B. said
C. my

_____ 7. Nevsky Prospekt is the main Boulevard near the Winter Palace in St. Petersburg.
A. Prospekt
B. Boulevard
C. Palace

_____ 8. Russians are fascinated by western culture but also strangely resist most change in that direction.
A. western
B. direction
C. no error

_____ 9. Even though Catherine hated moscow, it was still the center of Russian Orthodoxy.
A. moscow
B. center
C. Russian

_____ 10. Catherine once said of herself, "I had in my heart a strange certainty that one day I should, by my own efforts, become empress of russia."
A. herself
B. empress
C. russia

Titles, Proper Adjectives, and Common Nouns

Identify the word that is an example of a capitalization error. Write in the blank the letter that corresponds to the correct answer.

_____ 11. Catherine supported the ideals of the European Enlightenment.
A. ideals
B. Enlightenment
C. no error

_____ 12. Catherine married duke Karl Peter Ulrich of Holstein-Gottorp, later known as Tsar Peter III.
A. duke
B. Holstein-Gottorp
C. Tsar

_____ 13. Catherine hated Peter so much that one of her cossack guards eventually murdered him after she overthrew him in a coup.
A. Peter
B. cossack
C. him

_____ 14. Catherine realized the need for huge reform; she said, "people were careful not to talk of art or sciences, because they were ignorant about them."
A. she
B. people
C. sciences

_____ 15. Catherine's Peasants were divided in their support of her political tactics.
A. Peasants
B. political
C. tactics

_____ 16. The Sun was soon to set on one of Russia's most controversial leaders.
A. Sun
B. Russia's
C. leaders

_____ 17. Catherine the Great died on november 6, 1796.
A. Great
B. november
C. no error

_____ 18. Her body was buried in the Hall of pillars.
A. body
B. Hall
C. pillars

_____ 19. The inscription on her tomb reads, "divided in Life, United in Death."
   A. tomb
   B. divided
   C. no error

_____ 20. Catherine's elaborate funeral followed the traditions of the Russian orthodox Church.
   A. elaborate
   B. funeral
   C. orthodox

Chapter 15: Punctuation

End Marks, Periods, and Commas
Insert missing end marks, periods, or commas in each sentence.

1. Sweden is a beautiful country made up of many lakes forests and mountains

2. Did you know that some parts of Sweden have dark bitterly cold winters

3. Those crystal-blue lakes are amazing

4. Sweden is the fourth largest country in Europe and it is located on the eastern part of the Scandinavian Peninsula

5. Is Norway to the west of Sweden

6. Stockholm Sweden, the capital city, is an important sea port

7. Many Swedes of course are known for their blond hair fair complexion and blue eyes

8. Because Sweden is located by the water the Swedes' diet consists mainly of seafood

9. Because of their love for recreation Swedes do a lot of camping boating and fishing

10. Sweden's new constitution went into effect on January 1 1975

Semicolons, Colons, and Quotation Marks
Identify the punctuation mark missing from each sentence; identify also quotation marks that should be removed. Write in the blank the letter that corresponds to the correct answer.

        A. semicolon
        B. colon
        C. quotation marks
        D. remove quotation marks

_____ 11. Sweden has five universities Uppsla, Lund, Göteborg, Stockholm, and Umeå.

_____ 12. Midnight in Sweden is 6 00 p.m. in the eastern United States.

_____ 13. Swedes eat a lot of wild game they also enjoy reindeer steaks.

_____ 14. "I love wild rose hip juice, my sister told me.

_____ 15. My uncle said that "his favorite thing to eat in Sweden was ligonberries."

Quotation Marks, Italics, Apostrophes, and Hyphens

Underline the word or phrase in parentheses that is punctuated correctly.

16. Sweden's national anthem is (*Du Gamla, du fria;* "Du Gamla, du fria").

17. The Swedish number *sjuttiofem* is equivalent to our English number (seventy five, seventy-five).

18. Dag Hammarskjöld, a Swedish author, wrote the book (*Markings,* "Markings").

19. Swedish (*ä's, äs*) are pronounced differently than English *a*'s.

20. Lakes make up about (one-third, one third) of Sweden.

21. (Sweden's, Swedens) eastern border separates Sweden from Finland.

22. Recently, Swedes (haven't, have'nt) used the land for farming as much as in the past.

23. The (Swedes, Swedes') culture includes many celebrations and holidays.

24. Bernt Notke's sculpture (*St. George and the Dragon,* "St. George and the Dragon") is located in Stockholm's Great Church.

25. Hugo Alfvén's (*Midsummer Vigil,* "Midsummer Vigil") for orchestra follows the traditions of Swedish folk music.

Chapter 16: Spelling

Verbs and Nouns
Write the correct plural spelling of each underlined singular word.

_____ 1. A police officer enforces the laws of a <u>nation</u> and protects its people.

_____ 2. Informally, a police officer has sometimes been called a <u>cop</u>.

_____ 3. Some believe that this name was an abbreviation for *constable on patrol,* while others think that it came from an officer's copper <u>badge</u>.

_____ 4. Of the many types of police, the most common is probably the patrol officer, who prevents or responds to crime within an assigned <u>territory</u>.

_____ 5. A traffic officer works to ensure the safety of each <u>auto</u> and pedestrian.

_____ 6. A detective investigates crime, perhaps looking for a murderer, a <u>thief</u>, or a drug runner.

_____ 7. Often his evidence proves the <u>key</u> to a conviction in court.

_____ 8. An undercover agent monitors the <u>activity</u> of a suspected criminal.

_____ 9. A worker in the central <u>dispatch</u> office links people who need help with officers who can help them.

_____ 10. Special units contain many a <u>hero</u> who has rescued a lost person, freed a hostage, disarmed a bomb, or captured a criminal.

ie or *ei* and Suffixes
Identify the correctly spelled word to complete each sentence. Write in the blank the letter that corresponds to the correct answer.

_____ 11. American police operate at several levels, each one _?_ its place under a different division of government.
A. occupiing
B. occupying

_____ 12. City police enforce the laws within urban regions and range in size from the thousands of the _?_ force in New York City to just a handful in small towns.
A. busiest
B. busyest

_____ 13. County police patrol wider regions under the direction of their _?_ officer, the sheriff.
A. chief
B. cheif

_____ 14. State police, sometimes called _?_ , focus mainly on the highways.
A. trooppers
B. troopers

_____ 15. Federal agencies pursue people who break federal laws or who cross state lines after committing crimes like _?_ or murder.
A. robbery
B. robery

_____ 16. Private agencies _?_ licenses from the state to perform police work for individuals or organizations.
A. recieve
B. receive

_____ 17. In other parts of the world, police systems perform _?_ services.
A. comparable
B. compareable

_____ 18. Among those that may be familiar to you is our _?_ Royal Canadian Mounted Police.
A. nieghbor's
B. neighbor's

_____ 19. Another would be the Metropolitan Police of London, with its _?_ offices at New Scotland Yard.
A. controlling
B. controling

_____ 20. Most far-reaching of all is Interpol, an agency that fights international crime through its _?_ of cooperative effort.
A. achievment
B. achievement

Spelling

Questions 21-25: Circle the spelling errors in the following paragraph. In the blanks provided, correctly spell the words that you circled.

Soldiers typically performed police dutyes in ancient times. In 27 B.C. the emperor Augustus set up a nonmilitary police force for the city of Rome. However, it was the medeival Englishmans who placed law enforcement firmly in civilian hands by divideing their country into small groups and holding families accountable for each other. Britain also produced Sir Robert Peel, the father of modern police organizations and the source of the name *bobbies* for London police officers. Early law in America ranged from watch groups keeping peace in New England to vigilantes seekking justice in the Old West. Gradually, police work became more professional, and officers were better trained.

_____

_____

Glossary of Terms

Action verb   A verb that tells what someone or something does. (3)

Adjective   A word that modifies a noun. An adjective tells *what kind, which one, how many,* or *whose* about the noun it modifies. (5)

Adverb   A word that modifies a verb, adjective, or other adverb. An adverb tells *when, where,* or *how* about the verb it modifies. (6)

Antecedent   The word or phrase that a pronoun replaces. (4, 10)

Article   An adjective that shows whether a noun is being used in a definite or an indefinite sense. The definite article pointing to specific things is *the;* the indefinite articles pointing to nonspecific things are *a* (used before a consonant sound) and *an* (used before a vowel sound). (6)

Auxiliary   A verb that helps the main verb express a complete thought or special meaning. (3)

Being verb   A verb that tells what someone or something is. A being verb usually acts as a linking verb. (3)

Case   The characteristic of a noun or pronoun that reflects the way the word is used in the sentence. Pronouns have three case forms: subjective (sometimes called nominative), objective, and possessive. (4, 11)

Clause   A group of words that has both a subject and a predicate. Two types of clauses are independent and dependent clauses. (8)

Comma splice   The error that results when two sentences are joined by only a comma. (1)

Common noun   A general word for a person, place, thing, or idea; the opposite of a proper noun. (2)

Complete predicate   The complete verb and its modifiers and completers. It describes the subject or tells about the subject's action. (1)

Complete subject   The simple subject and its modifiers. It tells what the sentence is about. (1)

Complete verb   The main verb and any auxiliaries working together as the simple predicate in a clause. (1, 3)

Complex sentence   A sentence made of one independent clause and at least one dependent clause. (8)

Compound noun   A noun formed by joining two or more words to make a new word. (2)

Compound predicate   Two or more simple predicates joined by a conjunction. (1)

Compound sentence   A sentence made of two or more independent clauses. (3)

Compound subject   Two or more simple subjects joined by a conjunction. (1)

Conjunction   A connecting word that joins words or groups of words in a sentence. (7, 8)

Coordinating conjunction   A connecting word that joins sentence parts of the same type. Commonly used coordinating conjunctions are *and, but, or, nor,* and *yet.* (7)

Count noun   A common noun that can be made plural to show *how many.* (2)

Declarative sentence   A sentence that makes a statement and ends with a period. (1)

Demonstraßtive pronoun   A pronoun that points out the position of objects, persons, or places. *This, that, these,* and *those* are demonstrative pronouns. (4)

Dependent clause   A clause that cannot stand alone as a sentence. A dependent clause has a subject and a predicate but contains some other word that makes it express an incomplete thought. (8)

Direct object   A noun or pronoun in the predicate that receives the action of a transitive verb. (3)

Double comparison   An error created by using two comparative words together, such as *more better.* (5, 6, 12)

Double negative   An error created by using a negative word plus the adverb *not* to modify the same word. (12)

Exclamatory sentence   A sentence that expresses strong emotion and ends with an exclamation point. (1)

Fragment   A group of words wrongly punctuated as a sentence. (1)

Fused sentence   The error that results when two or more sentences are joined without punctuation or conjunction. (1)

Gender   The classification of third-person singular pronouns into masculine, feminine, and neuter. (4)

Imperative sentence   A sentence that gives a command or a request and ends with a period or an exclamation point. (1)

Indefinite pronoun   A pronoun that refers to persons and things in general terms. It refers to a large category, or part of a large category, without definitely specifying the particular individual or part. (4, 9, 10)

Independent clause   A clause that can stand alone as a sentence and that expresses a complete thought. (8)

Independent possessive   A possessive word that replaces a noun or a noun and its adjectives. (5)

Indirect object   The noun or pronoun in the predicate that (without a preposition) tells *to whom* or *for whom* the subject does something. It always appears after the verb and before the direct object. (3)

Intensive pronoun   A personal pronoun ending in *-self* or *-selves* emphasizing an already stated noun or pronoun in the sentence. (4, 11)

Interjection   A word that can stand alone and be punctuated as a sentence or can appear along with a regular sentence in which it takes no real part. It often expresses strong feeling and sometimes is called an *isolate.* (7)

Interrogative pronoun   A pronoun used to ask a question. These include *which, what, who, whom,* and *whose.* (4)

Interrogative sentence   A sentence that asks a question and ends with a question mark. (1)

Intervening phrase   A group of words that comes between the subject and the verb of a sentence. Common interrupters are negative phrases and prepositional phrases. (9)

Intransitive verb   A verb that does not need an object to express a complete thought. This verb does not send action toward anything or anyone. It occurs in the pattern S-InV. (3)

Inverted order   The wording that occurs when the verb comes before the subject in a sentence. Most interrogative sentences and some declarative sentences invert the normal subject and verb order. (9)

Linking verb   A verb that links the subject with a word that renames or describes the subject (a predicate noun or a predicate adjective). It functions something like an equal sign. It appears in either of these patterns: S-LV-PN or S-LV-PA. (3)

Modifier   A word that describes another word in a sentence. (5, 6)

Noncount noun   A common noun that cannot be made plural. (2)

Noun   The name of a person, place, thing, or idea. (2)

Number   The classification of noun forms and personal pronouns telling whether the noun or pronoun is singular or plural. (4, 9, 10)

Object of the preposition   The noun or pronoun (simple object) that follows the preposition and that the preposition relates to the rest of the sentence. The complete object of the preposition is the simple object and its modifiers. (7)

Person   The classification of personal pronouns into first person (the speaker), second person (the person spoken to), and third person (the person spoken about). (4)

Personal pronoun   One of the pronouns that are distinguished by person, number, gender, and case. (4)

Phrase   A word group that does not contain both a subject and a predicate. (8)

Possessive   A word that expresses ownership or belonging. It usually functions as a modifier. (5, 6)

Predicate   The part of the sentence that asserts something about the subject. It includes the main verb in the sentence. (3)

Predicate adjective   An adjective in the predicate that follows a linking verb and describes the subject. (3)

Predicate noun   A noun or pronoun in the predicate that follows a linking verb and renames or identifies the subject. (3)

Preposition   A word that relates its object (a noun or pronoun) to another word in the sentence. (7)

Prepositional phrase   A preposition and its complete object. An adjectival prepositional phrase functions as an adjective; an adverbial prepositional phrase functions as an adverb. (7)

Pronoun   A word that replaces a noun or a noun and its modifiers. (4, 10, 11)

Pronoun-antecedent agreement   Correct use of singular pronouns with singular antecedents and of plural pronouns with plural antecedents. (4, 10)

Pronoun reference   The relation of a pronoun to its antecedent. (4, 11)

Proper adjective   An adjective made from a proper noun. Proper adjectives must be capitalized. (5)

Proper noun   A specific name for a person, place, or thing. Proper nouns must be capitalized. (2, 14)

Reflexive pronouns   A pronoun ending in *-self* or *-selves* that is used as an object to refer to the same person or thing as the subject. (4, 11)

Run-on sentence   Two or more sentences joined with incorrect or no punctuation. It is usually called a *comma splice* or a *fused sentence.* (1)

Sentence   A group of words including a subject and a predicate that expresses a complete thought. (1)

Simple predicate   The main verb and any auxiliaries in the predicate. (1)

Simple sentence   A sentence made of one independent clause and no dependent clauses. (8)

Simple subject   The main noun or pronoun in the subject. (1)

Subject   The part of the sentence that expresses what the sentence is about. It includes the main noun or pronoun in the sentence. (1)

Subject-predicate pair   The two main parts, subject and verb, that go together in any given sentence. One subject may have two verbs, but they are still a pair. Compound and complex sentences have more than one subject-predicate pair. (8)

Subject-verb agreement   Correct use of singular subjects with singular verbs and of plural subjects with plural verbs. The first word of the complete verb agrees with the person and number of the subject. (1, 9)

Subordinating word   The word in a clause that makes that clause dependent upon another clause. (8)

Tense   Forms of a verb that indicate time, continuing action, or completed action or state of being. (3)

Transitive verb   A verb that needs a receiver for its action. It occurs in the sentence patterns S-TrV-DO and S-TrV-IO-DO. (3)

Understood *you*   The unstated subject of an imperative sentence. (1)

Verb   A word that expresses action or state of being. (3, 9)